Andrew Cohen is a lecturer in Imperial History at the University of Kent in the United Kingdom and a research fellow at the International Studies Group, University of the Free State, South Africa.

'The collapse of the Central African Federation in 1963 was the greatest failure of British colonial policy in Africa after 1945 and left a grim legacy not yet expunged in Zimbabwe. The causes of that collapse have been much debated and much mythologised. In this closely researched study, deploying the widest range of sources so far used by an historian of the Federation, Andrew Cohen has presented the most scholarly and persuasive account of its fall, and made an important contribution to the larger history of decolonization in Africa.'

John Darwin, Professor of Global and Imperial History,
Oxford University

THE POLITICS AND ECONOMICS OF DECOLONIZATION IN AFRICA

The Failed Experiment of the Central African Federation

ANDREW COHEN

I.B. TAURIS

LONDON · NEW YORK

For Helen

Published in 2017 by
I.B.Tauris & Co. Ltd
London • New York
www.ibtauris.com

International Library of African Studies 33

ISBN: 978 1 84885 882 4
eISBN: 978 1 78672 216 4
ePDF: 978 1 78673 216 3

A full CIP record for this book is available from the British Library
A full CIP record of this book is available from the Library of Congress

Library of Congress Catalog Card Number: available

Typeset in Garamond Three by OKS Prepress Services, Chennai, India
Printed and bound by CPI Group (UK) Ltd, Croydon, CR0 4YY

MIX
Paper from
responsible sources
FSC
www.fsc.org FSC® C013604

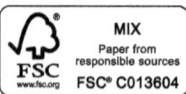

CONTENTS

Acknowledgements   vii

Map of Central African Federation, 1959   ix

Introduction   1

Historiographical Approaches to Federation:
Foundation and its Early Years   3
Historiographical Issues and the End of Federation   12

1. Conception and the Early Years of Federation   20

Acquiring the Charter   20
Company Days   23
Responsible Government   31
Towards Federation   38
Early Years, 1953–6   49
African Advancement   53

2. The Pipe Dream of Partnership, 1957–9   57

Welensky and Macmillan Take Office   57
Partnership in Practice   72
Southern Rhodesia: The Removal of Todd and
Arrival of Whitehead   75
Northern Rhodesia and Nyasaland: Dr Banda Returns   79
The 1959 Emergencies   82
Repercussions of the Emergencies   85

Devlin Commission   93
Preparing for the Federal Constitutional Review
and the British General Election   100

3. 'The Wind of Change', 1960–1   105

Macmillan Visits the Federation   105
Recasting the Federation's Public Image in Britain   107
Preparing for the Monckton Commission   110
The Monckton Commission in the Federation   115
Territorial Reviews   121
Southern Rhodesian Constitutional Conference and the
Northern Rhodesian Constitutional Review   126
The Mining Companies and the 'Wind of Change'   133
The United States and the Federation   149
The Federation in the United Nations   154

4. A Failed Experiment, 1962–3   160

Maudling and the Northern Rhodesia Proposals   160
Butler and the Central Africa Office   164
Preparing for the Northern and Southern
Rhodesian Elections   168
The Federation, the United States and the United Nations   170
Northern and Southern Rhodesian Elections   179
South Africa and the Federation   182
Dissolution   184

Conclusion   193

Notes   205
Bibliography   264
Index   285

ACKNOWLEDGEMENTS

This book began life in Sheffield and travelled through Pretoria and Bloemfontein before finally seeing the light of day in Canterbury. It would be impossible to thank all the people who have helped to shape the final version but some debts need to be repaid. Ian Phimister has steadfastly provided guidance, inspiration and friendship over the past 15 years. Ian has been, and continues to be, an inspiration. During my time at the University of the Free State, Kate Law, Daryl Gowlett and Ilse le Roux deserve special mention for making Bloemfontein feel like home. I retain a research fellowship at the institution and this work is based on the research supported in part by the National Research Foundation of South Africa (Grant Number 103547). Jonathan Jansen, the former Rector of the University, was instrumental in creating an environment that brought together early career scholars from across the globe. I have particularly benefited from discussions with Rory Pilossof, Cornelis Muller, Tinashe Nyamunda, Lazlo Passemiers, David Patrick, Clement Masakure, Dan Spence and Neil Roos. Jack Hogan and Duncan Money, new arrivals to the group, have also provided assistance and friendship. During my time in Pretoria, Alois Mlambo, Lize Kriel, Niel Roux, Johan Bergh, Karen Harris, Antony Goedhals and Duncan Hodge all proved invaluable in different ways. Other debts of gratitude are owed to Aldwin Roes, Paul Ashmore, Joanna Lewis, Marja Hinfelaar, Miles Larmer, Mucha Musemwa, Bizeck Phiri, Matthew Graham, Rachel Johnson, Jonathan Saha, Julia Tischler, Gerold Krozewski, Peter Cain, John Darwin, Philip Murphy and Lucy McCann. The friendships I made in Oxford during 2004–5 continue to nourish my academic work;

Vincent Kuitenbrouwer, Casper Andersen and Robert Fletcher deserve particular mention in this regard. I would also like to thank Tomasz Hoskins at I.B.Tauris for his assistance and Shani D'Cruze for copyediting the manuscript.

The final touches to this book were made at the University of Kent and I owe several debts of gratitude to those who have made me feel so welcome in Canterbury. Giacomo Macola has welcomed me into his 'Bantustan' and is truly a staunch 'Chief'. Jackie Waller, Christine Whyte, Leonie James, Ambrogio Caiani and Barbara Bombi have all made me particularly welcome in the School of History. Special thanks is due to my family. Helen Garnett provided the map for this book and all the support I could ask for, and more, when I most needed it. She is truly exceptional. Dave, Jude, Amy and Tom Cohen have all been invaluable over the years but my final thanks go to my parents, Peter and Eileen, whose unconditional love and assistance made it possible for me to write this book.

Leopoldville

TANGANYIKA

BELGIAN
CONGO

Dar es Salam

Elisabethville

NYASA
-LAND

ANGOLA

NORTHERN
RHODESIA

Broken Hill

Lusaka

Blantyre

Livingstone

MOZAMBIQUE

SOUTHERN
RHODESIA

Salisbury
Umtali

Beira

Bulawayo

INDIAN OCEAN

SOUTH
WEST
AFRICA

BECHUANALAND

Pretoria

Johannesburg

SWAZI
-LAND

Lourenço Marques

BASUTO
LAND

ATLANTIC OCEAN

UNION OF
SOUTH AFRICA

Cape Town

International Boundaries

The Copperbelt

0   200   400   600 Miles

Central African Federation 1959

INTRODUCTION

> I'm quite prepared to leave history to judge whether I was telling
> the truth or whether the British Government are honourable in
> what they say.
>
> Sir Roy Welensky, 12 March 1963[1]

The decolonization of European colonial empires after 1945 was a key
episode in the history of the twentieth century. This process, however,
was by no means inevitable. Britain's withdrawal from India and
Palestine in the late 1940s coincided with the formulation of plans for
the 'second colonial occupation' of many of its African colonies.[2] The
British also used military force to quell communist insurgents in
Malaya and Mau Mau fighters in Kenya during the early 1950s. This
contradictory approach was driven by a need to earn American dollars to
finance London's wartime debts, and a stark refusal to accept that
Britain's African colonies were 'ready' for independence under majority
rule. This view, combined with a wish to stymie possible Afrikaner
expansion, after the National Party's South African general election
victory in 1948, saw British policy align, albeit briefly, with settler
desires in Southern and Northern Rhodesia (Zimbabwe and Zambia) for
a closer association of the territories. Widespread African opposition to
the plan was overlooked, and on 1 September 1953 the Federation of
Rhodesia and Nyasaland came into existence. Nyasaland (Malawi) was
included on the insistence of the British government. The Federation
was a bold experiment in political power during the late stage of British
colonialism and constituted one of the most intricate episodes in its

retreat from empire. This book examines how and why the Federation lasted just over a mere ten years before its eventual dissolution at midnight on 31 December 1963.

Following an initial chapter which charts earlier ideas surrounding a union of British territories in central Africa, the foundation of the Federation and its early years, the main focus will shift to consider the political and economic factors that led to the Federation's failure after 1957. In many respects 1957 is a natural point on which to focus a study of this kind. In the British political arena Harold Macmillan replaced Anthony Eden as prime minister in January 1957 in the wake of the Suez crisis. In the Federation, Lord Malvern passed on the leadership of the Federal Party to Sir Roy Welensky in November 1956. Macmillan and Welensky would lead their respective governments for the remainder of the Federation's life. A further development in 1957 was the introduction of the Constitutional Amendment Act, despite the protestations of the African Affairs Board. This piece of legislation catalysed African protest against the federal experiment and inspired Dr Hastings Banda to return to Nyasaland during 1958 to organise African resistance. Furthermore, in the international arena 1957 saw the Federation of Malaya and Ghana gain membership to the United Nations (UN). Over the following six years a further 30 newly independent countries joined the world organisation. As a result the UN became a well-publicised arena where the case for self-determination for the Federation's African majority could be made. Finally, in the economic field the price of copper on the world market fell dramatically towards the end of 1956. It continued to fall during 1957 with devastating effect on the Federation's financial position.

Against the backdrop sketched out above, this book examines events in both Britain and Africa that led to the Federation's dissolution. Furthermore, it draws out a new interpretation of how multinational business adapted to this unstable political environment and for the first time situates the Federation fully into the wider international context of the period. In doing so, it sheds light on the Federation's complex relationship with apartheid South Africa, whilst also considering how the United States sought to influence events. The Federation as an issue at the UN in the early 1960s is also examined.

Historiographical Approaches to Federation:
Foundation and its Early Years

The existing literature regarding the Central African Federation has been written using varying methodologies and source materials, reflecting evolving viewpoints and the opening of relevant archives. There was a great deal of work produced by both contemporary critics and apologists for federation.[3] These works attempted to discuss the development of the Federation and their arguments engaged with ongoing debates over its future. As a result, they have become historical sources in their own right, offering insights into the contemporary discourse regarding the Federation. Accounts in support of the Federation placed more emphasis on the perceived economic benefits of association, while more critical appraisals focused on the failure of 'partnership' to address racial discrimination. There are also memoirs by the British and Federal politicians who were involved in deciding the Federation's fate.[4] These are often partisan in nature; however, as such they clearly illustrate the rapid divergence of opinion in the late 1950s and early 1960s.

A more historically rigorous analysis of events took place during the late 1960s and early 1970s, in which the Federation was assessed primarily as a precursor to the Rhodesian Front's unilateral declaration of independence (UDI) during 1965.[5] Juxtaposed with this school of thought, a further branch of scholarship moved away from a Eurocentric assessment of African history and attempted to reinterpret the period in the context of constructing national histories for the newly independent countries of Zambia and Malawi.[6] Much of this work, while commendable in highlighting African experiences, sidestepped the international nature of colonialism and focused inwardly on the new nation states, rather than locating their arguments in the wider colonial system, and created highly nationalistic 'useable' pasts.

This imbalance began to be addressed during the 1980s and 1990s with the development of a further strand of scholarship that primarily examined the Federation in the wider context of British and European decolonization.[7] One problem faced by these scholars was a lack of official primary sources, principally due to the 30-year release rule. This problem, of course, plagues any attempt to write a historical account of the more recent past. Recent broad surveys of decolonization have benefited from access to archival sources, yet constraints on space limit the extent to which they considered the Federation in any depth.[8] Both British and Federal government records only became available to scholars during the 1990s. With the exception of Richard Wood's authorised account, *The Welensky Papers*, most work from before the mid-1990s is based only on sources available in the public domain.[9]

During the mid-2000s, two sizable and valuable additions to the historiography of the Federation illustrated a renewed interest in this field. In one, Philip Murphy edited the central Africa editions of *British Documents on the End of Empire*.[10] Murphy's selection of documents comprises two volumes and offers an important introduction to relevant documents held in the National Archives, Kew. The other, *So Far and No Further!* represents the fruits of Richard Wood's privileged access to the papers of Ian Smith.[11] Wood's account, whilst broadly sympathetic to the settlers' plight, offers a valuable insight into the workings of the Southern Rhodesian territorial government in the final years of federation. Over the last few years aspects of the Federation's history have received attention in journal articles and book chapters.[12] In addition, Julia Tischler has published a monograph detailing the construction of the Kariba Dam.[13] More broadly, Jason Parker's work on the similarly ill-fated West Indies Federation offers an important comparative case study.[14] Also, highlighting British federal experiments and linking the creation of the Federation to wider imperial trends, Michael Collins has pointed to a 'Federal Moment' in the post-World War II period.[15]

Many of the early historical explanations detailing the formation of the Federation were based on contemporary views advanced by the Federal government in the late 1950s and early 1960s to justify its continued existence. The idea of federating Britain's central African territories enjoyed a measure of encouragement from both the Labour government of Clement Attlee and the Conservative government of Winston Churchill. This cross-party support for federation has been attributed to Britain's desire to halt the spread of apartheid after D. F. Malan's electoral victory in South Africa during 1948. This became increasingly important in the early 1950s as apartheid began to intensify and become solidly entrenched. In this respect federation was seen as a way to strengthen the forces of liberalism and racial partnership and counterbalance South African practices.[16] This hypothesis has been primarily used to account for metropolitan motives and has been very strongly advocated by Ronald Hyam who contends that:

> In truth, the explanation for setting up the Central African Federation is as nearly monocausal as any historical explanation can ever be. The motive was to erect a counterpoise to the expansion of South Africa, especially by checking Afrikaner immigration.[17]

Nonetheless, this view must be qualified with respect to local conditions. No mention is made of how Britain's unease with the Malan government was exploited by the pro-Federation settler faction who exaggerated South Africa's growing influence in Southern Rhodesia.[18] When redressing this imbalance Philip Murphy concluded that the influence of South African policy on British policy makers in Central Africa is moot in light of the problems introduced by Central African settlers.[19]

Many settlers also saw the Federation as a first step toward achieving dominion status and integration into the Commonwealth as an independent white dominion. To those in Northern Rhodesia a federation offered the chance to gain greater freedom from London through closer ties with Southern Rhodesia. In Salisbury, the attractiveness of closer association to the north had increased greatly since the 1920s due to the high financial returns from Northern Rhodesia's mineral reserves. Also, the perception that federation made dominion status more likely encouraged support.[20] It has even been argued that dominion status was 'the main drive' behind the decision to federate.[21] In this case, federation was not the ultimate goal of the settlers; it was merely a stepping stone to full independence for a white-dominated country. There was, however, also a section of the settler community in Southern Rhodesia that actively opposed federation. They would have preferred closer ties with South Africa rather than with the northern protectorates, as they felt the latter would lead to increased British interference in their affairs and consequently African advancement. Paradoxically, more liberal settlers also feared federation as it would slow down constitutional advance.[22] These arguments firmly place the locus of power with the settlers. It is clear that the settlers exploited British fears of South African expansion, although how far they exaggerated this threat is open to debate.

Settler organisation has also been identified as 'the key' factor in making federation a reality in 1953. This argument implies that Britain was susceptible to settler pressure at this point as it lacked a coherent African policy.[23] In this respect, the Federation has been described from a British perspective as nothing more than a hopeless play for time.[24] Further arguments have been put forward, however, for the influence of Britain's wider global commitments. In this period, Cold War concerns had been brought to the fore by the Berlin blockade and the start of the Korean War. These events influenced Whitehall policy. Barber saw a federation in Central Africa as 'a bastion against the spread of communist influence', allowing power to remain in 'responsible hands'.[25] This emphasis has been successfully critiqued by Butler, who has made a convincing case that there was no significant communist threat in the Federation, and that the Cold War was only relevant as part of the wider ideological battle being fought in the United Nations.[26]

One contemporary apologist for the Federation argued that its formation was little more than an attempt to find acceptable compromise between white domination influenced by South Africa and 'uncontrolled black democracy'.[27] Yet this assertion over-emphasised the fear of African nationalism during the early 1950s. Settler nationalism was of far greater importance, due to their greater 'organisation, solidarity and effectiveness'. This gave settlers a far better chance of attaining independence than any African political organisation, and federation was an attempt by Britain to rein in this force.[28]

Despite the ultimate ineffectiveness of African opposition to the campaign for federation, it receives strong coverage in the early historiography. In Southern Rhodesia many Africans were cautiously optimistic about the idea as association with the north held the potential to improve their political situation.[29] In the northern territories, however, many felt they had nothing to gain and everything to lose.[30] Moreover, they saw federation as amalgamation under a different name.[31] Resistance in the north focused on the fact that power would pass from the Colonial Office to European communities in general and to Southern Rhodesia in particular, ruling out the eventual opportunity for self-government.[32] Opposition to closer association with Southern Rhodesia has been linked to its reputation as a 'white man's country'. This reputation was widespread due to the Africans' own experiences there as migrant workers.[33] The federal campaign has been cited as the 'decisive stimulus' for the formation of northern nationalist political movements. This was not the case in Southern Rhodesia where it delayed the formation of a united movement.[34] Ultimately, it has been suggested that African opposition failed in 1953 because settler pressure and British belief in federation were too strong.[35]

Scholars have seen the early years of the Federation as leading to a relaxation of African protest in all of the territories.[36] This was especially true of rural areas in Northern Rhodesia. Africans here had anticipated that federation would lead to an influx of white settlers north from Southern Rhodesia. As this did not happen, the united front between rural and urban Africans in the fight to resist federation crumbled. This split was further exacerbated by the Federal government, which encouraged traditional leaders to ban political activities in their districts.[37] Yet disillusionment with the Federation and with Britain's inability to safeguard African rights would come to fruition by the end of the decade. Federal discrimination stimulated political action and provided a central issue which could unite opposing movements.[38] It is perhaps unsurprising that much of the scholarship which emphasises the influence of African nationalism was produced in the immediate post-colonial period. It tended to romanticise the role of the triumphant nationalist parties, and was often written by scholars who were themselves involved in the independence struggle. A long overdue reassessment of African nationalism in the late colonial period is now beginning to be undertaken, although much work still remains to be done.[39]

It has also been suggested that the desire to transmit the more liberal practices of Northern Rhodesia and Nyasaland to Southern Rhodesia may also have motivated federation. From this standpoint, federation would prevent both extreme African and settler nationalism by promoting a policy of racial partnership.[40] After Southern Rhodesia gained responsible government in 1923, Britain was precluded from directly legislating for greater liberal practices. A closer association with the northern territories was seen as a more subtle way of achieving this.[41] The confidence that this policy could succeed reveals metropolitan ignorance of the strength of settler self-belief and the realities of race relations in Southern Rhodesia. In fact, it implies that Southern Rhodesian settlers were 'genuinely unaware' of the discrimination against the African population and consequently already believed they were 'honouring liberal principles'.[42] This argument, prevalent in some contemporary accounts, lacks any archival basis and has failed to gain any traction in later historical interpretations.

A further theory advanced is that the federal policy of racial 'partnership' may alternatively be viewed as an attempt by the Rhodesian white elite at self-decolonization.[43] According to this theory, partnership had three main purposes in the eyes of the settlers. The first was to hinder African nationalist protest by co-opting the emergent African middle-class into the mainstream political system. Secondly, despite the gradual opening of the political system to Africans, the settlers wanted a system to ensure their continued domination for the foreseeable future. Finally, partnership was hoped to provide a brake to both Afrikaner nationalism in the south and the African nationalism of the north.[44] This argument correctly posits that the settlers wished to protect their way of life, but fails to explain adequately why, if partnership was crucial to this aim, few meaningful attempts were made to co-opt African politicians into the political system before the 'build-a-nation' campaign during the early 1960s. It could be argued that in the early 1950s 'self-decolonization' for the Rhodesian settlers could have been secured if they had avoided involvement with the Colonial Office-administered northern territories altogether, and campaigned solely for Southern Rhodesia to be advanced to dominion status.

A more convincing contemporary argument which has continued into later scholarship was the economic advantages that could be expected following federation. This argument maintains that the economies of the three territories complemented each other. Northern Rhodesia brought vast mineral wealth through its copper mines, Southern Rhodesia had a healthy agricultural base, and Nyasaland, although not an essential component for the settlers, could provide a ready supply of African labour.[45] The economic compatibility of the territories would enable diversification of the territories' economies and provide a more attractive proposition for foreign investment.[46] This prospect persuaded many liberals in Britain that federation was the best way to further economic development and combat the poverty in which many Africans lived.[47]

Scholars have also remarked that Britain saw economic prosperity as a way to overcome African opposition to federation and also influence settler policies. African opposition to federation would soon wane as the economic benefits improved their standard of living, and settlers would be forced to moderate their racial policy in order to receive the co-operation of Africans. Thus economic necessity would 'force accommodations between white and black interests'.[48] For Britain the economic benefits were twofold. The immediate postwar period gave rise to what has become known as the 'second colonial occupation', due to Britain's increased interest in making its overseas possessions contribute to its postwar reconstruction. Central African policy was influenced by this and it was assumed that a federation of British territories would encourage the production of colonial commodities, such as Southern Rhodesian tobacco, which would earn valuable dollars for the sterling market as a whole.[49] Secondly, a federation would also be advantageous for Britain's economy, as it would provide an improved trading block within central Africa for British goods.[50]

Economic incentives may have also spurred the settler campaign for federation during the late 1940s and early 1950s.[51] The major copper companies operating in Northern Rhodesia supported federation as an integrated transport system would ease the transport of coal from Southern Rhodesia to the Copperbelt. It has been noted, however, that whilst business could exert a level of influence over settler politics, the link was not as powerful as crudely deterministic analysis may suggest.[52] It is unclear whether or not any detailed economic analysis predicting the effect of federation was carried out before it was implemented. That is, economic advantage was assumed rather than proved. Therefore, according to Arthur Hazelwood, the interdependence of economies cannot be considered a major motivation for Federation.[53]

The Federation's early economic performance was encouraging for both British officials and the new Federal government. The African protest that accompanied the campaign to federate dissipated and the economy was strong, buoyed by high copper prices and increased foreign investment.[54] The boom in the federal economy has been cited as the predominant reason for the reduction of African protest, particularly in Southern Rhodesia, as it enabled the Federal government to 'buy off' opposition with higher wages and improved facilities.[55] Hazelwood has questioned the extent to which federation was responsible for this economic development. Although the economy grew at an impressive rate during its first few years, the evidence for how far this increase was a direct result of federation is negligible. Hazelwood's argument credits the growth to normal economic forces and postulates that in the long term, federation damaged the economic position of Africans.[56] Although this may be the case, the important point is that in its early years the Federation did receive the credit, both in London and Salisbury, and this successful start led to the state of overconfidence that began its downfall. In fact the Federation's early success has been labelled a wasted opportunity to consolidate settler control of power as it missed the chance to obtain African support for its policy of partnership whilst the economy was performing well.[57] More recent scholarship centred on British government archives adds further weight to Hazelwood's conclusion. Hyam states that '[o]ne of the most obvious conclusions to be drawn from studying the British archival record is to underline the lack of emphasis on economic motives for federation'.[58] It is clear, however, that a general belief in the economic benefits of association was prevalent during the Federation's lifespan. This can be evidenced as late as 1960 with the assertion by the majority of the Monckton Commission that federation held economic advantages for its constituent territories.

A further influence emphasised in earlier historiography is the theory of nation-building, which may explain both the settler and British drive to federate. Central Africa was not the only federation considered or even implemented by Britain in the post-war period[59] At this juncture, white settler communities were still seen as an asset and intended to consolidate Britain's independent world role.[60] Furthermore, it may have been seen as 'simple expediency' to provide a bulwark against South African expansion whilst offering political security to Northern Rhodesia and solving the problem of Nyasaland's economic weakness.[61] To the Colonial Office this looked the ideal solution for central Africa; however, it overlooked the racial realities of the situation.[62] This valuable hypothesis moves away from a narrow Afro-centric explanation, and locates the decision to federate squarely in relation to the influence of wider international factors on British metropolitan policy. The nation-building argument for federation must also be assessed in relation to settler motivations. Since the early 1930s many settlers had favoured amalgamation of the Rhodesias. Lord Bledisloe was given the task of leading a commission to investigate the feasibility of this idea and his report was published in March 1939. Although the majority report favoured greater political unity, it ruled against immediate amalgamation principally due to the wide differences in 'native policy' between Southern Rhodesia and the northern protectorates.

Combining states at different stages of constitutional development also posed a further difficulty.[63]

The importance of land alienation for the Federation's African inhabitants varied vastly between territories and whilst it was felt most keenly in Southern Rhodesia, it was barely an issue in the north. Contrary to expectations, the copper boom during the first years of federation did not spark the growth of secondary industry in rural areas. Development was primarily restricted to European areas adjacent to the railway lines and consequently the majority of Africans did not share in the Federation's initial prosperity.[64] Links were created between African urban and rural concerns through increased migration into cities in Southern Rhodesia. This helped foster a greater sense of shared grievance against the Federation and of national consciousness.[65]

A further key consideration which should be addressed in explaining the history of central Africa in this period is the territorial rivalry within the Federation. Southern Rhodesia was clearly the senior partner as two initial decisions taken by the Federal government illustrate. The first was the placement of the Federal capital in Salisbury. The second was the decision to build a hydro-electric dam at Kariba rather than Kafue.[66] The construction of the Kariba dam has proved a divisive issue for historians. Its creation has been called a 'sound decision' as it was necessary to meet the power requirements of the Copperbelt and enabled greater investment.[67] Blake labelled it as 'undoubtedly the most spectacular achievement of the Federation', and argued that only in 'hindsight' does the placing of the powerhouse in Southern Rhodesia appear to anticipate the break-up of the Federation.[68] Conversely, its critics have described Kariba as 'an economic disaster' as it tied the Federation to repaying a vast amount of foreign debt at a time when its economic productivity was falling. If the dam had been built at Kafue instead and the Federation had borrowed the same amount of capital, it would have had an extra 50 million pounds to 'put to more productive uses'.[69] Nevertheless, even if the Kariba dam was far too big for any possible demand, it created the world's biggest man-made lake and was a striking advertisement for the potential of the Federation.[70] Yet, whilst Jones recognises territorial rivalry, he argues powerfully that loyalties were primarily racial not territorial.[71] Tischler also highlights this point, arguing that the decision to favour Kariba over Kafue 'can only be understood in relation to its central role in white identity politics'.[72]

Overall, as the following chapter will demonstrate, the early performance of the Federation was judged to be a success and by 1956 the Federation's future looked bright. Investment was high and Salisbury was undergoing a major programme of development as money and increasing numbers of European immigrants arrived. Wage levels had risen for both African and European workers, although there was still a large difference between the two. Moreover, African protest against federation was relatively small and ineffective. These optimistic times would prove to be short-lived.[73]

Historiographical Issues and the End of Federation

The period from 1957 to the Federation's end has attracted much comment in the historiography and the debates which shape this book require detailed information. As highlighted earlier, the 1957 Constitutional Amendment Bill has been identified by some as the first sign of decline in the Federation's fortunes. The Bill was designed to enlarge the Federal parliament whilst ensuring European control. It gave an increased number of seats to Africans, though this move has been described as nothing more than 'a smokescreen of liberalism' as it also increased the ratio of European MPs to their proportion of the population, further entrenching their dominance.[74] The African Affairs Board was responsible for guarding against discriminatory legislature being introduced by the Federal government. It was included at the insistence of London in an attempt to allay African fears prior to 1953.

The Board had the power to refer any discriminatory Federal legislation to Britain for assessment. The Constitutional Amendment Bill was one such piece of prejudiced legislation as it was a direct attack on Africans' rights, and the Board duly referred it to parliament in London. Much to their surprise, however, their objections were overturned. This action by Britain has been credited by historians, particularly those writing in the 1960s, with destroying African confidence in Britain's ability to safeguard their rights. Moreover, it was seen as signalling their willingness to consider granting dominion status to a white-minority-ruled Federation, principally after Britain agreed to review the Federal constitution in 1960.[75] Thus, the implementation of the Constitutional Amendment Act has been seen as crucial in 'galvanizing African opposition to the Federation and giving the protest an urgent cause and a specific timetable to concentrate their efforts'.[76]

The Constitutional Amendment Act was not the only force driving growth of African nationalism in the late 1950s and early 1960s. By 1958 the African National Congress in Northern Rhodesia had revived again and organised branches that covered most of the country. This reorganisation was aided by increasing numbers of Africans emerging with a secondary-school education or further education obtained overseas.[77] The improvement of organisation within the nationalist movement led to the return to Nyasaland of Dr Hastings Banda to lead the Nyasaland African National Congress in July 1958. The Federal government's attempt to stifle African protest led to a state of emergency being called during 1959. The Nyasaland Emergency and the subsequent Devlin Report have together been identified as a crucial turning point for the Federation's fortunes.[78] The territorial government, with the support of the Federal government, persuaded the Governor, Sir Robert Armitage, to call an emergency in order to foil a Congress-led murder plot against settlers in the territory. The result was that 52 Africans lost their lives and the majority of Congress leaders and many of their supporters were imprisoned. Although the British government initially supported Armitage's actions, growing criticism at home led to an inquiry into the incident, headed by Lord Devlin. He concluded that although a state of emergency was justified, there was no evidence of a murder plot. Moreover, his most damning conclusion was that Nyasaland 'had been, albeit temporarily, a police state'.[79]

The embarrassment caused to Macmillan's government by this remark should be placed in the wider perspective of colonial policy. Previously, action in Suez, Cyprus and the deaths of Mau Mau detainees at Hola had given rise to international and domestic condemnation.[80] Historians have argued that the repercussions of the Nyasaland Emergency were responsible for Macmillan altering his African policy and bringing central Africa into line with the rest of the continent.[81] The emergency also had the effect of adding further impetus to African nationalism throughout the Federation. In Southern Rhodesia the National Democratic Party (NDP) was formed; in Nyasaland the Malawi Congress Party (MCP) replaced the Nyasaland African National Congress whilst in Northern Rhodesia, the United National Independence Party (UNIP) came to the fore. These parties were better organised, more disciplined and now had the support of many liberals at home and much of world opinion.[82]

In order to aid the Federal constitutional review due in 1960, London appointed a commission under Lord Monckton to make recommendations on the future of the Federation. The terms of reference for the report caused much contemporary debate and disagreement and when it was published it received a mixed reception.[83] For one scholar, the Monckton Report 'changed the course of the Federation's history'.[84] Monckton concluded that although it would damage their economies to dissolve the Federation, the individual territories should have the right to secede if they so wished.[85] After the report Britain agreed to discuss Southern Rhodesia's future separately to that of the Federation.[86] The commission's treatment of the economic benefits of the Federation, however, has been described as 'casual and amateurish'.[87] This argument asserts that the report overestimated the economic benefits of federation to the territories. Although Hazelwood does concede that the growth rate was 'probably faster' than it would have been without federation, he attributes this purely to 'psychological reasons'; as people believed federation was economically beneficial, there was a greater inflow of capital.[88] While the Monckton Report was in favour of a form of continued association between the territories, its recommendations stipulated that if federation was to succeed, almost every aspect of the legislature that guaranteed settler supremacy would have to be changed.[89]

One strand of later scholarship moved away from an Afro-centric approach and focused on metropolitan explanations for the end of the Federation. Harold Macmillan was appointed prime minister in the wake of the Suez Crisis, and his first three years in office were characterised by caution in his approach to colonial affairs.[90] The policy of gradualism was abandoned after the surprise Conservative victory in the general election during October 1959.[91] This enabled Macmillan to rethink his African policy; Alan Lennox-Boyd at the Colonial Office retired, and Macmillan replaced him with Iain Macleod. Macleod's appointment has been judged significant as it underlined Macmillan's change of policy with regard to handing power over to Africans rather than Europeans.[92] It has also been seen as an attempt by Macmillan to wrest control of the situation in central Africa back from the Federal government, as Britain's reputation was suffering from the fallout of the

UFP's policies.[93] Macleod has also been attributed with shaping Conservative policy, with the full support of Macmillan, towards greater African representation.[94] Blake, however, accepts at face value Macmillan's own facile comments regarding the Federation, concluding that 'the theory behind British colonialism had, it is true, always been that British rule was a preparation for indigenous self-government'.[95]

The Central African Federation has also received attention in respect of its influence in British domestic politics, primarily with regard to the Conservative party.[96] Although the Conservative party was broadly sympathetic to the settlers' cause, Macmillan was able to push through his African policy. As Simon Ball has noted, 'MPs might froth over their club claret but they were not going to risk their seats and emoluments over a very large country, a long way away, of which they knew little'.[97] Although Macmillan's African policies received a great deal of contemporary coverage, it has been suggested that his main political aim after 1959 was to secure Britain's entry into the European Economic Community (EEC).[98] This may have accounted for the speed with which he wished to disentangle Britain from its previous African initiatives. Running parallel to the desire to join the EEC, and perhaps leading to his eventual failure to negotiate British entry, were Macmillan's 'illusions of British grandeur'.[99] These illusions, enhanced by the US secretary of state John Foster Dulles' terminal illness, encouraged Macmillan to pursue a quasi-independent policy in world affairs during 1959. Richard Aldous and Sabine Lee argue that this policy was best illustrated by Macmillan's visit to Moscow early in 1959 and was also evident during the Geneva Foreign Ministers' Meeting during April 1959. Rather than enhancing Britain's international position, Macmillan alienated Germany and France which were both 'inherently suspicious of British reliability'.[100]

International affairs, more widely construed, have been credited with influencing the fortunes of the Federation.[101] By the early 1960s the international community was levelling increasing criticism against Britain's central African policy. The United States warned that the speed at which concessions were granted to Africans in the Federation was too slow.[102] Here, John Kent highlights the importance of the United States and wider tactical concerns of the Cold War. With Africa rapidly decolonizing, it was seen as tactically wiser to support independent African governments than attempt to hold up a regime based on white minority rule. The colonial policy of other European powers also influenced the fate of the Federation. The French experience in Algeria has been judged highly influential on Macmillan's colonial policy.[103] A further factor credited with shaping British, settler and African attitudes towards federation was the events in the Congo. Belgium's decision to abandon a colony that was seen as more backward than Britain's African possessions made a mockery of Britain's policy of gradual withdrawal.[104] It also instilled fear that violence might spread across the border into Northern Rhodesia, where African opposition to federation was increasing.[105]

African nationalism, particularly in Northern Rhodesia, was given a boost when Katanga's attempt to secede from the Congo ended in failure.[106] To the settlers, the chaos of the Congo provided a stark example of what happened when Africans were given power too early.[107] The worsening situation in Katanga drew greater attention to the role of big mining business in central Africa, and created a potential Cold War flashpoint on the Federation's doorstep. This interest reached fever pitch in September 1961 following the UN Secretary-General Dag Hammarskjöld's fatal aeroplane crash in Northern Rhodesia.[108] Suspicions still remain as to the precise cause of the crash and in 1992 Conor Cruise O'Brien, the UN's representative in Elisabethville, still believed that mining companies operating in the region were involved.[109]

Regarding the economic and political role of the mining companies, only RST has received attention.[110] There is, however, no major work on the part played by the other large company, the Anglo American Corporation, for all that Miles Kahler and Philip Murphy have briefly dealt with the relationship between Anglo, RST and the Federal government.[111] The greater role pursued by the UN in southern Africa during the late 1950s and early 1960s was of great concern to the Federal and the British governments alike. To the Federation, the UN appeared to cover for communist-inspired Afro-Asian conspiracy against the settler societies of southern Africa. The UN also provided a highly publicised environment where Britain's refusal to condemn South Africa's apartheid regime caused a good deal of embarrassment.[112]

Against this backdrop, the constitutions of both the Federation and the individual territories had to be renegotiated. Nyasaland had already been promised an African majority in its legislature in the wake of the emergency, and there were increased calls from Northern Rhodesian

Africans for the same. Welensky clashed with Britain violently over Northern Rhodesia not merely for political gain; he was fighting for the very survival of the Federation.[113] During December 1960 it was agreed to postpone the conference to discuss the Federal constitution until the Northern and Southern constitutions had been ratified. Initial negotiations in Northern Rhodesia stalled and against Monckton's recommendations, Britain made proposals that would ensure settler control for the immediate future. This led to violence by Africans throughout the territory and Britain looked into the feasibility of a military intervention if the situation further deteriorated. The Chiefs of Staff, however, concluded that this option was neither militarily nor politically feasible.[114] Britain, much to the settlers' disgust, reversed its initial decision and in February 1962 settled on a new constitution that gave Africans predominance in the legislature.

The Southern Rhodesian Constitution cemented Britain's unique relationship with Southern Rhodesia. Britain accepted Sir Edgar Whitehead's vague promises of 'equal rights for civilized Africans' against much African opposition. It has been argued that the final Constitution was little more than 'sophisticated cover' for British withdrawal from responsibility in central Africa.[115] Britain conceded to settler demands in Southern Rhodesia as it was not in a position to do anything else. The increasing hardening of settler opinion in Southern Rhodesia was not a problem that only Britain had to contend with. By the early 1960s, the Federal government viewed settler nationalism as a far greater threat to the Federation's future than African nationalism in Southern Rhodesia. By 1962 the Federal economy had slowed considerably, white immigration was falling, and white unemployment was becoming a problem for the first time since the 1930s. It is within this milieu that the Rhodesian Front formed from the amalgamation of several smaller Southern Rhodesian settler-nationalist parties in March 1962. The Rhodesian Front campaigned on the policy of independence for Southern Rhodesia and defeated Whitehead in the December 1962 Southern Rhodesian general election.[116] With African majorities in the governments of Northern Rhodesia and Nyasaland, and the Rhodesian Front in power in Southern Rhodesia the Federation's fate was sealed.[117]

By the end of 1962, the one issue that both the African nationalists in Northern Rhodesia and Nyasaland and the white settlers of Southern

Rhodesia could agree on was that the Federation should be dismantled. By this point, Britain was more than happy to oblige and in March 1963 the Federation's disbanding was formally agreed. A conference to formalise the articles of dissolution took place at Victoria Falls during June, and it was agreed that the Federation would be formally dissolved at midnight on the 31 December 1963. Northern Rhodesia and Nyasaland quickly gained independence during 1964, however, Southern Rhodesia was left in constitutional limbo. Horowitz contends that this was because it was the only territory where the two main themes of decolonization – disengagement without complication and coming to terms with African nationalism – conflicted with each other.[118]

Several explanations to account for the end of the Federation have been advanced by scholars. Blake contends that it failed because the Europeans did too little to make partnership a reality while, more damagingly, the African population was encouraged to fight for independence by the achievements of other African colonies.[119] Britain has also been blamed for naïvely imagining that federation could work 'in tune with British policy and thinking and colonial affairs'.[120] Creighton saw the failure of federation as a reminder that economic considerations are not always paramount in the minds of indigenous populations who are striving for self-government.[121] Furthermore, the Federation has also been accused of paving the way for Rhodesia's attempt at independence while making Zambia more vulnerable to Rhodesian economic manipulation.[122] Contrary to guaranteeing settler independence, the Federation has also been cited as the inspiration behind African nationalism in Northern Rhodesia and Nyasaland.[123] These explanations, however, while possessing several strengths, do not fully answer crucial questions regarding the final years of the Federation. The first concerns the locus of power: did London or the Federation hold the reins? If it was the Federation, did power lie with the settlers or African nationalists? Or, if metropolitan concerns took precedence, to what extent were decisions influenced by domestic or international concerns? Secondly, how significant were economic conditions in determining the Federation's future? Is there a correlation between its economic performance and its political success? Furthermore, how can settler and African *mentalities* be explained? Were they primarily conditioned by internal or external circumstances, or a combination of both?

In summary, recent explanations for the Federation's failure have moved far away from earlier simplistic accounts which cited the all-pervasive triumph of African nationalism, or alternatively credited its demise to the final fulfilment of Britain's unsolicited task as bearer of the 'white man's burden' in central Africa. Instead, as this book will demonstrate, the final years of the Federation were shaped by a complex interaction of African dynamics, metropolitan concerns and international pressures. In doing so, it will seek to make an important contribution to our present understanding of the dynamics of decolonization in the latter days of the Central African Federation.

CHAPTER 1

CONCEPTION AND THE EARLY YEARS OF FEDERATION

Political rights, after all, mean very little to a man with an empty stomach. If we are genuinely concerned about the Africans let us give them economic development and political rights can come later.

Roy Welensky to the Northern Rhodesia Legislative Council, 24 November 1949[1]

Acquiring the Charter

A federation of Britain's central African territories only became a serious consideration following the end of World War II. Yet ideas surrounding the political and economic integration of the region had a much longer and contested history. There had been little appetite in either Whitehall or Westminster for the formal expansion of British direct control north of the Limpopo River during the nineteenth century. This began to change, however, with the discovery of significant gold deposits on the Witwatersrand in the independent Boer South African Republic (ZAR) in 1886. Gold transformed the ZAR from a sleepy agricultural backwater to a position where it supplanted the British-controlled Cape Colony as the region's economic powerhouse. Unlike the diamonds discovered in Griqualand West two decades earlier, the Witwatersrand's geographical location in an internationally recognised 'white' republic presented legal barriers to its annexation to the British Empire.[2]

By 1887 it appeared that the ZAR was willing to flex its new-found economic muscle and expand its influence into the region after the Ndebele king, Lobengula, signed a treaty of friendship with the Boer republic.[3] It also allowed Pretoria to keep a consul in residence in Lobengula's capital city of Bulawayo. This provided Cecil John Rhodes, who held his own designs on the area north of the Limpopo, with an excuse to pressure the British into action, as the peace treaty signed to end the First Anglo-Boer War (1880–1) stipulated that London would control all of the ZAR's external relations.[4] Upon hearing rumours of a treaty Rhodes urged Sir Hercules Robinson,[5] the Governor of the Cape Colony and High Commissioner in South Africa, to declare the area a protectorate, following the precedent set by the case of Bechuanaland.[6]

Robinson knew the political climate in London would not allow him to accede to Rhodes' request, however, he did agree to dispatch an envoy to negotiate with the Ndebele king. Consequently, John Moffat, the Assistant Commissioner in Bechuanaland, who was already known to Lobengula through his missionary work, departed for Bulawayo. Moffat subsequently obtained Lobengula's mark on a document, which became known as the Moffat Treaty, on 11 February 1888. This document claimed Lobengula enjoyed suzerainty over parts of what became Mashonaland where in reality he had little influence. It also removed his right to conduct an independent foreign policy. When the treaty was publicised in London in April both the ZAR and Portugal refused to recognise its legitimacy.[7]

The British government faced the dilemma that although they held little appetite for an expansionist overseas policy; they could not afford to be seen to concede British paramountcy in southern Africa to the ZAR. Yet there was little desire held by the British taxpayer to fund another protectorate over seemingly economically questionable land in central Africa. Similarly there was little faith that the Cape Parliament could lead the way in region. The arguments over the extension of the Cape to Kimberley railway to Bechuanaland had displayed the reluctance of many of the Cape's members of parliament (MPs) in pursing expansionist policies. By April 1889, however, a potential answer to the problem appeared to have been found when Rhodes arrived in London to seek a royal charter for a company to develop and colonise lands both north and south of the Zambezi River.[8]

Before embarking for London, Rhodes had tasked a party led by Charles Rudd, his long-time associate from the Kimberley diamond diggings, to secure the mineral rights for Lobengula's kingdom.[9] The party had left Kimberley on 15 August 1888, ostensibly on a hunting trip but carrying £10,000 in gold sovereigns, an introductory letter from Sir Hercules Robinson and significant quantities of brandy, champagne and stout. They reached Lobengula's capital on 20 September and by 30 October had convinced the king to set his seal on a document.[10] The Rudd Concession, as it became known, stated that, in exchange for a monthly stipend of £100, one thousand Henri-Martini rifles and ammunition and a steamboat, Rhodes would get:

> the complete and exclusive charge over all metals and minerals situated and contained within my kingdoms, principalities and dominions together with full power to do things which may be necessary to win and procure the same, and to hold, collect, and enjoy profits and revenues, if any derived from the said metals and minerals.[11]

Marshall Hole, a Chartered Company official, found it 'inconceivable' that Lobengula later claimed that he had not been fully informed of the exact terms of the Rudd Concession.[12] Yet, more recent scholarship has demonstrated that Rudd acted with 'consummate duplicity' to obtain Lobengula's agreement.[13] A missionary witness to these discussions later revealed that verbal promises were made to Lobengula that no more than ten white men would enter his country to dig for gold. Despite this, the British government later upheld the Rudd Concession in the face of criticism from Lobengula and Rhodes' European competitors.[14]

With the Rudd Concession secure, Rhodes applied for a royal charter for his company on 13 July 1889. It was a laborious process yet also eventually successful. On 29 October 1889, 364 days after Rudd's triumph with Lobengula, the British South Africa Company (Chartered Company) received its Letters Patent from Queen Victoria. On 6 May 1890 Rhodes dispatched a pioneer column north from Kimberley with instructions to avoid a direct clash with the Ndebele by heading for the rumoured goldfields of Mashonaland.[15] The column arrived at what they initially named Fort Salisbury during

September 1890. In the context of the European 'scramble for Africa', competition in central Africa was fierce. The Chartered Company had to contend with interest from Germany, Portugal and the Belgian King Leopold's Congo Free State. During 1890–1 a series of conventions demarcated British, and consequently Chartered Company, interests in the area.[16]

Rhodes was successful in securing the territory that would later become the two Rhodesias, however, objections from the African Lakes Company and local missionaries prevented Nyasaland falling under Company control.[17] As a result, it became a separate protectorate in 1891. It was envisaged that eventually the lands secured by the Chartered Company would be amalgamated into a 'Greater South Africa' and, together with the Cape and Natal colonies, help secure British paramountcy over the Boer republics of the Transvaal and the Orange Free State.[18] As Alfred Milner,[19] British High Commissioner for Southern Africa pronounced in 1899: 'one thing is quite evident. The *ultimate* [emphasis in original] end is a self-governing white Community, supported by a well-treated and justly governed black labour from Cape Town to Zambesi'.[20]

Company Days

'I have no doubt of the future of the country as a gold producing state' Rhodes proclaimed, as he reassured Chartered Company shareholders in London on 2 May 1898.[21] Events since the arrival of the pioneer column in Mashonaland had led many of his shareholders to need a great deal of reassurance. The rainy season of 1890–1, a particularly severe affair, affected the transport of supplies from the south to Fort Salisbury. The large amount of rainfall also brought malaria and the fledgling settlement was also struck by an outbreak of horse sickness. The promise of a 'second Rand' was also proving elusive as early prospecting provided little evidence of any large quantities of gold. By December 1891 conditions were such that Chartered Company shares had fallen below their par value of £1.[22]

In response Company expenditure was slashed and further investment garnered from Rhodes' other business interests: De Beers and Gold Fields of South Africa. This kept the Chartered Company afloat in the short term. Large land concessions were also granted in an attempt to stimulate speculative investment in Mashonaland and a propaganda campaign was launched in London to counter negative newspaper commentary on the enterprise.[23] Fuelled by the effects of the stagnant local economy on settlers and the financial pressure on Company shares in London, the expansion of Company rule in Mashonaland was 'an unusually brutal process' that led to approximately one-sixth of the country's 96 million acres of land being expropriated by Europeans.[24] Inevitably this process led to clashes with the African population.

Attacks by a group of Ndebele on Shona cattle and settlements near Fort Victoria in 1893 drew calls for war from Company officials who coveted the potential riches of Matebeleland. Again, Chartered Company shares fell rapidly.[25] Dr Leander Starr Jameson, Rhodes' confidant who had become the Chartered Company's Administrator in 1891 used the incident as a *casus belli* to remove the Ndebele threat and restore the share price.[26] Men were formed into columns with the promise of further land and mining claims and set off for Bulawayo. The Ndebele army, suffering from a smallpox outbreak and weakened from extensive campaigning north of the Zambezi River could not withstand the power of the settlers' modern weapons and Bulawayo fell to Company control. Lobengula escaped the city but died shortly afterwards.[27] The victory removed some of the pressure of the Company's finances as the focus of the settlers moved westwards to Bulawayo. As Ian Phimister notes, 'the whisky-soaked frustration and wretchedness' of the previous few years in Mashonaland was soon swept away.[28]

Questions soon arose over the administrative position of the two territories after the end of the war. An agreement was reached between the Chartered Company and the British Crown over the unification of Mashonaland and Matabeleland. This was subsequently confirmed by an Order-in-Council on 18 July 1894, which placed both territories under the administration of the Chartered Company. There was now the issue of a name to cover the two unified territories. Rhodes favoured 'Zambezia', while Jameson preferred 'Charterland'. The majority of settler opinion, however, preferred Rhodesia which had entered common journalistic usage by 1891. The Company officially adopted the name in 1895 and it was finally recognised by the British government with the Southern Rhodesia Order-in-Council of 1898.[29]

The improvement in conditions was closely linked to the Rand boom of 1894–5 and the renewed confidence of speculative capital.

Chartered Company expansion into Mashonaland throughout the early 1890s had been gradual and uneven. The highly localised structures of Shona groups hampered any organised opposition in the face of Company aggression. Any resistance to the Company's encroachment on African lands was met by brutal reprisals against people and their possessions. Murder and theft were commonplace and used as a means of applying administration. When it became clear that there was no 'second Rand' in the area both the Chartered Company and European settlers resorted to outright theft from both the Shona and the Ndebele. It is estimated that between October 1893 and March 1896 between 100,000 and 200,000 cattle were seized from the Ndebele alone.[30]

Furthermore, an 'illegal' hut tax was introduced in 1893 in Mashonaland, with further collections taken when it became legal in 1894. Shona resistance to the hut tax was widespread and its collection was arbitrary and irregular, leading to it to be 'more like the levy of tribute than the collection of a civilian tax'.[31] Forced labour also became prevalent in this period as the demand for workers by mine owners and farmers garnered little enthusiasm with the African population. The reality of Chartered rule provided many reasons for Africans to resist. An opportunity to remove the European settlers appeared to present itself in 1895 when a substantial number of Company police left the territory to prepare for the Jameson Raid. Rhodes believed that with a little encouragement a revolution of the *uitlanders* in the ZAR could be fostered which would provide for the elimination of President Paul Kruger and his Transvaal state.[32] Jameson's men were expected to support the uprising, however, it failed to materialise. Jameson took matters into his own hands and entered the Transvaal from the Bechuanaland Protectorate with 600 Chartered Company police and volunteers but was forced into an inglorious surrender at Doornkop, fourteen miles from Johannesburg.[33]

The arrest of Jameson and a significant portion of his police force left Southern Rhodesia perilously underprepared for any African rebellion. Tensions had also been exacerbated by the outbreak of cattle disease in 1896 which placed further pressure on Africans in the territory.[34] The war of 1893 had not destroyed Ndebele society and in March 1896 Lobengula's son, Nyamanda, led his people in revolt. Rhodes realised that in order to save his Royal Charter the Ndebele rebellion had to be brought to a swift end. By mid-October 1896 a combination of war, rinderpest and famine and Rhodes' promises to recognise African communal tenure and purchase land between Bulawayo and the Matopos for the Ndebele to settle on brought the rebellion to an end.[35]

The Company was also faced by a series of uprisings in Mashonaland as the Shona also rebelled against Company rule. It took the Chartered Company until the end of 1898 to fully quell the resistance to their rule.[36] To Earl Grey, who arrived in Salisbury along with Rhodes in November 1896 to replaced Jameson as Administrator, the uprisings were caused by 'the incapacity of a warlike and aristocratic race to give up their old habits, and to accept their natural place in the peaceful and industrial organization of a settled civilized community' rather than the injustices of Chartered Company administration.[37] Rhodes also had to address growing settler dissatisfaction with the Chartered Company, which was particular strong in Salisbury against the backdrop of the Shona rebellion. In an attempt to calm these rising tensions, Rhodes gave a speech to an audience of leading settlers in November 1896 in which he informed them that he favoured a semi-elective system of representation in preparation for eventual self-government. He also promised to provide financial compensation to anyone who had suffered as a result of the rebellions.[38] With settler passions calmed, Rhodes returned to London to deal with his critics there.

It was clear to Rhodes that the Jameson Raid and the uprisings could threaten the Company's Royal Charter. Joseph Chamberlain, the Colonial Secretary who was also implicated in the failed coup, was unable to prevent a House of Commons inquiry into the circumstances of the raid.[39] He did, however, agree to defend Rhodes in exchange for Rhodes' silence as to his role in events. By the time the inquiry reported in July 1897, the changing political situation in South Africa and Rhodes' part in negotiating the end of the Ndebele uprising had dissipated some of the criticism against him. As a result the Company kept the Charter and Rhodes retained his membership of the Privy Council.[40]

With the Charter secure, a further reorganisation of the territory's government was initiated. Alfred Milner, the new High Commissioner of Southern Africa, embarked on a tour of Southern Rhodesia and agreed to a revision of the territory's constitution. Rhodes agreed that representation should be given to settlers under a resident commissioner, the first being Sir Richard Martin, responsible to the High Commissioner.[41] Consequently, The Southern Rhodesia Order-in-Council of 1898 led to the appointment of two administrators: William Milton, in Salisbury;[42] and Albert, Earl Grey in Bulawayo.[43] All communication with the London Board of the Company of the Colonial Office went through the Salisbury administration making Milton *primus inter pares*. Although the administrator in Bulawayo sat on the governing council during his visits to Salisbury, the lack of a rail connection in the early years made his attendance a rare occurrence. This Order-in-Council remained the governing instrument in Southern Rhodesia until responsible government was introduced 25 years later.[44]

Settler representation took shape through a new Legislative Council (LegCo) that contained ten members: the Administrator, five members nominated by the Chartered Company and approved by the Colonial Office, and four elected settlers who qualified via a basis of property ownership and literacy. In an attempt to keep poor whites from the Transvaal from influencing the process, only British subjects could qualify for the franchise.[45] A key early problem that needed to be addressed in the LegCo was access to land for both Africans and new European settlers. The speculative nature of early settlement had led to large swathes of the countryside being held by absentee landlords who had no intention of developing it for the good of the territory. This made it difficult to set aside a suitable area of land for African reserves and the process was laboriously slow. In the event it took until 1908 before the Colonial Office approved the creation of the reserves.[46] The early settler representatives on the LegCo enjoyed close connections with the large speculative land-owning companies and were opposed to any change. Numerous reforms were attempted to the system over the first decades of settlement, but to little avail.[47] By 1912 only one million of the eight million acres of land owned by companies had undergone any development.[48]

Rhodes had often used his vast wealth and charm to dampen down the fires of settler discontent during the early years of settlement. Following his death in 1902 and the end of the Second Anglo-Boer War (1899–1902) settler opposition to Chartered Company rule, particularly in Mashonaland, intensified. The difficulties involved in raising issues with the London Board without Rhodes' backing and the perennial complaints over land, mining royalties and railway rates all came to the fore. As a result, the Chartered Company agreed to a further elected member on the LegCo. This would provide parity with official members and was ratified by an Order-in-Council in 1903. Concessions were also given on royalties and railway rates. However the Chartered Company held firm on two important issues: that if the colony was to become independent it must accept responsibility for the Company's past administrative debts. Secondly, that all land not allocated to settlers, companies or designated as African reserves belonged to the Company. There was never an agreement on these issues between the Company and the settlers and the matter was only determined by a judgement from the Judicial Committee of the Privy Council in 1918.[49]

In October 1914 Sir Drummond Chaplin,[50] a protégé of Rhodes and a close friend of Jameson, replaced Milton as Chartered Company Administrator in Mashonaland.[51] By this point the debate as to the future of Southern Rhodesia after Chartered Company rule was intensifying. One view was that Rhodesia should be assimilated into the Union of South Africa. This view had powerful supporters in the Union, being advocated by the South African Prime Minister, General Jan Smuts.[52] It was feared by some settlers that if Southern Rhodesia joined the Union it would become dominated by Afrikaner nationalism which was increasingly taking hold south of the Limpopo. Many who held this view advocated a possible union with Northern Rhodesia and East Africa to create a 'Greater Rhodesia' that would act as a counterpoise to the growing Afrikaner influence in the south.[53]

The competing interests of the Chartered Company, the Colonial Office and the settlers came to the fore in 1917 when Dougal Malcom,[54] a director of the Chartered Company, secured support within the LegCo from Chaplin to push for amalgamation with Northern Rhodesia. This was a direct challenge to the majority of settlers in both territories who did not favour amalgamation. By the late 1910s the settler population in Northern Rhodesia stood at around 3,000 and they feared that their interests would be of little consequence, even with representation, to decision makers in Salisbury. In Southern Rhodesia, many settlers feared that the large African population north of the Zambezi would make it more difficult to persuade London to concede to their wish for responsible government.[55] In the event, the vote in the Southern Rhodesian LegCo was carried in favour of amalgamation, yet the overwhelming opposition from elected members forced Chaplin and Jameson to reconsider. Instead they proposed that both territories should come under the same administrator. This measure was still opposed by its elected members, particularly by Charles Coghlan[56] and consequently the Colonial Secretary, Walter Long,[57] rejected Chaplin's request.[58]

A development that augured the end of Chartered Company rule was the Privy Council's decision on the ownership of unalienated land during 1918. Although it did not challenge the title of those granted land by the Chartered Company, it ruled that all unalienated land would be owned by the Crown. It did, however, decree that the Chartered Company could claim against the Crown for administrative expenses once it ceased to govern the territory. If the Chartered Company was unable to sell the unalienable land to benefit its shareholders there was little incentive to continue to cover the bill of administration. Consequently, a claim for £7,866,000 was handed to the Colonial Office to cover their administrative costs in the territory to date. In response, the British government appointed a Commission of Enquiry under Lord Cave to assess the figure.[59] Much to the Chartered Company's distress, the Cave Commission fixed its compensation at a figure of £4,435,000. From this figure it was recommended that deductions were made to cover the appropriation of unalienable land by the Company for its farming and ranching concerns and grants of land made in lieu of cash.[60]

The almost certain removal of Chartered Company rule invigorated Southern Rhodesian politics. It was clear that there were two options for the post-Company period: either incorporation into the Union or 'responsible government', independent of South African interference. The Responsible Government Association (RGA) was founded in 1917 in support of the latter, while in 1919 the Rhodesia Unionist Association (RUA) was created in favour of the former. The RGA drew much of its support from the Rhodesia Agriculture Union whose members feared that they would lose out in a competition for labour with the Rand. They were also backed by Earl Buxton, High Commissioner and Governor General of South Africa who influenced Milner, by now Secretary of State for the Colonies, giving the campaign important support in British circles.[61]

The RUA, on the other hand, enjoyed the support of the mining companies, in addition to that of many Afrikaners and professionals.[62] The LegCo elections during April 1920 gave a further indication that the responsible-government campaign was in the ascendancy. Out of the 13 members elected, 12 supported responsible government.

The campaign did receive a blow in February 1921 as Milner resigned as Colonial Secretary and was replaced by Winston Churchill, who was not fully convinced by the plan.[63] Consequently, Churchill appointed a committee to advise him on the situation in both of the Rhodesias under the chairmanship of Earl Buxton. It did not take long for the committee to find in favour of granting the Southern Rhodesian electorate a referendum.[64]

The Chartered Company was incensed by the report of the Cave Commission and swiftly announced its preference for amalgamation into the Union. In South Africa, Smut's victory over J. B. M. Hertzog's National Party in the 1921 election had given him majorities in both Houses which were needed to formally request the incorporation of a new territory into the Union.[65] It was clear at this point that Churchill was in favour of amalgamation but the Buxton Committee had stressed that any solution could not be forced onto the Southern Rhodesian settlers without prior consultation. The most he could do was insist that the forthcoming referendum included an amalgamation option. On 25 May 1922, the LegCo set the date of the referendum as 27 October 1922 and required Smuts to provide details of his amalgamation offer by 30 June. Smuts subsequently managed to get this deadline extended until 30 July.[66]

Smuts offered Southern Rhodesia ten members in the House of Assembly and five in the Senate, to be increased as Southern Rhodesia's population rose. He also detailed generous financial arrangements for territorial development and compensation for loss of tariffs. The civil service would be amalgamated into its South African counterpart, however it was stressed that there would be no recruitment of Southern Rhodesia's African labour elsewhere in the Union. However, he did require that Dutch should become a co-equal official language and that all white South Africans should have free movement rights within the territory. Smuts offered the Chartered Company £6,836,500 for its land, public works and railways but was prepared to let the Company keep its other commercial rights.[67]

The European population at the time of the referendum was c. 35,000 and c. 20,000 individuals qualified for the electoral roll. Of the estimated c. 900,000 Africans in the colony, only 60 qualified to make their voice heard. When the referendum took place the vote was close, 8,774 votes went to responsible government, while 5,989 went for incorporation into the union.[68] After Southern Rhodesia gained self-government, the Chartered Company relinquished its administration of Northern Rhodesia and in 1924 administration of the territory passed to the British government who henceforth governed it as a tropical dependency. Despite their loss of administrative responsibility in both Northern and Southern Rhodesia, the Chartered Company retained extensive land and mineral rights along with an 86 per cent stake in Rhodesia Railways.[69]

Responsible Government

After the dust had settled on the referendum result, the Colonial Office announced the terms of its settlement with the Chartered Company. On 10 July 1923 the Company's shareholders were given just a fortnight to approve the Colonial Office offer of £3,750,000 in settlement for its claims. In addition, the Company would be awarded 50 per cent of land sales in the north-east of the territory. In return it was expected to renounce its claim on unalienated land and surrender its administrative infrastructure in the country. Its commercial, railway and mineral rights would remain, though it would cease to administer either of the Rhodesias. The new government would assume power in Southern Rhodesia on 1 October 1923 and during April 1924 the administration of Northern Rhodesia would be taken over by the Crown.[70]

The Letters Patent granting Southern Rhodesia responsible government were published on 24 September 1923 and their ambiguous nature was crucial to explaining the later history of the Federation. They stated that both executive and legislative power in Southern Rhodesia was subordinate to the British government which retained the right to appoint the territory's governor. In addition, legal appeals could be remitted to the Privy Council and there were substantial limitations on the new Legislative Assembly's ability to pass laws. Crucially the Legislative Assembly was forbidden to legislate in regard to the Native Department or African reserves. The new Legislative Assembly was to have 30 members and like its predecessor the franchise was based on a property or income basis together with a literacy test. Although there was no overt racial discrimination these rules resulted in a resoundingly white electorate with a few Indian shopkeepers and prosperous African farmers also qualifying.[71] Therefore, in reality the new system was responsible government subject to certain limitations, rather than self-government.

In practice, however, these limitations were purely theoretical. From the very beginning the Southern Rhodesian Assembly was treated by London as if it enjoyed responsible government. Westminster never used its right to legislate for areas not covered by the Legislative Assembly nor did it ever countermand any laws enacted in Salisbury. The Legislative Assembly did, by manner of convention, submit proposed law changes to London before raising them in parliament. It is important to note, however, that although the British government had input into legislation, all initiative came from Salisbury. This convention made the actual government of Southern Rhodesia far closer to that of a self-governing Dominion than a Crown Colony with self-government.[72]

The creation of the Dominions Office in 1925 was a mixed blessing for Southern Rhodesia settler aspirations. In their favour, was that the Dominions Office had been created to handle relations with those colonies considered by the Balfour Declaration of 1926 as 'autonomous communities within the British Empire'.[73] The Dominions Office treated Southern Rhodesia as if it had already been given self-government, rather than the more paternal approach of the Colonial Office. Initially both offices came under the same Secretary of State, however in 1930 a separate Secretary of State for the Dominions was created and given responsibility for Southern Rhodesia. Consequently Northern and Southern Rhodesia came under different jurisdictions and that metropolitan rivalry would further complicate inter-territorial relations during the federal period.[74]

With Southern Rhodesia's relationship with the Union of South Africa now decided, greater attention was placed on the territory's relationship with its neighbour north of the Zambezi River. Until close to his death, Coghlan retained the view that amalgamation with Northern Rhodesia would be a mistake. However, the difficulties involved in integrating the territories' railway systems had persuaded him to reconsider. His replacement as Southern Rhodesian Premier, Howard Moffat,[75] was also in favour of amalgamation. Moffat had previously supervised mineral exploration in Northern Rhodesia and appreciated the potential of the colony's copper deposits.[76] Coghlan's initial interest in Northern Rhodesia was solely confined to the railway strip running north-east of Livingstone to Broken Hill and then on to the Congo. The Northern Rhodesian LegCo was, however, against any dismemberment of the territory; as was Moffat who convinced Coghlan that the whole area should be incorporated as it would guarantee a ready supply of African labour.[77]

By the 1920s the fabled mineral wealth that had instigated European occupation of the region began to become a reality on the Northern Rhodesian Copperbelt. Twenty years earlier Edmund Davis[78] and Robert Williams,[79] two financiers with experience in mining, had played a key role in prospecting for mineral deposits in the region. Williams, however, soon shifted his attentions across the border to Katanga, leaving William Collier, a prospector working for Davis, free to peg claims on the Roan Antelope and Bwana M'Kubwa deposits during 1902, and on the Chambishi deposits the following year. At first glance it appeared that Katanga offered the greater return to investors as it contained far greater visible oxide-ore bodies than the Copperbelt. This began to change when the problems with transport on the Copperbelt were eased following the completion of a railway line north from Broken Hill to Katanga.[80]

The mineral wealth of the Copperbelt was predominantly that of sulphide copper, which was more difficult to exploit than the oxide deposits in Katanga. However, the dramatic increase in demand for copper after World War I, due to the growth of the automobile and electrical industries,[81] combined with technological breakthroughs in the metallurgical industry, such as aerial photography, made large-scale exploitation viable.[82] Medical advances also ensured it was now possible for Europeans to live in the region and remain reasonably healthy, as the benefits of the nineteenth-century scientific breakthrough of germ theory – the knowledge that malaria and sleeping sickness were transmitted through insects – began to be felt.[83] One financier who took advantage of these developments was Alfred Chester Beatty.[84]

Beatty, an American mining engineer based in London, provided nine-tenths of the £50,000 founding capital of Selection Trust Limited in 1914.[85] Preston K. Horner, another American mining engineer, and a former manager of *Union Minière du Haut Katanga* talked enthusiastically with Beatty over the prospects of finding large-scale copper deposits in Northern Rhodesia. Beatty agreed with Horner and soon after formed Copper Ventures Limited, a syndicate whose aim was to acquire rights for the application of the Perkins Process[86] in the treatment of copper ores in Northern Rhodesia.[87] The company soon acquired an option over Nkana Claims, and shortly after secured, with the assistance of Davis, the 1,800 square-mile Nkana Concession, which surrounded Nkana Claims, and the rights to over 50,000 square miles in the north-western part of the territory. Following this, the company floated Rhodesian Congo Border Concessions Limited (RCBC) to further explore the area.[88]

Large-scale development of the Copperbelt was given further impetus in 1922 as the Chartered Company decided to grant sole prospecting privileges over large areas to stable financial companies. Beatty sold a one-third interest in Roan Antelope mine to the American Metal Company (AMC) during 1927. American Metal originated in 1887 with financiers from Britain, Germany and the United States; however, after World War I it became an exclusively American company.[89] Beatty formed a subsidiary company, RST, in order to finance further development on the Copperbelt, and in 1930 sold a controlling interest of 50.6 per cent to the AMC. In return he received the largest single block of AMC stock.[90] Consequently, although Beatty became a British citizen in 1933, his company retained an American majority shareholding throughout the life of the Federation.

The second mining interest on the Copperbelt was Ernest Oppenheimer's[91] Anglo American Corporation.[92] Unlike RST, Anglo's primary business interests were located in South Africa. The company was predominantly concerned with control of the production and sale of diamonds on the world market, though it also held substantial interests in gold and coal mines on the South African Rand. During 1924, Edmund Davis, by now chairman of the small Bwana Mkubwa copper mine in which the Selection Trust had an interest, required fresh capital. Davis had been engaged in negotiations with the Portuguese government on behalf of Ernest Oppenheimer, who was attempting to participate in the development of diamond deposits in Angola.

Oppenheimer agreed to supply the capital provided Anglo American were appointed as consulting engineers, and at this time Oppenheimer entered into agreement with Consolidated African Selection Trust Limited (CAST) to sell its diamonds from the Gold Coast and Sierra Leone. Beatty further suggested that Oppenheimer should participate in the Rhodesian Congo Border Concession project. Consequently, on 1 January 1925 Anglo American were appointed as consulting engineers. Anglo thereby acquired control of the Nkana mine and a third interest in Mufulira. Rhodesian Anglo American Limited was founded during December 1928.[93] It was financed by Anglo American, the United States mining companies Kennecott and Newmont, other South African financial houses and the British South Africa Company.[94] In March 1931, further consolidation of mining interests on the Copperbelt was achieved when RCBC, Bwana M'Kubwa and Nchanga copper companies were merged to create Rhokana Corporation Ltd.[95]

The late 1920s also saw ideas around a closer association of Britain's central and east African possessions mooted in Westminster and Whitehall. Consequently, a Commission of Inquiry had been formed under the chairmanship of Sir Edward Hilton-Young to examine the whole question of closer association.[96] The Hilton-Young Commission published its findings in the form of a white paper in 1929.[97] In the event Hilton-Young refused to sign the majority report which dismissed out of hand any form of self-government for east and central Africa under settler control. Instead, it reaffirmed an earlier white paper from 1923 on Kenya (the Devonshire Declaration), which placed African interests as paramount and stated that the territories should be administered through a policy of trusteeship.[98] During his tenure as Colonial Secretary from 1924 to 1929, Leo Amery's failure to repeal any Southern Rhodesian legislation dealing with African Affairs confirmed that African paramountcy did not apply in Southern Rhodesia. Lord Passfield, Amery's successor, made it clear in a memorandum in 1930 that this was not to be the case in Northern Rhodesia.[99]

To many Northern Rhodesian settlers, Passfield's memorandum made it clear that if they wished to control their own affairs they needed to remove Colonial Office administration of their territory. As such, amalgamation with Southern Rhodesia became a far more attractive option. In July 1932, the British government responded to demands from the Northern Rhodesian LegCo for amalgamation with the South. London, while not ruling out amalgamation, stressed that conditions in the territories were not yet suitable for amalgamation to be considered. The main point of concern was the differing approaches to African affairs in the territories.[100]

From 1933 onwards three main issues defined Southern Rhodesian politics until the end of World War II: recovery from the economic crisis, the colony's 'destiny' and race relations. Economically the colony's performance began to improve, and was buoyed by the increasing demand for coal from the Northern Rhodesian Copperbelt. The Southern Rhodesian railways also benefited from the growing freight rates on copper transported on its infrastructure to the Mozambique port of Beira. Britain's, albeit late, decision to rearm against the threat of Nazi Germany in the late 1930s also helped Southern Rhodesia's export of base metals. Production of the key agricultural crop of tobacco had suffered greatly, declining from 25,000,000 pounds in 1928 to 3,500,000 pounds in 1931. It did, however, recover quickly, reaching 26,700,000 pounds in 1934, helped by the policy of imperial preference agreed at the Ottawa Conference in 1932 and British tobacco manufacturers' decision to mix cheaper Rhodesian tobacco in with its more expensive American counterpart.[101]

In regard to Southern Rhodesia's constitutional future, it was clear that the option of becoming the Union of South Africa's fifth province was still not favoured by the majority of the territory's settlers. Instead, a Rhodesian sub-imperialism with amalgamation with the north began to gain traction. The apparent wealth of the Copperbelt proved desirable to the south. In addition, amalgamation opened up the possibility of a coordinated railway system, a customs union and the creation of a larger market, which all proved attractive concepts to those favouring this option. There was, however, scepticism in some circles. In the case of Southern Rhodesian settlers there was the fear that amalgamation would threaten the territory's development as a 'white man's country' as amalgamation would significantly increase the black population. In Northern Rhodesia Africans feared that amalgamation would materially affect their positions by introducing the Land Apportionment Act[102] and other more restrictive racial practices from south of the Zambezi.[103]

Vocal settler opinion in both Rhodesias favoured amalgamation from 1933 onwards. They were eventually joined by the Chartered Company, which had opposed amalgamation at the time of the Hilton Young Commission but supported the move four years later. Similarly Ernest Oppenheimer's Anglo American Corporation was in favour. Even Smuts' coalition government in the Union indicated it would not oppose the development. Opposition to amalgamation was prevalent amongst Northern Rhodesian civil servants and 'officials' on the territory's LegCo, and most importantly from Africans in both of the territories. They were able to utilise the supporters among the clergy, missionaries and academics in both Britain and Africa to press their case.[104]

Whitehall was torn between its paternalistic stance and the desire to counterbalance the Union of South Africa which, even before 1948, appeared to be distancing itself from Britain. Indeed, there was the fear in some British circles by the late 1930s that a war with Germany would see South Africa opt for neutrality. In discussions around the future associations of Britain's central African possessions in this period the question of what to do with Nyasaland loomed large. The debate centred on whether Nyasaland should join with Northern Rhodesia or perhaps be included in a federation of Britain's east African territories. A further option was to include Nyasaland in a possible federation with both Rhodesias. Even the question of how an eventual federation between the two Rhodesias would take place was complicated.[105]

In January 1936 a conference at Victoria Falls was attended by representatives of the Northern Rhodesian LegCo and delegates of the three main political parties in Southern Rhodesia. The Conference passed a resolution calling for amalgamation of the two territories. This formed the basis of a motion subsequently carried in the Southern Rhodesian Assembly in May 1936.[106] Huggins visited London in 1937 to press the settlers' case. As a result, the British government agreed to another commission to contemplate the territories' future association. Although there was little expectation of success on the part of Huggins, he had convinced the British government to leave to the possibility of amalgamation under the Commission's terms of reference. The Commission was led by Lord Bledisloe, a former Governor General of New Zealand.

The Commission took evidence from across British Central Africa and it was clear that the majority of Africans consulted were opposed to amalgamation.[107] Its report was released in March 1939 and while the majority report recognised the appeal of closer association between the territories, it concluded that the territories' 'native policies' were too divergent to make amalgamation a viable option. Federation was also ruled out due to the constitutional differences between the territories being too great as well as the incompatibility of their legal status. The Commission did, however, recommend the immediate amalgamation of Northern Rhodesia and Nyasaland and the creation of an Inter-Territorial Council to co-ordinate administration, economic policy and development between the Rhodesias.[108]

Towards Federation

The outbreak of World War II resulted in discussions over the Bledisloe Report's conclusions being placed on hold. Huggins did manage to persuade the British government to assign Lord Hailey to examine the possibility of coordinating 'native policy' in the Rhodesias and Nyasaland.[109] In the event, however, this offered little comfort as it was clear to Hailey that the policies in place were vastly different and there was no guarantee that they would lessen over time.[110] Yet it was apparent to officials in Whitehall that settler calls for amalgamation would need to be appeased. In November 1943 Evelyn Baring, the governor of Southern Rhodesia, warned London that failure to make a positive step towards closer association could lead to Southern Rhodesia's amalgamation into the Union of South Africa or amalgamation on terms which would introduce the Southern Rhodesian colour bar into the Copperbelt.[111] Although immediate action was not taken, Oliver Stanley, Secretary of State for the Colonies, announced the creation of a Central African Council on 18 October 1944.[112] The Central African Council would be responsible for all development and welfare plans and for the allocation of Colonial Development Fund grants to Northern Rhodesia and Nyasaland. It did not, however, have any responsibility for African policy, which remained under the purview of the individual territories.[113]

Philip Murphy contends that the Central African Council's creation represented a 'double-blow' for those Northern Rhodesian settlers who wished for closer association by ruling out amalgamation. The constitutional changes announced for the territory added to their woes. Although they stipulated that unofficial members would be the majority in the LegCo, two of the four additional members would represent African rather than settler interests. The proposals, therefore, failed to offer representative government on Southern Rhodesian lines. Given the Bledisloe Commissions recommendation that if the territories were to amalgamate they needed to be at a similar level of constitutional development this was a significant setback.[114] Sir Andrew Cohen, Assistant Secretary in the Colonial Office, made it clear that he did not view the proposals for the creation of the Council as 'a step towards amalgamation'.[115] Rather it was intended to show that the British government did 'intend co-ordination between the [t]erritories to be a reality' rather than 'mere window dressing', as Britain's critics had suggested.[116] This was in direct contrast to Welensky who held a clear belief that if the Council was a success it could 'be the beginning, or foundation, of amalgamation between the territories'.[117]

During 1948 a delegation from Northern Rhodesia arrived in London to discuss the territory's constitution. The delegation included settler unofficial members and two Africans who had been selected by the African Representative Council. When they met with Cohen they found his attitude towards closer association had softened. Huggins' United Party had lost its overall majority in Southern Rhodesia during the 1946 general election, and consequently he had formed a minority government with the support of the opposition Liberal Party. Given that the Liberal Party opposed amalgamation Huggins had toned down his public support for the cause, which perhaps led Cohen to presume that settler leaders were prepared to accept a British designed closer association.[118]

Earlier in 1948 the decision had been taken by pro-amalgamation settlers in Northern and Southern Rhodesia to create a committee to promote their desired goal.[119] The United Central Africa Association (UCAA) was formed on 31 March 1948 and its chairman, F. E. Harris, was a close friend of Huggins. Members of the UCAA met with unofficial representatives from the Northern Rhodesia LegCo in Lusaka in June that year. Following discussions they decided that their best chance of securing the cooperation of the British government would be to push for federation rather than amalgamation. This changed approach found favour with Cohen who noted in a minute that he had 'for some time taken the view that federation of the three territories should be the ultimate aim of policy'. Cohen did recognise, however, that there would be potential administrative difficulties of linking a self-governing territory with two protectorates although in his opinion these difficulties were not 'insuperable'.[120] The day before Cohen penned his thoughts, Huggins had engineered the fall of his minority government in an attempt to win a clear mandate to push for federation.[121]

Roy Welensky also revealed that he had come to the conclusion that there was little to be gained by pressing for amalgamation after he had met with British officials, as part of the Northern Rhodesian delegation, on 30 July 1948. In these discussions the British delegation had stressed that under no circumstances would amalgamation be allowed. Arthur Creech-Jones,[122] Secretary of State for the Colonies, told Welensky in no uncertain terms that 'no government, irrespective of its political hue, would carry out that action today [placing the responsibility of Northern Rhodesia and Nyasaland's Africans into the hands of the Southern Rhodesian settlers]. The world wouldn't put up with it'.[123] This marked a shift in Welensky's attitude. In subsequent discussions he played to British desires, by pressing for a federation which would have all the economic advantages of amalgamation, but 'would not prejudice the advancement of the African population in Northern Rhodesia'.[124]

In order for a federation to be a serious proposition there needed to be an agreement from the Southern Rhodesian settlers. In the general election that followed on 16 September Huggins secured a safe majority which enabled him to re-enter discussions with renewed vigour. Shortly after the result was declared, he announced that he would use a forthcoming trip to London for the dominions' prime ministers' conference to press again for a closer association of Britain's central African territories.[125] It was during October 1948 that both Huggins and Welensky publicly came out in favour of federation.

Richard Wood suggests that the 'parlous state' of Southern Rhodesia's finances at this time 'were undoubtedly a major influence' on Huggins' decision to come out in favour of federation. The economic advantages of a link with the Northern Rhodesian Copperbelt have also been stressed in much of the literature surrounding the formation of the Federation.[126] As mentioned in the introduction, the economic compatibility of the territories would enable diversification of their economies and provide a more attractive proposition for foreign investment.[127]

This prospect persuaded many liberals in Britain that federation was the least worst way to further economic development and thus combat the poverty under which many Africans lived.[128] Britain also saw economic prosperity as a way to overcome African hostility to federation and also influence settler policies. As already highlighted, it was suggested that African opposition to federation would soon wane as the economic benefits improved their standard of living, and settlers would be forced to moderate their racial policy in order to receive the cooperation of Africans. Thus economic necessity would 'force accommodations between white and black interests'.[129] For Britain the economic benefits were twofold. The immediate postwar period gave rise to what has become known as the 'second colonial occupation', due to Britain's increased interest in making its overseas possessions contribute to its postwar reconstruction.[130] Central African policy was influenced by this and it was assumed that a federation would encourage the production of colonial commodities, such as Southern Rhodesian tobacco, which would earn valuable dollars for the sterling market as a whole.[131] Secondly, a federation would also be advantageous for Britain's economy, as it would provide an improved trading block within central Africa for British goods.[132]

Economic incentives also spurred the settler campaign for federation during the late 1940s and early 1950s.[133] It should be stressed, however, that although business could exert a level of influence over settler politics, the link was not as powerful as crudely deterministic analysis may suggest.[134] It is unclear whether or not any detailed economic analysis predicting the effect of federation was carried out before it was implemented. That is, economic advantage was assumed rather than proved.[135]

With Huggins and Welensky now united behind the idea of a Central African Federation, senior Colonial Office officials were 'broadly positive' about the prospect for discussions. Creech-Jones, however, remained cautious and gave the impression that the initiative for any scheme should come from settler leaders.[136] An initiative that was taken up on 20 December when Welensky announced that a conference on closer association would be held at Victoria Falls on 16 and 17 February 1949. It was clear from the outset that there were limitations as to what the conference could achieve. First, there were no representatives of the British government present. Secondly, only Huggins spoke for a government in office as the representatives for Northern Rhodesia and Nyasaland were drawn from settler representatives on their respective Legislative Councils. Thirdly, no Africans from any of the three territories were invited. Stuart Gore-Browne was invited to represent Africans in Northern Rhodesia, yet this was hardly a progressive demonstration of the willingness of settlers to give Africans a say in their own futures. The talks concluded by recommending that a committee of technical experts should be formed to draft a constitution and calculate the financial implications.

In addition, a further meeting should be arranged to decide on how the British government should be approached.[137]

To British officials, it was clear after the Victoria Falls conference that both Huggins and Welensky were prepared to use any means necessary to achieve federation. In February 1949, Welensky intimated to a visiting Colonial Office official that if the Colonial Secretary did not back the settlers' plans, he would ensure that the unofficial members of the Northern Rhodesian LegCo would attempt to disrupt the administration of the territory. Similarly, it was suggested that if federation was not secured the Southern Rhodesian government would refuse to continue to cooperate with the Central African Council. Consequently, London had to be proactive or risk losing control of the process.[138]

Eventually the Southern Rhodesian government forced the issue during January 1950 by placing a motion on the Central African Council agenda that called for the organisation's abolition in 12 months' time. This move was calculated to imply that Salisbury would look to foster closer relations with the Union of South Africa. Arthur Benson, the Chief Secretary of the Central African Council, informed Whitehall that he felt it was 'essential that every endeavour should be made to keep Southern Rhodesia looking north' and suggested the only way this could happen would be if 'some means of closer association between the three territories could be found'.[139] The issue of growing South African influence was an issue that became increasingly pushed by Welensky and eventually provided an area where Cohen and Welensky could agree: that closer cooperation between Britain's central African territories could help to stymie the influence of the Union of South Africa in the region. In this respect federation could be sold as a way to strengthen the forces of liberalism and racial partnership and counterbalance South African practices.[140]

By early 1951 the idea of a federation of Britain's Central African territories as a means to stymie the advance of Afrikaner influence north of the Limpopo was gaining increasing traction in British circles. Patrick Gordon Walker, secretary of state for Commonwealth relations, embarked on a tour of southern and central Africa between 18 January and 3 March 1951.[141] Although he was convinced that apartheid could not be supported, Britain's economic weakness meant that cooperation with South Africa had to remain the prime objective of British policy in the region.[142] In addition, Gordon Walker became convinced that there was a threat to the Rhodesias from the Union and that a federation of British colonies would be the most effective way to meet it.[143] To Hyam, Gordon Walker's tour was 'the most important single event in stepping up the commitment of the British government to federation'.[144]

Soon after Gordon Walker's return, a conference took place attended by officials from Britain and central Africa which was chaired by Herbert Baxter, the head of the British delegation. Baxter reported that the Southern Rhodesian delegates had arrived at the conference expecting to find 'a spirit of stonewalling and procrastination' from their British counterparts yet this proved not to be the case. Instead, Baxter suggested that the conference 'proceeded in an excellent atmosphere of cooperation and harmony'.[145] The conclusions of the conference were published at the end of March. They laid the foundations for the eventual federal scheme that would be implemented. Key issues such as territorial responsibility for the administration of the day-to-day lives of Africans and the creation of an African Affairs board to evaluate federal legislation were suggested here. The fear of Afrikaner influence was not explicitly mentioned in the report so as not to anger Pretoria, however a confidential minute from Baxter and Cohen stressed the potential threat to the territories' independence and 'British way of life'.[146]

As Hyam suggests, the Baxter Report taken in conjunction with Gordon Walker's assessment of the situation in the region was 'striking, and it proved decisive' in convincing the Colonial Secretary, James Griffiths,[147] to support federation.[148] Consequently, there was the rare occurrence of agreement between the secretaries of state for the Colonies and Commonwealth Relations with both Griffiths and Gordon Walker backing federation. Baxter and Cohen drafted a memorandum which Griffiths and Gordon Walker jointly presented to Cabinet. Murphy suggests that this memorandum was 'as notable for what it did *not* say as for what it did'.[149] The fear of encroaching Afrikaner influence was clearly acknowledged yet there was little attention given to settler pressure for closer union. Consequently, the central African settlers became increasingly cast as the 'upholders of British values, under threat from an illiberal alien culture'.[150]

Despite the perceived threat of South Africa, it was becoming increasingly clear that many Africans in Southern Rhodesia were cautiously optimistic about the idea as association with the north held the potential to improve their political situation.[151] In the northern territories, however, many felt they had nothing to gain and everything to lose.[152] Moreover, they saw federation as amalgamation under a different name.[153] Resistance in the north focused on the fact that power would pass from the Colonial Office to European communities in general and to Southern Rhodesia in particular, ruling out the eventual opportunity for self-government.[154] Opposition to closer association with Southern Rhodesia has been linked to its reputation as a 'white man's country'. This reputation was widespread due to the Africans' own experiences there as migrant workers.[155] The federal campaign has been cited as the 'decisive stimulus' for the formation of northern nationalist political movements. This was not the case in Southern Rhodesia where it delayed the formation of a united movement.[156] Ultimately, African opposition failed in 1953 because settler pressure and British belief in federation was too strong.[157]

Gordon Walker returned to Central Africa in September 1951 for a ministerial conference at Victoria Falls to discuss the proposals that had emerged from the officials' conference chaired by Baxter. These had been previously published as a white paper during June.[158] The conference, however, was not a success. The British government were still reluctant to come out fully in favour of a federation. Furthermore, the decision by the British Prime Minister, Clement Attlee,[159] to call a general election on the second day of the conference further undermined it. Given the Labour government's slim majority, settler representatives had little incentive to make concessions given the probability that they would be faced after the election by a more sympathetic Conservative party.[160] In the event the settlers were proved right, as Winston Churchill's Conservatives were returned to power. The new Colonial Secretary, Oliver Lyttelton,[161] wasted no time in expressing the view that there was an urgent need for a federation along the lines of the officials' report.[162]

By January of 1952 there was a growing acceptance in Whitehall that African opposition in the northern territories would not be enough to stop the creation of a federation. It was clear that it would be impossible to create a federation that would satisfy both settlers and Africans and the British government's decision to discount African opinion left only the settlers to appease. Consequently, Huggins and his finance minister, Sir Edgar Whitehead,[163] and the Governors of Northern Rhodesia and Nyasaland, Sir Gilbert Rennie[164] and Sir Geoffrey Colby[165] respectively, travelled to London for secret talks. The side-lining of African interests was clear as it was confirmed that the British were prepared to remove the necessity of a minister for African affairs from the proposed federal structure. This was a major step in satisfying settler concerns and as a result the discussions 'went all too cosily'.[166] In further public discussions it subsequently became clear to critics of the federation that the British government would no longer provide assurances that any federation would not be imposed against African opinion.[167] Consequently, Northern Rhodesian and Nyasaland Africans withdrew from discussions to shape the agenda for the next proposed conference.[168]

In an attempt to reach a definitive conclusion it was decided to bring forward the next scheduled conference by four months; consequently officials met again in London on 23 April. The conference at Lancaster House attempted to set out fiscal structures for the Federation. It was recognised that in order for the polity to function effectively it should possess the power to collect taxation above its immediate requirements and distribute to its composite territories according to their needs. It was decided to appoint a Fiscal Commission of experts to advise as to how this would operate in practice. As Murphy notes, the dilemma facing the British was that a strong federation would potentially increase Southern Rhodesian influence and consequently endanger African interests. Yet a weak federation would run the risk of being unable to improve the financial fortunes of Nyasaland, which could also increase African unrest.[169] The conference also confirmed that the proposed post of minister for African affairs was to be removed. Instead, the governor-general would appoint a private individual to be chairman of the African Affairs Board. The Board, was eventually comprised of six appointed members, rather than the originally proposed nine members, and would would be solely responsible for securing African interests.[170]

There were two other important changes to the scheme first proposed by the officials. The first Federal government was given the power to fix the terms of the federal franchise and any bill affecting the federal constitution or any bill affecting the electoral law had to receive a two-thirds majority in the Federal assembly. As a contemporary commentator noted, given that under the scheme Europeans held 29 of the 35 federal seats in the Federal assembly, 'it is not difficult to see how little value this device had as a safeguard for African interests'.[171] In addition to the three proposed members for African interests, two were voted for by the Southern Rhodesian electoral roll, of which 99 per cent of the registered voters were European.[172] The appointment of Lord Salisbury to the post of secretary of state for Commonwealth relations also boosted the settlers' chance of a satisfactory conclusion to the discussions.[173] Salisbury was an avowed imperialist and later resigned from the government after Harold Macmillan allowed Archbishop Makarios to return to Cyprus.[174] Upon his resignation Salisbury was promptly offered a position on the board of the British South Africa Company.[175]

African opposition to federation relocated to Britain in May 1952 with a delegate conference of the Northern Rhodesia and Nyasaland African National Congresses being facilitated in London by the Africa Bureau.[176] In the discussions that followed, Paramount Chief Chitimukulu of the Bemba in Northern Rhodesia stressed his fear of the expansion of racial discrimination practiced by Europeans in the territory. Instead, he argued, 'the British Government has a further duty of educating us in the running of our own government'; a potential federation was little more than an 'obstacle to the advancement of Africans in Northern Rhodesia'. Chief Msamala of the Yao in Nyasaland also stressed the more oppressive racial policies of Southern Rhodesia and invoked the service of his people to Britain during World War II. He stressed that Nyasalanders had always 'fought side by side with the British and not complained because they knew they were defending their country in doing so'. During the second session of the meeting Harry Nkumbula,[177] president of the NRANC, focused solely on the situation in Northern Rhodesia, suggesting that it was unfair that 40,000 Europeans should determine the lives of two million Africans. Nkumbula also inadvertently followed the line pursued by Huggins and Welensky, noting that 'in the last three years the flow of people from South Africa had increased considerably and most of the Europeans now came from there'.[178]

In Britain, the publication of the proposed federal scheme in a white paper during June led to attacks from the Labour and Liberal parties, and left-leaning clergy and academics.[179] The Labour party MP, Leslie Hale, began canvassing the doyens of left-wing liberal opinion to rally support against the Federation.[180] He proposed the presentation of a signed memorial from concerned individuals expressing 'concern' over the government's plans for closer association.[181] It was planned that the memorial would be delivered to the Prime Minister. The final document, while not disputing the possible economic advantages of federation, stressed the signatories' opposition to the imposition of federation against the wishes of Africans in the territories. It stressed that the example of South Africa highlighted 'the inadequacy of entrenched clauses and constitutional safeguards' in securing African interests.[182] The final document attracted the signatures of upwards of 500 individuals and was ready to be presented by March 1953. In the event, Churchill refused to meet with the delegation. They did, however, secure an appointment with the secretaries of state for the colonies and commonwealth relations.[183] Hale's campaign in March 1952 can be seen as indicative of the end of a bipartisan approach in central African policy in the British political sphere.

As the dust settled after the publication of the federal proposals in the June 1952 white paper, Henry Hopkinson, minister of state at the Colonial Office, departed London for central Africa in August 1952.[184] Hopkinson held 68 meetings with African leaders and canvassed informal opinion on the streets in Northern Rhodesia and Nyasaland. His conclusion was that the vast majority of Africans cared little about federation and would happily follow the lead of their chiefs. Therefore the British government needed to provide the chiefs with firm guidance. Nkumbula also recognised the importance of support from traditional leaders.

During the same month as Hopkinson's visit NRANC held a chiefs' and delegates' conference in Lusaka where again he stressed the difference between settler administration in Southern Rhodesia and Colonial Office administration in the north. To Nkumbula, Africans in Southern Rhodesia were 'subjected to humiliation, social disabilities and political castration'.[185] Nkumbula was representative of those who feared that federation would sound the death knell for African self-government similar to that instituted in the Gold Coast in 1951. Opposition to federation was also intertwined with ongoing grievances amongst workers on the Copperbelt over issues surrounding the industrial colour bar. In Nyasaland, opposition stemmed more from 'nascent nationalism' which was inspired by events in West Africa and elsewhere. Opposition in Southern Rhodesia was slight and Hopkinson concluded that a multiracial federation would provide a favourable solution.[186]

In October 1952 the Fiscal Commission convened the previous April submitted its report. It suggested that the collection of customs and excise duties and income tax across the three territories should be the responsibility of the federal government. It would retain 60 per cent of this revenue; the governments of Northern and Southern Rhodesia would each receive 17 per cent, leaving the Nyasaland government with 6 per cent of the revenues.[187] As Murphy notes, considering the small contribution Nyasaland would make to federal revenues, a 6 per cent return was extremely generous. The lack of a sizable European community meant it lacked a significant tax base and the prices of the territory's two principal exports – tea and tobacco – were in decline.[188] Despite this, it was clear that opinion in the Colonial Office was mixed as to the financial advantages of federation to Nyasaland. It was debateable as to whether the economy of Nyasaland would benefit greatly from federation or whether the British government would make any significant savings from the territory's inclusion. Yet, for all of the mystery surrounding the financial implications of the scheme, it was clear that, as one treasury official noted, 'finance is not the rock on which this scheme [federation] may founder'.[189]

As 1952 drew to a close any objections raised by the Federation's critics in central Africa and London were increasingly sidelined. The decision in Whitehall and Westminster to implement federation without the support of the African majority in effect made its creation a certainty. A further conference was held at Carlton House in London, opening on 1 January 1953 to hammer out the shape of a future federation. It allocated the division of powers between the federal and territorial governments. An Executive List was proposed, which comprised matters of common interest across all of the territories that became the responsibility of the federal government. There was also a Concurrent List of matters which both the federal and individual territorial governments would enjoy a measure of jurisdiction. All other matters remained the responsibility of the territorial govern-ments. Both Northern Rhodesia and Nyasaland would remain under the special protection of the Crown while Southern Rhodesia retained its responsible internal self-government, in accordance with its constitution.[190]

The conference also further weakened the powers of the African Affairs Board by bringing it under the aegis of the Federal parliament as a standing committee of the legislature, rather than its previously proposed incarnation as an independent entity. In addition, it was decided that during the first decade of the Federation's existence there would be no change in the division of powers between the federal and territorial governments without the full agreement of all three territorial legislatures. Furthermore, it was proposed that there would be a constitutional review between seven and nine years after the implementation of the federal scheme. Welensky was later adamant that promises were made to the effect that this review would not have the power to dissolve the Federation.[191]

The conference drew to a close on 31 January and its conclusions were published as a white paper.[192] There still remained substantial criticism of the federal scheme within the Labour party which managed to secure a Commons debate on the proposed scheme on 24 March 1953. During the debate Lyttelton publicly stated that the proposed federal review would 'not [...] decide whether federation has succeeded or failed, or whether it should be abolished or continued'.[193] Given Southern Rhodesia's existing de facto self-government it had been agreed that no scheme of closer association would be implemented without the support of the territory's electorate. Consequently a referendum on the federal proposals took place on 9 April. With 25,570 votes in favour of federation and 14,729 against, the final hurdle in central Africa had been cleared. The finishing line was crossed on 9 May when the Federation Bill passed parliament, with 247 MPs backing the scheme, against 221 in opposition.[194] The subsequent Rhodesia and Nyasaland Federation Act received Royal Assent during July and the Federation was inaugurated on 3 September 1953.

Early Years, 1953–6

The creation of the Federation led to the reshaping of the political landscape in central Africa. Godfrey Huggins stood down as Southern Rhodesian Prime Minister on 7 September, a post he had held for almost 20 years, to take up the position of interim Federal Prime Minister. Garfield Todd replaced Huggins as Southern Rhodesian Prime Minister, after narrowly beating Julian Greenfield in the August election for the leadership of the United Party.[195] There was also a further consolidation of settler political power as the United Party merged with the Rhodesia Party on 5 November to create the United Rhodesia Party which would secure 26 of the 30 seats in the LegCo following the announcement of the election result on 27 January 1954. At federal level the first election was scheduled for 15 December 1953 and Huggins' new Federal Party secured 24 of the 26 seats, giving a clear mandate to govern.[196]

The early federal period was marked by an increased clash between the interests of Southern Rhodesian and Northern Rhodesian settlers. The final federal financial scheme adopted had given all customs and excise duties to the Federal government in addition to the majority of revenue raised through income and profit taxes throughout the Federation. The rest was to be distributed to individual territories according to a set formula. Until mid-1957 this formula gave 64 per cent of monies raised to the Federal government; 17 per cent to the Northern Rhodesia government; 13 per cent to the Southern Rhodesia government and the remaining 6 per cent to the Nyasaland government.[197] In the postwar period, the United States' decision to stockpile copper combined with the outbreak of the Korean War (1950–3) had pushed up the price of the base metal.[198] This resulted in many Northern Rhodesian settlers accusing the Federal and Southern Rhodesia governments of using the wealth of the Copperbelt to finance the development of Southern Rhodesia.

The financial health of both territories was, however, interconnected, with the Copperbelt mines of RST and Anglo American reliant on coal sourced from the Wankie colliery in Southern Rhodesia. Ever since the end of World War II there had been acute problems with supply, leading to the periodic closure of the mines. RST had fared a little better than Anglo, having introduced wood-fired boilers at Roan, Mufulira and Rhokana.[199] Initially the colliery company placed the blame for their inability to meet the requirements of the Southern Rhodesian economy and the Northern Rhodesian Copperbelt squarely at the door of Rhodesia Railways' shortage of trucks. In part to address this problem, the Southern Rhodesia government had purchased Rhodesia Railways during April 1947 and embarked on a huge programme of capital expenditure, placing a £2 million order for 60 heavy locomotives and investing another £4 million in rolling stock. Yet when this stock was introduced it became clear that the railways were not the problem. Wankie was not producing enough coal to meet its commitments.[200]

Prior to World War II, both mining companies had promised not to develop hydro-electric power. The problems with coal supplies led to a re-evaluation of this commitment. Of the potential options: a dam on the Kafue River or on the Zambezi River at the Kariba Gorge, the former option was the early favourite.[201] Harold Cartmel-Robinson, deputy chairman of the Federal Party and an RST director, felt confident enough to write in September 1953 to Sir Ronald Prain,[202] that 'the prospects for getting the Kafue scheme started seem much brighter' he continued 'the politicians here have made up their minds to Kafue taking precedence over Kariba and they all seem keen on the former scheme being started at the earliest possible date'.[203] Kafue was cheaper to build and closer to the Copperbelt, and, even as late as February 1955, Prain still hoped that 'the decision will be taken on the availability of money, because this decision should mean Kafue'.[204] Yet little under a month later Huggins announced to the Federal Assembly that the Kariba project had been chosen, much to the surprise of the majority of his audience. Julia Tischler has covered in great depth the resulting furore from Northern Rhodesian settlers who viewed the decision, particularly after the decision had been made to site the Federal capital in Salisbury rather than Lusaka in March 1954, as further proof of Southern Rhodesian bias in federal circles.[205]

Following the announcement of the decision to go forward with Kariba, the Federal government approached Anglo American and RST, both buoyed with profits from the high price of copper, to help finance the dam's construction. The Federal government viewed this as a mutually beneficial proposal. The copper companies depended on an increased and more reliable power supply, and so it was in their interests for the dam to be completed on schedule. When they met during December 1955, the government was represented by Welensky and Huggins, who was awarded a peerage in February 1955 and adopted the title of Lord Malvern of Rhodesia and Bexley. Ronald Prain of RST and Harry Oppenheimer, managing director of Anglo American, represented the copper industry. Malvern revealed that the shortfall in financing the scheme would total £20 million over the following five-year period, and that the railways would require a further £10 million. He suggested Anglo and RST should cover this shortfall in the form of loans. Should the companies not agree to this, Malvern proposed instigating an export tax on copper to the value of 50 per cent of all profits.[206]

Together, RST and Anglo American were in agreement that this would 'have disastrous effects on the credit of the country', as it would 'kill new investment' and offer no incentive for the companies to keep production costs low.[207] As a result of these 'unnecessary strong-armed tactics', as Prain later recalled, the companies agreed to provide £10 million each towards financing the Kariba project, and agreed to accept a surcharge on the power produced by the new dam until a further £10 million had been paid.[208] To this was added a loan of £4 million from the BSAC which brought the total amount invested in Kariba to £34 million.[209] R. M. Taylor, secretary to the Federal Treasury, later revealed the relative ease by which he obtained the loan. Taylor noted that negotiations were 'entirely between Sir Ellis Robins and myself and very much on an "old boy" basis. He virtually asked me how much I wanted and how I wanted it and I told him.'[210] The tactics adopted by the Federal government illustrate the confidence with which it viewed its position in 1955. At this time it was possible for the government to adopt 'strong-arm tactics' in its dealings with the copper companies to secure their co-operation.

In May 1956 discussions took place between the Federal and British governments and the International Bank for Reconstruction and Development (IBRD) to finalise the financing of the project. Ever since Malvern had announced the decision to favour Kariba over Kafue the estimated cost of the project had been continually revised upwards. By November 1955, only eight months after the decision had been announced, the estimated cost for the first stage of the scheme had risen from £53,400,000 to £78,000,000; the cost of the completed scheme, with a power house on the north bank in addition to the initial power house on the southern bank, rose from £85,800,000 to £111,780,000.[211] Despite this, there was little appetite on the British side to reopen the debate over the respective merits of the Kafue and Kariba schemes.[212] Construction began in 1955 before the loan from the IBRD had been secured. Negotiations were, however, successful and their support was confirmed on 19 April 1956, with the loan of £28.6 million approved by June 1956.[213] As the IBRD's economic advisor on Africa, Andrew Kamarck had earlier noted, the result of the loan was that there were 'few areas in the world' where per capita debt 'will be as heavy as in the Federation'.[214]

African Advancement

The failure of the anti-federal campaign had led to a relaxation of African protest on a national level, and in all individual territories.[215] This was especially true in Northern Rhodesia's rural areas. Africans there had anticipated that the scheme's success would lead to an influx of white settlers from Southern Rhodesia. When this failed to materialise the united front between rural and urban Africans in the fight to resist federation crumbled. This split was further exacerbated by the Federal government, which encouraged traditional leaders to ban political activities in their districts.[216] Despite this promising situation, the Federal government failed to live up to their promise of 'partnership'.

The importance of land alienation for the Federation's African inhabitants varied vastly between territories. It was felt most keenly in Southern Rhodesia, yet was barely an issue in the north. Contrary to expectations, the copper boom during the first years of federation did not spark the growth of secondary industry in rural areas in the northern territories. Development was primarily restricted to European areas adjacent to the railway lines and consequently the majority of Africans did not share in the Federation's initial prosperity.[217] African urban migration increased after World War II in Southern Rhodesia as the colony's secondary industry grew in towns and cities.[218] Urban life for Africans during the 1950s was often characterised by 'extreme deprivation' as any improvement in their income gained from leaving the countryside was often offset by higher living costs.[219]

These conditions fostered urban discontent which mobilised into African opposition. In Salisbury this took the form of the City Youth League which campaigned for greater African self-reliance rather than multiracial cooperation between 1955 and 1957.[220] The growing urbanisation of Africans created links between urban and rural concerns that helped to foster a greater sense of shared grievance against the Federation, and of national consciousness.[221] In an attempt to project a more moderate image, the City Youth League combined with the Bulawayo-based African National Council to become the Southern Rhodesian African National Congress (SRANC).[222] The party had a balanced ethnic mix amongst its senior officials and Joshua Nkomo was elected president in an attempt to project a moderate image.[223] Nkomo had no link to the Youth League and had a record of multiracial cooperation.[224] The SRANC was able to expand its support into the countryside as it opposed the Land Husbandry Act (LHA),[225] introduced in 1951, and described by George Nyandoro[226] as 'the best recruiter Congress ever had'.[227]

In the early years of the Federation, however, many African elites in Southern Rhodesia had bought into the rhetoric of 'partnership' and attempted to engage with the system. Many of these doctors, lawyers, teachers and preachers saw their interests as different to those of uneducated Africans living in the townships.[228] This section of African society produced those individuals who became involved in the multiracial political organisations that were founded at this time. The most prominent included the Inter-Racial Association and the Capricorn Africa Society. Although multiracial in nature, these groups were infused with white paternalism and in no way challenged the dominant position of western civilisation. As such they were the mid-twentieth century expression of Cecil Rhodes' dictum: 'equal rights for all civilized men'.[229] As it became clear by the mid-1950s that partnership had not sufficiently addressed the fact that Africans were treated as second-class citizens in the Federation, many left these organisations to take leading roles in the growing African nationalist movement.[230] In the context of Southern Rhodesia, Alois Mlambo suggests that Garfield Todd's – the one politician many Africans thought sympathetic to their interests – ruthless suppression of the Wankie Colliery strike in 1954 was a key factor in re-orienting many African elites away from white liberals towards a more militant African nationalist movement.[231]

There was a similar experience for Africans in Northern Rhodesia. In Lusaka, Africans suffered the indignity of being unable to enter most European shops. Instead, they were obliged to stand on the street and purchase goods through a hatch in the wall. When the shop assistants chose to serve them, they had to accept what was given without question.[232] This practice ended following an African boycott of businesses in 1954. Nonetheless it was indicative of a general level of discrimination which was commonplace during the Federal period.[233] Herbert Chitepo, the first African advocate in Southern Rhodesia, remarked: 'let it be said that partnership failed, not in parliament or in industrial relationships, but in the shops, on the staircases, and at office counters where someone denied to the African his essential dignity as a person and violated his sense of justice and self-respect'.[234] Discrimination stimulated political action and provided a central issue which could unite opposing movements.[235] The unwillingness of most of the Federation's European population to engage seriously with African political opposition critically illustrates the central problem with the 'partnership' policy in the Federation: namely the majority of settlers' inability to view Africans, even potentially, as their equals.[236]

Both mining companies on the Copperbelt also struggled to satisfy their African workers' demands for greater equality given their European workers' refusal to allow their own privileged position to be undermined. Prain cautioned in 1954 that the buoyant economic condition of RST at that time could not be allowed to be 'impaired by the reckless financial advancement, in the mass, of Africans'.[237] He then continued by summarising that 'the gross disparity between individual European and African earnings is not due to the African being underpaid but to the European being overpaid'.[238] Harold Hochschild would later recall how the high remuneration of white labour was due to the difficulties in the early days of the development of the Copperbelt of attracting skilled labour to 'this primitive, unhealthy and unknown corner of Africa'. To attract skilled labour the companies 'had to offer extraordinary inducements' to enable to the development of the areas copper deposits. Thirty years later:

> The European miner in the Copperbelt lives at sub-economic rent in a comfortable modern house with one two or three African servants. He enjoys subsidized amenities and other substantial perquisites. His living standard is higher than that of any group of workmen I know of anywhere else in the world, not excluding the United States.[239]

As Phimister has argued, and subsequent chapters of this book demonstrate, African advancement on the Copperbelt was intimately linked to maximising profitability of the copper industry.[240]

For all of the growing African discontent bubbling under the surface of the Federation, few realised by the beginning of 1956 that the Federation would be dismantled in only seven years' time. Buoyed by the high price of copper, its early economic performance was judged to be a success and its future looked bright. Investment was high and Salisbury was undergoing a major programme of development as money and increasing numbers of European immigrants arrived. Wage levels had risen for both African and European workers, although there was still a large difference between the two. Moreover, African protest against federation was relatively small and ineffective.[241] Yet these optimistic times for the Federation's leaders would prove to be short-lived. Later that year the price of copper slumped which made the Federal government – as Welensky who would become prime minister of the Federation in November 1956, would later recall – 'conscious of the fact that we must count every penny we spent'.[242] As the next chapters will detail, the faltering economic situation in the Federation combined with growing political discontent in both African and European communities would fatally undermine the embryonic federal experiment.

CHAPTER 2

THE PIPE DREAM OF PARTNERSHIP, 1957–9

It is we, here in Africa who will have to make the decisions which will determine our future, and those decisions will not be in the ultimate made in Westminster as some think.

Roy Welensky to the Salisbury Executives Council,
5 November 1959[1]

Welensky and Macmillan Take Office

Sir Roy Welensky succeeded Lord Malvern as federal prime minister in October 1956. He had entered politics by representing the interests of his fellow white workers in the railway workers' union before graduating to become the leader of the unofficial members of the Northern Rhodesia Legislative Council. Welensky firmly supported closer association between the Rhodesias and was widely seen as Malvern's natural successor.

As Welensky settled into his new role as prime minister, Britain embarked on its ill-fated Suez adventure. This apparent reversion to nineteenth-century gunboat diplomacy met with disappointed silence, if not outright condemnation, from many of her friends on the world stage. Sir Pierson Dixon,[2] Britain's permanent representative to the United Nations, tongue firmly in cheek, noted that 'flanked by our faithful Australians and New Zealanders, we wandered about the UN halls like lost spirits. Our best friends averted their gaze or burst into tears as we passed'.[3] Britain's 'faithful Australians and New Zealanders' may have stood firm over Suez, but a striking feature of the international influences on the Federation is the way Commonwealth influence faded as the Federation waned.[4] This is perhaps indicative of the changing nature of the organisation. Macmillan allegedly complained that Commonwealth membership was 'no longer like gaining admission to Brooks's but joining the R[oyal] A[utomobile] C[lub]'.[5]

This apathy was underlined by his commitment to take Britain into closer association with Europe. As Max Beloff mused in 1963: 'eventual entry into Europe must mean a sacrifice of one aspect of Britain's world role; namely, the potentialities of development inherent in an alternative grouping of countries based upon the existing membership of the Commonwealth'.[6] Stuart Ward has noted that Britain's desire to play a full economic and political role in Europe 'hardly seemed compatible with being leader of the Commonwealth family of nations'.[7] Similarly by 1960 Welensky could be found questioning the utility of the organisation that he had been so keen to secure the Federation membership of only three years previously:

I really believe that the Commonwealth has come to the crossroads. If Macmillan is as able as I think he is, I think he can preserve it. If not, I think we see the beginning of the end. It does look as if Malaya is determined to discuss South Africa's affairs. Ceylon had a blood bath a little over three years ago, and I don't have to tell you how they deal with their language and minority problems. Pakistan is a military dictatorship. Can these people really sit in judgement on South Africa? I am seriously hoping that common sense will prevail. If it doesn't then the future, Commonwealthwise, [sic] is a grim one.[8]

There was no serious threat of a Commonwealth split after South Africa's exit in 1961, as the Afro-Asian members found the United Nations a far more effective arena for their opposition as confirmed by the Assembly's reaction to Suez.

The Suez crisis caused embarrassment as it demonstrated that Britain had attempted to undermine the purpose of the UN itself. This was particularly damaging as, as one official summarised, the British position was 'based not so much on our [...] material power as on our reputation for wisdom, honesty, fair dealing and restraint'.[9] Criticism in New York over colonial policy was not only confined to the British. It has been remarked that 'the French were equally notorious, but with a difference. No one at the United Nations expected anything but colonialist behaviour from the French.'[10] Britain's record in southern Africa, particularly with regard to South Africa, attracted criticism in the General Assembly. South Africa had been a live issue at the United Nations prior to the National Party's election victory in 1948.

Despite this rising international criticism, Welensky's belief in Britain did not waver and one of his first acts as prime minister was to offer Britain the Federation's unqualified support. This generated warm feelings towards the Federation from many within the British government. In fact, this period has been described as 'the zenith of the Anglo-Federal relationship'. Relations were further strengthened by Welensky's close relationship with the Governor General of the Federation, Lord Llewellin,[11] who supplied valuable advice for dealing with British politicians.[12] The Suez debacle saw Anthony Eden step down as British prime minister to be replaced by Harold Macmillan in January 1957.[13]

The new Prime Minister was faced with two immediate challenges: the need to repair the damage caused to the Anglo-American 'special relationship' after Suez, and also to rebuild Britain's relationship with the Asian members of the Commonwealth.[14] If Britain was to retain any influence in world affairs it was vital that both these tasks were met. Macmillan clearly identified Anglo-American relations as the most pressing task, and, in effect, 'did little to mend fences with the Commonwealth'.[15] This was in part, perhaps, due to the Commonwealth's declining importance and the increasing influence of the United Nations, and his desire that Britain should start to move towards a closer relationship with the European Economic Community.

The United States, a former colonial possession itself, enjoyed a mixed reputation in Africa. Its tradition of anti-colonial resistance was juxtaposed against a history of racism and lynchings.[16] British suspicion of America's anti-colonial tradition waned during the early 1950s, as the United States hesitated to criticise the remaining European empires since they were viewed as useful as a bulwark against communist infiltration.[17] Some British mistrust lingered, however, as demonstrated by a Colonial Office Report from early 1957. It noted that American scepticism of 'so-called "British Colonialism"' had coloured American attitudes toward such issues as the Baghdad Pact, Cyprus and Suez. Therefore it was essential for British interests that the Americans were made to realise that 'what we are doing in our colonial territories has no relation to their out-of-date conception of "Colonialism" but is, on the contrary, a constructive job of *nation-building* [emphasis in original] which is of the utmost importance to the free world and which they have a duty as well as an interest to support'.[18] One such case of nation building was the Central African Federation.

When Macmillan took office Eisenhower had just embarked on his second term as president. As mentioned above, one of Macmillan's first priorities was restoring Anglo-American relations following Suez, and with a view to this end he met with Eisenhower twice in 1957.[19] Following these discussions, Macmillan agreed not to enter into any major military operation without American approval.[20] While in the colonial sphere both countries agreed that the transference of power to friendly indigenous regimes was the best way to prevent communist penetration in Africa, they nonetheless both expressed doubts over how ready most African countries were for independence.[21]

An earlier indicator of Africa's rising importance in Washington was the reorganisation of the State Department following the end of World War II. Previously all of Africa, except Egypt, Ethiopia and Liberia, came under the jurisdiction of the Bureau of European Affairs. Over the following years the Africa Office was divided into offices of Northern and Southern African Affairs and the position of Assistant Secretary of State for African Affairs was created by the Senate Committee for Foreign Relations in June 1957.[22] This increased interest in African affairs was met by 'ingrained suspicion' and 'widespread condescension' by many in Whitehall. This was certainly reflected in the British minister in Washington's patronising comments on the issue:

> Their enthusiasms may strike us as occasionally misdirected and their methods as not always wisely chosen, and we should not hesitate to explain our views to them firmly but politely when this happens. But in general I am sure that we should welcome their closer involvement in African affairs.[23]

Welensky's honeymoon period as federal prime minister was not to last long. The slump in the price of copper had in March 1956 brutally exposed the weakness of the federal economy's overdependence on a single commodity.[24] A further worry for the federal government was that the reduced price of copper also affected the copper companies' tax contributions. By 1958 taxation revenue from the Northern Rhodesian copper industry was worth just of half the amount received during 1957.[25] 'I need hardly say how anxious we are about the copper situation' remarked Welensky, 'we have tightened our belts as much as we possibly can. I don't know what else we can possibly do', he lamented.[26] Only in 1960 did overall taxation revenue rise to equal the amount received in 1957.

In addition to the Federation's worsening financial position, during January 1957 Welensky's wife, Elizabeth, suffered a coronary thrombosis and his troubles were further compounded by the death of Lord Llewellin two days later.[27] Welensky described the former Governor General's death as a 'tremendous loss' and thought 'he would be most difficult to replace'. He believed that 'of all the people I can think of who might be the nearest to the type of Governor [to] Llewellin [. . .] is Walter Monckton, who is about to go to the Lords'.[28] In the event, Monckton was not appointed, although he would later provoke Welensky's ire as chairman of the federal review preparatory commission.[29]

The importance of contact with leading figures in the American business and political worlds was abundantly clear to the Federal government. As a result Sir Edgar Whitehead was sent to Washington, DC during March 1957 to represent the Federation's interests. The American Consul General in Salisbury believed Whitehead to be 'a very mature and experienced man' who would 'make an excellent impression in his new assignment'.[30] An important part of the federal representative's role was to attract new investment capital into the Federation. This campaign had some early success: during July 1958 a $6 million bond issue was floated on the New York market, and this was followed by a $10 million loan from Chase Manhattan Bank in June 1960.[31] American investment in the Federation was predominantly in Northern Rhodesian mining interests, chrome production in Southern Rhodesia, and help with railway infrastructure.[32] Despite their best efforts the Federal government had little success in changing this pattern. Notwithstanding the encouraging start in attracting American capital by June 1961 Welensky bemoaned 'nothing the Americans have done has replaced the risk capital that [the] British provided in the nineteenth century. The Americans certainly don't provide it, they do nothing without adequate security and guarantees'.[33]

In an attempt to ease the Federation's precarious financial position, Keith Acutt,[34] a director of Anglo American and a close friend of Welensky, indicated that Anglo American had large sums of short-term money available for the government to borrow.[35] The Federal Prime Minister asked his minister of finance Donald Macintyre to assess the impact of such a loan. Macintyre's findings were hardly promising. He speculated that the money Acutt had offered was the reserve that they held to pay their income tax and warned against borrowing the Federation's own future income tax receipts. Macintyre admitted that 'copper mining is the engine which drives our economy', and informed Welensky that 'at the moment we have a gear box in that drive which gives us time to adjust ourselves for any shocks. If we did what Acutt suggested we should be in direct drive and this might be very unpleasant'.[36] Welensky appears to have lost interest in the idea following this advice.

Despite these challenges, Welensky began to prepare the Federation for greater independence from Britain by reorganising the federal electoral system through the introduction of the Constitutional Amendment Bill and the Federal Electoral Bill.[37] These Acts were designed to ensure that the European settlers maintained control of political power in the Federation. Yet, the Federal government underestimated the effect that legislation designed to reassure Europeans would have on the Federation's African population. The introduction of these Acts, together with the mounting distress of growing unemployment, helped reinvigorate the moribund African opposition to federation in all three territories.[38]

The discussions that followed between representatives of the Federal and territorial governments illustrate some of the problems they faced in agreeing on a suitable franchise. The Southern Rhodesian representatives stressed the need for qualifications that would ensure that 'civilized and responsible persons' would be eligible for the upper, or 'A', roll. They did not believe, however, that these qualifications alone would be satisfactory indicators, and wondered if people with criminal records could be taken off the roll. The Nyasaland representatives favoured a single roll arrangement and suggested that the income level should be £400 instead of £500, as this was a more realistic level for Africans to reach. They believed that an adequate knowledge of English was essential, and suggested that a form could be completed in the presence of the registering officer to ensure voters' eligibility. The Northern Rhodesian representatives also stressed the importance of minimum educational and income levels, although they believed exceptions should be made for 'deserving Africans in the older age group' who would not otherwise qualify under these rules.[39]

This dialogue reflects the broad concerns of Europeans in the Federation in crafting both the Federal and territorial franchises. The somewhat vague term of 'partnership' had been selected as the cornerstone of federation policy on race relations.[40] The intention was that the Federation would adopt a more moderate position on the issue of race than that pursued by its southern neighbour, South Africa. In practice, however, most Europeans in the Federation were in no hurry to advance Africans economically, politically or socially, hence the above reference to 'civilized and responsible' Africans and minimum levels of education and English proficiency. As a result, this language was not far removed from Cecil Rhodes' dictum of 'equal rights for all civilized men' which, like 'partnership', hinged on how 'civilized' was defined.

In addition, the governments encountered vociferous opposition from those educated Africans who met the criteria for voting rights. Many found they were discriminated against in the workplace and grew frustrated that their qualifications appeared to count for very little. In contrast, the settler governments often found less-educated Africans easier to co-opt. For example, many traditional elites, such as chiefs, enjoyed advancement of their personal positions under settler rule. This inspired the Northern Rhodesian representative's concern for 'deserving Africans in the older age group' who would be unlikely to have the necessary educational attainment. The settlers' conundrum was spelled out plainly in a later meeting by Sir Robert Tredgold,[41] the federal chief justice, who thought that 'the Africans could be classified into two groups – one minority group which was extremist in outlook, and the other, larger group which was anxious to co-operate with the European'.[42] Consequently, a way to include less qualified but more loyal Africans on the voters' roll would ideally be found.[43]

Discussions over the federal franchise proposals continued into March, as Welensky hoped that all the territories could agree on a common solution. The Southern Rhodesian Cabinet believed their territory's different status, under the jurisdiction of the Commonwealth Relations Office, unlike the northern territories which were the responsibility of the Colonial Office, entitled it to formulate its own independent policy on the matter. In fact, the Southern Rhodesian Cabinet believed Welensky's attitude was 'dictated very largely by political expediency' as he had the forthcoming federal election to navigate.[44] Welensky favoured a dual-roll approach to the franchise, while Garfield Todd, the Southern Rhodesian Prime Minister, highlighted a serious shortcoming in that a minority of Europeans would only qualify for the B roll, and thus would only be able to vote for an African representative. The dual-roll system would consolidate the racial basis of representation instead of abolishing it. In response, Welensky offered the caveat that his proposals could be reviewed and adjusted as necessary after a ten-year period.[45]

Welensky visited London for the first time as federal prime minister during April 1957 to hold discussions with British ministers regarding the future of the Federation. He wished to secure support for the Federal government's proposals for a new constitution and franchise proposals. Already the Federation's critics in Britain were beginning to stir. Prior to Welensky's arrival the Labour Party published a pamphlet entitled *Plural Society*. This publication demanded that full adult suffrage be introduced immediately in the Federation and that Britain should retain ultimate political control until full democratic elections took place.[46] This was a line of attack which would become all too familiar to the Federal government over the following years. A further blow to the Federation's future, although not immediately apparent, was Lord Salisbury's resignation from Cabinet, during March, over the decision to release the Cypriot nationalist leader, Archbishop Makarios,[47] from his exile in the Seychelles.[48] Five years later Welensky described Salisbury's resignation as 'one of the tragedies of the present period', when the Federation was in desperate need of influential friends.[49]

Welensky was joined in London by Julian Greenfield, federal minister of law,[50] and over the course of their visit they met with Alec Douglas Home,[51] secretary of state for Commonwealth relations, and Alan Lennox-Boyd,[52] secretary of state for the colonies on five occasions.[53] Greenfield later recalled that Home and Lennox-Boyd 'were both well-disposed to the Federation and sympathetic to our proposals', although the concessions gained by the federal delegation 'did not come easy'.[54] The concessions secured included confirmation that the federal constitutional review conference would be held in 1960 and also that a programme to enable the Federation to progress to full membership of the Commonwealth would be considered.[55]

Lord Home speculated that the urgency behind Welensky's request was driven by his fear that the timing of the review conference would fall to a new Labour government. Welensky's trepidation was by no means unfounded: in April 1957 the Labour Party led the Conservatives by ten points in a Gallup opinion poll and was widely expected to win the next general election.[56] Welensky viewed his visit as 'genuinely constructive'[57] and before he returned to Africa he addressed a press conference at which he attacked Labour's call for 'one man, one vote', labelling it 'mischievous and dangerous' and he made clear that no such system would be introduced in the Federation in the near future.[58]

The economic situation in the Federation continued to cause concern. The ongoing poor performance of copper prices led RST to announce a cut in production at Roan Antelope and Mufulira mines during May 1957. Chibuluma was allowed to continue at full capacity as it was a new mine and still had metal repayment obligations to make to the United States government for its initial finance.[59] RST's announcement was greeted with a degree of trepidation within the Federal government. A memorandum to Welensky from the Federal Economic Section reminded the Prime Minister that 'in view of the scope of their activities', the copper companies 'seem to have national responsibilities beyond that of ordinary private undertakings'.[60] Consequently, they argued, the Federal government should be given advance notice by the copper companies regarding their policy towards production.

Production cuts were feared to affect the wider economic prospects of the Federation, particularly the demand for railway transport and its subsequent revenue. A policy of retrenchment was 'considered as particularly disturbing to the economic prospects of this country if production of the most important export commodity is to be reduced for any lengthy time in such circumstances'.[61] Soon after this statement was released RST and Anglo American announced that they had agreed to a common basis of pricing on all copper sold to British consumers. Although the details were not clear, *The Economist* reported that 'the impression is that Anglo American has moved much closer to RST than this group has moved to Anglo American'.[62] Previously, Anglo American had traded based on the price quoted on the London Metals Exchange while RST had sold at a fixed price of £240 per ton.[63]

The decision to cut copper production was taken against the backdrop of European industrial unrest in the Copperbelt. Between January 1956 and July 1957 there were 14 separate strikes called by the European mining trades unions.[64] The *Union News* saw the mining companies' policies as an 'all out attempt by the mining companies – Rhodesian Selection Trust as well as the Anglo American Corporation – to SMASH THE NORTHERN RHODESIAN MINE WORKERS UNION!'.[65] The European miners were very highly organised and enjoyed an uneasy relationship with the copper mining companies, particularly RST, over their perceived sympathetic attitudes towards African advancement in the Copperbelt.[66]

During the postwar period in Northern Rhodesia European trade unionists and artisans had combined to ensure that some positions were 'European' and stayed that that way. This had been achieved through the educational advantages enjoyed by Europeans and restrictive entry into industrial training.[67] This situation did not preclude Africans obtaining these skills, however it was expected that the copper companies would provide the Europeans with further training to maintain their position at the top of the industrial ladder.[68] Prain later recalled in his memoirs that it was very difficult to pursue long-term polices towards African advancement when short-term considerations argued against the wisdom of trying to implement them. 'Public opinion always had to be considered as well as the attitudes of our own employees', he concluded.[69] Resistance to greater African advancement was a fixture throughout the life of the Federation. The actions of both the government and the copper companies were considerably restrained by the increasing obstinacy of the European population.

Meanwhile, in London, Labour Party opposition to the Federal Party's Constitutional Amendment Bill continued into the summer. James Callaghan,[70] the shadow colonial secretary, led the attack in the House of Commons contending:

it is awfully difficult for him {Welensky} to persuade his African electorate or would-be electorate that the idea of the alterations of the franchise is to increase their share in the government of the country, or when he has to go to a by-election – and we all know what by-elections are like – to explain to his electors that what this enlargement of franchise has meant in Southern Rhodesia is that only 600 Africans have managed to secure the vote in 33 years.[71]

Callaghan was referring to the recent Federal by-election in Mrewa, which the Federal Party had recently lost to the Dominion Party.[72] Archer Baldwin,[73] the Conservative member of parliament (MP) for Leominster recounted a recent statement by Welensky when he informed the chamber that 'the tendency was developing for the African to look over his shoulder to London instead of to the Government of the Federation'. Baldwin continued 'I hope that we shall abolish the idea that we in London propose to take on the responsibility of Government in those countries where we wish to see multiracial self-government'.[74]

Welensky obtained qualified support from James Johnson,[75] Labour MP for Rugby, who had recently visited the Federation. Johnson proclaimed that the Federation was suffering from its initial creation against the wishes of the majority of its African population. Johnson recognised that progress had been made: 'it is an excellent thing that Africans are now able to have a meal in the dining car on the Federal railways', however he continued 'it would be a much better thing if Africans were also on the footplate and had jobs as drivers and stokers on the railways'. In Johnson's view there was 'social apartheid' in place in the Federation and revealed how he was 'tempted to say that many people in the administration think that Lord Lugard is still alive. They are working by indirect rule through the chiefs and headmen.' He did believe there was some hope for the future adding 'in my view a lead is awaited from the liberal Europeans, particularly Sir Roy Welensky at the head of the administration. He is the only one who can give this lead.'[76]

Welensky returned to London at the end of June for the Conference of Commonwealth Prime Ministers, and he was able to resume discussions with Home and Lennox-Boyd. The secretaries of state expressed reservations over the recent announcement that British Protected Persons[77] would have to take an oath when registering to vote. Lennox-Boyd stated that after Mau Mau, oath-taking had fallen into disrepute.[78]

However, Welensky maintained that the oath was necessary to try to address the unpopularity of his party with the electorate.[79] It was agreed that any oath should be a pledge of loyalty to the Queen and the British government would draft it.[80] Welensky again expressed satisfaction at the success of his London talks and labelled them 'constructive and helpful'.[81]

The dual-roll proposals were formally adopted as the Constitutional Amendment Act by the Federal Assembly on 31 July 1957. Crucially, criticism of the Constitutional Amendment Act was forthcoming from the African Affairs Board. They believed the Act 'differentiated' against Africans, and demanded that the Act be placed before both houses of the British parliament before being granted royal assent.[82] Philip Murphy notes that the British government was placed 'in the embarrassing position of having to persuade the Commons to accept a bill that had effectively been judged to be racially discriminatory'. The Act was eventually backed by the British government, and became law the following November. As a consequence this incident 'heightened the British left's suspicion of the Federation'.[83]

The caution displayed by American investors was also echoed in their government's attitude towards diplomatic relations with the Federation. There was a debate in the State Department in September 1957 over whether the United States Consulate in Salisbury should be upgraded to a Diplomatic Agency in advance of possible Dominion Status being granted by Britain in 1960. The promotion did not take place, and the memorandum discussing the issue illustrates American thinking on the Federation at this juncture. The memorandum makes clear that while the attitude towards the Federation in Washington had been one of 'friendship and sympathy' from its birth in 1953, this attitude had been tempered 'with a distinct reserve, and implicit policy of "wait and see"'. Four years later there appeared to be no strong reason to revise this policy. African opposition to the Federation in Nyasaland and Northern Rhodesia appeared to be strengthening. Potentially more worrying for Sir Roy Welensky was the opinion that his party was 'following rather than leading the attitudes of the Rhodesian white electorate', and had not done enough to implement its policy of racial partnership.[84]

The report made clear that at this time the United States' ability to influence the racial policies of the Federation was 'limited at best'.

Consequently, it was important that the United States 'should not appear eager to grant the Federation an enhanced international status which would tend to strengthen its hand in dealing with the UK'. A further worry for the State Department was that if it was judged to be endorsing a 'white minority government' it would attract criticism from groups within the United States and could damage their relations with other nationalist groups in Africa.[85] It is particularly important to recognise the influence of the domestic civil rights movement on American policy regarding Africa.[86]

In October 1957 the Federal government received news that the position of copper was improving. Keith Acutt wrote to Welensky from London, reporting he was 'most heartened' to find the demand for copper was improving and argued that the statistical position revealed that there was not a great over-supply of copper. He did caution, however, that the 'main cause for concern is, of course, the possibility of an economic recession in the United States and a very definite slowing down of development plans here'.[87] Welensky revealed that Acutt's remarks were contrary to the information he had received in Salisbury. 'Need I say that I was quite heartened to read your remarks about copper. Mac [Donald Macintyre] is so gloomy about everything that I almost feel like the proper thing for us all to do would be to go and jump in the lake', Welensky reflected.[88] Macintyre's gloom provides a further indication of the financial pressure the federal economy was under after the fall in the price of copper.

During each of the first six years of the Federation both Anglo American and RST contributed £5,000 to UFP funds. By the end of 1957, however, Harold Hochschild, Chairman of AMAX, RST's major shareholder, expressed concern to Welensky over the future of the Federation. Hochschild's concern centred on the controversy surrounding the Constitutional Amendment Bill and the decision by the head of the African Affairs Board, Sir John Moffat, to refer the matter to the British government. Hochschild perceived the affair to be discriminatory against Africans. He agreed with Welensky that maintaining European standards was of 'vital necessity', though he worried that the unwillingness of Europeans in the Federation to make any concessions towards Africans would 'endanger' such standards.[89] Welensky, while recognising 'the wisdom and justice' of Hochschild's remarks replied 'I have gone as far as the electorate will permit me to go at the moment'.[90] This would become an all-too-regular refrain from Welensky over the following years. Torn between the Africans' desire for greater equality, Britain's increasing commitment to realpolitik when dealing with its colonial possessions and the settler population's ever-increasing intransigence, he seldom felt left with a choice to make.

The Constitutional Amendment Bill was published by the Federal government during May 1957. Despite African representatives walking out of the debate the Federal parliament passed the Bill on 31 July, and the African Affairs Board duly declared it a 'differentiating measure' as it reduced the proportion of effective African representation. The British government announced that it did not agree that the measure was discriminatory in October and a Labour Party amending motion was debated in the Commons on 25 November.[91]

During the debate, Callaghan suggested that there was a cross-party consensus in favour of blocking the Bill.[92] This was an overestimation of the strength of feeling against the Bill on the Conservative benches. Two days earlier the Bow Group, a Conservative think tank whose members were drawn from the more liberal wing of the party,[93] declared that the Act should be approved, although they recognised that in its present form 'it will be many years before a sizable number of Africans get on the 'A' roll, and before political parties find a strong urge to appeal to all races'.[94] Callaghan further argued that if the government was to force through the Bill 'it will be regarded in Africa as further proof that the British Parliament has deserted the African people'.[95] John Dugdale, Labour MP for West Bromwich and a former minister of state for the colonies agreed with Callaghan, pronouncing that 'it was nothing short of hypocrisy' to say that the Bill was a step towards racial partnership.[96] Dugdale took particular issue with the idea that whether someone was 'civilised' could be judged on income or property ownership and further reminded the Chamber that:

> during the course of European civilisation there have been many poor writers, scientists, artists and musicians who have contributed much to it. Yet such men as Rembrandt, who was in the bankruptcy court, and Mozart, who was given a paupers burial, would be regarded as uncivilised and not worthy of having a vote on these standards if they really meant anything [...] they are merely a device to keep Africans from getting the vote.[97]

Speaking for the government was 'Cub' Alport,[98] the under secretary of state for commonwealth relations, who claimed 'not by the widest stretch of imagination' could the Bill be described as providing a predominantly European electorate with an opportunity to vote for the new African members.[99] The Conservative MP for Torquay, Frederick Bennett[100] also spoke in favour of the Federation, stating 'many hard things are sometimes said about Sir Roy Welensky, I think they are sometimes too hard. He is, after all, a very loyal friend to this country'.[101] The Labour amending motion was defeated, and after a further debate in the Commons on the 18 February 1958 the Act was passed at the end of the month.

The British government received support from some quarters in Britain over its ratification of the Constitutional Amendment Act. The Joint East and Central Africa Board[102] concluded that Lord Home's decision over the Constitutional Amendment Bill was 'a difficult one to make' and agreed with his decision.[103] Critics of the Bill in Britain were disappointed when the government overruled the African Affairs Board's objections. The Labour Party adopted the opposite position and released a statement which 'deplored' the passing of the Constitutional Amendment Act and stated that 'the passing of this legislation marks a new stage in the history of the Federation'. Labour believed that the decision to override the African Affairs Board had weakened African confidence in the Board's ability to protect them from discriminatory legislation. Therefore, they argued that the franchise in both of the northern territories 'should be broadened immediately as an instalment of progress towards a common roll and full adult suffrage'.[104]

Following the defeat, Jayne Symonds of the Africa Bureau astutely advised Kenneth Kaunda,[105] secretary-general of the Northern Rhodesian African National Congress, that 'although we did not succeed in our immediate aim I think we did succeed in awakening people to some of the dangers threatening in Central Africa'.[106] Kaunda, who would later lead Northern Rhodesia to independence and majority rule, had spent six months in Britain as a guest of the Labour Party. He used the opportunity to study how the party functioned on a day-to-day basis and spoke to audiences around the country about the Federation. Kaunda's visit also enabled him to cultivate contacts with Labour politicians and party activists such as

John Hatch, commonwealth officer of the Labour Party.[107] These contacts proved useful during the following years as an outlet in Britain for his party's views.[108]

The Conservative Party also attempted to cultivate links with African nationalists in the Federation through the Conservative Overseas Bureau.[109] In 1959 the Bureau's president wrote to Mainza Chona,[110] the acting president of the Northern Rhodesian African National Congress, and stated that Chona should regard him 'as an unofficial channel along which to express your views, however frank'. In addition, he informed Chona that he was 'quite wrong in your judgement of the political situation here [Britain] if you expect more effective help from the Labour Party rather than ourselves'.[111]

The passage of the Bill demonstrated clearly to Africans in the Federation the ineffectual nature of the African Affairs Board. Its failure to stop a clearly discriminatory piece of legislation acted as a catalyst for more and better-organised African opposition to settler rule throughout the Federation.[112] It gave opposition to the Federation a focus that eventually transformed opposing African movements into national political parties. The widespread disappointment over their failure to prevent the creation of the Federation, combined with the downward trickle of economic benefits from the copper boom, had turned many Africans' protest into grim resignation.[113] The debates over the Constitutional Amendment Act and the Federal Electoral Act[114] helped further to revive the waning African nationalist movements in all three federal territories.

Partnership in Practice

The unwillingness of most of the Federation's European population to engage seriously with African political opposition clearly illustrates the central problem with the 'partnership' policy in the Federation: namely the majority of settlers' inability to view Africans, even potentially, as their equals. European liberals and African intellectuals did attempt to promote multiracial partnership, initially through the Capricorn Africa Society and from 1959 via the Central Africa Party.[115] This organisation provided European liberals with the opportunity to work with educated Africans.[116] They pursued a policy closer to other African nationalist parties, except they advocated a qualitative franchise and the retention of white leadership. Despite some initial success, however, they failed to attract mass support as the federal political landscape rapidly polarised along racial lines from the late 1950s.

Discrimination was, however, entrenched across all levels of society, and made it difficult for Welensky's government to take even small steps towards removing more formalised discrimination. Resistance to the implementation of partnership can be illustrated through the difficulties faced by the opening of a new multiracial cinema in Lusaka. The strict censorship laws, which differed between races, meant that the cinema struggled to find any 'good films' that were cleared for viewing by both Africans and Europeans. Guidelines on censorship reveal that Africans were forbidden from viewing films that included scenes of 'women in scanty attire, prolonged embraces, and crimes readily understood by Africans [and] scenes of drunkenness except for deliberate and obvious comedy'. There were strict guidelines on violence which led to the banning of films showing scenes of 'deliberate murder, wanton killing, knife scenes, scenes including Europeans of both sexes being tied up by natives, including North American Indians'. Films depicting war were banned outright, but the censorship panel, perhaps unsurprisingly, saw no harm in Africans watching 'newsreel scenes of military, naval and air force manoeuvres and exercises'.[117] The result was that a European child could watch a film deemed unsuitable for an African adult.

Welensky was clearly aware that the 'indignity' suffered by Africans and Asians from the lack of multiracial facilities was 'one of the most bitter criticisms of the Federation'. This caused particular embarrassment in the Federal capital of Salisbury and he felt compelled to bring one example directly to the attention of the Southern Rhodesian Cabinet. The case in question related to an Asian businessman from Uganda – 'a man who was accustomed to staying in the Dorchester or Park Lane in London' – who refused to invest in the Federation after being unable to find a suitable hotel in Salisbury in which he was allowed to stay. Welensky's wish for a suitable multiracial establishment to be opened in Salisbury was complicated by the Land Apportionment Act, which expressly forbade African or Asian use of buildings in the centre of Salisbury. The Liquor Act set further restrictions on which hotels Africans were allowed to use.[118] After 1958 there was a 'slow, very incomplete, yet unmistakable thaw' in the segregationist policy contained within the Act.[119]

A further failure of partnership was the continuing disparity between wages paid to African and European employees. A memorandum presented to the Southern Rhodesian Cabinet recognised that Europeans would have to ultimately 'accept the principle of "rate for the job" since this is the only way of avoiding racial enmity and developing the satisfactory relations among the races'. Furthermore, it acknowledged that greater educational and social equality was a prerequisite for equal wages. The author, an advisor on technical education, suggested that 'it is in the best interests of both the European and the African first to aim at high productivity in industry so to strengthen the economy and secondly to improve the educational, social and economic status of the African as fast as we can afford to do it'.[120] The secretary for labour and social welfare went further, arguing 'I feel that many of the European jobs are overgraded [sic] at present'. He believed that the colour bar should be removed immediately and opportunities found for Africans to embark on apprenticeships.[121] This mirrored developments on the Copperbelt during this period. An amendment to the Apprentice Ordinance Act (1946) was passed that extended the scheme to Africans. The low price of copper meant that separate training facilities could not be opened for Africans and it was suggested that the most economical course was to use the existing facilities. This move was opposed, however, by the federal minister of education who refused to allow Africans into European technical colleges in Salisbury and Bulawayo. This problem was not solved until 1962 when the Copperbelt Technical Foundation was opened to all races providing that they could reach the entrance requirements.[122]

The Federal government faced two major problems in opening more positions for Africans. First, once Africans had secured employment, European workers were reluctant to take similar positions.[123] Secondly, and perhaps more importantly, the UFP needed to fight – and win – elections. As discussed earlier, the electoral system was skewed in favour of the white minority so that any party that directly advocated removing their privileged place in society, or lowering their standard of living, would soon be in opposition. The UFP faced the impossible task of trying to move swiftly enough to appease African aspirations while allaying European fears.

Southern Rhodesia: The Removal of Todd and Arrival of Whitehead

The difficulty facing the UFP of reconciling African demands for equality with European fears was a constant problem for Welensky. This dilemma was underscored by the removal of Garfield Todd as Southern Rhodesian prime minister by his own cabinet. Todd held liberal views on issues such as the 1916 Immorality Act and over the Southern Rhodesian franchise and was viewed by many as a liberal.[124] Herbert Baxter,[125] chairman of the Rhodesia and Nyasaland Committee,[126] was worried that this issue would be raised by the Labour Party in the House of Commons and 'play straight into the hands of the more besotted and intransigent elements (of both colours)' in Africa. Baxter wrote to Major Patrick Wall in an attempt to neutralise this danger.[127] Wall, a stalwart supporter of the Federation, did not appear to be the obvious choice for this task. Baxter asked Wall to use his influence with Callaghan and persuade him to rein in the rest of his party. This may have been rather a desperate move, but given that Wall had joined Callaghan on a Commonwealth Parliamentary Association trip to the Federation during September 1957,[128] Baxter thought they 'must have found many points in common, to produce that admirable report'.[129]

Callaghan did not subsequently raise the issue in the Commons; however, the Labour Party MP Barbara Castle[130] did criticise the settlers' removal of Todd in the final debate over the Constitutional Amendment Bill.[131] Welensky, however, suggested that it was Todd's personality that had led to his fate. 'What is not generally understood', he wrote to a friend, 'is that the basic issue, whatever they may say about it, was never one of liberalism. For your own ear Todd had developed rather autocratic tendencies which I must confess I would not like to inflict on any Cabinet'.[132] Yet Todd's removal was seen by many Africans as further evidence that partnership was an empty term.[133]

Welensky's Federal Party had voted to merge with Todd's United Rhodesia Party on 23 November 1957 to create the United Federal Party. This merger allowed considerable economies of scale, as the membership of both parties in Southern Rhodesia was virtually identical.[134] As the merger occurred only a few months before Todd's removal, however, political gossip in Salisbury suggested that Welensky was behind the move. Welensky categorically denied this rumour and there is no evidence to implicate him in any such plot.[135] As he wryly noted, 'on the one hand I am accused of having got rid of Todd and of having engineered his removal, yet only a short while ago I was just as strongly accused by another section of keeping him in office. It does show that the middle-of-the-roader generally gets into trouble from either one side or another.'[136] His position as a 'middle-of-the-roader' brought increasing criticism over the next few years as anti-federation African opinion strengthened and the European population in the Federation galvanised, moving further to the right.

Todd's replacement as Southern Rhodesian prime minister was Sir Edgar Whitehead. As Whitehead was not a sitting member of the Southern Rhodesian Assembly, he required a parliamentary seat. It was agreed that the member for the Hillside constituency in Bulawayo, J. M. Macdonald, would resign his seat so that Whitehead could stand in the by-election.[137] This transition faltered, however, as Whitehead lost the subsequent election. This loss precipitated a decision by the Southern Rhodesian Cabinet to call a general election as soon as possible.[138] Although Todd initially agreed to join Whitehead's interim cabinet, after failing to convince Whitehead to remove the more right-wing members at the UFP Caucus on the 24 April, he resigned and formed the Central Africa Party to fight the in forthcoming general election.

The UFP managed to retain power after the June 1958 election, winning 17 seats to the Dominion Party's 13.[139] This victory was a not as resounding as it seemed. The Southern Rhodesian election allowed voters to choose a second preference candidate, and the UFP won based on the second preference votes of Todd's supporters. In fact, the Dominion Party secured a majority of just over a thousand on first preference votes alone.[140] This illustrates that there was a high level of resistance against further African advancement in Southern Rhodesia as early as 1958. Welensky was fully supportive of Whitehead's victory and, during the election, had released a statement which stated that the new Southern Rhodesian prime minister 'was following the tradition, already long established in Southern Rhodesia, of progress through evolution and not by revolution'.[141] This did little to convince the Africans who were dismayed by the settler government's swift replacement of a perceived liberal. A number of European voters 'were also soon alarmed by the programme of the awkward, partially deaf, poor sighted, unmarried, academically-minded and somewhat unpractical

Whitehead'.[142] Lord Alport, the future high commissioner in Salisbury, believed that the differences between Welensky and Whitehead 'were as contrasting as their qualities were complimentary [sic] and any deep mutual understanding, or real personal friendship was difficult for either to achieve'.[143]

Sir Roy Welensky contacted Ellis Robins prior to the 1958 Federal election to ask for financial aid for the UFP campaign. The money was to be paid into the 'chairman's fund', which was used to finance the election campaigning of UFP candidates. The chairman's fund was useful as it was not administered through the party and therefore deposits could be made in relative anonymity. The money was intended to help UFP African candidates who did not have the money to pay their own deposits or fund their travel. He suggested that the chairman's fund was used as these expenses were 'not the kind of thing we can put through the usual Party machine'.[144] Welensky asked for a payment of approximately one thousand pounds. Although the documentary evidence does not reveal the final amount Robins agreed to pay, a payment was made.[145] The chairman's fund would subsequently play an important role as the channel through which Anglo American could continue to provide Welensky with financial support, particularly in the 'build-a-nation' campaign.

A link between the Federal government and RST was provided by David Cole, a journalist, who left Sheffield in 1948 to take up a position at the Argus Group's newspaper, the *Johannesburg Star*. He moved to Rhodesia soon after and subsequently held the editorship of the *Northern News* and the *Bulawayo Chronicle* and a place on the editorial board of the *Central African Examiner*. By the mid-1950s he had established himself as a public relations consultant in Salisbury after Prain agreed to fund an advisory position for the Federal government. Consequently he drew his salary from RST, yet answered to Welensky.[146] Cole has been described as 'a Welensky man first and last' and less sympathetically as 'Welensky's doormat'.[147] Though he was instrumental in securing the British public relations firm, Voice and Vision, to run the government's public relations campaign in Britain, his close links to RST meant he was never fully trusted within some quarters of the Federal government. This air of suspicion led the director of the Federal Intelligence and Security Bureau (FISB), Basil 'Bob' de Quehen, to warn Welensky's principal private secretary, Stewart Parker, about Cole during March 1958.

De Quehen notified Parker that he had 'good reason' to believe that RST, through Cole, was pressing Welensky to call an early general election.[148] This allegation was particularly disturbing as Cole's advice was offered against the backdrop of the Southern Rhodesian political crisis which saw Garfield Todd, prime minister of Southern Rhodesia, lose his position to Edgar Whitehead after a protracted power struggle within his party during February 1958. RST would later be accused of financing Todd's United Rhodesia Party during the subsequent general election, though Prain emphatically denied its involvement.[149] De Quehen did not doubt who was to blame for Cole's advice, and wrote 'we know that the copper mining companies, especially the RST Group, are pushing with all their might for much greater measure of African advancement in industry'.[150]

African advancement in the Copperbelt was seen by de Quehen as advantageous to RST as he speculated that it would reduce production costs. Lower production costs would have 'the effect of pleasing American interests' as it would result in a higher share dividend. Consequently, he argued that 'PRAIN is playing the HOCHSCHILD [emphasis in original] line very carefully'.[151] Harold Hochschild held a particular interest in race relations in central Africa, and consequently favoured RST adopting a progressive policy towards African advancement on the Copperbelt.[152] The 'Hochschild line', according to de Quehen, was a test of the Federation's future viability. This highlights the distrust in which certain sections of the Federal government held American influence on their affairs. A strong economy was critical for the survival of the Federation and a loss of faith in the project from foreign investors had to be avoided at all costs.

The next flashpoint in Anglo-settler relations occurred over the Northern Rhodesian constitutional changes. Sir Roy Welensky and the leader of the UFP in Northern Rhodesia, John Roberts, held divergent views on how the constitution should evolve.[153] The matter was further complicated by disagreements on the British side between the Commonwealth Relations Office and the Colonial Office on how far concessions to Africans should go.[154] Roberts, who visited London in July 1958, reported to Welensky that he was 'stunned' at the Colonial Office's attitude towards negotiations. According to Roberts they had adopted a policy of 'expediency' rather than acting on any long-term considerations; consequently the Colonial Office appeared to be pursuing a course that would please the Labour Party.[155] In contrast the Commonwealth Relations Office adopted a far friendlier attitude to the Rhodesian settlers during 1958. Lord Home contended in a Cabinet memorandum, in November 1958, that 'we are in danger of losing the sense of purpose which led us to establish the Federation in 1953'. He further argued that it should be made clear to Welensky when he visited London later in the month that British belief in the principle of federation was undimmed. Home believed that this course of action would provide Welensky with a secure position to push through greater reforms for Africans which, in turn, would reduce tension in the Federation.[156]

Northern Rhodesia and Nyasaland: Dr Banda Returns

Following the Southern Rhodesian election, events in the two northern territories began to overshadow those in the south. In Nyasaland, Dr Hastings Banda returned from Britain, via the Gold Coast, to popular African acclaim during July 1958.[157] Banda was subsequently elected leader of the Nyasaland African Congress (NAC) on 1 August 1958.[158] Banda's mandate was to secure an African majority in the Legislative Council at the forthcoming Nyasaland constitutional review. Britain had agreed to open discussions over the constitution during 1959 and this, along with the forthcoming federal review due for 1960, helped create a sense of momentum and urgency within the African nationalist movement of Nyasaland.[159] This urgency was likely driven by the belief that they had a better chance of success negotiating with London than with Salisbury.

In Northern Rhodesia, the constitution was due for revision during 1959, and with a territorial election set to occur in March 1959 the task of agreeing on its replacement was paramount. This task fell to the territory's Governor, Sir Arthur Benson.[160] Since assuming the position in 1954, Benson had frequently clashed with settler politicians in the territory although his own approach to African political development was deeply paternalistic. Benson was sceptical of the Northern Rhodesian Africans' ability to engage with western-style political institutions, and preferred that Africans were represented through their traditional elites and native authorities.[161] Benson's proposals were eventually published as a white paper in March 1958.

In the event, the document pleased no one as it drew criticism from Welensky, African nationalists and the British Labour Party.[162] It contained proposals for a Legislative Council composed of 30 members and a speaker. Of these, it was expected that 14 members would be European and eight African. They would be joined by a further six official and two nominated members. Members would be chosen by a complicated system of cross-voting, which was based on the federal model of a dual-roll system. It consisted of 'ordinary' votes, which were expected to be held predominantly by Europeans, and 'special' votes with lower qualifications which would be held mainly by Africans. Benson's belief in traditional African elites was evidenced by the clause he inserted that any African wishing to stand for a seat on the 'special' roll had to have the support of two-thirds of the constituency's chiefs. Benson further proposed that the Executive Council would consist of ten members: the Governor as well as four official and five unofficial members, of which four of the latter would be elected.[163]

Welensky arrived in London in November for a series of eight meetings with Lennox-Boyd over the Northern Rhodesian constitution.[164] Towards the end of the visit Welensky and Greenfield watched the parliamentary debate on the government's constitutional proposals from the Strangers' Gallery in the House of Commons. Callaghan followed Lennox-Boyd's explanation of the proposals by stating that the Command Paper,[165] on which they were detailed, struck him as being 'a compound of bureaucracy run mad plus prejudice', and continued 'It is designed to prevent the African from having too large a say in the affairs of Northern Rhodesia.'[166] Callaghan also drew attention to Sir Roy Welensky's influence suggesting:

> that the Federal Prime Minister whom we see on television is a very different person from the Prime Minister who speaks in Salisbury. One would hardly recognise him as the same man. Here we have a liberal, bluff man of honest common sense who is doing his best for everyone. The story is very different when one reads the speeches delivered in Africa.[167]

James Johnson, Labour MP for Rugby, backed Callaghan and stated that now Welensky had won the Federal election he must demonstrate that he was as liberal as he claimed.[168] Patrick Wall defended the proposals claiming that as:

> every member of every party in Northern Rhodesia, and right hon. and hon. Members of all three parties in this House, have criticised certain aspects of it. It may be that this shows that it is a reasonably fair one, since everybody can pick holes in it and everybody is pleased with certain parts.[169]

In the event the Conservatives won the debate with a majority of 296 to 238.

Welensky had also agreed to address the Commonwealth Affairs Committee during this visit. Patrick Wall advised Welensky of the federal issues which were worrying many of the Conservative Party backbenchers. The majority of backbenchers recognised the desire of the settlers for full admission to the Commonwealth; however there were two main issues which they viewed with concern. The first related to the promises Oliver Lyttleton, former secretary of state for the colonies, had given to the northern protectorates and secondly, whether the Federal government would be strong enough to handle the inevitable African opposition – 'either administratively or physically' – that such a move would create. Concerns also circulated over the possible repercussions across the rest of the Commonwealth that a conflict between settlers and Africans in the Federation would raise.[170]

Welensky's broad attack on Benson's proposals was made on the grounds that they would entrench racial representation and therefore betray the principles of partnership. He criticised the vetting of 'special' candidates by chiefs and believed that it would strengthen the African position 'without making any advance towards responsible self-government substantial enough to satisfy European aspirations.[171] In contrast African leaders and the Labour Party attacked the proposals for granting insufficient representation, as the new constitution only enfranchised approximately 7,000 new African voters.[172] Kaunda was 'deeply shocked' by the constitution, and later recounted how Harry Nkumbula had publically burnt the white paper.[173]

The Colonial Office made small changes to Benson's initial proposals – for instance, insisting on two African members for the Executive Council instead of one – and published their amendments in a white paper on 17 September. This version was adopted. Welensky continued to protest the vetting of special roll candidates until the eve of the March election in which the UFP secured 13 of the 22 elected seats, including two of the special seats reserved for Africans.[174] This provided Welensky with a second successive victory in the polls, adding to the UFP's victory in the November 1958 federal election. Welensky, buoyed by his electoral success, believed that he 'could face the difficulties and dangers which undoubtedly lay ahead with a reasonable degree of optimism'.[175] His optimism would soon be tested by the worsening security situations in all three territories.[176]

The 1959 Emergencies

Of all the federal territories, Nyasaland contained the most effective African political opposition to federation by the late 1950s. In many respects this was not surprising. The Nyasaland Africans had been at the forefront of the anti-federal campaign prior to 1953, and the territory's European settlers were far less numerous and powerful than in either of the other two territories. Additionally, the territory's land was under higher population pressure and, consequently, Nyasaland was at the forefront of experiments with new agricultural techniques which often upset peasant farmers.[177] After Banda's return in 1958 nationalists in the territory finally possessed a charismatic and well-qualified leader.

In Northern Rhodesia the centre of anti-federation protest was much more contested. The nationalist movement in Northern Rhodesia was split between the ANC, which wished to contest the March 1959 territorial election under the leadership of Nkumbula, and the newly formed Zambia African National Congress (ZANC) led by Kaunda. Nkumbula, it was suggested, was known to enjoy 'the pleasures of life' and became increasingly lax in organising party affairs.[178] A further cause for the divide was Kaunda's belief that Nkumbula had led the ANC 'to the verge of dictatorship' in his attempt to keep hold of power in the party.[179] In Southern Rhodesia, the nationalist movement, SRANC faced far greater difficulties than its northern neighbours due to the size and power of its territory's settler population.

By December 1958, however, the growing confidence of the movement and its increasing influence on the African population convinced Whitehead and his cabinet that they would have to act.[180]

It is within this milieu of growing African confidence and assertiveness that the emergencies in Southern Rhodesia (25 February 1959) and Nyasaland (2–3 March 1959) should be placed.[181] A state of emergency was not called in Northern Rhodesia, however, ZANC was banned on 11 March 1959. Across the Federation, African political unrest and civil disobedience increased.

The tension in Nyasaland was heightened at the end of January 1959 when Governor Armitage announced his proposals for the new constitution.[182] Armitage favoured a Legislative Council in which only 14 of the 29 members would be elected. Under the dual-roll system, Africans were expected to win eight of the elected seats while the Europeans would hold six. This fell far short of Banda's wish for an African majority in the Legislative Council and further exacerbated strain within the territory.[183] Acting Chief Secretary to the Nyasaland government, Peter Youens, believed that if Banda had accepted these proposals he would have failed in his promise to bring majority rule swiftly and consequently could have been in 'Queer Street' with his party.[184] Therefore, he speculated that Banda was attempting to provoke his own arrest as 'perhaps on way of buying time' with his supporters.[185]

Reports began to reach the Nyasaland government of a 'meeting in the bush' between senior NAC leaders – minus Banda – at which a plot to murder Europeans and Africans sympathetic to the Federation was conceived. The Nyasaland Police Commissioner would later inform Government House of the plot, remarking that his special branch source claimed that 'the NYASALAND AFRICAN CONGRESS has prepared plans for the mass murder throughout the Protectorate of all foreigners, by which is meant all Europeans and Asian, men, women and children, to take place in the event of DR BANDA being killed, arrested or abducted' [emphasis in the original]. The Police Commissioner was convinced of the severity of the situation, which was complicated by a further rumour that 75 per cent of the police force and King's African Rifles were expected to defect and join with Congress if the 'R' Plan was implemented. The Commissioner conceded that 'there is nothing to indicate these forces would be anything other than loyal, although it is known that certain of the younger men are in the police are in sympathy with the aims of Congress'. He therefore recommended that 'urgent action is necessary now to prevent the situation becoming out of hand'.[186] Two days after this letter, African nationalists seized control of the airfield at Fort Hare and by the time the government had reasserted its control five Africans had died.[187] This appeared to add further credence to his informer's claims.

The Nyasaland government feared it would be unable to cope with a widespread African insurrection without help from outside its borders. Law and order were the responsibility of territorial governments while defence came under the federal remit. Consequently if Armitage, wished to deploy soldiers to keep the peace he would need the support of the Federal government. The governors and prime ministers of the four governments in the Federation met in Salisbury on 20 February 1959. Sir Edgar Whitehead revealed that he was planning to call a state of emergency in Southern Rhodesia in due course in order to detain leading SRANC members, ostensibly so that his territory could be secured before troops were moved from there to Nyasaland. Armitage did not confirm that he too intended to call an emergency although he informed the room of the rumours regarding 'R-Day'.[188]

Whitehead called a state of emergency on 25 February and managed to successfully detain 430 leading SRANC members, although Joshua Nkomo, SRANC's leader, avoided detention as he was out of the country.[189] Despite this success, Whitehead faced embarrassment over the arrest of Guy Clutton-Brock,[190] who had jointly authored SRANC's constitution with Nkomo.[191] Clutton-Brock held joint Federal and British citizenship, and his detention had led to questions being asked in the British House of Commons. This moved the Southern Rhodesian cabinet to consider whether Clutton-Brock should be released to end the matter.

It was decided that if he was to be released there should be 'a token release of African detainees, if such were available, so as to avoid any racial discrimination'. They hesitated to allow a wider release as doing so would cause 'some dislocations in the preparations which included an elaborate ceremonial release of detainees and public admonition in the presence of their chiefs at which the regulations and the illegality of the African National Congress were to be explained.[192] Consequently it was agreed that 'a few Africans' should be released along with Clutton-Brock on 24 March.[193] Benson resisted pressure from the Federal government to declare an emergency in Northern Rhodesia, preferring instead to continue discrediting ZANC's decision to boycott the forthcoming election.[194] He changed his approach, however, on 11 March 1959 when he banned ZANC, but not the ANC, after claiming that African nationalist leaders from all the Federal territories had prepared a joint plan for violent revolution at the Accra Conference during 1958.[195]

Meanwhile, the situation in Nyasaland had continued to deteriorate rapidly and on 25 February Armitage felt compelled to cancel the visit of Lord Perth, minister of state for the colonies, who was due to arrive at the end of February to discuss constitution proposals.[196] The following day he notified Perth that he intended to declare a state of emergency at midnight on 3 March.[197] Macmillan blamed the emergency on 'a most unstable division of responsibility between the various governments concerned', and speculated that he must 'take a lead in this affair' as it was becoming 'politically damaging at home'.[198]

A further politically damaging event that day was the arrest of John Stonehouse MP[199] by federal immigration officials at Lusaka airport.[200] Stonehouse had met with African nationalist groups in Southern Rhodesia earlier in his visit to the Federation and had been informed four days earlier by Malcolm Barrow, the federal minister for home affairs, that he would be prevented from travelling to Nyasaland. If Stonehouse would not leave the Federation of his own accord he would be declared a 'prohibited immigrant' and be expelled from the Federation immediately. Stonehouse refused to co-operate and was arrested by Federal immigration officers in Lusaka while he waited for a flight to Nyasaland.[201] A supplementary event which also helped to move opinion against the Federation in Britain was the death of 11 Africans at Hola Camp, a Mau Mau rehabilitation facility, in Kenya. Ronald Hyam goes as far as to state that 'if one had to choose a single fateful date which signalled the moral end of the British empire in Africa it would thus be the 3 March 1959'.[202]

Repercussions of the Emergencies

By 1959, Harold Hochschild's earlier concern was replaced by action. In the wake of the publicity surrounding the Nyasaland emergency, RST and Anglo American announced that their donations to the UFP would henceforth cease. The *Guardian* later called this announcement a sign of the 'liberal influence' that big companies could have in the region. The article further mused: 'once it used to be said that the Rhodesias consisted of "white ants and the British South Africa Company"; to-day it is truer to say that the only certain permanencies are big business and Africans'.[203] According to Harold Taswell, Stewart Aitken-Cade, leader of the Dominion Party in Southern Rhodesia believed:

> the mining companies were possibly divorcing themselves from recognising political parties with the idea of playing up to the natives in Northern Rhodesia [...] By showing the natives that they are on their side now the companies might be able to save their copper interests in the same way that the cocoa companies have apparently saved theirs in Ghana.[204]

Aitken-Cade thought, however, that 'the companies would lose out in the end anyhow and find the mines nationalised by any native government which came into power'.[205] Taswell also noted that there were rumours of friction between the two mining companies. He believed this had occurred as RST were 'in favour of a far more liberal policy towards the Bantu while Anglo American are hesitant of moving too quickly – possibly because of their wider experience and greater knowledge of native mentality'.[206]

The political fallout during the aftermath of the emergencies called in February and March 1959 has been labelled 'a major turning point' in the history of British colonial rule in Africa.[207] In addition to the political ramifications, the emergencies also engendered serious economic consequences for the Federal government. Reports reached Welensky, that investment opportunities in the Federation were not viewed in the same light as they once were in London. Much to Welensky's chagrin, a British insurance company revealed it now thought of the Federation as part of 'Black Africa' when considering where to invest its pension funds.[208] Harry Oppenheimer, chairman of Anglo American, took a rather different view as he believed the Federal government's actions demonstrated a 'determination to govern' and the ability to see that law and order was maintained.[209] Consequently, the declaration of a state of emergency would be a boon to potential investors.[210]

Prior to RST's decision to withdraw its financial support from the UFP, Sir Ronald Prain had written a long and detailed letter to Sir Roy Welensky in which he summarised his views on the Federation's current and future positions. Having expressed his continuing belief in the future of racial partnership he asked what road Welensky planned to take to implant it in the Federation. In Prain's opinion the best course of action would be 'to get alongside these African movements and bring along Africans as partners and not throw them into the opposing camp'.[211] This should be a priority, according to Prain, as it was becoming increasingly difficult to attract foreign investment into the Federation. Prain saw it as 'partly a question of the chicken and the egg', in that without economic development there would be political trouble in the Federation, yet without political stability it would prove difficult to attract investment.[212]

Political stability in the Federation was increasingly important in the context of ongoing riots in Leopoldville in the Belgian Congo. The Belgian government announced plans for the independence of the Congo a mere week after rioting began and, although Prain recognised that independence was the culmination of several turbulent months, he saw it as a mistake because 'to the simple African mind the connection between the two will be too obvious; all you have to do is riot one weekend and you get independence the following weekend'.[213] Consequently, Prain urged Welensky to make concessions immediately to dissipate the chance of a similar occurrence in the Federation.

Welensky's reply dealt first with the question of the future of the Federation. He noted Prain's concerns and agreed that the economic and political situations in the territory were intertwined. Welensky also revealed that there was a section of the settler community that was 'anxious to create an impression that the position in the Federation is unstable', as they wished for at least a portion of the Federation to become a fifth province of the Union of South Africa.[214] Welensky commented on the question of African advancement by describing the numerous advances that federation had introduced to the civil service, although he asserted that there were 'not the Africans of quality to fill the posts that I want to put them in'.[215]

African advancement on the railways, Welensky argued, was complicated by the assurances given to the European trade unions regarding African advancement prior to federation being introduced. He also pointed to the advances that had been secured in the mining industry. With regard to Prain's opinions on the Congo, Welensky wrote 'quite frankly I don't share your view'.[216] He reasoned that in the Congo the policy was 'to treat the African like an animal, feed him well, house him well and you would get good work out of him, but little consideration was given to his needs other than his material ones'.[217] This was in direct contrast to how Welensky viewed Africans' position in the Federation, citing the fact that out of the federal parliament of 59 there were 15 African representatives. Welensky concluded his letter by bemoaning his position, writing:

> I am sniped at from every quarter; I lack the reliable backing of a press organisation; I have to walk on ice that is so thin that occasionally it frightens me, but I do have faith in the things I am trying to do and I believe that any dispassionate historian who looks back at the last five years and evaluates circumstances will say that our advancements were by no means small.[218]

Welensky's reference to his lack of backing of a reliable press organisation referred directly to his disappointment with the *Central African Examiner*, the failure of which he laid squarely at the door of RST. The *Central African Examiner* had been founded in 1957 as a fortnightly journal of liberal thought with the aim of promoting racial partnership in the Federation. For the first three years of its existence it was financed by RST and was often critical of the slow pace of African advancement.[219] Therefore, the *Central African Examiner* often caused friction between the UFP and RST, and as early as October 1957 Prain felt compelled to write to Welensky to make clear that the *Examiner* was completely independent from RST commenting:

> I am most grateful for your continued refutal of any idea that the CAE [*Central African Examiner*] in anyway reflects RST or RLP [Ronald Lindsay Prain] thinking on policy. I think you know, Roy just where I stand – I am solidly behind the Fed[eral] Party (as I need hardly demonstrate) and one of your staunchest supporters.[220]

As the end of RST's three-year commitment to finance the *Examiner* drew near, sales had not reached a sufficient level to cover the cost of production. This concerned some sections of the government because, although the *Examiner* had often been critical of the government it had significance, as Donald Macintyre summarised, as an 'indicator to people overseas of a degree of economic, social and – dare I say it – mental development. The *Examiner* therefore has definite prestige value'.[221] This assessment moved Welensky to contact Keith Acutt of Anglo American to see if they could provide any help.[222] Acutt promised to advertise in the *Examiner* if Anglo American was not doing so already.[223]

The Colonial Office also recognised the potential damage that the Nyasaland emergency could have on public opinion in Britain. Julian Amery, under secretary of state for the colonies, notified Lennox-Boyd he was not in favour of a parliamentary enquiry into the disturbances.[224] Amery wrote that there were 'very strong feelings' in the Conservative Party which were not confined only to the right wing, against any enquiry. Amery further contended: 'I don't believe in the good faith of the Opposition in all this. They have been looking for a battle-ground with us for months and think at last they have found one. They would also like to wreck the Federation on the merits of the case if they could.'[225] Consequently Lennox-Boyd offered his full support to Armitage over his decision to call the emergency.

Rumours, however, were growing in Britain that Armitage had succumbed to pressure from Welensky and the Federal government. Andrew Thompson has demonstrated that public awareness of both Hola Camp and the Nyasaland emergency was quite high – 90 per cent of people knew of troubles in Kenya, while 80 per cent were aware of the Nyasaland emergency – however support for the authorities' actions differed markedly. The government's treatment of the Mau Mau was approved of by 40 per cent of people polled, and opposed by 23 per cent. In this and all other polling data mentioned here, the views of the remainder of the sampled population were not given. Only 25 per cent backed the handling of the Nyasaland emergency, while 23 per cent did not. Arguably of more importance to the Federal government was the fact that British sympathies were directed more towards the Africans (30 per cent) than the settlers (18 per cent).[226]

This shift in opinion was noted by Jack Thompson, an employee of RST who was in Britain during the Nyasaland emergency. He recognised the danger of unchecked negative press coverage in Britain and commented:

you will no doubt have seen the outpourings and headlines appearing in the UK Press, which seems to have gone a little hysterical about the whole thing [the Nyasaland emergency]. Whatever may be the feelings of the people in Rhodesia and Nyasaland, current events have not done the Federation's cause any good at all.[227]

Welensky later recalled how the events in Nyasaland 'roused the Socialist Opposition in the House of Commons, and our British newspaper, wireless and television critics, to a higher pitch of indignation than any other action of the Federal Government during my whole term of office as Prime Minister'.[228]

The declaration of emergencies in Southern Rhodesia and particularly Nyasaland provoked criticism in many parts of the world, including the United States. The disturbances in Nyasaland were of prime concern to the State Department prior to Assistant Secretary for African Affairs, Joseph Satterthwaite's proposed visit to Salisbury in June 1959.[229] It was assumed that Satterthwaite would be invited to speak with Welensky and it was suggested that Satterthwaite emphasised that the situation in Nyasaland had damaged the Federation's reputation in the United States. This damage had been further compounded with the introduction of draconian legislation in Southern Rhodesia such as the Unlawful Organisations Bill. While the United States government accepted that this was a territorial rather than a federal matter, it seemed necessary to make clear to Welensky that in the outside world distinctions were not always correctly drawn.[230]

Nyasaland was still a major issue when Satterthwaite met with the British ambassador in Washington the following August. They were concerned that the Nyasaland disturbances had set in motion a train of events which could lead to the break-up of the Federation. The danger was that an independent federation would move closer to South Africa or become 'an erratic and easily subverted African government'. The Americans made clear they believed that onus for the current crisis fell on the 'inordinate slowness' of the Federal government in implementing its partnership policy.[231]

It was the view of the State Department that American interests would suffer if Britain handed control of Northern Rhodesia and Nyasaland to a settler-dominated government in Salisbury. It was recognised that Britain might be forced to concede self-government, outside the Federation but within the Commonwealth, to Nyasaland.

While this would generate enormous pressure in Northern Rhodesia for a similar arrangement and consequently would affect the short-term stability and economic development, it was judged 'more in keeping with long range US (and UK) interests than a federation in which "stability" rested on the power of a dominant white minority to impose its will on an overwhelming African majority'.[232]

These examples demonstrate a distinct disenchantment in Washington with the way in which the UFP was implementing its policy of partnership well before John F. Kennedy assumed the presidency in 1961.[233] Satterthwaite was to end his discussion with the British ambassador with the following recommendations:

In general, we hope the UK will find it possible to (1) resist European demands for more power at this stage of the Federation's history, when Africans are extremely suspicious and bitter because of the handling of the recent 'emergencies' (2) make soon the difficult but necessary decision to deal with the detained African nationalists from Nyasaland, who must be consulted, eventually, and (3) advance Africans politically in Nyasaland and Northern Rhodesia as [... has] been done elsewhere in non-settler Africa when events clearly dictated the necessity for such moves.[234]

While these conclusions closely follow the line adopted by the British government, it would be an overstatement of American influence to credit the State Department with dictating British colonial policy. The British Cabinet Future Policy Study Working group noted two months later that the Americans had come to 'respect' British African policies and collaborate increasingly with them. 'In the case of America', however, it was still necessary to provide 'skilful presentation of our steady progress towards agreed goals'. That is, any difficulties in the Federation that the British faced 'will be worse if we try to keep the Americans at arms' length'.[235]

The shared Anglo-American approach to the federal situation spurred Welensky to attack the ease with which an African nationalist could 'find there what I can only describe as monumental support for his aims'.[236] Welensky's case was not helped by the reaction from federal authorities to instances such as the proposed United States trade delegation to Salisbury. The problem arose when a rumour reached the

Federal government that the delegation would contain a black representative. The problem was such that Welensky had to approach the American Consul General, Joseph Palmer, to discuss the matter. Palmer reported that:

> Roy was quite correct in his discussion of this matter with me. He said that I would understand that he personally had no objection to a Negro member and reiterated that the policy of his government was one of partnership. He said he wanted me to know, however, that Whitehead was very upset about the possibility and feared that any Negro member might be subjected to slight or incident which would detract from the impact of the mission.[237]

Consequently, Palmer recommended that no black Americans should be present on the mission. Satterthwaite replied to Palmer, agreeing that in light of Whitehead's reservations it might be 'counter-productive in some circles' to push the matter.[238] It was difficult for the UFP to counter outside criticism of its racial policies when instances such as this demonstrated that it could not guarantee equality to a visiting black delegate.

In light of the above, it is unsurprising that, by the end of Eisenhower's presidency, the State Department believed that the Federation could not work under its present constitution. They believed the wisest course of action for the British was to 'play for more time in which to bring its influence to bear while avoiding an outright racial conflict'. The United States hoped to prevent the worsening of 'current trends' by encouraging Britain to commence talks immediately with the Federal and Southern Rhodesian governments. During these discussions, Britain should firmly set forth the following points: firstly, that the policy of partnership was a failure and thoroughly discredited; that the worsening situation called for 'the re-imposition of UK authority in her role as imperial arbiter'; and finally that the rapid advancement of Africans was necessary on a broad front, for which Britain and the United States should assume a greater share of the cost.[239]

Eisenhower's Republican administration developed an increasingly liberal approach in its policy towards the Central African Federation. The meetings between Macmillan and the American president in 1957 led to the acceptance that the best approach to combating communism in Africa was through advancing pro-western African leaders to power in the remaining colonial territories. The Federation was not excepted from this rule, and consequently the settlers were a liability, rather than an asset, in the war against communism in Africa.

Devlin Commission

In an attempt to end public outcry over the Nyasaland emergency the Conservatives 'turned to a favourite British device',[240] in Welensky's words, and appointed a commission of inquiry headed by Lord Devlin.[241] It was also decided to appoint a preparatory commission in advance of the proposed 1960 Federal review, in order to ensure the Devlin Commission did not exceed its remit and consider the wider question of the Federation's future. Lord Home telegraphed Lord Perth, minister of state at the Colonial Office, who was in Lusaka, and asked him to convince Welensky to agree to this approach. Home suggested that Perth warn Welensky that the political situation in Britain was 'very difficult and bad and a lot of Conservative opinion deeply disturbed and in need of re-assurance'. There was also a danger that Labour would commit themselves to a policy of secession without a preparatory commission, which would seriously prejudice the 1960 review, and this could be avoided if Welensky acceded to Home's request. Finally, a preparatory commission would help remove the British public's ignorance of the Federation and assist Welensky in his aim of Commonwealth status in 1960.[242]

It was judged important to remove the Federation as an election issue in case a new Labour government insisted on a parliamentary commission.[243] Combating criticism from the Labour Party was important to both the Conservative and Federal governments. Julian Amery judged that the Labour Party were not 'acting in good faith' over the Nyasaland enquiry. This he attributed to 'Colonialism' having become 'the main issue in party politics'.[244] Indeed, he went as far as to speculate that 'it is about the only issue the Labour Party can still campaign on'.[245] Macmillan was of the opinion that 'if the Labour Party gets in here, I have no doubt that they [the Federation] will secede and either proclaim their independence or join S. Africa'.[246]

There were also problems developing for Welensky within the Conservative Party. In July 1959 the Bow Group released a memorandum entitled *Central Africa: The Challenge of 1960*. The document called for a Commonwealth commission to prepare for the 1960 Federal review. It contended that the commission should be comprised of Privy Councillors representing all British political parties as the Federation was ultimately a British parliamentary responsibility. Crucially, the document suggested that this commission should be prepared to consider a rapid move towards full adult suffrage without transitional safeguards for Europeans.[247] The Bow Group consisted of around 50 members with a median age of 28 in 1960 and as Philip Murphy observes they 'represented a young and ambitious section of the party'.[248] Welensky subsequently recalled how 'colonialism [...] among all progressive-minded young Conservatives in the later 1950s, was a dirty word, which they wished to expunge from their consciences'.[249]

The prospect of a commission of inquiry was also not popular in Salisbury. M. R. Metcalf, the British High Commissioner to the Federation, warned that he was 'completely convinced by my talks here that any hint of [a] UK inquest into the activities in relation [to the] Nyasaland disturbances would have disastrous effects on European opinion'.[250] Despite this fear, Sir Patrick Devlin arrived in Nyasaland on 11 April 1959 after he was chosen to lead the commission.[251] In many respects Devlin could have been expected to produce a report that was favourable towards Armitage and his Conservative party supporters back in Britain. Devlin had attended the University of Cambridge with Lord Perth and the two men were life-long friends; he was a cousin of the wife of Sir Peveril William-Powlett, the governor of Southern Rhodesia, and a member of the Carlton Club, the spiritual home of establishment conservatism.

The other members of the commission should also have been sympathetic to Armitage's plight. Sir Percy Wyn-Harris was 'an old Africa Hand', having served as an administrator in Kenya and also as former governor of the Gambia.[252] Also chosen was E. T. Williams, the Warden of Rhodes House and Field Marshall Montgomery's chief of intelligence during World War II.[253] The final member selected was Sir John Ure Primrose, a former Lord Provost of Perth who served with the Royal Navy during World War I and MI5 during World War II.[254] Consequently, while Harold Macmillan may have harboured personal doubts about Devlin due to his Irish-catholic heritage and his failure to be appointed Lord Chief Justice, Devlin's fellow commissioners should have been expected to produce a suitable report.

The Devlin Commission collected its evidence by soliciting written submissions by anyone, European or African, who wished to make their opinion heard. They further interviewed the main protagonists on both sides as well as any of the written contributors who they thought could be of greater value. Although the Commission's terms of reference forbade it from considering the future of the Federation, many African witnesses made clear their unhappiness with the present situation. As one young NAC member related:

> Our peace, loyalty, obedience has been destroyed by the introduction, or to be correct, by the imposition of the Federation founded in 1953. Yes the word Federation by itself is quite innocent, but the type of Federation is the question to debate upon, because the Federation can either be bad or good, judging from the constitution's point of view governing it. Therefore, [that] this Federation was shuffled in our mouths, but not as yet swallowed, is terrifying! There is much danger in it, though Partnership is a catchy word meant to magnetise us towards it. We definitely know that at the end, this catchy-word would be eliminated and 'Segregation' would come in. Some of the dangers are:- 'White Domination', and 'Apartheid'.[255]

A further witness believed that Africans in Nyasaland had 'a real belief and conviction' that the Federation was not in African interests:

> We knew when this catchword 'Partnership' was introduced, that it was designed to hoodwink people in Britain, and in fact the designers succeeded to deceive or rather cheat them. Partnership was a mere passport to their so-called Federation. That in the recent past, the planters and their governments began to shout for dominion status; that in itself, was enough and sufficient evidence to change the temper of the normal person to retaliate on physical provocation kindled by the police and some Government officers which is so frequent in this doom ridden country of our ancestors.[256]

This witness anticipated the most damning charge against the Nyasaland government within the Devlin Report, proclaiming:

> If ever there was a Police State, this is one of those states which are worse than useless. We have paid voluntary police and security members everywhere in the African locations, place of work and at meetings. Nearly every European Federationist is a security member of the secret branch of the Police. We have no freedom of speech and the relative freedoms [sic]. This is one of the worst grievances we have here.[257]

Lennox-Boyd had made clear to Armitage before the Commission's arrival that 'the crucial point is that witnesses should not fail to come forward from fear of subsequent victimisation'.[258] Despite this, several African government employees alleged that they had been 'encouraged' not to talk to the Commission. One man, who refused to remain quiet, alleged that 'many [witnesses] have been intimidated by an enormous number of full-time detectives who go about the government rest house to see who will give evidence'.[259] This corresponds with the experience of another government employee, who later told the Commission:

> I wished to give evidence on the Nyasaland disturbances but I could not do so due to intimidation attitude (threats of dismissal from work) shown by the Government generally and in particular the immediate supervising European Officers. It is only when a telegram was received in this office safe guarding a civil servant who gave or would give evidence that I felt I would give the evidence appended below, though of course too late.[260]

The above witnesses were all NAC members and uniformly denied any knowledge of an 'R-Plan'. They blamed Nyasaland's troubles on the imposition of the Federation. Of course, it is unlikely that these comparatively junior members of the organisation would have been privy to any high-level plan. However, as one witness pithily summarised:

> African leaders are not fools to plan such a thing when in fact they know that they have no guns, no rifles, no planes, no armoured cars etc. They are not fools to let their people get into such troubles when in fact they know that if they attempt they will be the losers.[261]

By contrast European statements to the Commission illustrate clearly the sense of unease in the community which had been growing over the previous few months. The provincial commissioner for the Southern Province, Mr Nicholson, expressed that he had no doubt that there was a murder plot. He claimed his province had 'been batting on an uneasy wicket here for some weeks'. Consequently he had judged it prudent to 'be prepared for any sort of disturbances which broke out'.[262] The Bishop of Nyasaland reported a similar rise in tension. In his opinion, the Africans in the territory, 'a rather Scottish body of people, stolid quiet folk', had been angered by a very vigorous anti-soil erosion campaign which left them 'rather hot under the collar'.[263] The reference to the anti-soil erosion campaign corresponds with John Darwin's assertion that 'the growing appeal of nationalist movements may have owed a good deal to the desire of both urban and rural interests to protect themselves against the increasing intervention of the colonial state in their local affairs, especially through its efforts to regulate agriculture'.[264]

All the members of the Commission attended the interviews of Dr Hastings Banda and Sir Robert Armitage. Banda was interviewed first on 16 May, and was accompanied by Dingle Foot, his adviser and friend.[265] During the first section of the interview Foot asked Banda about his activities since returning to Nyasaland the previous year.[266] Banda confirmed that after two years of negotiations over constitutional reform, by January 1959 'the people were expecting something'. Despite the frustration over the failure to secure an African majority in the Legislative Assembly he dismissed the notion of an 'R-Plan'. 'Definitely not, there was no such thing, not a thing, not a truth in that', he protested, 'it was all a fabrication by somebody who wanted something'. He stated that his tactics had always been based on the Indian model of peaceful non-cooperation. After all, he remarked, 'the Government have no gold mine of their own and I thought if we did that it would make them believe we meant this when we said secession from the Federation and Self-Government for Nyasaland'.[267]

Banda informed the Commission that, in his opinion, the decision to deploy Federal and Southern Rhodesian troops in Nyasaland indicated that 'the die is cast and the Rubicon is crossed'. He believed it demonstrated a complete lack of willingness to compromise by the Nyasaland government, as:

to bring troops from Southern Rhodesia, one of the Federal territories, was like the waving of a red flag before a bull, or putting oil on a fire, because as far as we were concerned that is what we had to say against Federation, that is proof of our case, that Europeans in Southern Rhodesia wanted our land, and therefore were bringing soldiers in to terrorise people and make us submit to their Federation.[268]

Sir Robert Armitage appeared before the Commission during May 1959 and was questioned by Devlin, who informed him that he would 'simply put the criticisms as we had heard them', although Devlin assured him that 'it does not of course mean we have necessarily adopted them'. Devlin began by asking Armitage if he had pursued a deliberate policy of delay when dealing with the NAC's claims for constitutional reform. Armitage denied this, stating that any delay had come about through Banda's own reluctance to enter into discussions with the other races in the territory.

Devlin then came to the rationale behind the state of emergency and questioned: 'It would be fair to say, would it not, that the object of the emergency measures that had been put into force was completely to suppress Congress?' Armitage curtly responded that the emergency measures had been introduced 'completely to suppress those responsible for creating disorders, and I do not think any other organisation had shown itself wishing to do so'. Continuing on his line of questioning, Devlin then inquired as to whether emergency measures had already been decided on and, consequently, whether the murder plot was merely a convenient 'frontispiece' for the emergency. Armitage refuted this strongly, contending that the information regarding the 'R-Plan' had been corroborated by several sources and he had no reason to doubt it. 'It seems to me,' replied Armitage, 'quite unreasonable for anyone, as the days went by, to look at that plan and to say that because no one has been murdered yet we will put a red pencil through the murder part of it this, and we will discount it. The plan was being carried out in a variety of ways, who was to say it wouldn't be carried out in that way?'[269]

The Devlin Commission's findings were published on 13 July 1959 and were highly critical of the government's actions on three main counts. First, it found that the hostility of politically conscious

Africans towards the Federation had been a major factor behind the unrest. Secondly, it cast considerable doubt that there had been a murder plot at all. Finally, it concluded that the security forces had used illegal force in executing 'Operation Sunrise'.[270] The most damning line of the report was the oft-quoted sentence that 'Nyasaland is – no doubt temporarily – a police state'. With memories of Nazi Germany still fresh, any mention of a 'police state' in a description of a British colony could not help but attract severe criticism. This resulting censure was further exacerbated by events in Kenya. The parliamentary debate on the Devlin report took place the day after the government had faced fierce criticism in the Commons over the deaths of 11 detainees at the Hola detention camp in Kenya. The convergence of these two incidents has been credited with persuading many in the British government that it was far too costly to prop up settler colonies in east and central Africa.[271]

Devlin's conclusions were not taken well in the Federation. Sir Roy Welensky dismissively remarked, 'I haven't very much regard for it as a document. It's contradictory and I think it shows more than anything else that one should not pick people from the British judicial scene and set them down in Africa, and expect them to produce a reasonable result'.[272] Julian Greenfield later stated that the report had 'killed any faith we [the Federal government] might have had in Commissions appointed by the British Government'.[273] Furthermore, the South African high commissioner to the Federation, Harold Taswell, reported that the Devlin Report had come as a 'great shock' to the people of Salisbury. Africans believed that the findings would result in Banda's imminent release from prison. The Federal authorities responded to the news by sending Northern Rhodesian policemen to the Nyasaland border. They were told 'to show the flag and remind would be trouble makers that they are nearby'.[274] Despite the settlers' fears, Banda would only remain in gaol until 1 April 1960.

The internationalisation of anti-colonial groups led the Federal government to approach the South Africans following the 1959 Nyasaland emergency, to ask for intelligence on the Nyasaland African Congress (NAC). The South Africans were keen to assist, as they already had information-sharing agreements in place with police forces in the neighbouring Portuguese territories. Unfortunately for the Federal authorities, in this instance the South African reports, revealed very little of direct relevance to NAC's activities in Nyasaland.[275] This connection later proved more useful when documents seized by a South African police raid on offices used by NAC members in the Union were passed to the Federal government.[276] In return, the Federal Intelligence and Security Bureau sent the South African government regular reports on the security situation in the Federation.[277]

The sharing of intelligence is indicative of the sympathy for the Federal government's plight amongst South African politicians. It was understood, however, that South Africa would not assist the Federation's case if this support was made public. Accordingly, when a rumour reached South African Prime Minister Hendrik Verwoerd that the opposition United Party (UP) would raise the issue of the Nyasaland disturbances in the South African Assembly, he moved quickly to try and stop it.[278] Any such question would undoubtedly bring a high level of support from the floor for the Federal government's actions. This publicity would be contrary to both South Africa's and the Federation's interests, and he had Sir de Villiers Graaf, leader of the UP, approached and asked to refrain from letting his party ask any questions on Nyasaland.[279] The leader of the opposition agreed to this on the condition that information received by the NP on the Federal situation was shared with his party.[280] Furthermore, it was also decided to stop 'a well-intentioned proposal by a group of Government Members to send Sir Roy Welensky a telegram of support' as it could be well-imagined 'how the news of such a telegram would be seized upon by the Socialist Opposition in Britain'.[281]

Preparing for the Federal Constitutional Review and the British General Election

Welensky visited London in July 1959 and the South African High Commission in London reported that Sir Roy Welensky was 'very satisfied' with the talks he had held with Labour Party leaders over the 1960 preparatory commission. Welensky was against a purely parliamentary commission as 'it would give the impression that the [Federal] government was being "put in the dock"'. The South Africans believed that Sir Roy had 'made a deep impression on the MPs by his sincere approach to the problem', and that chances of a bi-partisan approach to the Federation's problems had improved significantly.[282] Welensky later reported that the 'atmosphere was tense' in London and Macmillan 'was more harassed than I had ever seen him'. Welensky credited this to the worry that events in the Federation were having on the Conservative Party's electoral prospects in the forthcoming election.[283]

Further pressure over the Federation was applied to the government in a six-hour debate over the federal review preparatory commission in the Commons during July 1959. The Labour Party leader, Hugh Gaitskell began the debate, and highlighted the international nature of the Central African problem.[284] Gaitskell recognised that progress towards 'genuine racial equality' had been made, although it was being implemented far too slowly and the decision by the Federal and territorial governments to ban the leading African nationalist parties in the Federation was a worrying development. In conclusion, Gaitskell posited that government throughout federation 'rests today even more upon force and less upon consent than in 1953'.[285]

Harold Macmillan then spoke. He criticised those members of the Labour Party who had called for the Federal constitutional review to be postponed and argued that 'to postpone it now would seem to raise the maximum of suspicion for the minimum of advantage'. Furthermore, any such decision would be 'based merely on an unwillingness to grasp a difficult problem. It would not be standing up to the danger but, rather, running away from it.'[286] Finally, he concluded:

> If we were to announce our intention now to disband the Federation, or form a new one, or to divide it into different units without waiting either for the Commission or for the 1960 Review; if we were to tear up, without much thought, an experiment which is only seven years old and which was started with a good deal of good will on all sides, and an experiment which has made very considerable progress, we should be guilty of an act of treachery towards the high ideals and purposes which we set ourselves.[287]

Patrick Wall concurred, and noted that in his opinion the central African settlers felt that 'their future is being made the plaything of party politics in this country'.[288] John Dugdale recognised that the government could use a preparatory commission as a 'political dodge' when he asserted:

It is very useful to have a Commission of this character set up just before a General Election and to be able to say that everything is now *sub judice*, that the Commission is discussing the matter and it cannot be brought into politics and made use of during the election.[289]

Macmillan's Conservative Party were returned to government after winning 365 seats to Labour's 258 in the general election on 8 October 1959. This was welcome news in Salisbury. Whitehead wrote to congratulate Home on his party's 'splendid victory', and also to inform the secretary of state for Commonwealth relations that now the election was over he was keen to visit London to discuss the removal of the reserved clauses in the Southern Rhodesian constitution.[290] Sir Roy Welensky also greeted the news of Macmillan's victory. In a speech to the Executives of Central Africa Association, he announced that the Conservative Party was 'exceptionally well led'. Welensky credited the strong leadership of Macmillan and the 'sound common sense' of the British electorate in ensuring the 'emotional appeals' by the Labour Party in regards to recent events in Nyasaland and Hola had little effect.

Following the general election result, the Conservative Research Department, assessed the new parliament's comparative strengths in addressing colonial questions on east and central Africa. The report recognised that over the next few years there would be 'continuous and bitter warfare over Africa' and therefore it was important that the Conservatives 'should have a team of well-informed members capable of putting over our point of view'. The report acknowledged that the Labour Party were in a strong position:

The Opposition have great talent at their disposal – Messers Callaghan, Dugdale, Creech Jones, Brockway, Stonehouse, Soskice, Mrs White and Mrs Castle, are regular speakers in African debates while Gordon Walker, Ungoed Thomas, Paget, Thomas and Hale make up a good 'second eleven'. All have visited Africa; and – what is more – have kept up their knowledge. All are fluent speakers. Since the Election only James Johnson of their colonial experts is lost to them.

The Conservative Party position was not seen as comparable. They could boast 12 MPs who had visited Africa, but their quality did not match that of the Opposition. The report noted that of the MPs 'one never speaks: two are so reactionary as to be a liability: two know only Tanganyika: and two have lost interest'. Patrick Wall was judged 'a tower of strength, but taken on the whole our side has not the knowledge, oratorical or debating powers of the Opposition'.[291]

The South African High Commissioner also alluded to the influence of Labour Party criticism in Britain during 1959. A Federal government official had reportedly stated, to Taswell, that he had stopped reading the *Digest of South African Affairs*, as the more he read it 'the more convinced I become that you are right and we are wrong'.[292] To Taswell, the statement was 'typical of the doubts which have been crossing the minds of Rhodesians during the last few months'. He credited this swing in opinion to the shifting policy of the British government, and particularly attacks by the Labour Party. The 'accelerated pace' at which racial barriers were removed and the liberal policies of former Southern Rhodesian Prime Minister, Garfield Todd's, Central Africa Party (CAP) caused further concern.[293]

The necessary 'antidote' to any CAP threat was provided by the Dominion Party (DP). 'Although the party has shown signs of division and internal collapse in recent months, its backbone has been stiffened somewhat of late', Taswell enthused, citing a speech in the Legislative Assembly by Aitken-Cade, regarding the amount of Southern Rhodesian taxpayers' money which went towards implementing partnership. Aitken-Cade remarked: 'we of the Dominion Party renew our pledge to the people of Southern Rhodesia that will terminate the exploitation of the Europeans of this country. Unless we make a stand it will be too late to preserve what little we have left in Southern Rhodesia'.[294] Aitken-Cade again caught the attention of Taswell in July 1960, after introducing a motion which contended that it was not in the best interests of Southern Rhodesia to remain in the Federation.

In Taswell's opinion, however, Aitken-Cade 'was not at his best and his speech was dull and repetitious'. The speech did raise the question of Southern Rhodesia joining the Union, which drew a sharp reaction from the United Federal Party members. Mr Pittman, UFP member for Marimba, contended that white South Africans were divided into two distinct groups, with some being 'anti-British, anti-Monarchical and anti-Commonwealth', and that South Africa 'was an unhappy and disunited country amongst the white people'. Sir Edgar Whitehead argued that if South Africa's racial policies were allowed to move north they would inevitably lead to war with the black African nationalism prevalent in the rest of the continent. Whitehead believed the Federation 'is quite capable of forming a buffer state of service to all'.[295]

While the debate did not reveal much support on either side of the Assembly for amalgamation with South Africa, Taswell believed it was part of an underlying trend in Southern Rhodesia towards a political sentiment closer to that of South Africa. 'I have gained the impression that the English speaking Rhodesian's extreme pro-British sentiment and his fear of so-called "Afrikaner Nationalism" are diminishing', mused Taswell. 'Many Rhodesians are deeply disillusioned by the attitude of political parties in the United Kingdom. The movement for closer politically unity with the Union can, therefore, by no means be disregarded.'[296]

Welensky's assertion that opened this chapter, namely that those decisions taken in Africa would determine the Federation's future looked increasingly like wishful thinking by the end of 1959. The price of copper, the Federation's key export, was dictated by the London Metals Exchange and Westminster still retained the right to determine the Federation's constitutional future. As the early Monckton Commission would subsequently show, Welensky's faith in the successful implementation of partnership to secure the Federation's dominion status would prove to be little more than a pipe dream.

CHAPTER 3

'THE WIND OF CHANGE', 1960–1

I have thrown my full weight behind Whitehead trying to get people to support change. The Europeans have sheltered long enough behind the myth that the Africans have the same freedom as we do in this country. It is true that there is nothing preventing an African becoming Prime Minister or getting into Parliament, except the fact that economically he doesn't stand a snowball's chance in hell of achieving it.

Letter from Sir Roy Welensky to Pieter van der Byl, 24 July 1961[1]

Macmillan Visits the Federation

On 5 January 1960 Harold Macmillan embarked on his famous 'wind of change' tour of Africa.[2] The Prime Minister visited Ghana, the Federation and the Union of South Africa. In Accra on 9 January Macmillan first announced that 'the wind of change is blowing through Africa'.[3] The comment did not attract much attention until 3 February when Macmillan again used the phrase in an address to the South African parliament in Cape Town. This speech has been seen as an announcement of 'British abdication in Africa and the cynical abandonment of the white settlers'.[4] Yet this was not the impression gleaned by Welensky earlier when Macmillan visited the Federation during the previous month. Soon after Macmillan arrived in Salisbury, Welensky had pressed the British prime minister on the impending Monckton Commission, which was due to arrive in February, and more generally on the Federation's future. Macmillan assured Welensky that the Commission had not been appointed to 'destroy the Federation' and promised to clarify this publicly when he addressed the Rhodesia National Affairs Association the following day.[5]

True to his word, Macmillan's speech made clear that the Commission would abide by its terms of reference and advise the Federation on the best way to progress. Welensky described Macmillan as 'a most polished performer' although he confessed his difficulty in concentrating on Macmillan's speech 'because he speaks slowly and every word is read'. Many in the audience also expressed disappointment, as Macmillan did not go as far as they wished in offering support to the Federation. Welensky, however, was not too downhearted, as Macmillan had made clear that 'he'd come to look and learn, and not to discuss constitutional matters other than in private with me'. Welensky noted that Macmillan received 'an extremely good reception from both black and white'.[6] Following his time in Southern Rhodesia, Macmillan moved on to Northern Rhodesia and Nyasaland where he pursued a different tack. In Northern Rhodesia he 'immediately damaged the Federal case further by meeting Kenneth Kaunda and members of his new United National Independence Party (UNIP), conferring on them official recognition hitherto withheld'.[7]

Macmillan's ambiguous approach to the Federation's future continued throughout his visit. When the South African High Commissioner in Salisbury, Harold Taswell, enquired with the British High Commissioner, Maurice Metcalf, as to what impression Macmillan had taken from his visit, Metcalf replied 'quite frankly I don't know. He has not expressed any opinion that I know of.' The federal minister of finance reported that Macmillan was 'the finest skater on thin ice I have ever seen', while a former Federal civil servant reportedly mused that '[Macmillan] delighted his audiences wherever he had spoken and had held their attention throughout. When one analysed his speeches afterwards however one came to the conclusion that he had really said nothing at all.'[8] By the end of Macmillan's visit even Welensky thought he had left 'a very odd impression on the people here [...] in a lot of his statements there was a lot of good stuff, but he created such an impression of polish that people felt everything was slippery'.[9]

Recasting the Federation's Public Image in Britain

Macmillan trod carefully with his statements to audiences in the
Federation as his speeches also had to satisfy British public opinion.
The Federation's image had been tarnished in Britain by its response to
the Nyasaland emergency.[10] Lord Home, the secretary of state for
Commonwealth relations, also noted this and informed Macmillan
that the British public was becoming 'more and more doubtful as to
whether their government were backing the wrong horse' in central
Africa. Home claimed that the Federation's 'inept public relations' had
led to its becoming viewed in the same light as South Africa.[11] In
response to this problem the Federal government decided to employ
Voice and Vision, a professional public relations company.[12] The need
for the Federal government to appoint professional public relations
consultants in Britain reveals the weakness of its existing connections to
the British establishment. Philip Murphy has demonstrated that the
Europeans in central Africa differed markedly from their east African
compatriots. The Kenyan settlers exploited their 'close links' with the
British elite and preferred to 'exert pressure directly through informal
contacts'. This was possible in the Kenyan context due to the social
composition of the settlers in each colony. Kenya enjoyed a large
proportion of civil servants, farmers and businessmen. Central African
settlers, on the whole, lacked a significant number of upper-middle-class
settlers and therefore could not pursue their interests through the same
channels as the Kenyans.[13]

The appointment of Voice and Vision appeared to offer an excellent
opportunity for the Federal government to bolster its faltering image.[14]
The company was a subsidiary of Colman, Prentis and Varley, a leading
public relations firm that was fresh from securing a surprise victory for
the Conservative Party in the 1959 British general election.[15] David
Cole[16] recognised that under Colman, Prentis and Varley the election
campaign had been 'brilliantly handled'.[17] Moreover, Cole argued that
the fact they handled the Conservative Party account 'means that they
already have contact with every Conservative MP, with every
Conservative Party organisation and all eight fingers on the pulse of
the British electorate'.[18] This sentiment has subsequently been echoed
by scholars such as David Goldsworthy who contends that Voice and
Vision 'gave Welensky not only a medium for public campaigning in

Britain but also an excellent institutionalised link with the parliamentary party'.[19] Furthermore, the Conservative government could 'hardly object', as by hiring a public relations firm 'the settlers were only doing what they themselves had done'.[20]

The campaign proposed by Voice and Vision encompassed a total reorganisation of the Federation's existing arrangements in London. The estimated cost for implementing these changes was £40,000 and it was expected that results would begin to be seen after three months.[21] Overall, the initial aim of the campaign would be to improve background knowledge in Britain of the Federation's achievements and its leading personalities.[22] The idea that knowledge of the progress the territories had made under federation would woo public opinion was not new. This idea had first been suggested to Welensky by Lord Home, as early as 1957. Home later recalled how he had 'urged them to try and sell their case'.[23] His suggestion, however, was not well received and he remarked how 'they weren't impressed, they thought they were doing pretty well and it was self-evident'.[24]

The Federation's success was far from self-evident to Iain Macleod, who had replaced Lennox-Boyd as colonial secretary following the 1959 general election. Almost immediately after his appointment Macleod quarrelled with Welensky, as well as many of his Cabinet colleagues, over his desire to release Hastings Banda from detention. Welensky expressed grave concern that if Banda was released while the Monckton Commission was in Nyasaland, Africans who were in favour of the Federation would be too intimidated to give evidence. Lord Home, who was in the Federation at this time, replied that the Federation could only work if the cooperation of the northern territories was secured, and he believed in the case of Nyasaland this would only happen if Banda could talk to the Monckton Commission as a free man.[25] Macmillan viewed Macleod as 'very clever and very keen and enthusiastic', but believed that he was also quite 'inexperienced', and this had led Macleod to threaten to resign over the issue. Home, Macmillan wrote, was 'a really splendid fellow' who understood the 'political dangers and embarrassment' which would follow such a ministerial resignation.[26] Macmillan finally acceded to Macleod's view as he returned from his African tour.[27]

Despite Welensky's defeat by Macleod over Banda's release he was still in a defiant mood and maintained the belief that Banda's 'efforts on TV and with the newspaper men will begin to bring home to the great

British public the kind of fellow he is'.[28] Although his supporters may have agreed with him, the influential *Times* newspaper had already decided that 'Dr Banda is not an evil man, he honestly works for the good of his people'.[29] This view of Banda was to remain consistent throughout press coverage though Welensky's remark is an indication that he had misjudged political realities and British attitudes towards settler colonialism. Welensky was informed of a further setback by 'a very decent Tory MP', namely that politicians who supported the Federation in Britain were 'generally tainted' because they had financial interests in the Federation.[30] This certainly applied to Patrick Wall who had purchased 'a few acres near Salisbury' during his visit in 1958.[31]

Further criticism was levelled at British MPs who had taken advantage of trips to the Federation organised though Voice and Vision.[32] They hoped the visitors would express favourable opinions of the Federation through television and the print media, put down questions in the House of Commons, participate in debates and finally influence their colleagues and constituents.[33] The MPs were chosen based on both their parliamentary connections and their 'special sphere of influence'.[34] These extra-parliamentary activities included access to publishing, trade unions and 'a fondness for public speaking'.[35] Voice and Vision also chose MPs who were sympathetic to federation, or at least open-minded.

The visits did not go unnoticed in Britain and a Complaint of Privilege was raised in the Commons by Frank Bowles, Labour MP for Nuneaton. Bowles saw the trips as an attempt 'by improper means to influence members in their parliamentary conduct'.[36] He had been made aware of the trips through an article in *Reynolds News* which led with the headline 'Beware the PR men as they invade the shrinking world of hard news!'[37] The article revealed how Voice and Vision 'offered free trips to MPs of all parties to see for themselves the wonders of partnership', after which 'they warmly backed the Federation and deplored any talk of secession'.[38] Bowles concluded by remarking 'I suspect that this is as gross and grave a breach of privilege as I can imagine'.[39]

The following day the matter was raised again and two of Voice and Vision's guests defended their visits. F. J. Bellenger likened it to that of the Monckton Commission, stating that through Voice and Vision he and other MPs had been 'afforded an opportunity, at no expense to themselves except in time, hard work and inconvenience to their own affairs at home, to see for themselves on the spot what is happening in the Federation'.[40] G. H. Rogers felt no particular need to explain his motives, curtly commenting 'if anyone thinks my advocacy is bought by a free trip to Africa, he seriously under-rates the price of my corruption'.[41]

The Complaint of Privilege was not upheld, however jibes about the impartiality of MPs taking advantage of the trips continued to be made. Sir Godfrey Nicholson, Conservative MP for Farnham, retorted to one MP who had benefited from a Voice and Vision trip: 'he spoke of new voices, and I was only expressing the hope that there would also be new vision'.[42] Although there was concern over the rising cost of these visits, they continued and were judged to be a resounding success by both Voice and Vision and the Federal government. However, their impact back in Britain was slight at best. Although MPs and journalists often wrote and spoke favourably about their experience in the Federation – the Labour MP for Rochdale, Jack McCann, was reported to have given approximately 40 talks on his visit to the Federation – their message was only received by a limited audience.[43] Furthermore, regional rather than national press tended to carry their reports.

Preparing for the Monckton Commission

Lord Home visited the Federation during February 1960 to discuss the future of the Federal and Southern Rhodesian governments. When Home left on 26 February he believed that his talks had been 'fruitful and encouraging',[44] while Welensky thought Home had left 'a much wiser man than he arrived' as he was 'pretty shaken about what he discovered here'.[45] Sir Edgar Whitehead, the Southern Rhodesian Prime Minister, did not share Home's optimism and, little over a week later, notified the secretary for Commonwealth relations that the situation in Southern Rhodesia had 'deteriorated considerably' since Home's visit. Whitehead believed political uncertainty in the colony had caused people to reduce their spending, in favour of saving in case they have to leave the country in the near future. The house-building industry had slumped and the vacant property rate in Salisbury was estimated at between 10 and 15 per cent of the total. Unemployment was high and increasing further. Whitehead believed that the cause of this trouble was 'entirely political' because the public were refusing to spend their income, despite record levels of Southern Rhodesian exports, because 'as they are all in the process of trying to get themselves into a completely liquid position'.[46] It was also reported by Taswell that Home's visit had caused one Federal MP to remark that there was truth in Napoleon's comment that the British were 'a race of shopkeepers who would sell their souls for a sixpence'. Following this visit, the Federal MP had come to the conclusion that the British were only concerned with preserving 'sufficient influence in this part of the world to continue selling their products, they couldn't give a damn what colour government was in power'. Tellingly the MP believed the white settlers were 'a pain in the neck to the British government', and consequently 'they would be prepared to write us off at any moment'.[47]

Although Taswell did not name his source, he told Pretoria that the MP had been born in Britain, but had lived in South Africa and Rhodesia for roughly 40 years. Taswell believed 'that he should have expressed himself so strongly against the British Government is just indicative of how strong feelings are here'.[48] He continued by linking this attitude to a generally more sympathetic feeling towards South Africa from Europeans in the Federation. This sympathy apparently arose from the 'friendship and understanding' that was building between the two countries, and was nurtured by South Africa neither interfering in the Federation's affairs nor actively encouraging them to move closer to the Union. Consequently many in the Federation 'believe that if all goes wrong here they can turn to us as a last resort. They are becoming less critical of our policies [and] more friendly towards us'. Taswell conceded that 'in certain quarters there is still much antagonism and anti-Union feeling but the goodwill is mounting'.[49]

In a similar vein Taswell reported during the following month that, despite a growing anti-British feeling in the Southern Rhodesian settler community, 'support for the Union was not very great [...] Rhodesians would rather be independent even if it means leaving the Federation and going it alone'. This was not, in Taswell's opinion, necessarily bad for the Union. There was no noticeably growing animosity towards South Africa, and he ventured that 'solidarity' between the Rhodesians and South Africans was increasing. Taswell believed that 'a strong "join the Union" movement would be an indication of despair, a sign that he saw no future here and that his only refuge was to turn to us'. Consequently, he argued that 'it is in our interests to see the White man maintaining a strong independent foothold here'.[50] This deterioration spurred the formation of organisations advocating a national government pledged to immediate secession. Whitehead captured the mood by stating, 'public opinion in our country, which has always been very loyal, is becoming frankly anti-British'. He linked this more broadly to events in Nyasaland, 'apparent anarchy in Katanga' and the 'irresponsible utterances' of the Labour Party in Britain. Therefore, any move to release Banda from detention 'may prove to be the last straw'. Whitehead prophetically speculated:

> I firmly believe that the action you are now proposing in Nyasaland will have fatal consequences in the Federation. The fact that my Government may be swept from office as a direct consequence of your actions in Nyasaland is of less importance than the fact that for the first time in our political history the real reactionaries are likely to be handed on [sic] a good working majority on a plate. This will obviously entail the break-up of the Federation within a matter of months.[51]

He ended by stating that, if Banda's release was followed by a breakdown in the Southern Rhodesian Constitutional talks, 'I fear that the Federation will very soon cease to exist and the British Government alone would be responsible for its break-up'.[52]

Whitehead's pessimistic view can be traced to two points: disillusionment within his own party over his leadership, and the resurgence of African nationalist protest throughout all three Federal territories. Welensky judged at this time that Whitehead 'walks a very slippery slope with a narrow majority'. Welensky credited this to the fact that European opinion in Southern Rhodesia was moving further to the right of centre, and noted that many UFP members in the territory doubted that they would be able to defeat the Dominion Party (DP) in a straight fight in any imminent election. In Welensky's view, the rightward shift was symptomatic of the growing anti-British feeling in the Federation.[53] Lord Home held similar fears to the federal prime minister. 'The absolute inevitable result, and I cannot stress this too strongly, would be the transfer of the frontier of South Africa to the Zambezi and that frontier would be armed', he wrote to Lord Monckton, 'the result would be certain and when you all go to Southern Rhodesia, I am sure you will be convinced of it'.[54] Sir Edgar Whitehead later attempted to play on Home's fear in discussions with Duncan Sandys to press Southern Rhodesia's case prior to the publication of the Monckton Report.[55] He informed Sandys that South Africa's attractiveness fluctuated in inverse proportion to how safe settlers felt in Southern Rhodesia. Worryingly, this was also said to apply:

> Even for persons who had no sympathies whatsoever with Union politics, there was the economic attraction that a boom would result from the Colony's joining the Union; prices of property would rise and many people would be able to sell up with advantage and retire to England.[56]

Whitehead's problems were added to by the resurgence of African nationalist protest in Southern Rhodesia. The banned SRANC was replaced by the National Democratic Party (NDP) on 29 December 1959. Unlike SRANC, which did not emphasise political advancement above other demands such as land reform, the NDP made 'one man, one vote' its primary political philosophy.[57] In Northern Rhodesia the banned ZANC was reborn as UNIP on 1 August 1959.

UNIP originated from two African nationalist splinter groups, the African National Independence Party and the United National Freedom Party, both of which were formed during the summer of 1959 in the wake of ZANC's banning.[58] After the new party's initial national meeting Mainza Chona was appointed as provisional leader. A conference was scheduled for the end of January 1960, at which time it was hoped Kenneth Kaunda would be released from prison and win election to the role of party leader.[59] UNIP was reported to have absorbed all ANC branches on the Copperbelt, except Mufulira, leaving Nkumbula with a greatly reduced presence. Lawrence Katilingu[60] reportedly still held the confidence of the African Mine Workers Union, but according to one UNIP source he was widely mistrusted by the majority of the African population as he was rumoured to be a government stooge.[61] UNIP's aim was to use 'all legitimate constitutional means based on the absolute principle of non-violence' to achieve independence.[62] UNIP's attitude towards the Monckton Commission was summed up as follows:

The Commission may take all our evidence but it is not allowed to recommend secession though there is abundant evidence supporting secession. So why do we waste our time? Is the attitude of the Africans towards Federation going to be to accept it in principle and help improve it? This is the stand we would not like to take. We stand by what we have always said. That is to say, Africans hate Federation and want it broken down. We are not prepared to compromise on this.[63]

Welensky's dominant personality in central African politics and his unwavering support for the federal experiment often led anti-Federation protests to make personal attacks against the federal prime minister. At one UNIP protest at Fort Jameson one UNIP member carried a placard proclaiming:

Vilinsky you are a Pole from Poland. Your father left Poland in nineteenth century for America and from there for South Africa then on foot to Southern Rhodesia. Your father had no education and the American immigration officer mispelt [sic] Vilinsky for Welensky. Thus Welensky usually known as Mazambani. You Welensky with kindergarten education you can hardly know your village in Poland. You are not a master but we can call you a destitute. Our rightful leader is Kaunda.

Another announced 'Roy Welensky you are no better than our heroes Kaunda or Banda. You are a foreigner from poverty stricken Poland. Away with your satanic and bogus federation now.' A further declared, 'Days of imperialist rule in Africa [are] finished. Roy go back to Poland. No foreign rule here.'[64] By 1962 these attacks had reached an overtly anti-Semitic level. *The Voice of UNIP*, a nationalist newsletter, proclaimed:

Our poor Boer-Jew friend by the name of Rolland [sic] Welensky is terribly warned. He and his British Government now realise the fact that Federation as opposed by the rightful owners of the soil is finished. In fact, we as Africans can now rightly say that it is an accomplished fact that Federation is dead.[65]

Welensky had previously suffered anti-Semitic attacks while working on the Rhodesian railways in the 1920s and would do so again when he ran for election in the Arundel by-election in Southern Rhodesia in 1964.[66] By June 1960 it was clear that Macleod had significantly misjudged the mood of the settlers. In the wake of recent events in the Federation, the Congo and South Africa, he believed that the majority of settlers 'are willing to see pretty rapid constitutional advance in Northern Rhodesia and Nyasaland and that they would be reconciled to see African governments there within ten years'.[67] This was certainly not the view of Welensky or his supporters in the British parliament, led by Lord Salisbury, and explains why Macleod became something of a hate object. Press coverage provided the focus of Welensky's anger during August 1960. He wrote to Lord Salisbury declaring:

> I feel that I am almost alone these days in speaking up for what I believe to be right. The extent to which Hollywood influences public opinion and the way the press, aided by the BBC, on every occasion they can, see nothing else but virtue in every leftist movement, shocks me.[68]

Shortly after this outburst, Voice and Vision released several newspaper advertisements on behalf of the Federal government.[69] They did not appear to have had much effect on the perception of the Federation, as a later report highlighted how 'the press and the BBC are increasingly adopting the rather nauseating attitude that we must save the white Rhodesians from themselves'.[70]

The Monckton Commission in the Federation

All the events of the first half of 1960 took place against the background of the Monckton Commission's visit to the Federation. If the settler governments had believed the 1959 emergencies would ease the Federation's route to dominion status by decapitating African protest prior to the federal review, they were sorely mistaken.[71] Macmillan realised he could not simply rubber-stamp Welensky's call for dominion status at the federal review in 1960, and during March 1959 his Cabinet decided to establish a commission to decide the terms of reference for the forthcoming conference.[72] Over the next four months

London and Salisbury argued over the exact composition of the Commission until agreement was finally reached on 8 July 1959.[73] Welensky was adamant that the Commission should not be able to consider the issue of secession. As a result, Macmillan's hope that the Commission would be a bipartisan undertaking was thwarted as the Labour Party refused to take part in a process which ruled out secession from the very beginning.[74] Monckton's biographer, however, claims that several British members of the Commission left for the Federation determined to consider secession.[75]

Many settlers would have been quite happy to see Nyasaland leave the Federation yet its continued presence was crucial from a British perspective. As Julian Greenfield would later recognise, it was the 'keystone in the federal arch comprising itself and the two Rhodesias'.[76] Welensky concurred with this view, and feared that if Nyasaland was allowed to secede it would set a precedent which an African-led Northern Rhodesia would be sure to follow.[77] Unlike the wrangling over the composition of the Committee, its chairmanship was solved remarkably easily. Lord Monckton of Brenchley proved to be a satisfactory choice for both Britain and the Federal government. The Monckton Commission – dubbed the 'Circus Commission' by Welensky – arrived in the Federation on 15 February and spent three months collecting evidence from each territory.[78] After much debate between Macmillan, who was under pressure from Macleod, on one side, and Welensky, Whitehead and Armitage on the other, it was decided that Dr Hastings Banda should be released from detention on the 1 April so that he could give evidence to the Commission as a free man. Larry Butler has argued that 'this move had enormous implications, effectively being an endorsement of Banda and his aims, and an implicit recognition that in the wake of the Devlin Report, the use of coercion against Nyasaland nationalists was no longer an option.'[79]

Iain Macleod's first visit to the Federation coincided with Banda's release. This gave Welensky the opportunity to meet with the colonial secretary, whom he subsequently described as 'a very able man, but an obstinate one and someone who is perhaps going to have to learn things the hard way. He and I got on quite well.'[80] Following his release, Banda arrived at Government House for talks with Armitage and Macleod, where he impressed the need for fresh constitutional talks for Nyasaland. Macleod, after leaving the Federation, announced that talks would be held in London during the summer.[81] It has been suggested that Macleod's decision to open talks on Nyasaland jeopardised the Federation's survival even before the publication of the Monckton Report.[82] The Nyasaland constitutional conference took place between 20 July and 5 August, at which it was agreed that an African majority would be introduced into the territory's Legislative Council. A Federal Intelligence and Security Bureau report contended that Banda's release immediately 'stimulated much nationalist fervour' against a 'superficially peaceful background'. On Banda's return to Nyasaland in May, an estimated 10,000 supporters greeted him at Blantyre's Chileka Airport and a further 15,000 at MCP headquarters.[83] It was estimated by the Federal authorities that MCP membership stood at 420,000, although 'some of these may not be active members and a considerable number have joined only to avoid victimisation'.[84]

The final report, described by Welensky as 'the most dangerous blow the Federation had so far suffered' – and by Monckton's biographer as containing 'an element of almost desperate optimism' – was passed to Macmillan on 7 September 1960, although it was not published until 11 October.[85] Like the Devlin Report before it, the Monckton Report noted widespread opposition to the Federation amongst Africans, particularly in the two northern territories. It recognised the economic benefits federation had brought to the region and stated it was desirable that these links remain. It also suggested that, like Nyasaland, Northern Rhodesia should concede political power to an African majority. This, however, would likely encourage the territory to request the right to secede from the Federation. It also called for a wider franchise in Southern Rhodesia to secure greater African representation. Finally, despite the assurances earlier secured by Welensky, the Report argued that the Federation could not survive if its people felt that they were there against their will, and consequently it suggested that 'under certain conditions there should be an opportunity to withdraw from the association'.[86]

The report was eventually published during the Conservative Party Conference on 11 October 1960. Voice and Vision actively tried to foster opposition to its more negative findings by distributing a selective summary of its contents two hours before the report was officially released.[87] Welensky received word of the Conservatives' reaction through Patrick Wall who summarised that, although most people considered that the Federation was an economic success 'it has been a political failure and that there is now little hope in preserving it in its present form'.[88] Welensky furiously wrote to Macleod stating that he found the Report 'a disaster' and, furthermore, its publication would make the continuation of the Federation 'virtually impossible'.[89] He believed that Monckton had gone beyond his terms of reference by considering the Federation's future.[90] Welensky's reaction had been identified by Macmillan prior to the Report's publication when he informed an official who believed that there was 'no doubt that Sir Roy Welensky has been badly treated in this matter'. Macmillan also advised that the report 'should be carefully examined immediately so that there will be a reply to any complaints by Sir Roy about lack of faith, or any public statements of that kind'.[91]

The Monckton Commission's members did not unanimously accept all of the report's recommendations. Only eight members of the Commission accepted the Report in full without making any notes of reservation, and two African members submitted a Minority Report.[92] Welensky expressed his dismay at the Commission's findings in a letter to Patrick Wall:

> The Commission, from my own point of view, could not have done a worse thing because the recommendation is, in my humble opinion, a lingering sentence of death, and frankly I'm not going to be party to it. Break up the Federation now if that's the view of HM Government, but don't let it bleed to death.

Welensky concluded by speculating that 'it will only be a matter of time before Southern Rhodesia will link up with the Union of South Africa, and as I've already said, the Union Jack will not fly anywhere on this continent'.[93] Welensky's fear of a lingering death for the Federation would, in some respects, prove accurate. The federal review conference scheduled in London for December 1960 was suspended after two weeks as it was judged necessary to await the outcome of the individual territorial reviews before considering the Federation as a whole.

Welensky was determined that the break-up of the Federation should not be discussed at the review conference and believed that the Federal and British governments should issue a joint statement which would show 'a united front and a determination not to allow the Federation to be sold down the river' in response to the Monckton Report. Sandys managed to persuade Welensky that separate statements should be released although Welensky warned Macmillan that if secession was discussed at the review conference 'all the assurances that I have had are worthless and we will undoubtedly face an exceedingly grave situation'.[94]

In Britain, pressure continued to build on the Federal government during November following the resignation of Federal Chief Justice, Sir Robert Tredgold. Wall informed Welensky that the resignation of the well-respected, liberal-leaning Tredgold had helped swing public opinion in Britain against the Federal prime minister. Furthermore, Wall gloomily wrote that opinion in the House of Commons was that 'the Federation had had it'. The Federation's friends on the right of the party were still behind Welensky, but Wall was worried about recent speeches made by MPs in the centre of the Party, such as Roland Robinson and Nigel Fisher, who were now beginning to have their doubts.[95] Wall's comment that MPs from the centre of the Conservative Party were openly questioning the Federation was a worrying development. This adds weight to John Darwin's claim that the Monckton Report was a reflection of new thinking in London towards central Africa.[96]

Welensky received further rumours on opinion in Parliament from a report on two meetings passed to Voice and Vision from Brigadier Clarke, Conservative MP for Portsmouth West. The first meeting was the Conservative Central African Committee, chaired by Patrick Wall and attended by around 50 MPs. The meeting was solidly behind maintaining the Federation although questions were raised over whether force should be used if necessary. Three members of the Monckton Commission were also in attendance and they were criticised for not considering evidence from all sides. Lionel Heald, a member of the Commission stated that all sides had been consulted and suggested that Welensky 'well knew, or should have known, that secession was being considered'. Overall, the meeting concluded with the members, including those representatives of the Monckton Commission, agreeing that the Federation must continue, although, as Clarke noted, 'no-one produced a satisfactory solution as to how it could be made to continue without the use of force'.[97]

The second meeting was attended by 'a lot of elderly ladies and gentlemen [. . .] all of whom had either recently been in the Federation or had been there at some time or another'. Also in attendance were three members of the Bow Group. Similarly, the room was in favour of federation 'except the youths from the Bow group who seem to have decided that Federation must stop'.[98] Patrick Wall also noted the Bow Group members' dissent in his report on the meeting and expressed to the secretaries of state that the overall conclusion of the meeting was 'that Her Majesty's Government should give a firm lead and should make it clear that their intention at the Constitutional Conference was to preserve a modified form of Federation'.[99]

Welensky left for London at the end of November and vowed he would fight for the continuation of the Federation at the review conference.[100] The conference was quickly adjourned as it was decided that agreement had to be reached on new constitutions for Northern and Southern Rhodesia before the Federal structure could be considered. Following the failure of the Southern Rhodesian constitutional talks, which opened in London on 16 December, it appeared that the Federal talks would not re-open in the near future. During his visit Welensky addressed the Conservative Commonwealth Committee and his performance received a rather mixed review from an MP who was present: 'one could not help liking him as a person [. . . although] his arguments did not seem to hang together and were not very convincing', he wrote, and concluded that 'the majority gave him their support but not as warmly and enthusiastically as I would have expected'.[101]

Lord Salisbury formed a Watching Committee to 'keep an eye on developments in Africa' early in 1961.[102] The Committee was modelled on the Watching Committee his father had founded in 1940 of which Macmillan himself had been a member. Salisbury assured Macmillan that 'there is no intention of opposing or even criticising government policy as such'.[103] This however seems unlikely considering the nature of the MPs, who were mainly drawn from the old Suez Group and the fact that Welensky had previously asked Salisbury to launch an attack on Macmillan.[104] The Watching Committee remained in place for the rest of the Federation's life. Rather than appearing formidable to Macmillan, however, its reliance on the usual suspects in its composition ultimately rendered it 'a little comical'.[105]

Territorial Reviews

Sir Edgar Whitehead failed to secure the removal of Britain's reserve powers from the Southern Rhodesian Constitution during his visit to London in April 1960. On his return to Southern Rhodesia early in May, he sought to arrange for a British delegation to come to Salisbury to achieve his aims. Home used the Monckton Report as a delaying tactic and promised that talks would resume when both governments at least had a draft copy of the Report.[106] The security situation in Southern Rhodesia, however, worsened and Whitehead authorised the arrests of three leading NDP activists. Had Joshua Nkomo not been out of the country, he would have shared the same fate. Protest soon spread. A strike in Bulawayo on 25 July involved three-quarters of the city's African workers and led to arson and widespread damage to property.[107] By the time order was restored on 27 July, 13 Africans had been shot dead and the damage incurred was estimated at £100,000.[108] Whitehead and Nkomo's poor relationship nearly hamstrung the constitutional conference before it began. 'Whitehead regarded Nkomo as an agitator and Nkomo regarded Whitehead as a tyrant', noted one commentator.[109]

As a new constitution was agreed for Nyasaland during August 1960, the South African high commissioner was reporting 'numerous signs' of a hardening of opinion amongst the European population in Salisbury. Taswell concluded that 'nervousness' had increased amongst the white population, and 'the determination of the white man to stay and defend his interest has been noticeable'.[110] He believed, however, that it was 'too early' to predict a change of policy from the Federal and Southern Rhodesian governments. 'Liberal and Government thought here is against the Union's policy,' he wrote, 'I cannot help feeling that the press will deliberately resist any movement in the direction of agreeing with us'. Furthermore, he believed the firming of white attitudes would lead to a campaign by the Federal government to show South Africa 'in as bad light as possible' to influence public opinion against the Union. Taswell alleged that the Federal government considered 'their success rests in proving to the rest of the world that their "island of sanity" follows a policy basically different, more enlightened and definitely better than ours'. For all these efforts, though, he believed 'that people in the Federation are going to do some serious rethinking'.[111]

African protests continued to grow throughout Southern Rhodesia during 1960. Whitehead attempted to counter this by adopting a 'carrot and stick' approach. Whitehead's concessions culminated in his attempt to reform the Land Apportionment Act in the Legislative Assembly on the 16 August 1960. This brought him into direct opposition with the majority of white settlers who saw the Act as their Magna Carta.[112] This proposal was vociferously criticised by the Dominion Party which vowed to repeal any alteration to the Land Apportionment Act when they came to power.[113]

Despite Whitehead's attempts at reform, protest and rioting worsened in Southern Rhodesia. Welensky believed that the problem was that 'Whitehead has a poor Ministry. I think he is an able man but he ought to have a few strong men around him who disagree with him, and it is not happening'.[114] In an attempt to stifle protest and restore order Whitehead banned all meetings in African townships for a month and on the 18 October introduced the Emergency Powers Bill which, amongst other measures, permitted arbitrary arrest and detention in the public interest. He also introduced the Vagrancy Bill, which would enable the arrest of anyone who could not prove they were living by 'honest means'.[115] The most controversial change was to the Law and Order (Maintenance) Bill one week later, which even Welensky opposed. Amongst other measures, the Bill proposed that there should be a minimum (and no maximum) sentence of five years for setting fire to buildings or cars during a disturbance; throwing (or threatening to throw) objects at a motor vehicle would be punishable by between three and 20 years imprisonment. Intimidation of a person because of their political beliefs would attract a sentence of between three and ten years and a sentence of from two to seven years for taking part in a political boycott.[116] Whitehead's new policies also attracted comment from UNIP. Sipalo wrote to Nkomo that 'the recent activities of Sir Edgar and his henchmen have shocked even his own voters. I am sure he is tip-toeing to his downfall propelled by his own blindness.'[117]

The South African High Commissioner also passed comment on Whitehead's recent policies. Taswell believed Whitehead was:

> playing a political game of give and take, of mixing liberalism with toughness. On the one hand he is going out of his way to abolish racial discrimination against the non-white. On the other

he is seeking powers to control any chaos and confusion which this liberalism may bring in its wake. But his general trend is more to the left than the right. It will be interesting to see whether the next elections in Southern Rhodesia show that he has underestimated the hardening strength of the forces of the right in this country.[118]

Whitehead's problems grew after Sir Robert Tredgold resigned from his position as chief justice so that he could protest publicly against the Emergency Powers Bill. The South African high commissioner thought that Tredgold's potential entry into politics came during a mounting 'lack of confidence in Southern Rhodesia and uncertainty regarding the future'. He ascribed this uncertainty to the Southern Rhodesian Constitution being 'in the melting pot', given the Monckton Report, constitutional review, the increase in the number of parliamentary seats bringing in greater African representation, greater implementation of partnership and Africans taking positions in the civil service. For all the publicity accorded to the 'entry of a new and impressive figure' to the Southern Rhodesian political arena, Taswell doubted Tredgold's chances, describing him as 'scrupulously fair and honest [...] intellectually he is outstanding and his knowledge of Southern Rhodesian and its peoples is exceptional [...] Sir Robert is looked upon as a liberal'. Taswell believed these qualities to be a disability in Southern Rhodesian politics as 'the white population here generally are becoming increasingly dissatisfied and worried [...] a strong lead from the right would seem to have more appeal at the moment'.[119]

Duncan Sandys, who had replaced the Earl of Home as secretary of state for Commonwealth relations, agreed that Alport, minister of state in the Commonwealth relations office, should return from Ceylon via Salisbury on the 22–23 November and discuss with Whitehead the removal of the reserved powers. Sandys, however, later informed Whitehead:

I have been considering further the question of Alport's visit in the light of the latest developments in Southern Rhodesia. It seems to me that the political situation which existed when I saw you in Salisbury in September has now greatly changed as a result of your new legislation, the resignation of Tredgold and the state of

African and European opinion. We have accordingly come reluctantly to the conclusion that it would be inadvisable for Alport to go to Salisbury at this juncture.[120]

Whitehead regretted Sandys' decision as he was still convinced that the Southern Rhodesia talks must be held before the federal review. He dismissed Tredgold's resignation as a matter of 'purely internal concern' and did not find the reasons for delaying discussions 'entirely satisfactory'.[121]

Whitehead notified Welensky of Sandys' concerns over the security situation, and Welensky wrote separately to Sandys remarking, 'It appears to me that you are not being kept abreast of the situation here – it is quite clear to me that as far as Whitehead and his Government are concerned the state of African and European opinion has improved.' He further called into question Sandys' comment on Tredgold's resignation, believing it was obvious that Sandys 'had not been given the history of the affair'. Welensky agreed with Whitehead that the Southern Rhodesia constitutional review should take place before the federal review, commenting 'I must therefore press you strongly to adhere to the original promises in this matter'.[122]

The Southern Rhodesian constitutional conference finally opened in London on 16 December 1960. However, it swiftly reached an impasse after Whitehead banned the NDP delegates from attending, following the Africans' decision to walk out of the earlier federal review conference. Whitehead and Nkomo eventually agreed to hold another conference on the 30 January 1961 in Salisbury.[123] In the event the conference appeared surprisingly successful, as all parties except the DP accepted the conference's final conclusions.[124] The Dominion Party's statement to the Southern Rhodesia constitutional conference made clear their belief that after 37 years of self-government there were 'no grounds whatsoever' for withholding independence provided reasonable constitutional amendments could be devised. Therefore:

Unless Southern Rhodesia is to gain her full independence from the United Kingdom, the Party holds the view that the Conference is no more than an academic discussion and has resulted in giving African Nationalist leaders unnecessary publicity and an importance magnified to a point of unreality, and that the unjustified provision of seats for Africans sets a precedent for the future.[125]

Consequently they found it impossible to recommend to the people of Southern Rhodesia that independence would be gained through discussions of this nature and therefore they could not support the report of the conference.[126]

In an attempt to allay European fears, Whitehead broadcast to his electorate in an attempt to reassure them that they were not being 'sold down the river' and that no constitution for Southern Rhodesia could come into effect until it had been endorsed through a referendum. He stated that in order for the British to relinquish their reserved powers it was necessary to establish safeguards appropriate to a multiracial state. Under the existing constitution, however, only Africans were provided with constitutional safeguards, whereas the new constitutional safeguards would be relevant for all races. Although the new constitution would not give complete independence, Whitehead believed it would 'bring us to a position where we are more than 90 per cent independent'.[127]

It became clear however that Nkomo was having second thoughts about the constitutional proposals. Since the end of the conference he had come under increased pressure from the more militant members of his party, and UNIP also denounced him for 'letting down the Africans in Southern Rhodesia'.[128] When this news reached Whitehead's cabinet, they believed it was crucial to obtain confirmation that the British government would still adhere to the agreement before the Southern Rhodesian United Federal Party Congress later that week. The Southern Rhodesian cabinet decided to inform the British government that, if the rumours proved true, they were no longer prepared to discuss land and any other problems left over from the constitutional conference with the NDP or any other dissenting parties.[129] Whitehead expressed these thoughts in a message to Sandys, commenting that he was 'not surprised' at Nkomo's decision as 'this is quite normal form for our leaders of extremist parties'.[130] In reply, Sandys stated he was glad that Whitehead was going to go through with the agreement that was reached at the conference and confirmed that 'You may naturally count on us to do the same and you may so inform your Congress on Wednesday.' However, Sandys asked that Whitehead did not announce that Southern Rhodesia was not prepared to discuss the land problems with the NDP at the present time.[131] Nkomo formally withdrew his support from the constitutional proposals at a press conference on 17 February 1961.[132]

Southern Rhodesian Constitutional Conference and the Northern Rhodesian Constitutional Review

John Day has argued that the convening of the Southern Rhodesian constitutional conference in 1961 was the 'summit of the African nationalists' achievement, from which they subsequently declined'.[133] Day believes that the NDP's decision to boycott the conference proposals – which were later embodied in the 1961 Constitution and 'virtually assured' Africans 15 seats in a Legislature of 65 – led to there being no more African influence under the new political system than the old. Furthermore, he argues that an important consequence of the NDP delegates misjudging the mood of their party and repudiating their franchise agreements was that both the British and the Southern Rhodesian governments thereafter viewed the NDP as an ineffective political organisation.[134]

Whitehead managed to achieve acceptance for the constitutional proposals at the UFP Congress although he was forced to warn Sandys that 'I and my Party are by no means out of the wood.' Over the last couple of years Southern Rhodesian Europeans had become 'extremely critical' and Whitehead was worried that 'the present temper of the electorate is such that they are simply not going to support anything which is not clearly set out in black and white and fully endorsed by the Governments concerned'. Consequently he believed it would be crucial to publish a detailed white paper in advance of the referendum which would publicly guarantee 'without alteration or amendment' that the proposals would be included in the Constitution. Without this step, he could not envision the proposals receiving the support of the electorate.[135] Whitehead's next test was to take the proposals to the Southern Rhodesian electorate, which he did on the 26 July 1961. Meanwhile, Welensky feared Whitehead's growing unpopularity would hamper his chances:

> There is an element among the electorate who say they will vote against the referendum not because they disagree with the

proposals, but because it will help get rid of Whitehead. I have pointed out time and time again that it is like sinking the ship because you don't like the way the cook has cooked dinner, but unfortunately people do not think like that, whether or not one likes it.[136]

Welensky's fears, however, proved unfounded when Whitehead won approval for the constitution by 41,949 votes to 21,846.[137] The NDP, who were boycotting the referendum, held an African vote on the proposals which found 467,189 votes against with only 584 votes in favour of the proposals.[138]

The negotiations that took place over the Northern Rhodesian Constitution have been seen as the 'definitive trial of strength' of the future of the Federation.[139] Holland, agreeing with this, suggested that after the Monckton Report the Federal government were resigned to losing Nyasaland and, subsequently, Northern Rhodesia became 'the focus of Central African Affairs'.[140] Macmillan also appeared to recognise the importance of Northern Rhodesia. He feared Welensky would refuse to attend as the Federal prime minister had declined to make any amendments to the proposed opening speech by Macleod, instead calling for a postponement altogether. Macmillan supposed that, if the UFP withdrew, they would publish Britain's proposals for the conference and concentrate on the 'rallying of press and public opinion' in both Rhodesia and Britain against any outcome.[141]

If Macmillan conceded to Welensky's demands and postponed the conference, he feared there would be 'consequent danger of serious riots or clashes between the two sides'.[142] The key was therefore to make sure everyone actually attended the start of the Conference as 'once proposals are made and discussions are joined adjournments from time to time are tolerable'.[143] This philosophy was typical of Macmillan's approach to negotiations between Britain, Welensky and the African nationalist groups. While all the parties were involved in the dialogue over the Federation's future, it was easy to fend off any criticism from Welensky or his supporters in parliament. If the negotiations were to break down, however, and Britain was shown to be at fault, Macmillan's support from more moderate MPs would be threatened.

Julian Greenfield, the federal minister of law, and John Roberts, the leader of the UFP in Northern Rhodesia, went to London to discuss

Macleod's proposals in February. Patrick Wall informed Welensky that their visit had gone 'extraordinary well'. Furthermore, he added that he thought 'the corner had been turned' as it 'was increasingly clear that the Conservative Party would react strongly against any question of an African majority at this time'.[144] Wall changed his opinion that very afternoon, however, as he lunched with Julian Greenfield and was 'shocked to hear that not only had little progress been made but that relations were deteriorating'. Wall stated that it was extremely difficult 'even for informed Back-bench opinion, to gauge exactly what is happening'. Wall's conversation with Greenfield had convinced him that matters between the Federal and British governments were 'extremely serious'. Wall believed that there had been a 'swing of opinion' on the backbenches against the British government granting 'too many concessions to Africans in Northern Rhodesia', however, matters 'were not sufficiently clear' to enable the backbenchers to decide 'whether or not the limit of concessions has been reached'.[145]

On the same day Wall, who was acting chairman of the Commonwealth Affairs Committee, briefed Macmillan that all [backbenchers] with very few exceptions, 'fully support the policy which has become known to us as "wind of change" but a growing number are becoming anxious at the speed in which power is being transferred to relatively immature African political parties'. Wall continued by stating that the Committee would oppose any move towards giving Northern Rhodesian Africans a majority in the new constitutional talks, although 'some form of parity might be acceptable but only if it was acceptable to a reasonable selection of white Rhodesian opinion'. Wall concluded by reminding Macmillan that 'it is the solid, middle of the road, Conservative Back-benchers who are now expressing these views'.[146]

In the Federation Kenneth Kaunda continued to press the British government for a new constitutional review for Northern Rhodesia following his release from gaol in January 1960. Macleod, under pressure from Welensky and the territory's new Governor, Sir Evelyn Hone, initially resisted Kaunda by declaring that no review could take place until after the federal constitutional talks. Following a meeting with Kaunda in March 1960, Macleod conceded to Macmillan that: 'I left Northern Rhodesia with a very uneasy feeling indeed and I am by no means sure that we can hold the position of refusing to have constitutional talks until after the Federal Review'.[147] Reports from Northern Rhodesia that Kaunda ran the risk of being replaced as leader of UNIP by a more intransigent individual if he could not secure any concessions from the British increased Macleod's unease. Kaunda's wish to reopen discussions was also aided by the publication of the Monckton Report which recommended an immediate conference and the introduction of an African majority in the Legislative Council.[148]

Macleod approached Welensky to discuss his ideas for constitutional reform in late 1960 and met with a hostile response when he suggested an African majority in Northern Rhodesia. These acrimonious discussions continued into early 1961, and although Macleod remained committed to a constitution which would obtain an African majority, he was prepared to lower the number of Africans he wanted to enfranchise. Welensky continued to resist Macleod's proposals, and in February Macmillan corresponded directly with Welensky in order to break the deadlock. Richard Wood speculates that Macmillan was forced to intervene because Welensky and Macleod's relationship had deteriorated markedly over this issue.[149] Macmillan's suggestion envisaged a legislative assembly made up of 45 members.[150] Welensky later described his belief that these proposals had a 'customary thick coating of Macmillan treacle and cotton-wool', yet underneath lay a 'nakedly dangerous Macleod scheme'.[151] Macleod's actions over Northern Rhodesia led Welensky to describe him as 'completely and utterly dishonest politically'. Welensky continued:

> He [Macleod] knows full well the scheme he is producing is to introduce political apartheid in the Northern Rhodesia legislature and to go back on everything Alan Lennox-Boyd achieved. I can only assume that Harold Macmillan knows and condones what he is doing, but if Alec Home and Duncan Sandys have any guts in them, then what is happening must be pretty unpalatable.[152]

The Northern Rhodesian constitutional discussions in early 1961 marked a particularly low point in Anglo-Federal relations. Welensky, in view of the worsening situation across the border in Katanga and the possible need to secure Northern Rhodesia by force, approached South Africa for military equipment and personnel, while Britain drew up a contingency plan – KINGFISHER – to deal with any serious outbreak of unrest in Northern Rhodesia over the constitutional negotiations.[153]

Macmillan, who understood the importance of keeping Welensky at the negotiating table, told Macleod to keep his white paper proposals vague. Macleod would not, however, support a constitution which did not give Africans at least parity in the legislature and threatened to resign. According to Wood, Welensky saw parity as an indication that 'a "Kenya" was about to be perpetrated and, he warned he would fight it with everything at his disposal'.[154] Macmillan managed to talk Macleod out of resigning, and negotiations continued until June 1961 when their proposals were published. Welensky, still angry over the whole process, confided to Harry Oppenheimer, the chairman of Anglo American:

> I never thought I would live to see the day when Her Majesty's Government and a member of the Commonwealth would have to resort to a type of haggling which I should imagine was seen in few places in the world other than an Egyptian bazaar.[155]

The Northern Rhodesian constitution was debated in the House of Commons on 22 February 1961. Iain Macleod opened for the government and expressed his belief that there was little difference between the course he was pursuing and the view of the Labour Party over this issue. Macleod stressed the importance of advancing African political rights in the two northern territories of the Federation and warned:

> At all times when one has to study Colonial Territory problems there are those – these are the faint hearts – who look for the course in which there is no risk. There is no such course. There is no safety for us in any particular course. Every course that one can put forward is fraught with danger, including the one that I am recommending to the House now.[156]

Callaghan questioned how far Macleod was prepared to go in satisfying African political aspirations and stated 'if the Colonial Secretary really wants blessings and hosannas to fall upon him, he ought to at least get the encouragement of those who are to benefit from the blessings which he is intending to confer'. Callaghan did agree with Macleod that he 'had not been conscious of any gulf' in colonial policy between the Labour Party and Macleod 'for the last eighteen months', and speculated there was a far wider division between Macleod and Robin Turton.[157]

Robin Turton, Conservative MP for Thirsk and Malton, had tabled an Early Day Motion demanding that Macleod adhere to the principles in a white paper drafted by the previous colonial secretary, Alan Lennox-Boyd, in 1958. According to Salisbury, Turton's Motion had come as a 'considerable shock' to the Government, and also indicated that 'the rank and file of the party in the country is becoming more and more worried'.[158] Within a few days, 101 Conservative MPs had signed the Motion, which equated to over one-third of the party's backbench membership.[159] This was the first time a pro-federal motion had attracted significant support in the centre of the party.[160] Moreover, Gallup polling demonstrates that an important breakthrough was made in attracting support from the British people at large. Between 1960 and 1964, respondents were asked which of 12 responses, including 'colonial affairs', was the most important problem facing the country. During this period, 'colonial affairs' was consistently chosen by 1–6 per cent of the sample. It jumped, however, to 18 per cent in January, February and April 1961 and 19 per cent in March.[161] Ideally, this poll would have provided a more accurate appraisal of the relative importance of colonial affairs by asking people to rank the issues in order of importance. Even the results above indicate, however, that the British public's indifference towards its colonies was challenged during a time of increased pressure from Conservative MPs. Ultimately, Macleod defended his proposals in Parliament and in two meetings of the Colonial Affairs Committee. Gradually Turton's moderate supporters withdrew their signatures and by the end of February it was estimated that only 40 members would still support Turton if it came to a test of strength.[162] Wall judged that 'the centre of the Conservative Party was 'excessively worried' and would 'close its ranks as it always does in a crisis'.[163] Consequently Macleod was able to ride out the storm, though the damage to his personal reputation over this incident would return to haunt him.

The final paper on Northern Rhodesia's constitution, however, proved remarkably friendly to the Federal government and included two concessions which made it extremely difficult for Africans to gain a majority. The first was the creation of a separate Asian seat, while the second stated that successful candidates on the joint roll would have to secure 20 per cent of the votes from both other rolls.[164] Even Welensky conceded that although it was not the constitution he would have chosen – 'the thing is far too damned complicated' – it would 'at least keep government in responsible hands, and that is what matters'.[165]

The white paper was greeted by UNIP with dismay and widespread rioting. A UNIP publication indicative of this response made clear that:

> there can neither be peace nor security in N. Rhodesia without freedom and political stability. For as long as any group in England denies the chief demand of the majority inhabitants in this country, so long will the future remain gloomy; if it uses authority to retain the UFP in power.[166]

Welensky was subsequently informed by Lord Alport that the British government were considering announcing that they would reopen talks on the Northern Rhodesian constitution, if violence in the territory immediately ceased.[167] Macleod was replaced by Reginald Maudling as colonial secretary in October.[168] Lord Alport later stated that the 'hatred and contempt' with which many of the central African settlers held Iain Macleod was 'merely a measure of their own lack of political balance'.[169] Any joy they received from Macleod's exit from central African politics, however, was soon dissipated as his replacement pursued a policy even more pro-African than his predecessor.

Maudling confirmed that discussions on the Northern Rhodesian constitution would be reopened despite Welensky's protests that the British government had promised that the July proposals would be upheld.[170] He had specifically demanded this confirmation 'so that we would not face the accusation during the [Southern Rhodesian referendum] campaign that something terrible was going to emerge and was not being held back purely because it was so bad that the people of Southern Rhodesia would not have supported the Referendum had they known what was coming'.[171] According to Welensky the British had conceded his point, then proceeded to make an apparent volte-face with the announcement that further talks would take place with Kaunda. Welensky despaired: 'twice in eighteen months I have had publicly to admit that I have been misled by the British government. I said openly in our House the other day that I have no confidence whatsoever in my dealings with HMG. I didn't believe that the time would ever come when I would say that kind of thing, but unfortunately it's all too true'.[172]

Welensky's pessimistic mood was further fuelled by the result of the Nyasaland election during August 1961, in which the MCP secured a majority in the legislative council. He attempted to put a brave face on the result, arguing that Nyasaland had been 'lost' as soon as Macleod had become colonial secretary. He trumpeted:

I never wanted Nyasaland in the Federation. It was forced on us by Her Majesty's Government. I wanted the amalgamation of the two Rhodesias but we gave way when we were told it was this or nothing. Just at the moment I am watching the game that HMG are playing with Nyasaland. They would like me to make a move; I don't intend to. The next move is theirs.[173]

By the end of 1961 Welensky's hope of leading the Federation to dominion status was shattered. In Southern Rhodesia, the settlers had become increasingly dissatisfied with Whitehead's approach to African advancement. Neither the Northern Rhodesian nor federal constitutional talks were further forward than they had been a year previously and in Nyasaland there was an African majority in the legislative council led by a man who was determined secede from the Federation.

The Mining Companies and the 'Wind of Change'

The Anglo American Corporation had publicly joined with Rhodesia Selection Trust (RST) in withdrawing financial support from the UFP in 1959; however their actions in private were very different. They continued to provide both funds and personnel to Welensky in secret. This divergence of policy seems somewhat surprising considering that Harry Oppenheimer had written to Ronald Prain, chairman of RST, only the previous year commenting that it was 'highly desirable' for the copper companies to work together, as it would 'contribute greatly to our mutual advantage and that of the territories in which we operate'.[174] Furthermore, Prain revealed in October 1959 that Oppenheimer 'agreed with all the views I expressed about race relations'.[175]

A key factor that may account for the difference in the companies' policy is the difference in their principle areas of work. RST's operation was primarily concentrated on the Copperbelt, whereas Anglo's Northern Rhodesia business was merely an offshoot of its principal business interests in South Africa. Oppenheimer had long attracted the wrath of the South African National Party, being a wealthy South African of non-Afrikaner heritage. During his period in the South African parliament Oppenheimer had been referred to as their 'Number One bogeyman on the Oppositions' benches'.[176] He was further vilified by many Afrikaners over his family's wealth and Jewish background. His father, Ernest, had previously experienced similar attacks. Anti-Semitism was never far beneath the surface of white South African society in this period and was brought to the fore in relation to the Oppenheimer family. 'Hoggenheimer the Jew' was a character from a satirical pamphlet distributed by striking miners in the 1920s. It was meant to represent the archetypal South African capitalist and although it was a composite character of various 'Randlords', it is unlikely that its nominal proximity to 'Oppenheimer' is mere coincidence.[177] Therefore, it is likely that Anglo's actions on the Copperbelt were in part driven by domestic considerations in South Africa. Ronald Prain certainly believed that this argument was valid, when he informed Harold Hochschild that 'it just cannot be argued that their [Anglo American's] decisions are not ultimately made in South Africa.'[178]

A further consideration influencing Anglo's decision was Welensky's close personal friendships with members of the Anglo board, particularly Keith Acutt. Acutt moved to Salisbury in 1953 from Johannesburg and held the position of resident director of Anglo's operations in the Federation. He began working for the company in 1928 and swiftly climbed the corporate ladder.[179] This was in part due to Acutt securing the patronage of Ernest Oppenheimer who, reported *Optima*, the company's in-house magazine, 'took him under his wing'.[180] Acutt appears to have taken every opportunity to help Welensky in the final years of the Federation. For example, Welensky wrote to Acutt in February 1960 regarding his son Michael. He thanked Acutt for the employment he had secured for Michael in Southern Rhodesia; however, despite Welensky's protests his son was considering giving in his notice as he did not believe he could support his wife and two children on the salary. 'I don't want you to do anything about it' wrote Welensky, 'I just wanted you to be kept in the picture'.[181] There is no record of whether Acutt provided Welensky's son with a more suitable position in 1960, however in correspondence during 1962 Acutt indicated that another Anglo employee 'was going to fix Michael up with a job'.[182] Additionally, in May 1960, Acutt donated a car to the UFP to assist in the party's upcoming campaigns.[183] Welensky thanked Acutt and took pains to stress that 'it has been an extremely well-kept secret that you made this contribution'.[184]

In a third instance, Welensky tentatively approached Anglo, through Acutt, for a personal loan. Welensky had been given a boat on Lake Kariba by sympathetic supporters. He wished to exchange it, however, for a slightly larger vessel with two engines instead of one. In typical forthright fashion, Welensky wrote '[t]he real purpose of mentioning this to you is that I will need to find some money and, if I can't get my bank manager to provide the necessary overdraft, I might ask you for some money from investments'.[185] Anglo also made their aeroplane in the Federation available for Welensky's use.[186] Further evidence of Welensky's close relationship with Acutt lies in Welensky's invitation for Acutt to join himself, his wife Elizabeth, Federal High Commissioner Sir Albert Robinson and his wife Mary for a few days holiday in Paris.[187] Robinson was a close friend of both the Welensky and Oppenheimer families. He was formally chairman of Central African Airways and following the demise of the Federation he became chairman of Johannesburg Consolidated Company Limited, a subsidiary company of Anglo American.[188]

Welensky could also rely on the support of the British South Africa Company following RST's withdrawal of financial support. He wrote to Ellis Robins implying that in a recent meeting Prain had implied RST's abandonment of funds was prompted by ethical questions from their shareholders in the United States.[189] Robins replied expressing sympathy, and reassured Welensky in no uncertain terms that the Chartered Company had approved Robins' suggested contribution of £5,000 per year to UFP funds, for an initial period of three years.[190] This attitude is unsurprising considering the close links between the Chartered Company and Anglo American,[191] the 'dubious validity' of the Chartered Company's claim to mineral rights in large areas of Northern Rhodesia,[192] and the fact that they had the most to lose from the failure of the federal experiment.[193] The continued support for the UFP from Anglo American had been correctly predicted by Winston Field, the Dominion Party Federal MP for Mtoko, in a conversation with Taswell, who reported to his superiors in Pretoria how Field was 'certain that the companies would continue supporting the UFP but would do so in a more secretive manner'.[194]

The Monckton Commission gave Prain another opportunity to discuss the future of the Federation with the British government, much to Welensky's chagrin. Prain viewed Macmillan's decision to appoint Walter Monckton as head of the Advisory Commission in advance of the federal review conference as 'a stroke of genius'.[195] Prain and Monckton had been friends for a number of years, so much so that Prain recalled that Monckton was 'one of my favourite people'.[196] In his memoirs, Prain records that he met with Monckton 'practically every week' from September 1959 until he departed for Rhodesia in February 1960.[197] During these meetings Prain offered Monckton assistance with contacting Africans in the Federation. Monckton later thanked Prain for his efforts and, although he felt 'bound to say they [Prain's Africans] could not be described as key witnesses', he was keen for Prain to continue to encourage African participation.[198]

Prain, while eager to exploit his contact with Monckton, did not wish to serve on the Commission himself. He wrote to Harold Hochschild, drawing attention to the amount of his time it would take, and worrying 'it might prejudice one in the eyes of Africans, as I am sure that its composition will not command African confidence'.[199] Meanwhile, the Federal government attached Athol Evans as federal liaison officer to the Monckton Commission. Welensky was later to recollect that Evans was 'one of our ablest senior officials'.[200] Following the Commission's completion, he became chairman of the Official Review Conference Committee, and it was in this role that he contacted Prain in November 1960. Evans wanted to elicit Prain's views on the findings of the Monckton Report, and on three issues in particular: the secession recommendation, the composition of the Federal Assembly, and the relocation of the major functions[201] of the Federal government.[202] Prain was naturally willing to help and replied:

[y]ou may ask why I support the Monckton type of solution and my reasons are quite simple, namely, that I am a strong supporter of the Federation and I am most anxious that it should continue in some form or other rather than break up. I regard its continuance on the present form as highly problematical and I believe this to be a realistic view [...] I believe the Monckton

type of recommendations provide the most realistic bridge between African and European opinion.[203]

Prain then addressed Evans' specific questions. He found that the merits of the secession question had 'been obscured by the political heat engendered, understandably, as to the Commission's terms of reference'.[204] Prain believed that if the report was read dispassionately it would be found to be a 'well-reasoned argument'. Furthermore, he mused, 'I would rather have a Federation with a secession clause than a break-up of the Federation because of [a] refusal to grant such a cause'.[205] He was less supportive of the recommendations for the composition of the Federal Assembly and the relocation of the Federal government's major functions. Prain recognised that his views may have been contrary to those of the Federal government, concluding that '[a]ny difference in our views as to the Monckton Report probably is due [...] to our differing assessments of what is necessary for a Federation based on consent and not on force'.[206]

Against the backdrop of Prain's recent statements regarding the Federation, Welensky had good reason to fear the content of Prain's statement to the Monckton Commission. Sir Albert Robinson was one of the Federal representatives on the Commission and he, perhaps unexpectedly given the recent press, reported that 'Ronnie Prain [...] put on a very good show and was on the whole moderate and helpful [and] made a very good impression'.[207] Welensky also appeared to have not placed a great deal of stock in the recent press reports as he replied to Robinson:

> I was particularly interested in your account of Ronnie Prain's evidence. I was waiting to hear what he had to say, because, as you know, at this end there are grave doubts as to whether he really does support Federation, though I think he made it clear to me that he does.[208]

This statement suggests that Welensky could still not decide whether to believe his advisors who warned him of RST's activities or to keep faith in his previous friendship with Prain. It seems that Prain had no such worries as he wrote to Iain Macleod, the colonial secretary, two days after Welensky penned his response to Robinson. Prain notified Macleod that in his opinion the current African nationalist leaders were unlikely to maintain their leaderships if they advocated a policy of moderation. Prain opined that the majority of Europeans in the Copperbelt accepted the 'virtual inevitability' of an African majority in government, however, they failed to understand 'the corollary of this acceptance, namely that they must prepare themselves to give up something'.[209] Having spent two weeks in Southern Rhodesia, Prain was continuing his tour in Northern Rhodesia, spending five days in Lusaka and the Copperbelt. Prain's initial reaction was that the situation in Northern Rhodesia 'appears to have calmed down considerably,' however he added the caveat that all the factors[210] were present to recreate 'tension at sudden notice'.[211] Furthermore, he noted that the omens for this taking place were not good, commenting:

> the problem is that the moment violence ceases and moderation on the part of the Africans take its place, the European population sits back, relaxes, and does not pay further attention to the urgent necessity of making concessions in return for this policy of moderation. Thus you have a vicious circle. If events are to develop here in a moderate and orderly evolution, concessions by the European are, in my opinion, essential; without them I cannot see an alternative to a return to disorder.[212]

Prain's connectivity with all levels of the British government establishment was unique among colonial situations. White contends that in Malaya 'British businessmen played little part in the political process [...] they did not figure in the complex set of international, metropolitan and local variables which shaped decolonization'.[213] RST cultivated contacts with both the British government and African nationalist leaders.

The previous November, Harold Hochschild, chairman of the American Metal Company which was RST's major shareholder, drew Prain's attention to the investment plans of their rivals in Africa. He remarked that the United States Steel Corporation and Bethlehem Steel Company were considering a $500,000,000 investment in the former French Congo. 'European and American investors will prefer to take the risk of doing business with new African governments in countries where no race conflict exists', penned Hochschild, 'to dealing with a country in which a 4 per cent white minority clings to mastery over an increasingly resentful 96 per cent African majority'.[214] Hochschild's pragmatic approach to conducting business in Africa demonstrates that there was a subtle difference between the roles pursued by mining companies. Walter Rodney provides a counterpoint: 'the big mining companies [... were] manned by individuals capable of consciously planning the exploitation of resources right into the next century, and aiming at the racist domination of the black people of Africa until the end of time'.[215]

There is little doubt Rodney was right about the mining companies' long-term view of exploitation. Capitalism in Africa, however, was at its most efficient when operating in a politically secure environment. RST was not driven by 'the racist domination of black people in Africa'. Their primary concern was profit, and consequently they were quite willing to work with newly emergent African governments if it was considered the best way to protect their concerns. Hochschild still believed there was time for a system of racial partnership to work in central Africa. He believed that African protests in the northern territories would wane if Welensky swiftly addressed the grievances of Africans in Southern Rhodesia. Furthermore, Hochschild warned Prain, it would be in the Southern Rhodesian settlers' best interests to compromise in Northern Rhodesia and Nyasaland as '[i]f really serious and continuous disaffection spreads through Nyasaland and Northern Rhodesia it isn't going to stop short on the north bank of the Zambesi'.[216]

As Larry Butler highlights, by April 1960 Sir Ronald Prain's contact with African nationalist leaders and disillusionment with the UFP was an open secret.[217] The *African Mail* published an article with the headline 'Top Copper Men turn to Kaunda' in which they revealed that Prain had met with Kaunda several times. The article reported that Harold Hochschild, 'an admirer of Mr Julius Nyerere', was also chairman of the African American Institute, a leading United States organisation with liberal views on Africa.[218] In London, the *Daily Herald* reported that Ronald Prain attributed the problems in the Federation to 'unwillingness by Europeans to relinquish obsolete tradition', as well as 'political immaturity' amongst many Africans.[219] Prain's comments caused one Federal official to warn 'if one has any regard for Prain at all, he ought to be seriously warned at the quite incredible irritation some of his recent activities and statements are arousing round here'.[220]

Three days later the Federal minister of works observed that 'Prain's habit of speaking in a derogatory manner about the Federation to the outside world is rather infuriating'.[221] Prain's comments received praise in more liberal quarters. The American quaker George Loft, hoped 'that Sir Ronald can keep up the momentum and initiative, and that it might encourage other business leaders to do likewise'.[222] Loft was employed by the American Friends Service Committee (AFSC), was used by Macleod as an intermediary for discussions with Dr Hastings Banda while the leader of the MCP was in detention, and regularly attended African nationalists' meetings outside the Federation as an observer.[223] Furthermore, Loft's frequent correspondence with Harold Hochschild provided another route by which information from Africa could reach Hochschild, independent from Prain. Prain had a positive view, however, of Loft, and 'spoke in the highest terms' to Harold Hochschild about Loft's assistance in 'establishing and maintaining contact with African opinion'.[224] Loft informed Harold Hochschild that the AFSC were 'keeping their fingers crossed' on the appointment of Macleod as colonial secretary, but in their opinion two 'discouraging developments' had occurred. First, the Federal government's proposals for African advancement on the railways were only vague. Secondly, and more importantly for Loft, Welensky gave a speech to a Salisbury directors' group in November 1959. According to Loft, Welensky claimed that 'the whites in the Federation have done more to advance the African than any outside influences', and continued by 'damning the US and the UK for criticizing and meddling. The future of the Federation, Welensky said, will be worked out in Salisbury, and not in Westminster'.[225]

Loft also exchanged correspondence with Taylor Ostrander regarding the ongoing situation in Africa. Ostrander worked as Harold Hochschild's political advisor, and appears to have taken a special interest in events in the Federation under Hochschild's patronage. Loft relied on Hochschild's backing, as shown by a letter from Loft to Ostrander during August 1961. 'This is a personally added note' began Loft, 'I do hope it will give Harold and Sir Ronald the information they need to reach a decision – hopefully favourable – about continuing RST/AMAX support of this work.'[226] Loft then appraised the situation in both Kenya and Northern Rhodesia. He believed that Macleod's policy in Kenya was far more important for the future of Europeans in the Federation than the ongoing negotiations over the Northern Rhodesia constitution. Consequently, it is clear that Prain was not the only conduit through which information flowed to RST's American ownership. Hochschild's view was shaped by both Loft's and Prain's reports, and was further refined by his own personal experience. Although Butler draws attention to Sir Ronald Prain's independence of action, specifically with his success in resisting American pressure to transfer RST's domicile from London to Lusaka during the late 1940s,[227] this is in fact the only instance in Prain's voluminous correspondence where he explicitly opposed his American backers on a major issue. It would be misleading to overstate the autonomy enjoyed by Prain.

Hochschild's experience stemmed from his chairmanship of the African American Institute (AAI), which provided him with the opportunity to meet aspirant African leaders. One such occasion was provided by the reception, lecture programme and dinner, arranged by the AAI for Hastings Banda and Kenneth Kaunda, in Washington, DC during April 1960. During dinner, Hochschild was seated between Banda and Kaunda, and subsequently had an opportunity to promote the RST cause in the Federation. According to Hochschild, Banda was initially hostile, attacking RST over the fact that a £50,000 portion of RST's £1,000,000 loan to the Northern Rhodesian government had been spent on policing. Hochschild made clear to Banda that his company had no idea that the money would be used for that purpose and assured him that the remaining balance had helped Africans. Banda also criticised the remaining colour bar on the Copperbelt. Hochschild again defended RST, drawing attention to the fact that the company had been instrumental in breaching the colour bar in 1955. Banda recognised this, but was still adamant that there were too many discriminatory regulations left. While Hochschild agreed, he did however draw Banda's attention to the copper companies' grant to the Northern Rhodesian government for African education and referred Banda to Ronald Prain's company statement of the previous year.[228] Following this less-than-auspicious opening, Banda's belligerent manner became a little friendlier. Banda requested to meet with Prain on his return to the Federation, and stipulated that it would have to be in Blantyre, as he was still considered a prohibited immigrant in the Rhodesias. He asked for details regarding RST's assistance in the Northern

Rhodesian coffee development scheme, and Hochschild reported that Banda recommended that:

> in future when RST gives or lends money for African development it should insist that the project be administered by a commission rather than by the Government and that the commission's membership include Africans not considered government stooges. 'Otherwise', he said, 'you will never get credit for helping the Africans'.[229]

RST would later withdraw their support from the coffee development scheme, after African coffee growers in the Northern Province rejected their offer of help under pressure from the MCP.[230] Banda then blamed the copper companies in Northern Rhodesia for helping to create the Federation, and continuing to support it by assisting the Federal government's public relations campaign in Britain. Hochschild denied any knowledge of RST's involvement in this scheme, commenting that he 'had seen some of the material put out [. . .] and that it seemed [. . .] money wasted'.[231] Banda then brought the conversation to a close warning Hochschild: 'Welensky is trying to make you European property owners feel that you are safe only with a white government. He's trying to frighten you about us, to convince you that an African government will confiscate your properties. Don't you believe him; it isn't true'.[232] At the end of the dinner Banda thanked Hochschild and noted he was glad to have met him as he placed great value in personal contacts. '[Banda] had gained a better understanding of our views and actions', recorded Hochschild, 'but I don't think he will ever publicly give us any credit for them'.[233]

Hochschild's conversation with Kaunda was concerned with more general political and social questions than RST's actions in the Federation. His general opinion was that 'in private conversation both, particularly Kaunda, show much more moderation. Banda is the more genial and easy to talk to, Kaunda rather reserved and perhaps more impressive'.[234] He continued by stating that in their respective lectures, they were both 'not without aptitude for demagoguery', although he noted dryly 'neither was the late F. D. R. [Franklin Delano Roosevelt]'.[235] Hochschild noted that there was potential for rivalry between Banda and Kaunda, as when Banda made clear he intended to lead the fight for the freedom of Africans in Southern Rhodesia and the Union of South Africa 'Kaunda did not join in the applause'.[236] This account indicates that RST's sympathetic attitude to African nationalism in the Federation was not just driven by the personal views of Prain. Harold Hochschild used the African American Institute to make contacts with African nationalist leaders, to whom he argued RST's case as an open-minded business organisation in central Africa with which they could do business.

Prain's possession of Hochschild's report suggests that his grasp of the political situation in the Federation was in part influenced by nationalist leaders' meetings with his superiors in the United States. Consequently, the British government also benefited indirectly from these meetings through Prain's regular reports on the Federation, as detailed by Larry Butler. These interactions between RST and African nationalists contrast markedly with those involving the Federal government. Welensky would have no doubt been apoplectic at Hochschild's labelling of Kaunda as a 'moderate'. He later fumed to the South African author Sarah Millin that he was 'finding it increasingly difficult to keep quiet when I see our friend K. K. [Kenneth Kaunda] described as a moderate. The man is a blatant and un-mitigated liar'.[237]

The actions of RST's American backers in the United States had caused the Federal government further discomfort the previous December. The Office of the Minister for Rhodesia and Nyasaland Affairs, at the British Embassy in Washington, DC, received a complaint about the treatment of Enoch Dumbutshena, an African journalist who was refused permission to stop over in Ghana and Nigeria on his return flight from London to Salisbury. Dumbutshena had intended to cover the Nigerian elections during December and the letter stated that 'if the Federal concept of political unreliability extends to a man like Dumbutshena, then I am more depressed than ever before about the prospects of forging any practical bond to African opinion'.[238] The letter caused particular concern as it was written on the official paper of AMAX by Taylor Ostrander. In the eyes of the official dealing with the case, American Metal Climax 'on its own and in conjunction with Sir Ronald Prain, appears to me to be assuming authority in regard to our affairs'.[239]

Ostrander featured heavily in a Federal 'secret report' that was compiled during July 1960. The report stated that David Cole had written to Ronald Prain with what was assumed to be an appraisal of the political situation in the Federation. Prain passed the letter on to RST in New York where Cole's views were 'obviously unacceptable' to Ostrander and consequently he forwarded it to Hochschild.[240] It was then alleged that, after making comments, Hochschild passed the document to the UNIP representative in Los Angeles, Arthur Wina, who arranged for the document to be smuggled through to UNIP headquarters in Lusaka. The report drew four conclusions. The first was that RST had decided that partnership and federation could not coexist. Secondly, it stated that, since Africans would dominate the Federation, RST had chosen to align itself with the African nationalists. The third conclusion was that RST would not change its mind if violence were employed because the European settlers were to blame. Finally, it stated that RST saw European opposition to their new policy as 'inescapable'.[241] Furthermore, it was argued, Kaunda would be less likely to compromise with the Federal government in the future if he realised that violent protest would not forfeit RST's support.

The African American Institute and the AFSC were not the only liberal pressure groups in the United States which were linked to Harold Hochschild. The American Committee on Africa (ACOA) was formed in the early 1950s as a reaction to racial discrimination in South Africa although it soon expanded its mandate to include the Federation, amongst other countries. The ACOA had financed the visits of both Banda and Kaunda to the United States after they were released from prison.[242] In January 1961, Harold Hochschild found it necessary to write to Prain to make clear that there was no truth in the rumours that there were any financial dealings between ACOA and AMAX. Hochschild conceded that he was briefly in contact with ACOA when he was asked to contribute an article for their magazine *Africa Today* during 1957, However, after consultation with his brother Walter, it was decided that David Cole should write the article and it was subsequently published in July of that year.[243]

Banda and Kaunda's access to influential international figures through Hochschild in the United States did not go unnoticed in Salisbury. During May 1961 the Federal government recognised that AMAX rather than the State Department had arranged for Kenneth Kaunda's recent meeting with President Kennedy.[244] Ostrander was apparently behind this move and also orchestrated a lunch at which Kaunda met with representatives of the World Bank.[245] Stewart Parker reported that Kaunda was initially told that 'the World Bank did not chanell [sic] money through organisations such as his'; Parker reflected that Lejeune of the World Bank 'changed his tone to some extent after the lunch and gave Kaunda more encouragement than he should have done'.[246]

Hochschild's ability to facilitate these opportunities reflected the close relationship which AMAX enjoyed with the State Department in Washington. In September 1961, Ostrander met with an official in the African Affairs Department to discuss the prospects of constitutional development in Northern Rhodesia. Ostrander expressed the opinion that the British government was constrained in its dealings with Kaunda by 'clever pressure' exerted by Welensky. As a result, at least one-fifth of the parliamentary Conservative Party was in favour of Welensky's government. Furthermore, Ostrander then angrily claimed that Welensky had an Achilles heel: 'the Federal Prime Minister started his political career as a poor man but that during the last few years has been very careful to "feather his own nest"'.[247] Ostrander hypothesised that following this revelation Welensky's support would melt away. He was willing to make the speech himself, but at present did not have enough reliable evidence. This contrasts sharply with Donal Lowry's assessment of Welensky as '[p]ersonally incorruptible'.[248]

It should be made clear, however, that the State Department archives contain no evidence of corruption on Welensky's part. It seems likely that Ostrander was referring to the assistance provided by Anglo American to Welensky and his family mentioned above. Further evidence of the connection between AMAX and the State Department can be found in the authorship of State Department briefing papers which were prepared by AMAX employees, including Taylor Ostrander.[249] Ronald Prain's attitude towards events in the Federation undoubtedly influenced these papers, as did Harold Hochschild's and George Loft's. These reports enabled AMAX to help shape American foreign policy towards central Africa, and thus may have influenced British policy through official channels.

The close personal and ideological links between Welensky and Anglo American enabled the UFP to tap the company's resources for its 'build-a-nation' campaign during 1961. The Nyasaland election in August 1961 secured an overwhelming victory for the MCP much to Welensky's dismay.[250] This loss made it very clear that the UFP needed to foster greater African support if the party was not to suffer the same fate during forthcoming elections in the Rhodesias. Welensky informed Keith Acutt that 'we had better do something and do it without delay'.[251] Welensky estimated that, for a chance at victory, the UFP required 50,000 Africans to be registered on the lower roll in Southern Rhodesia and 100,000 in Northern Rhodesia. He then reported that Federal sources had discovered that the three major African nationalist parties in the Federation – UNIP, the MCP and the National Democratic Party – had spent close to £200,000 on campaigning over the last 12 months. In later correspondence with Ellis Robins, Welensky accused RST of providing this money.[252]

Welensky was clearly attempting to elicit a similar amount of money from both Anglo American and the BSAC towards what would become known as the 'build-a-nation' campaign, and to that end he wrote 'you may think I'm shameless about this but quite frankly the stakes are so big that I do not believe that Anglo and BSA can afford not to help me in what is really our greatest hour of need'.[253] Welensky considered this a last desperate gamble and finished by stating 'we just cannot face the next year or two believing that we can compete with the African nationalist parties in this field if we are going to be so limited in regard to finances. I do ask your help on this occasion'.[254] Having received this plea Acutt quickly consulted with Ellis Robins and replied to Welensky, having found Robins 'naturally as willing to help as we are'.[255]

Both Anglo American and the BSAC were prepared to help provided their support was kept a secret, although Acutt acknowledged 'it is, of course, not easy to find very large sums without disclosing information to too many people in the organisation'. He was also keen that there should be no indication in the press of Anglo's support as 'we might have a few stupid shareholders who think they have a right to object'.[256] Acutt and Robins agreed that their companies should contribute £50,000 each to the UFP's campaign.[257] Robins confirmed his agreement to this and Welensky replied suggesting that the money be paid into the chairman's account following 'the previous arrangement'.[258] The 'previous arrangement' to which Welensky referred, related to the deposits made by the Chartered Company towards the financing of the UFP's 1958 Federal election campaign. Robins agreed and on 19 September he confirmed that an initial payment of £25,000 would be paid 'anonymously to the chairman's fund'.[259]

In addition to funds, Robins suggested that 'we should purge ourselves of the leading subversive elements in our midst, beginning with Walter Adams, [Terrence] Ranger, [John] Reed and Theodore Bull'.[260] Prain and RST also warranted a mention in this company as Robins continued:

> I would go far as to warn a certain prominent knight [Prain] and his associates that, unless they cease supporting the subversive elements in Northern Rhodesia they will be shown up, they ought to be shown up anyway for the hypocrites they are.[261]

This counsel illustrates the contempt that Prain and the RST warranted from the Chartered Company and the Federal government, and also how closely RST policy had come to resemble the African nationalist position over the previous two years. Welensky and Robins had both, two years earlier, been disappointed when RST and Anglo American had decided to discontinue payments to UFP funds. However, they had both understood as pressure to withdraw funding grew on both companies from outside of the Federation. Now, while Anglo still supported Welensky, albeit secretly, with payments towards the 'build-a-nation' fund, RST was perceived to be actively working to bring down the Federation.

The 'build-a-nation' campaign received financial assistance not only from Anglo American but also from its chairman, a director of the company named Dennis Etheridge. Having spoken with Oppenheimer, Philip Brownrigg of Anglo American informed Welensky that Etheridge could be seconded to the Federal government, or allowed to resign from his position so he could concentrate on the campaign. Welensky was assured by Brownrigg that Anglo 'would make the necessary arrangements to keep him going and he would be able to rejoin us after his term of duty'.[262] Brownrigg helpfully remarked 'it would be a very profitable way of using his talents and would not bring him in to [sic] the limelight, which I am sure is important'.[263] Brownrigg thus reminded Welensky of the mutual benefits of keeping Anglo American's support of the UFP out of public knowledge. Welensky replied that he thought Etheridge need not resign from Anglo American as he hoped 'he can do it in his spare time and no one will know about it'.[264]

Welensky was soon concerned by the cost of running the campaign, which during December 1961 alone incurred expenses of £6,000.[265] Consequently, it was decided that further funds would have to be raised. To this end a committee was organised in London comprised of businessmen sympathetic to the Federation, chaired by Alan Lennox-Boyd, the president of Arthur Guinness and Sons, and former colonial secretary. Keith Acutt of Anglo American and Harry Grenfell of the Chartered Company were also present on the committee. Lennox-Boyd's involvement was understandable in light of his support of Welensky's campaign for federation in Britain prior to 1953.[266] One attendee of the inaugural committee meeting summarised that it had been 'well worthwhile and the sheckles [sic] will pour in slowly but surely'.[267] During the meeting it was noted that literature produced on 'build-a-nation' must avoid any mention of the UFP,[268] and in a consequent meeting Lennox-Boyd argued that the campaign should be completely non-political.[269] Sydney Sawyer, a federal politician, mentioned that though £50,000–£60,000 had been raised in the Federation to finance 'build-a-nation', with costs running at £8,000 per month these funds would be exhausted by May. It is unclear whether or not Sawyer included the money paid by Anglo American and the Chartered Company in his estimate, as no mention was made of their financial support.

The businessmen present agreed to attempt to raise £50,000 between them towards the campaign on the condition that 'all contributions would be treated as confidential and there would be no publicity at all'.[270] Etheridge, however, was not sure that the money could be raised in time. He reasoned that 'many of the companies have to wait for Board meetings, and while everything is being done to press them, it is simply a matter of being patient'.[271] Etheridge was worried because the large insurance company Pearl Assurance, from which he had expected a contribution of several thousand pounds, had sent a cheque for only £250.[272] The assistance given to Welensky by Anglo American and the BSAC was mirrored by directors of another company whose predominant area of business was the Federation. The Northern Rhodesia based Susman Brothers & Wulfsohn did not make direct donations towards political parties, although its directors were free to make personal contributions. Hugh Macmillan reveals that the directors were broadly sympathetic to the idea of 'partnership' in the Federation and, furthermore, that one of the company's partners, Maurice Rabb, became actively involved with the UFP-backed Barotse National Party in the 1962 Northern Rhodesian general election.[273]

The United States and the Federation

John F. Kennedy's election in January 1961 brought a Democratic Party Administration to the White House.[274] Kennedy's election was met with some trepidation in Whitehall as he was known to be critical of colonial rule and sought to identify himself with anti-colonial struggles.[275] Kennedy appointed G. Mennen 'Soapy' Williams[276] as assistant secretary of state for Africa to demonstrate his commitment to African issues. Soon after his appointment Williams told a reporter in Nairobi that what America wanted for Africa was what Africans wanted for themselves. The headline the reporter attached to this statement was 'Soapy Says Africa for the Africans'.[277] This angered many settlers in the Federation, despite Williams' later clarification that he meant both black and white Africans, so much so that he was later punched on the jaw at Lusaka airport by an enraged European settler.[278]

Williams pledged to visit every African country during his first year in office and, following his first African trip, he set out his views on how the United States should approach African problems in March 1961.[279] He believed the 'most important' aspect in Africa was the progress being made by the governments there and the expectations of their people. He believed that the United States could assist the governments, noting:

the first step towards this is continuing and expanding our friendship and support. Unless we are in a position not only to preach but to practice racial equality we shall be seriously handicapped. What we do in regard to our race problem in the United States is as important as how we deal with Africans in their own country.[280]

Furthermore, Williams advocated that the United States should 'return to our earlier anti-colonial position'. Therefore, the United States should oppose Soviet colonialism as well as that of 'our own European cousins if they fail to move slowly forward on such problems as Algeria and Portuguese areas, the Federation of Rhodesia and Nyasaland, and

South Africa'. Williams believed that 'our current image is frequently blurred by the feeling that in recent years the once revolutionary United States has aged into a pro-colonial posture'. He understood that although a more anti-colonial attitude would 'create stresses and strains and often unfavourable comment in conservative European circles, I believe that the future of our position in Africa and throughout the free world requires our taking a firm stand in support of the reasonable aspirations of all Africans who seek freedom'.[281]

In advance of the Anglo American talks on Africa in early 1961, the State Department anticipated that the British position would be driven by three themes. Firstly, it would stick closely to the statement made in December 1960, which clearly announced that Britain had a duty to all races in central Africa, but that this duty could only be discharged if both Africans and Europeans were prepared to work together toward making partnership a success. Secondly, the British were satisfied that the federal system had promoted economic and social progress throughout the Federation and they did not wish to pursue any policy which would slow down further economic advance. Finally, the British would emphasise that if the Federation was to win the confidence of the whole population, Africans would need to play a greater role in the running of the country.[282]

The American position was consistent with that of the previous administration, contending that federation could not succeed without the support of the majority of its African population. It stated that the United States should continue to urge Britain to 'reassert its role as imperial arbiter until power can be peaceably transferred to responsible Africans'. They planned to assist Britain in this task through an expanded training programme for Africans. This failed to evoke a markedly favourable response during the November 1960 discussions, although Britain had welcomed limited American technical co-operation programmes in the fields of education and agriculture.[283]

The Federal government sought to clarify the intent of the new administration and wrote to the State Department requesting a detailed explanation of their policy. They asked whether United States support for the Federal government hinged on its reconstitution in a manner acceptable to African nationalist leaders. According to one State Department official, the tenor of the note was 'emotional, conveying reproach, fear and some belligerence at the same time'. State Department officials concluded that they did not owe the Federal government any explanation of their policy and, were they to give one, any such explanation 'would probably only infuriate and frighten them further, while decreasing our ability to exercise a moderating role in the racial accommodation which we prefer to see in the Federation'. Consequently, they wrote a short reply which stressed the United States' positive belief in the principles of self-determination, democracy and human rights for all peoples.[284]

Federal worries over the direction of American policy were in part driven by the ease with which African nationalists from the Federation could be heard in Washington. It was State Department policy that if the president met with one leader, the same courtesy would have to be extended to other visiting recognised national leaders. Consequently, following Kenneth Kaunda's visit during April 1961, the State Department recommended that Kennedy meet with Hastings Banda and Joshua Nkomo if the opportunity arose.[285] In comparison to this ease, the State Department questioned the 'usefulness' of a proposed visit by Welensky to Washington during June 1961. The visit was proposed at a time when colonial items could potentially have been debated before the United Nations (UN), and could be 'embarrassing to say the least'. Although the State Department was not 'uninviting' Welensky, the American consulate in Salisbury was requested to make it clear to the Federal government that he should be in the United States for another 'valid reason' and would merely be taking the opportunity to make calls in Washington while visiting.[286]

Despite this lukewarm and ambiguous message, a telegram sent later that day reflected that an unofficial visit would give the State Department an 'opportunity to express our views in a frank and more extensive exchange'. Furthermore, the Americans believed that talks would more likely succeed 'if conducted in Washington rather than the emotional climate of Salisbury'.[287] Williams had earlier recognised the opposition in certain circles to Welensky meeting with the president, however it was his feeling that the United States 'cannot refuse to listen to his side of the story, particularly having received African leaders from the Federation and in view of the fact he is Prime Minister'.[288]

Williams' qualified support for Welensky's visit may have been given as the State Department's relations with the Federal government had been 'under some strain because of the high-level attention which the forces of African nationalism have received recently'. This was not helped by the official decision in the Department to officially celebrate African Freedom Day. Williams believed it was important to stress that the United States wished 'to see a peaceful transition to African majority rule in the Federation which would permit the white minority to continue their valuable economic, administrative and political contributions'.[289] This message was conveyed by Dean Rusk, the Secretary of State, to Mr Jeffries, Federal representative in Washington, when they met in May 1961, with additional emphasis that that the United States 'does not believe any race or group is expendable'.[290]

Williams visited central Africa during August 1961 to develop a better appreciation of the problems in the area. The American consulate in Salisbury judged the visit a success and reported it had significantly improved attitudes towards the United States in the Federation. Both European and African press coverage had been favourable and the Europeans were pleased that Williams had established a relationship with Welensky. 'My own reactions to Williams were that I rather liked him personally' later mused Welensky, 'He said he hadn't made up his mind on the Federation, but he did admit publicly that we were going in the right direction though there might be some doubt about our going fast enough, whatever that may mean.'[291] The reception given to Williams in Nyasaland by Banda had created an extremely favourable impression among Africans throughout the Federation. The 'vehement' declarations against the Federation by African nationalists left no doubt about the difficulties facing Britain in keeping the Federation together. Welensky's failure to secure a sense of value in the northern territories was 'painfully obvious'. In Southern Rhodesia, Whitehead's 'logical problem of racial progress sharply contrasted with NDP [National Democratic Party] demands while Dominion Party ideas of waiting for Africans to develop their "capacity" sounded totally unrealistic'.[292]

The telegram did express some fears for Nyasaland if it was to secede from the Federation. While 'Banda's autocratic position and effective organisation [was] striking', the economic future of Nyasaland outside the Federation was a 'sobering thought'. Northern Rhodesia presented a 'sad picture'. Kaunda was trying to effect constitutional change while, according the American consulate, the unrest developed 'probably beyond his control'. The other UNIP leaders were described as 'unimpressive' while the Liberal Party lacked 'influence, organisation and personnel. They believed that unless Britain could produce a situation in which Kaunda and the Liberal Party would participate in elections, Northern Rhodesia's future 'appears uncertain for some time to come'.[293]

The State Department did not obtain its information only from leading protagonists in the Federation. American businesses operating in the Federation also supplied information. Taylor Ostrander, of AMAX, reported that 'the most serious deliberate African violence in the history of any of the three Territories' erupted on the 4 August 1961. This, he reflected, demonstrated that some UNIP members were making a concerted break with Kaunda's policy of non-violence. He found it 'hard to conceive that Kenneth Kaunda and his closest lieutenants, including Simon Kapwepwe, participated in the planning of this action'. The violence had exploded out of the negotiations regarding Northern Rhodesia's new constitution.[294] Ostrander did not confine his report to events in Northern Rhodesia. He analysed the UFP's victory in the Southern Rhodesian referendum, speculating that it represented some progress in the territory and '[it] was certainly noteworthy that the recalcitrant white right wing opposition of the Dominion Party was shown to be so much smaller than at the time of the last general election three years ago'. Ostrander believed that, despite African opposition, the new constitution gave a practical grant of independence to Southern Rhodesia, although Britain retained the right to legislate by its own initiative if the country was in 'palpable chaos'. Consequently 'the complex and unwieldy Rhodesian Federal structure has thus become even more complex by the grant of virtual independence to one of its three subordinate territories'.[295]

In his final evaluation, Ostrander reported that 'the net effect [. . .] after a year and a half of preparation for and negotiation of political change in Rhodesia, is that African bitterness is heightened'. He contrasted Britain's handling of the situation in Kenya with that of the Federation concluding that the copper and tobacco of the Federation were more important to Britain's economy than anything Kenya had to offer. Therefore, the British had a 'disinclination to antagonize Welensky to the point where he would either take Southern Rhodesia out of the Federation or [. . .] bolt away from British control with both Northern Rhodesia and Southern Rhodesia in his pocket'. Consequently, 'so long as Welensky controls Northern Rhodesia and benefits from the tax revenues that flow from copper, he is powerful – so powerful that he can work his will on London'.[296] This would change in the long term, according to Ostrander, as other developments in Africa and the need to combat communism would 'ultimately weaken Welensky's position and increase the need to accommodate the Africans of Central Africa'. Britain's short-term policy, in Ostrander's view, was ultimately driven by other pressures: Macmillan's desire for a closer association with Europe, pressures in West Berlin, and the country's 'chronic economic illness'. These factors 'forced Macmillan to shy away from a show-down with Welensky now – or with his own right wing.[297]

A State Department official met with the colonial attaché at the British Embassy to discuss the violence highlighted in Ostrander's report. The colonial attaché replied to a question about the measures Britain was taking to deal with the disturbances by stating 'that the British Government was attempting to treat the current unrest as a police matter and wanted to avoid giving exaggerated impressions of the seriousness of the problem'. If, despite this, the violence continued, the governor could call for Federal or British troops to restore order. The colonial attaché was worried that 'At this juncture in the constitutional talks the introduction of Federal troops could well drive moderate Africans to join radical Africans.' He further added that 'some of the white Federal troops might be eager to impose a harsh military regime on the Africans in Northern Rhodesia'. If British troops were introduced, there was the problem that 'Sir Roy Welensky could be expected to react rather violently. He would look upon the introduction of British troops as a move to undermine his authority.'[298]

The Federation in the United Nations

The United Nations (UN) provided a further minefield of international opinion for the Federal government to tip-toe through. In the General Assembly there was a divisive split in the African membership between the Casablanca and Brazzaville blocs. The former contained most of the more radical African states, whilst the latter was made up of some ex-French colonial possessions. This split was potentially damaging, as the influence that the African states could wield necessarily depended on a degree of unity.[299] Despite this tension, if the members agreed on an issue, as was a common occurrence in the case of colonial questions, they possessed an effective veto in the General Assembly as a two-thirds vote was required to carry substantive issues.[300]

One resolution supported by all factions of the Afro-Asian movement was 1514 (XV), the Declaration on the Granting of Independence to Colonial Countries and Peoples. Resolution 1514 was passed in December 1960, and exhibited a 'definitive expression of anti-colonialism' from the Assembly, as it provided formal recognition that colonialism could no longer be regarded as legitimate.[301] The Soviet Union had initially proposed a declaration demanding immediate freedom for all non-self-governing countries. There was, however, a general fear within the Afro-Asian group that Soviet sponsorship of an anti-colonial motion would result in a Cold War vote, in which the Latin American countries would side with the west and endanger the resolution. Consequently, a watered-down Afro-Asian version was eventually submitted and adopted by a unanimous vote of 89 to 0, with nine countries – including the United Kingdom, the United States, France, and Belgium – abstaining.[302] Resolution 1514 was couched in the language of the Bandung conference, and called for 'the end of colonialism in all its manifestations'.[303] This success for the Afro-Asian bloc in the Assembly was reinforced during 1961, when the Special Committee on the Situation with Regard to the Implementation of the Declaration on the Granting of Independence to Colonial Countries and Peoples was established under Resolution 1654 (XVI). The committee was, perhaps unsurprisingly, more commonly known as the UN Committee of Seventeen, or after December 1962, the UN Committee of Twenty-Four.[304]

The composition of the Special Committee was weighted strongly in favour of the anti-colonial bloc.[305] For example, in 1963 12 of its members were Afro-Asian, four, including the Soviet Union, were drawn from the communist bloc, and three were Latin American. Only five members represented the west – the United Kingdom, the United States, Italy, Denmark and Australia. Following these developments, Afro-Asian anti-colonial policy generally adopted a three-pronged attack. Colonialism was condemned as it denied fundamental human rights, was contrary to the UN Charter, and impeded the promotion of world peace. Yet, for all that:

> no quantity of UN resolutions could force Portugal to acknowledge that its territories were non-self-governing and

must therefore be reported on, compel South Africa to change its ways in relation to apartheid or South West Africa, or to make the United Kingdom admit a UN Mission of investigation to Aden or order Southern Rhodesia to democratize its constitution. The result in part was a stalemate.[306]

This was not always obvious to the British government of the day. Reginald Maudling, Secretary of State for the Colonies, was 'very worried' at the situation developing at the United Nations. He found it 'not improbable' that Britain could be 'faced with Mr Kaunda arguing about the Northern Rhodesia constitution; Kenyatta arguing about the independence of Kenya, or Mintoff about the Malta constitution' at the United Nations.[307] Furthermore, he was 'convinced that if we do not make a stand at this moment on a clear matter of principle the slippery slope down which we may have been moving for some months will grow rapidly and disastrously steeper'.[308]

Wider regional problems were also linked to the Federation, and exerted pressure on the Federal and British governments alike. The Congo gained its independence from Belgium at the end of June 1960, and five days later the army mutinied against its Belgian officers, which led to outbreaks of violence throughout the country. The widespread breakdown of order peaked with the declaration of independence by the mineral-rich south-eastern province of Katanga, on 11 July 1960.[309] Northern Rhodesia and Katanga were connected through both human and natural geography. The border between the two states crossed the Copperbelt, which provided each territory with mineral wealth.[310]

Although Macmillan thought it was natural that Moise Tshombe, the Katangan president, should enjoy the moral support of Sir Roy Welensky and the government of the Central African Federation, who were anxious to see a reasonably stable regime in a territory so intrinsically connected to Northern Rhodesia, he still aligned Britain behind UN action in the Congo.[311] This greatly annoyed Welensky. Britain, he claimed, was more concerned with following the American line, and causing no offence to the 'very noisy leaders of the Afro-Asian bloc' in the UN, than defending her interests (i.e., the Federation) in central Africa.[312] Welensky later recalled how his relationship with the British government which was 'already delicate enough, not to say strained' deteriorated further after Britain supported UN intervention in the Congo.[313]

Welensky's criticism of UN activities in Katanga resonated with some quarters of the British press. During September 1961 the *Daily Telegraph* asked '[w]hy has the United Nations now abandoned conciliation for a policy of force?', and concluded that '[w]e have now been deliberately confronted with a "last resort" that bears every appearance of having been deliberately engineered'.[314] Two days later it built on this theme in an editorial, arguing that '[i]n ruins at the moment is the whole conception of the United Nations as an austere and impartial force, standing above the quarrels of the nations, not the servant of any one nation or group of nations but the servant of all'.[315] *The Times* noted 'it seems odd to attack Katanga to prevent civil war'.[316] The *Daily Mail* asked 'is a gun-slinging *coup d'etat*, engineered by outsiders, any way to secure lasting unity and stability?'[317] The *Daily Express* directly linked the unfolding crisis in Katanga to events within the Federation:

> One man emerges from the Katanga crisis with enhanced reputation: Sir Roy Welensky [...] time after time he warned of the dangers of [UN] activities in the Congo [...] There is only one way in which the British Government can redeem its wretched blunders in Africa. That is to support Sir Roy Welensky in the tremendous – but not yet hopeless – task of holding the front for civilisation.[318]

As welcome as this support was, a mere 48 hours after the *Daily Express'* rallying-call, events in Northern Rhodesia dramatically intensified criticism of the Federation in the UN.

On 17 September 1961 an aeroplane carrying the United Nations' Secretary-General, Dag Hammarskjöld, crashed 12 kilometres from the Northern Rhodesian town of Ndola.[319] Hammarskjöld was flying to the Federation to meet with Tshombe. Prior to the accident, the Federation had been accused of allowing Katangan forces to use its airfields for fighter planes, and Hammarskjöld's death inevitably cast suspicion on the Federation. Welensky reflected on the day after the crash that '[t]he Federation has taken the place of South Africa and this morning I had a fairly difficult time with the United Nations in Southern Rhodesia'.[320] He did, however, continue to vigorously deny any Federal involvement in the crash, and lamented that 'the death of Hammarskjöld has not made our task any easier'.[321] His protestations, however, went unheeded and Afro-Asian suspicions were voiced in the UN when the Guinean Minister of Foreign Affairs announced:

> there can be no doubt whatever that Secretary General Hammarskjöld fell a victim to the same colonial and racist forces whose united front, organized and financed in broad daylight, after having murdered Patrice Lumumba and his companions, is now endeavouring to prevent at any cost the inevitable decolonization of Central and Eastern Africa.[322]

The Federation was also accused of supplying both arms and men to support Tshombe against UN forces. Since the crisis began, the UN repeatedly requested that Britain allow UN observers into the Federation to supervise the border. This was not an unreasonable request. Correspondence between the Federal and South African governments the previous year demonstrates that Pretoria was providing Tshombe with weaponry, with all identification marks removed, via the Federation.[323] Mercenaries played a key role in Tshombe's forces. Initially, predominately French and Belgian ex-servicemen were recruited, though as the crisis wore on the focus shifted to Southern Rhodesians and South Africans. Criticism in New York was such that Britain applied pressure on the Federal government to restrict mercenary recruitment in Salisbury and Bulawayo, however it made little difference. Recruitment was temporarily displaced to South Africa where lax visa controls allowed mercenaries to travel through the Federation unhindered.[324]

This chapter has reinforced John Darwin's claim that by the early 1960s 'the British regarded their "imperial" interests as quite distinct from the local interests of their kith and kin, the white settlers'.[325] The Federal government's failure to significantly influence Macmillan's government corresponds to Andrew Thompson's view that between 1959 and 1964 there was a 'third implosion of empire' as people were less likely to hold any opinion about empire, never mind offer it outright support.[326] Macmillan highlighted that the Conservative Party's interests were not as similar to those of the Federal government as they had been in 1957, with his 'wind of change' speech early in 1960. The defeat of Robin Turton's Early Day Motion signalled that the Federal government was unable to raise enough support within the Conservative Party to significantly influence the Party's leadership. Macmillan's liberal policy towards African political advance placed the government closer to the position adopted by their Labour opposition and isolated Welensky's support to the right wing of the Conservative Party. Porter has also highlighted the indifference of the British public and politicians during this period. He notes that MPs of all parties 'mostly accepted the general principle of colonial [African] self-government and went along with the unexpected pace of it with no great qualms'.[327]

CHAPTER 4

A FAILED EXPERIMENT, 1962-3

It's a sad world in relation to what was our Empire. Occasionally at night when I'm restive, I turn to a selection of speeches. They range over a period of nearly fifty years and cover some of the greatest figures of the end of the nineteenth and the beginning of the twentieth century. The other night I read one of Winston Churchill's and one of Cecil Rhodes' [...] After I'd read, I lay and wondered what the British press would say about any Englishman who got up and tried to speak on those lines today.

Sir Roy Welensky to Sarah Gertrude Millin,[1]
16 March 1962[2]

Maudling and the Northern Rhodesia Proposals

At the beginning of 1962 the Federal government faced an almost impossible task in keeping the Federation together. No date had been set for the federal review conference to resume, the Northern Rhodesian agreement looked far from secure and Hastings Banda continued to demand the immediate secession of Nyasaland from the Federation. In his memoirs Sir Roy Welensky provides a rare example of understatement when he described the outlook for the Federation as 'far from sunny'.[3] In the first instance Welensky had to contend with Reginald Maudling, Iain Macleod's successor as secretary of state for the colonies. It soon became clear that any hopes Welensky held that Maudling would offer his government respite over Northern Rhodesia proved little more than wishful thinking.

Despite Welensky's later recollection of Maudling as 'amiable, completely ignorant of Africa, not aggressively opinionated, but certainly neither strong enough nor independent enough to make any stand against the majority of his senior colleagues'.[4] The new secretary of state for the colonies in fact pursued a line of policy which was even more liberal than his predecessor's, and that against the wishes of many of his cabinet colleagues.[5] His opponents believed that any amendment to the June proposals could lead to accusations that government policy could be influenced by violence.[6] Furthermore, Duncan Sandys, the secretary of state for Commonwealth relations, contended that it would expose the government to a 'charge of bad faith' from the Federal government.[7] Even Harold Macmillan was startled by Maudling's desire to tear up the June agreement, which he considered morally, if not legally, binding.[8] Maudling would later suggest that he moved more quickly than Macleod in order to 'avoid that degree and form of violence which would make a solution satisfactory to both races virtually impossible to obtain'.[9] Maudling had formulated this view whilst he – in Welensky's words – 'bustled cheerfully around the Federation'.[10]

In addition to information from his ministers and civil servants, Macmillan's policy towards the Federation was, in part, influenced by Sir Ronald Prain, the chairman of the Rhodesia Selection Trust (RST) mining company. In early 1962 Prain informed Macmillan that '[t]here can no longer be any doubt that there is not a compromise solution which will satisfy both African opinion and European opinion'.[11] Prain believed that if both sides could not be mollified, the British government should base their decision on what would be best for Northern Rhodesia, rather than for the Federation as a whole. This, he argued, was necessary for two reasons. First, it was the best guarantee that the Federation would continue in some form. Secondly, he predicted that if Northern Rhodesia was not the primary concern in any settlement then 'your government will have an extremely difficult security problem on its hands'.[12] Prain clearly recognised that his company's best interests would be served by a stable transition to majority rule in Northern Rhodesia. He was adamant that any opposition from settlers in the territory would be 'short lived in comparison with the opposition which any other form of Constitution would bring about on the African side'.[13]

Maudling's initial ideas on the Northern Rhodesian issue had been circulated to the Federal cabinet during the December of the previous year. It was immediately apparent that he intended to remove every concession that Welensky had previously won from Macleod. The Federal government wasted no time in rejecting Maudling's suggestions in the strongest possible terms. Welensky believed that the British should have had more faith in the Federation and that Maudling's proposals were 'a body-blow to the Federation [... which] would make the task of the Federal supporters impossible, while making that of its enemies easier'.[14] Lord Alport agreed with this sentiment and advised Whitehall that African nationalists in Southern Rhodesia would inevitably conclude 'that direct action was the most effective way of obtaining power and all arguments about the value of gradual, constitutional processes [were] simply a rather cynical attempt to pull wool over their eyes'.[15]

By the end of February it became clear that Maudling was going to announce changes to the Northern Rhodesian agreement in spite of the opposition from the Federal government. Welensky, retaliated by leaving Salisbury for London against the wishes of the British government.[16] The Federal Prime Minister still had faith that in Britain 'the man in the street' would back him even though 'papers like the *Observer* and the *Guardian* hate my very guts and believe everything I do is very wrong'.[17] It is clear that Welensky believed his appearance in London would strengthen the Federation's bargaining position.[18] Yet crucially he had misjudged his own influence in the matter. Macmillan did not meet with Welensky until after Maudling's announcement, and, when Welensky finally secured an audience with the British prime minister, he was bereft of ideas on how to move the situation forward.[19] No progress was made and, as a result of Welensky's actions, Patrick Wall, a stalwart supporter of the Federation in Westminster, gained the impression that 'Sir Edgar's stock is up and Sir Roy's is down'. Wall did not believe this had caused any major problems as 'this presented two sides of the same picture and served to impress upon those responsible the dangers of the situation'.[20] Welensky's protests, however, were ineffectual, and the final proposals were announced at the end of February.[21] As a result of Maudling's revised proposals the United National Independence Party (UNIP) agreed to contest the Northern Rhodesian territorial election scheduled for later in the year.

Welensky was bitterly disappointed by his failure to stop the renegotiation of the Northern Rhodesian constitution and on 8 March he

called a federal election in an attempt to buttress his political position in
the Federation and secure a public vote of confidence.[22] He believed that
he had been left with few options and that his hand was 'really forced
in the sense that I couldn't get the British government to really do
anything'. Welensky described the ensuing political situation in the
Federation as 'quite amusing' as his political opponents had been caught
off-balance. Welensky believed he would do 'fairly well' in the election
although he was worried about Whitehead's fate in the forthcoming
Southern Rhodesian contest.[23] Welensky's decision to call an election in
March 1962 provided an opportunity for the United Federal Party's
(UFP) opponents in Southern Rhodesia to reorganise themselves into
a far more formidable force. For them, the UFP's attack on the Land
Apportionment Act in combination with increased African violence
threatened the very fabric of European existence in the territory and on
13 March 1962 the four main right-wing parties in Southern Rhodesia
– the Federal Dominion Party, the Southern Rhodesian Dominion Party,
the Southern Rhodesian Association and Ian Smith's recently formed
Rhodesian Reform Party – united as the Rhodesian Front (RF) under
the leadership of Winston Field.

Tellingly for the Federation's future the RF refused to stand against
the UFP in the Federal election as they saw the imminent Southern
Rhodesian election as far more important.[24] Although the UFP won 54
of the 59 seats in the legislative assembly, Welensky could not claim a
clear mandate because the opposition refused to take part, and only
13,397 voters of an estimated 120,000 exercised their right to vote.
On hearing the result Harry Nkumbula is said to have announced
'Hallelujah – Sir Roy has killed the Federation himself',[25] while a UNIP
publication announced:

Look at the standard of the election! The mandate he got is
hopeless because it has no blessing from the English people or the
Africans. It is a sham mandate as most of those who voted are sons
and daughters of Boers who have packed half of their essential
properties – ready to jump into South Africa.[26]

This period also saw Banda move closer to agreeing a process with
London for Nyasaland's secession from the Federation. In order to secure
Banda's attendance in London for talks during April, Sandys is believed

to have offered an assurance that the terms would be settled before Banda's arrival.[27] Philip Murphy has noted, however, that this view was not unanimous and Home still believed that it would be possible to hold the Federation together by force.[28] Banda met with Sandys during February 1962 and convinced the Secretary of State for Commonwealth Relations that his wishes should not be delayed. Sandys initially wanted Welensky to arrange Nyasaland's secession with the British government himself, but was talked out of this action by Sir Norman Brook, the cabinet secretary, as it would mean an end to the Federation.[29] Welensky was still dead set against Nyasaland's secession at the beginning of March 1962.

Butler and the Central Africa Office

If Welensky's intransigence and Sandys promise to Banda appeared to put the British and Federal governments on a collision course over Nyasaland, the creation of a Central Africa Office under R. A. Butler[30] appeared to provide space for manoeuvre.[31] Welensky would later say that Butler was 'the best British Minister I dealt with in the years from 1957 onwards'.[32] Welensky's attitude was unsurprising as Butler was broadly sympathetic to the settlers' plight. In his memoirs he revealed that he never supported the Monckton Commission's appointment, and upon assuming his new post he cancelled Banda's visit – thus heading off Sandys' alleged promise.[33] He also announced an inquiry to consider the consequences if Nyasaland were to withdraw from the Federation, and of alternative forms of association between Nyasaland and the two Rhodesias.[34]

The creation of the Central Africa Office was a result of Macmillan's desire to centralise responsibility for the Federation under a single secretary of state. As he subsequently noted, 'divided Ministerial responsibility has given rise to difficulty in the past; and, with the recent constitutional development in the northern territories', Macmillan informed Alport, who was now British high commissioner in Salisbury, that 'the balance of advantage now lies in transferring all responsibility for the Federation and its constituent territories to a single Minister'.[35] Alport agreed, judging that there was 'great advantage' in having a single secretary of state to deal with the Federation.[36]

Support for the move was also forthcoming from Patrick Wall who thought 'Rab's appointment is a very good augury for the future as he is certainly a friend of the Federation and an extremely shrewd politician'.[37] Less predictably, African nationalist sympathisers were also broadly sympathetic to this development. Thomas Fox-Pitt, secretary of the Anti-Slavery Society and a member of UNIP's London Committee, informed a UNIP official that the Party should not be too worried by the appointment of Butler.[38] Fox-Pitt had talked with several left-wing members of the Conservative Party who believed that the rationale behind Macmillan's decision was 'to have a Minister with enough authority to carry through the changing of the Federation from a political federation to an economic federation'.[39] Furthermore, it was suggested that many Conservative MPs were trying to protect their financial interests in Southern Rhodesia by ensuring that the Northern Rhodesian copper mines remained linked to the Southern Rhodesian economy. Welensky also came in for criticism:

> The Conservatives are no longer as keen on Welensky as a great Commonwealth statesman as they were. I am told that it is not so much his threat to use force that has put them off as his reference to 'my Federation'. I don't know if this made them angry because it was the Queen's Federation and not his or because they saw a hint of megalomania and dangerous conceit in it. They, of course, think of it as a shareholders' Federation. It has always been understood by them that the whole thing was been run for the benefit of the money interests and it was a shock to find a personal claim being put forward which might conflict with their established rights.[40]

Simon Zukas saw Butler's appointment as recognition by the British government that 'the situation is too complex to be handled by their traditional machinery'.[41] Furthermore, he concluded that 'the move must be aimed at achieving a rapid FINAL solution to the Federal Problem of the winding up of this newly created Office and strange responsibility for a Home Secretary' [emphasis in original].[42] This apparent optimism was short lived, however, as Zukas revealed three months later that none of the UNIP London committee 'feels we can place any faith in Butler [... as] while Nyasaland may be released that does not apply similarly to us'.[43]

In early May 1962 Butler arrived in Salisbury for the first time in his new role. The Southern Rhodesian government wasted no time in trying to impress on the secretary of state the urgency of the territory's financial situation. They reported that African unemployment had reached 50,000, and as no unemployment benefits were paid to any race in the colony 'a grave deterioration in the security situation can be anticipated with a corresponding loss of confidence by private investors'. Consequently, 'complete economic collapse is a real possibility if a solution for the future of Central Africa is postponed again after the past three years of uncertainty'.[44] Their memorandum also alleged that in the three years prior to federation in 1953 Southern Rhodesia had been able to borrow £31,535,589 externally, yet during the eight years of federation Southern Rhodesia's share of federal external borrowing had only been £11,308,000. The Federal government's inability to raise loans on the open market in London due to the political instability in the Federation had not helped the situation. Financial collapse would have such dire consequences that the Southern Rhodesian government believed that 'if a final settlement of the Central African constitutional problem cannot be reached by July this year, Her Majesty's Government will have to buy time or they will find there is nothing left to Federate'.[45]

When Butler met with Welensky and the Federal government it was against a backdrop of growing African violence in Salisbury. Butler swiftly ruled out any partition of Northern Rhodesia. The idea of joining the Northern Rhodesian line of rail, the Copperbelt and Barotseland to Southern Rhodesia had moved from being an idea backed by the Confederate Party during the 1950s to being given serious consideration by the Federal government, especially during the Northern Rhodesia constitutional crisis. Despite Butler's refusal to consider a territorial settlement, Welensky seemed buoyed by their encounter, believing the Secretary of State to be:

of a different calibre to a lot of the other people I have had to deal with. First of all, he does seem to be an honourable man, and that counts for something in one's dealings with a man. He has been frank and I think, has an appreciation of the position here that I have found few British politicians to have. He has certainly come with few, if any, preconceived ideas and almost no illusions about the troubles.[46]

Welensky hoped Butler had found his visit to the Federation instructive
in three ways: first, that Kaunda was not the leader Macleod believed
him to be; secondly, that there were no easy solutions to the future of the
Federation; and, finally, that Britain needed to reach an agreement with
Welensky or 'they're going to have a row on their hands and it will be a
first class one'.[47]

Perhaps Welensky's enthusiasm over Butler's visit would have been
tempered had he been aware of the impression Butler had made on African
nationalists in Northern Rhodesia. According to one UNIP member, 'One
thing that must be mentioned is that Mr Butler left Central Africa fully
convinced that Federation was dead'.[48] Mainza Chona also expressed
UNIP's pleasure in Butler's appointment: 'we are glad Federation and its
constituent territories are in the hands of one person. This time, we won't
have one Minister trying to keep alive a dead duck while the other one is
proceeding on the basis that the duck is dead.'[49] Butler also gave Banda
a private assurance that the British government understood that the
Malawi Congress Party was not prepared to let Nyasaland remain the
Federation.[50] Having secured this concession Banda agreed, during a visit
to London in July, to attend a Nyasaland Constitutional Conference
scheduled for November.[51] Butler credited his progress in moving
forward negotiations on all Federal territories to his 'composite approach';
this he later revealed was 'designed not to leave any one territory out on a
limb – creating an explosion in Northern Rhodesia, for example, because
I had gone too far in Nyasaland – and to keep the territories as far as
possible together, economically if not politically'.[52]

Butler's approach secured support in Westminster as well as the
Federation. Wall reported that he had 'made a great impression on
Parliament' and had managed to satisfy 'the right, the centre and the left
– with the possible exception of Humphrey Berkeley who wants the
Federation destroyed immediately!' Consequently 'whatever Rab Butler
makes his mind up to do he will get the support of the party and carry it
through'.[53] John Darwin has suggested that 'perhaps with its own
backbenchers in mind, London shrank from being the Federation's
public executioner'.[54] Yet the highpoint of danger from the backbenches
had been reached with Turton's Early Day Motion during the previous
year.[55] Since then opposition to the government had been confined to the
usual suspects on the right of the party. Welensky would later note that
Butler was:

a much more dangerous opponent than Macleod, because he's been able to handle the Tory back bench in a way that the former gentleman never got anywhere near doing. As a matter of fact Butler, to a very large extent, has dissipated any support we had among the Tory back benches as a result of his tactics[56]

In June 1962, the British cabinet agreed that Butler could offer Banda a constitutional conference in the autumn. Butler, however, believed that the right of secession should not be granted until after the Northern Rhodesia election in December. Nonetheless, by October it had become clear to Butler that the constitutional review would not succeed unless the right of secession had already been granted. Welensky strongly refuted Butler's opinion and argued that any statement made before the conference, which was due to begin on 12 November, would damage his party's chances in forthcoming elections in both Rhodesias. Butler conceded this point to Welensky and announced that Nyasaland had the right to secede from the Federation on 19 December 1962. It was September 1963 before Britain finalised the date for Nyasaland's independence.

Preparing for the Northern and Southern Rhodesian Elections

Welensky's inability to secure firm support from the British government for the Federation's future was increasingly attracting criticism from his own supporters in Britain. On the same day that Macmillan announced Butler's appointment at the Central Africa Office, Sir Albert Robinson, the Federation's high commissioner in London, expressed concern that Welensky's approach to negotiations with Britain was too 'rigid'.[57] Robinson's view was also shared by Lennox-Boyd and Lord Salisbury. Welensky vigorously denied this charge in correspondence with Salisbury and maintained that his hand had been forced 'by being in the embarrassing position of having a mandate from the electorate to do a particular thing and I have failed'. Furthermore, Welensky admitted that he 'felt so strongly about the way I have been double-crossed by Her Majesty's Government in the last two years that at some stage even a worm would turn, and on this occasion I was the worm'.[58] Welensky later revealed to Patrick Wall that he was 'a bit shaken' at this accusation being adamant that 'the last three or four years had shown only too clearly how fluid my thinking was'.[59]

As Welensky's earlier impromptu flight to London following Maudling's Northern Rhodesia proposals demonstrated, British public opinion was a key battleground over the future of the Federation. In July, Welensky instructed Stewart Parker, his principal private secretary, to arrange for a parliamentary question to be asked in the Commons. Parker duly wrote to Voice and Vision, the public relations company retained by the Federal government, requesting that questions be asked:

> specifically on the fact that the British taxpayer is to provide the sum of 5 [shillings] out of every £1 Nyasaland spends on Current Account. Perhaps the questioner might enquire whether it is normal practice for the British taxpayer to subsidise the running of Government-owned newspaper.[60]

Sydney Wynne of Voice and Vision promptly made arrangements and one week after the request had left Salisbury, Roy Mason[61] tabled a written question identically phrased to Butler.[62] UNIP also used sympathetic MPs in this way. Barbara Castle had been contacted in April 1962 and asked to enquire why prisoners at Broken Hill were not allowed reading material to undertake private studies.[63] Two weeks later she was asked to enquire about the enrolment of voters for the forthcoming territorial elections.[64] UNIP correspondence indicates that Barbara Castle raised both points with Butler upon receipt of the requests.[65] Likewise John Stonehouse was requested to raise the issue of electoral registration; this he did.[66]

Welensky returned to London again during September in an attempt to press the Federation's case and meet with British officials for further discussions. He made little progress and flew back to Salisbury with 'some very unhappy feelings about the future'.[67] One such feeling had been aroused by the possibility of Britain applying to join the Common Market.[68] Butler had raised this issue during September and took the opportunity to describe the advantages and disadvantages that the Federation could expect from associate membership of the Common Market. Welensky later explicitly linked Britain's desire to join the Common Market with influencing events in the Federation.

'The British are very anxious to get rid of us', he mused on his return to Salisbury:

> we are an embarrassment. All white people on the continent today are an embarrassment to their former home countries and this, to a large extent aided and abetted by Britain's desire to enter the Common Market, was part of the reason for the 'Wind of Change' speech and what flowed from it.[69]

The Federation, the United States and the United Nations

The uncertainty over the Federation's future led to increased attention from the United States as G. Mennen Williams, the Assistant Secretary of State for Africa, attempted to ensure his country came down on the right side of any political settlement.[70] Williams notified the United States' Consulate General in Salisbury, Paul Geren, that as the eventual settlement was far from certain it was important for the United States to retain 'good contact with all shades of political opinion'. Williams understood that 'the Europeans may have real or imagined grievances against the United States'. He believed that although the consulate should go some way to soothe European feelings it should not give the impression it supported their cause. 'The reason that the President received Banda and Kaunda was to demonstrate American sympathy for African self-determination', he wrote. Consequently, if the president was to see a representative of the Federal government, the Europeans 'might be misled into believing the United States somehow supported the Welensky Government'. Williams believed that while allowing a Federal official to visit President Kennedy would help American/Federal relations, 'the recommended cure is worse than the disease'.[71]

Towards the end of the Cuban missile crisis in October 1962, the difficulties facing the United States in the Federation, and Southern Rhodesia in particular, were judged 'perhaps the most difficult situation for the United States in Africa today'. For Mennen Williams, although the partnership programme had started well, it had moved too slowly to accommodate African nationalism in the Federation over the last five years: 'the winds of change have now proved to have blown stronger and faster than Sir Roy Welensky's ability to accommodate and perhaps even with greater velocity than Sir Edgar Whitehead has felt himself able to cope with'.[72] Furthermore:

> The political problem which confronts Great Britain is that they are convinced that the Southern Rhodesian whites will not accept a more liberal constitution than the one under consideration and that if there is any liberalization of the constitution, then Sir Edgar Whitehead will fall. They state the case very boldly that it is Sir Edgar or apartheid.[73]

It was believed that if changes were not made to the constitution, however, there would be increasing dissatisfaction from Africans which would increase the level of violence. This would also provide a rallying call for the Afro-Asians in the United Nations to further increase pressure on Britain. The United States, while sympathetic to Britain's problems, hoped that a policy which would satisfy both parties could still be found.[74] Mennen Williams' concern over the position of the Afro-Asian bloc in the United Nations (UN) reflects the growing importance of the UN as an awkward arena of international protest during the final years of Federation.[75]

The political situation in Southern Rhodesia deteriorated rapidly during the summer of 1962, bringing the territory under increased scrutiny from the United Nations. In an attempt to stem the growing tide of African nationalism, Whitehead banned ZAPU during September in an attempt to calm the situation, with some early success.[76]

The Federal government exploited its contacts with South Africa with regard to the UN. In June 1962, the South African High Commissioner in Salisbury divulged to Welensky and Parry, federal secretary for external affairs, that Britain was considering abstaining from, or not even participating in, the forthcoming United Nations vote on Southern Rhodesia. Welensky was 'most surprised' at this news and immediately approached his high commissioner in London for more information.[77] The South African information was duly confirmed: London preferred non-participation. The South African High Commissioner believed that whatever Pretoria was to do:

> it should not be weak-kneed. Britain has earned the reputation here of being only too ready to let the Federation down and to

compromise with the Afro-Asians. If she shows an inclination to vacillate now strong action on our part would contrast favourably with her action in the eyes of people here.[78]

By 1962, Africa was thoroughly intertwined with the procedure and policy of the United Nations, to the extent that 42 per cent of the sixteenth *Annual Report of the Secretary General* (1962) was devoted to African issues. By comparison, the first 66-page long *Annual Report* contained only two sentences on Africa.[79] One issue attracting increasing attention was the situation in Southern Rhodesia. This change in priorities was not welcomed by Welensky. He began the year in a deflated mood, writing how he had 'been having one of my recurring rows with Her Majesty's Government. I don't have to tell you that, of course, they quake every time the United Nations say anything. I know that we are a tremendous embarrassment and, after having chewed up South Africa, the United Nations are now looking for fresh victims.'[80]

Welensky was proved correct. Much to the surprise of the British government, the question of whether Southern Rhodesia had received 'a full measure of self-government' was referred to the Committee of Seventeen, after a vote on the last day of the Sixteenth General Assembly. For the first time Southern Rhodesia was a topic of formal discussion at the UN. Britain had three main points for opposing this action. First, they had cooperated with colonial issues on the condition that there would be no intervention by the UN in British territories; secondly, Southern Rhodesia was self-governing in its internal affairs and completely responsible for its own economic, social and educational policies; and finally the British government was not in a position to provide information as it could not demand such information from the colony. The Ghanaian representative responded to these claims by suggesting that if Britain could not control the situation in Southern Rhodesia, then the United Nations should 'come to the rescue'. Scorn was also poured on British assertions of self-government for the territory:

How can a colonial territory in Africa be self-governing when the three million Africans have no say in the administration – which is in the hands of only 280,000 European settlers who, by the grace of the British Government, have been allowed to maintain a racist regime, comparable only to the apartheid state of South Africa?[81]

Ghana was not the only country to voice its displeasure during the March debate. The representative of Sierra Leone accused Britain of upholding 'a mockery of democracy' in the Federation. Much to British incredulity, the USSR and Bulgaria also argued that the principle of one-man-one-vote should be recognised and independence given to the Africans of Southern Rhodesia rather than the white settlers.[82] In response, the British representative again claimed a lack of jurisdiction over the territory and categorically denied that Southern Rhodesia was another South Africa. He referred to Southern Rhodesian Prime Minister, Sir Edgar Whitehead's recent comment that 'white supremacy is as dead as a dodo [in Southern Rhodesia] and that those who wanted to perpetuate white supremacy can get another Prime Minister'.[83]

Only Canada and the United States supported Britain on this issue. A State Department report maintained that one explanation for the Afro-Asian bloc's 'surprising success' in securing the referral of Southern Rhodesia to the Committee of Seventeen was 'the effective lobbying' of African nationalist representatives in the United Nations. This lobbying was characterised quite differently by Sir Roy Welensky, who found Kenneth Kaunda's 'performance of wailing before the Committee of Seventeen in New York [...] nauseating'.[84] The State Department report further recognised that:

This move in the General Assembly lends moral support to the African nationalists in Southern Rhodesia and could subject Southern Rhodesia to a barrage of external agitation and propaganda from Africa's nationalist statesmen at a time when delicate negotiations on the Northern Rhodesian and Federal Constitution are under way[...].[85]

These points succinctly illustrate the problems facing Britain in the international community. Southern Rhodesia was too easily linked to events in neighbouring countries and the publicity provided by the UN encouraged African nationalists still further. Welensky alluded to this in correspondence to a friend, writing that 'the nationalists here now no longer look to the United Kingdom; they look to the Afro-Asian Group at the United Nations'.[86] He was, however, forced to admit that Britain did its best to resist open interference by the United Nations in the Federation.[87]

Events during March 1962 caused further consternation among the Afro-Asian bloc. The debate over Southern Rhodesia's 'self-governing' status was still ongoing when Whitehead's government decided to ban the Zimbabwe African Peoples Union (ZAPU). Lord Home informed Secretary of State, Dean Rusk that while he fully regretted Whitehead's decision to ban ZAPU, he felt sure that the Rhodesian authorities must have done it with the 'greatest reluctance'.[88] Home made clear that if Britain was forced to enter into any undertakings at the UN it would be 'most damaging' to securing any success in the Federation. Whitehead was apparently 'particularly sensitive' to the 'danger that any appearance of yielding to the United Nations pressures could well lose them the election'.[89] As a result of the ZAPU ban, the Special Committee decided to make Southern Rhodesia its first order of business. This consistent focus on Britain's colonial record continued to place the United States in a difficult position. Mennen Williams believed that the issue was so contentious that '[t]he US position on the Southern Rhodesia question will to a large extent determine our effectiveness in pressing for moderation on subsequent "colonial" issues and in exercising influence with the Afro-Asians on the whole range of the UN Agenda'.[90] The problem facing Washington was that if the Afro-Asian bloc believed that the US had not fully pressured Britain over Southern Rhodesia, it could move them closer to the Soviet Union. In the Cold War context of the early 1960s this was to be avoided. Consequently, Mennen Williams concluded that:

[i]n the absence of any ameliorating action by the UK or the Southern Rhodesian Government, we should express in the UN General Assembly, in restrained terms, and avoiding criticism of the UK, our dismay and dissatisfaction with the course of events in Southern Rhodesia. While urging moderation in corridor conversations with Afro-Asians, we should not conduct a campaign on behalf of the UK or the Southern Rhodesian Government.[91]

By the end of the month the Southern Rhodesian question had still not been satisfactorily addressed and, according to the South African representative's report to Pretoria, 'the end is not yet in sight'.[92] At least 13 of the 17 members of the Committee were convinced that Southern

Rhodesia was not self-governing. Only the United States, Australia and Italy accepted that there were constitutional problems facing Britain. The British official then argued that it would be impossible to solve Southern Rhodesia's problems without widening the debate to consider Northern Rhodesia and Nyasaland. The Committee agreed to this on the condition that Southern Rhodesia was discussed first. The South African representative believed Britain was attempting to blur the issue. He noted that 'it is already absolutely clear that the whole Southern Rhodesian issue is now on the United Nations' plate and will probably stay there as long as Southern Rhodesia exists in its present form'.[93]

Discussions followed on Northern Rhodesia and Nyasaland and the Special Committee concluded a series of meetings in May by approving 12–4 in favour of calling for immediate independence for Northern Rhodesia.[94] The Special Committee's report was described by the United States representative described as 'excessive and emotional'. The State Department contended that Britain feared UN interference would 'hinder' their efforts to find a solution to the problems in the territory as it would 'stimulate African nationalist agitation' for immediate independence. Not only would UN action encourage African extremists, it would also encourage reactionaries among the European population. If 'serious conflict and violence' ensued in Southern Rhodesia, and Britain could not devise a new constitution acceptable to the majority African population, Southern Rhodesia would also be added to the Assembly's programme. Furthermore, it was 'virtually impossible to discuss any of the individual territories of the Federation without becoming involved in the question of the Federation itself'.[95] This was a key concern to Welensky, particularly in the case of Nyasaland. He was well aware that '[i]f Nyasaland goes [. . .] how does one refuse Northern Rhodesia the right?' The only argument he could offer was the size of Northern Rhodesia's European population, however, he was realistic enough to realise that this would carry little weight in the eyes of the Afro-Asian bloc.[96]

As expected, a vote in June passed the debate over Southern Rhodesia to the General Assembly. Welensky tartly noted that of the 61 nations voting for the debate, 22 were dictatorships, 23 were in arrears with their subscriptions to the UN and in two – Saudi Arabia and the Yemen – slavery was openly practised.[97] The debate began on 14 June with a resolution tabled by 38 Afro-Asian countries, including all the African and Asian members of the British Commonwealth. The resolution claimed that, as 'the territory of Southern Rhodesia is a non-self-governing territory within the meaning of Chapter XI of the Charter of the United Nations', Britain should convene a conference with 'the full participation of all political parties'. The resolution also requested the UN Committee of Seventeen continue its efforts to ensure that Southern Rhodesia emerged as an 'independent African State'.

During the week-long debate, the Ghanaian representative argued that Southern Rhodesia presented 'one of the most urgent colonial problems of Africa', which could produce 'a colonial conflict of the Algerian or Angolan type'. This sentiment was echoed by other Afro-Asian delegates. Britain continued to deny it had any power to intervene in Southern Rhodesia, an assertion that was supported by Canada and Australia. Furthermore, the British representative warned that any UN action would only increase difficulties, harden attitudes and widen existing divisions in Southern Rhodesia. Britain, he avowed, had faith in the genuine intention of the Southern Rhodesian government to eliminate racial discrimination and to build a multiracial society based on tolerance and goodwill. In any case, he declared, the organisation had no authority under the Charter or elsewhere to intervene in Southern Rhodesia. The resolution was 'objectionable in principle and dangerous in practice'.[98] The General Assembly disagreed and adopted the resolution by 73 votes to one (South Africa) with 27 abstentions. An amendment by Bulgaria was also adopted which called on the Southern Rhodesian franchise to be based on the principle of one man one vote.[99]

Britain suffered further embarrassment later in the year when Sir Hugh Foot, Britain's Ambassador to the UN, resigned during October. Foot's reason for his decision was that he could no longer defend Southern Rhodesia's policies in the Assembly. The British Conservative press denounced his action as a 'stab in the back'. However, Foot was unrepentant and revealed that he was honouring a pledge to Joshua Nkomo, the leader of ZAPU, to resign if Britain refused to intervene in Southern Rhodesia.[100]

A further issue that attracted criticism in the United Nations was the suspicion that the Europeans in Rhodesia would annex the Katanga province of the Congo and create a territory centred around the line of rail and the mineral wealth of the Copperbelt. Philip Brownrigg, a director of Anglo American, visited Salisbury during February 1963 where he met with Ronald Prain and drew his attention to a paper produced by Taylor Ostrander of the American Metal Climax Company entitled 'The corporate structure of Rhodesian Copperbelt mining enterprise'. Brownrigg wished to raise Anglo American's 'strongest possible objections to it'. While he understood its purpose was to refute charges of a conspiracy between mining companies in southern Africa in the UN he believed Anglo should have been consulted before it was produced.[101] Furthermore, 'it was a biased and unfair picture [. . .] the general implication was to smear Anglo American'. Moreover, 'it was a hit below the belt [. . .] libellous [. . . and] Harry Oppenheimer took a very serious view of it'.[102] Brownrigg believed that the paper's intention had been to deflect attention away from RST by presenting 'Anglo American in an unfavourable light as a corporation governed by South African policies'.[103] In wake of this, Hochschild wrote to Oppenheimer reiterating that the intention behind the publication was to rebut the alleged conspiracy between the Copperbelt mining companies and *Union Minière du Haut Katanga* to maintain white supremacy from 'Cape to Katanga'. Harold Hochschild further attempted to calm the waters, remarking that he was:

[w]ell aware of the risks a company chairman in South Africa takes in expressing liberal views in opposition to government policy and I am happy to have had the opportunity to testify to your courage in doing so - a quality that surprises no one who knows you.[104]

The accusations in the UN were not completely fanciful. In July 1959 Harry Grenfell, a director of the British South Africa Company, wrote to Parker suggesting that with the chaotic situation in the Congo, there were 'advantages and dangers' to attracting the Katanga Province into closer association with the Federation. He highlighted the advantages of 'keeping the Katanga mines and the Benguela Railway route in the hands of the European-led parts of Africa', and suggested that 'the big mining interests on both sides [Federation and Katanga] might be encouraged to do so as that would not implicate governments'.[105] Ellis Robins raised this point with Welensky in February 1960 by stating that the Chartered Company 'have reason to believe from some of our Belgian friends, that the Katanga Province (which is largely dominated by *Union Minière*) will not accept control by a central administration in the Congo'.[106] Robins went on to suggest:

> ought we not (in the Federation) give some indication that we would welcome a closer association with these near neighbours whose interests and the basis of development are so linked with our own? I feel that it is worth while for us to make a pretty definite approach to them.[107]

Welensky urged caution and replied that he had spoken to some Europeans in the Congo who were 'frightened stiff' because if it were known that they had spoken with him 'anything might happen to them'.[108] Nonetheless Welensky continued:

> I have let it be known that I would welcome any approach from them. It's got to come that way, Ellis. I can't say anything or do anything that would give the impression that we are trying to grab any part of Africa.[109]

The close connection between *Union Minière* and both the British South Africa Company and Anglo American has previously been highlighted by Philip Murphy.[110] The British company Tanganyika Concessions Ltd. ('Tanks') held 20 per cent of the voting rights in *Union Minière*.[111] 'Tanks' was well connected to both the British South Africa Company and Anglo American. Although the Chartered Company had disposed of its Katanga holdings soon after trouble began in the region, Ellis Robins and his successor as Chairman, Paul Emrys Evans, both remained on the board of 'Tanks', where Harry Oppenheimer also sat; Anglo American was also reputed to hold a controlling interest in the company.[112]

A study of issues referred to the Security Council during the period shows, in addition to time spent discussing the Congo, over 47 per cent of the UN Security Council's remaining time for the period 1960–3 was spent debating questions of white supremacy or European colonial rule in Africa.[113] This demonstrates that the increased number of Afro-Asian states in the General Assembly meant they had enough votes to ensure that issues of immediate concern to them remained on the UN agenda.[114] The western powers, however, tended not to argue about many of these issues, preferring instead to register reservations. Britain used its veto only once during this period, during September 1963, to reject a resolution calling for Britain not to turn over control of the Federation's armed forces to, or grant sovereignty to, Southern Rhodesia. The British representative later announced that his government had the choice of vetoing the resolution or announcing its refusal to follow this 'invitation', and consequently it had chosen to veto.[115]

Northern and Southern Rhodesian Elections

Two days before the Northern Rhodesian election in October 1962, Butler speculated on the possible course of events in central Africa were the Federation to fail. He believed the consequences of failure would be 'extremely grave' as it could lead to an alliance between Southern Rhodesia and South Africa. Although it was tempting to announce firm proposals to keep the Federation together, to do so would probably destroy hope of obtaining African agreement for any kind of continued association.[116] Following the announcement that all territories would have the right to secede, however, Macmillan was confident that the Southern Rhodesian settlers would not declare their independence from Britain. Furthermore, he believed that many settlers in Southern Rhodesia were still too much in favour of 'more liberal racial policies' to consider closer association with South Africa.[117]

The Northern Rhodesian election saw another blow to Welensky's hopes for the Federation's future. When the votes were counted they revealed that Welensky's UFP had secured 16 seats, Kaunda's UNIP 14 seats and Nkumbula's ANC seven seats. This allowed an African coalition government to be formed, which was a satisfactory outcome according to British opinion. It however meant that if the UFP was to have any power at territorial level within the Federation, Whitehead had to win the Southern Rhodesian election.

Whitehead's expected success in the December 1962 Southern Rhodesian election was considered crucial by State Department officials, if race relations were to improve in the territory. It cited Sir Roy Welensky as a handicap encountered by Whitehead in implementing swifter changes: 'Although Welensky is on record as favoring non-racial political development [. . .] he seems to be opposed to the swiftness with which Whitehead is advancing Africans in Southern Rhodesia.' The influence of the Rhodesian Front was said to diminish or increase as Whitehead took a firm or lenient line respectively with the African nationalists.[118] The report noted that while Southern Rhodesian African nationalists had gained strength despite numerous banning orders, they still lacked the strength of other comparable movements in colonial Africa. The African nationalists were considerably bolstered by the support they had received in the United Nations. Britain was not prepared to intervene as actively in the problem as the United States wanted. 'In typical fashion, the British are knocking off one colonial problem after another in Africa and Southern Rhodesia's turn has not yet reached the center of the stage despite the focus of attention by the UN.'[119]

The report concluded by stating that the United States should continue to pressure the British to publicly assert their authority over the Southern Rhodesian settlers; reaffirm that the current pace of political developments was too slow; expand aid programmes to promote racial cooperation; offer increased encouragement to liberal members of Whitehead's government; and finally, make clear to African nationalists that United States support was conditional on a continuation of a policy of non-violence. It speculated that if Whitehead lost the December election, any move towards a South African position would be resisted due to:

the striking 'Britishness' of the average Southern Rhodesian. He may be critical of UK policy, but he is still loyal to the Queen and very proud of Southern Rhodesia's historic association with the Commonwealth now maintained through its links with the Federation of Rhodesia and Nyasaland.[120]

The British also agreed that Whitehead's victory was 'essential' and excused themselves from exerting greater pressure on him by purporting that doing so would prejudice the electorate against him. It was anticipated that after Whitehead's victory he would push forward reforms toward an African majority government in the area. The Americans would assist in this by providing resources to train Africans so that they could occupy newly influential positions.[121]

On 1 November parliament was dissolved in readiness for the Southern Rhodesian election which was scheduled to take place that

December. Welensky believed that Whitehead was 'cock-a-hoop' about his election prospects in late November, but personally believed that:

> unless I can swing the Europeans round to supporting our Party we won't win. I have seldom struck a man who occupies a high political position who is more divorced from reality than Whitehead. I suppose the fact that he's deaf and almost blind compels him to live in a sort of dream world of his own.[122]

Welensky was proven right when the RF won the election by a majority of five seats and took control of the government.

Writing to a friend in Johannesburg, Welensky stated that Whitehead's defeat was a 'serious blow', but that to a large extent the UFP were to blame for it. He believed 'our side had got the impression that Southern Rhodesia, because of the outcome of the Referendum campaign, had become all liberal and that you could say almost anything and get away with it'.[123] The election result put Welensky in a very difficult position in future negotiations with the British. As he reflected, 'in view of the decision at the election in Southern Rhodesia who do I really speak for now?'[124] Welensky believed that only Southern Rhodesia's precarious economic position had led Winston Field to state he had no desire to see Southern Rhodesia leave the Federation. Welensky summarised his personal opinion of Field:

> Field is the most moderate member of his Party. As a man he is a pompous individual, but I think a man of integrity, but I don't say that in an unkind way, I say that after having faced him for nearly five years in the Federal Assembly. He is a man who cannot tolerate any opposition or criticism, a firm believer that what he is doing is right, and frankly, would fit in very neatly in the Nat[ional Party] philosophy of South Africa.[125]

The RF's election victory all but guaranteed that the Federation would come to an end. Southern Rhodesia joined Northern Rhodesia and Nyasaland in having a legislature opposed to the continuation of the Federation. While Field may have offered public support for an association of sorts into the future, his first priority was to ensure that, if the two northern territories were to receive independence, Southern

Rhodesia would not be left behind. Harry Oppenheimer met with Kenneth Kaunda for the first time during December 1962, and on Christmas Day wrote to Welensky that Kaunda 'makes, on the surface anyway, a good impression'.[126] Oppenheimer reported that he had been careful to avoid expressions of political opinion though Kaunda had made it clear that he would be prepared for economic links with Southern Rhodesia but only if 'there was [sic] no political links whatsoever'.[127] He explained to Welensky his reasons for meeting with Kaunda: 'from a business point of view we must do our best to adapt ourselves to whatever political changes may come'.[128] Oppenheimer admitted that this was:

> very difficult in Rhodesia however, where one has always felt ourselves & still feel ourselves to belong to the country – just as much as we do in South Africa [. . .] The idea of Federation is still sound economically and politically and the ideal of racial partnership still seems to me fine and right. These things shouldn't be sacrificed to nationalism black and white.[129]

Oppenheimer clearly identified his views on the future of central Africa with those of Roy Welensky, since Welensky arguably sensed as much danger in extreme settler nationalism as in African nationalism. Oppenheimer finished his letter with a statement that could easily have been penned by Welensky:

> I wish I could see more certainly how matters are going to develop and what men of good will should do next. What does seem clear to me is that a fair and lasting solution to these problems will not be possible until 'the imperial factor has been eliminated'.[130]

In his response to Oppenheimer's letter Welensky made explicit his belief that if Nyasaland was allowed to secede from the Federation it would be impossible to refuse Northern Rhodesia the right to do so too.[131]

South Africa and the Federation

The Rhodesian Front's victory in the Southern Rhodesian election of December 1962 further strengthened links between South Africa and the Southern Rhodesian government. Meanwhile Nyasaland rapidly moved through the gears towards independence – Butler announced its right to secede in December 1962 and Banda became Prime Minister in February 1963 – while Southern Rhodesia appeared to be coasting in neutral. By April Welensky was commenting how you 'seldom hear anyone say a good word for Great Britain. Of course, Macmillan's name is an anathema to everyone and Butler's is almost as bad. This country is now looking to South Africa and her Portuguese friends and frankly, I think this is now the only course'.[132]

Despite Welensky's growing sympathy towards South Africa, it was mentioned in a Southern Rhodesian cabinet meeting that the South Africans were 'alarmed at any possible coalition with the United [Federal] Party' that the RF was considering. Additionally, the South Africans believed that the new Southern Rhodesian Prime Minister, Winston Field, should announce on the day of any declaration of independence for the other Federal territories that his government 'would take appropriate action unless similar independence was granted to Southern Rhodesia'.[133] The link between the RF and NP was such that Field briefed Harold Taswell, South Africa's special emissary to Southern Rhodesia, on the points Welensky intended to raise in his visit to Henrick Verwoerd, the South African prime minister, during May, a visit that Welensky believed demonstrated that he had 'crossed the Rubicon' and underlined that Europeans in the Federation 'had to look to South Africa and the two Portuguese states for our friends'.[134] This was a complete volte-face from the conclusion of a Federal memorandum in 1958 which concluded that South Africa 'is becoming characterised as the "funk hole" of the white man in Africa. The destiny of the Federation is otherwise, as it must at once come to terms with the rising lake of a politically conscious black majority.'[135]

Field advised Taswell that Welensky would raise two main points: to what extent could South Africa assist Southern Rhodesia through its present spate of financial difficulties; and if Southern Rhodesia was legally unable to make a defence pact with South Africa, to what extent would South Africa nevertheless back them? This latter question was part of an ongoing debate within British circles about how useful Southern Rhodesia was to western defence. Field revealed his closeness to the South Africans, telling Taswell that 'Sir Roy is one hundred percent behind us in everything he does [...] I trust him. He is one of us.'[136]

Economically, Welensky intended to ask for a more favourable trade agreement with South Africa.[137] Taswell advised Field that it was not the right time for Rhodesia to approach South Africa for a new agreement as many South African businesses believed that the terms of the current agreement already weighed in favour of the Federation. Taswell informed his superiors in Pretoria: 'if Southern Rhodesia does ask for a revision of our agreement we should find ourselves in a much stronger bargaining position than when the last negotiations took place', due to the weakness of the Southern Rhodesian economy. Taswell further highlighted that 'present indications are that while the London money market has much sympathy for Southern Rhodesia it is not likely to pour funds into this part of the world'.[138] Welensky later viewed this visit to Verwoerd as 'an unqualified success'. He gave no indication that he was aware of Field's conversation with Taswell. On the whole he was reassured that South Africa had no plans to bring Southern Rhodesia formally into its political orbit, although he hoped 'economic and the other associations that are necessary in the years ahead will develop along harmonious lines'.[139]

Lord Alport, the federal high commissioner, believed that there was minimal danger that Southern Rhodesia would succeed in pursuing closer economic integration with South Africa. He was certain that any connection between the two territories would be severely limited as South Africa had no desire to increase its African population and many of Southern Rhodesia's secondary industries would be destroyed if opened up to unlimited competition. Furthermore, he reported that 'as a senior Southern Rhodesian civil servant told a member of my staff last week, thinking people here still regard Britain as Southern Rhodesia's best friend'.[140]

Evidence of military cooperation between the Federation and South Africa was used to attack the Federation throughout its remaining days. In March 1963, Ndabaningi Sithole, answering a question on the 'unholy alliance' between Southern Rhodesia and South Africa, alleged that South African troops had been seen operating across the border in Southern Rhodesia during recent disturbances there.[141] Furthermore, he alleged that Federal troops had received military training in the Republic.[142]

Dissolution

By the end of 1962 Welensky's continuing support for Federation was out-of-step with the majority of both African and settler opinion.

There were now African majority governments in both Northern Rhodesia and Nyasaland, and the Rhodesian Front had come to power in the Southern Rhodesian election of December 1962 campaigning on a platform of independence free from Federation.[143] To Macmillan, the main British objective now was to not to 'let ourselves be manoeuvred into a position in which it could be alleged that it is we who have destroyed the Federation. We must try to manage things in such a way that the Federation dissolves of its own accord, preferably as a result of the expressed wish of the two Rhodesias.'[144]

With all three territorial governments opposed to the continuation of the Federation, its fate was sealed and negotiations over its dissolution took centre stage. The South African ambassador quoted a senior official in the State Department who was acknowledging that there was 'muted optimism' regarding the possibility of a compromise by the 'four signatories to the last will and testament of the Federation'. State Department officials believed, however, that there were potential problems ahead. First they accused Field of showing a 'regrettable lack of statesmanship' by not insisting on a British concession of Southern Rhodesia's independence as a *sine qua non* for his participation in any future quadripartite talks. Butler, however, believed a peaceful transition relied on economics, a view apparently shared by the State Department. 40 per cent of Southern Rhodesia's exports went to Northern Rhodesia and Nyasaland, so these markets needed to remain open if Southern Rhodesia was to remain economically viable. It was reported that Banda 'has already made his peace with the Portuguese in the course of a two-day visit to Lisbon some two years ago'. Similarly, Kaunda was 'expected to have made the right noises in that direction also, either himself, or through the agency of Nkumbula, who "has been bought body and soul by the white entrepreneurs"'. Butler was thought to be 'jingling money bags' in Field's direction, offering to increase British participation in development schemes in Southern Rhodesia.[145]

Butler visited the Federation again in late January 1963, Welensky revealed that his previous battles with the British government had left him with 'no scruples about bringing things out in the open and standing up to them, and that in itself has been a tremendous weight off my own mind, because I've been fighting like a boxer with one hand tied behind his back. I feel much freer now'.[146] He was concerned, however, over the position Field would adopt, stating 'the trouble is I don't really know where he stands'. Although Field stated in public that he wished the Federation to continue, Welensky believed Butler would attempt to isolate him from the territorial governments. 'That will not be difficult in regard to Nyasaland and Northern Rhodesia', he believed 'but it should not have been as easy as it may prove to be in Southern Rhodesia'. Field's apparently close relationship with Hastings Banda also caused Welensky concern: 'I don't pretend to understand what Field is doing. He's released all the detainees, some of them that had been restricted for something like five years have all been freed.'[147]

Welensky was right to be concerned. When Butler met with the Southern Rhodesian cabinet, Field outlined his government's attitude towards the future of the Federation. Although Field recognised that the 'Federation had not worked' they did not intend 'to do anything which would contribute to the break-up of the Federation'. The secession of Nyasaland, however, 'posed the question as to whether it did not automatically break-up the Federation', while the introduction of a non-racial government in Northern Rhodesia would 'sooner or later lead to an African government'. Therefore, his party 'saw no durability in a continuing association of political character with Northern Rhodesia'.[148] Field highlighted the damage to Southern Rhodesia's economic and employment situation caused by the uncertainty over the Federation's future. Despite his earlier assertion that his government would not do anything to contribute to the break-up of the Federation, he added that:

> the realistic view in the existing circumstances was that the Federation was finished and that no political tie-up was possible for the future between the three Territories. He would be prepared to give these reasons in public, or in private, but speed of decision was vital to enable his Government to prepare and adopt effective plans for the problems which were ahead.[149]

Butler was worried that Welensky's preoccupation with keeping the Federal armed forces intact indicated that he would hold the Federation together by force. Field assured Butler that he had never received any such proposal from the Federal government, and if he did it would be rejected as 'the loyalty of Southern Rhodesians is to their own country first'. Despite this, Field indicated that Southern Rhodesia's political uncertainty was having a detrimental effect on its Europeans, and 'any tendency on the part of the farmers and persons who were needed within the country to emigrate from the Colony would have to be prevented and the only sure way to do so was to restore stability to the country'. Butler replied that he appreciated the difficulties facing Field, however 'Her Majesty's Government had a distinct feeling of responsibility for the Federation and they would hesitate about promoting any rapid destruction of the Federation.' Therefore he was unable to give Field a 'snap answer' but would have to consult with his Cabinet colleagues in London.[150]

Welensky believed that Butler was only concerned about 'making certain that the British taxpayer doesn't have to pay for anything and that I don't make too much trouble for him in the United Kingdom Parliament'. Field had told Welensky the previous day that although he would do nothing to prevent continued association between the two Rhodesias, he thought it would fail due to opposition from Kaunda. The best Welensky could hope for was a form of economic association, and Welensky reported that Field 'then made a plea for me to accept this as inevitable'.[151] During these discussions Field reported to his cabinet that he had found Welensky in a 'belligerent mood and the general impression which Sir Roy had given him was that he was toying with ideas of unconstitutional action designed to find out whether the Rhodesian public would be behind him in a decision to make a stand'. The Southern Rhodesian Cabinet believed the best course of action was to encourage Welensky to find a means of disengaging from the present difficulties to 'ease the transition towards a new form of association'.[152]

When Butler met with the Southern Rhodesian cabinet later that day he made clear his hope that a conference could be arranged between the respective governments before March, as the longer the time taken the further relations between the territories would deteriorate. He was worried that Welensky would refuse to cooperate and asked Field if he knew what 'Sir Roy's present attitude was and what plans he had to propose'. Field said he would prefer that Butler ask Welensky directly. He indicated, though, that Welensky's attitude had 'not improved recently and that he was smarting from what he claimed was the bad treatment he had received'.[153]

Butler left the Federation on 1 February 1963, the day of Hastings Banda's inauguration as prime minister, and promised that he would appoint a working party to consider the future association of the Rhodesias. The prospect of this association was not helped the following day when Kenneth Kaunda, Simon Kapwepwe and Reuben Kamanga flew into Salisbury on transfer to Lusaka. The three men were classified as Prohibited Immigrants in Southern Rhodesia, but Kaunda believed their positions as ministers of the Queen should entitle them to visit the city. Unfortunately the British South Africa Police did not take this view and Kaunda was not allowed to leave the airport. Instead, he attempted to sleep on a bench in front of the assembled press.[154] Despite this, the Federal government attempted to convince the Southern Rhodesian government to 'fall in behind' Welensky in his struggle with the British government to preserve a political association between Southern and Northern Rhodesia.

Welensky assumed that this association would give Southern Rhodesia 'breathing space' to consolidate its own independence. The Federal government believed that Kaunda was prepared to cooperate in such a venture, while the Southern Rhodesian cabinet believed that 'the Federal proposals amounted to nothing more than a last ditch stand' and emphasised the importance of Southern Rhodesia's independent position.[155] Mennen Williams, who met again with Welensky during February 1963, described the occasion as both 'tragic and historic'. Williams further remarked that he 'couldn't help but be reminded of the last gallant charge by the old bull leader of the herd. Sir Roy saw and served the light in his day but it is unfortunate that time has passed him by'.[156]

According to a British official in Washington, Williams returned from this visit to the Federation 'very despondent about the outlook for Southern Rhodesia'. He admitted that he had no solutions to place before the British and that 'he and the State Department hold strongly to the view that Central Africa is a British responsibility and that, on the strength of our record as responsible decolonisers, we can and will discharge our responsibility successfully'.[157] Oliver Bennett, the federal representative in Washington, found Williams on his return to Washington 'a changed man; courteous and cautious in his approach, thoughtful about the difficulties, and hesitant about proposing solutions to our problems'. Bennett also believed he detected a change in broader American attitudes: 'the Americans are having some doubts on the speed with which events have been moving in the Federation in the last year or two'.[158]

Following his return from Africa, Williams penned a report to the secretary of state in which he described Southern Rhodesia as a 'new African time bomb'. He believed that there would be a 'major flare-up' if African nationalist aspirations did not achieve some level of fruition. He thought Northern Rhodesia's future looked politically and economically secure although secession from the Federation was 'probable'. There was the likelihood of continued economic links with Southern Rhodesia, providing that the government there was 'not too white-supremacist'. Nyasaland was politically sound but it was looking for help from the United States and Britain with its 'considerable' budgetary deficit. 'Southern Rhodesia may wreck Britain's decolonization record and produce a white-black showdown', believed Williams. This confrontation might be delayed by weak African nationalist leadership in the territory, but 'Britain must move Southern Rhodesia to more equitable franchise prior to granting of independence'. He concluded that 'while Britain has recouped some of its reputation for responsible actions in its colonial areas of Africa, this gain will be seriously set back if the Southern Rhodesian situation deteriorates much further'.[159]

Securing a satisfactory solution for Southern Rhodesia was a priority for the United States. Their aims were spelt out in a report and took the form of four main objectives: maintain close contact with the British over the problem; make clear to the British 'US readiness to render appropriate support for any reasonable solution acceptable to the Africans'; enter dialogue with all parties in the territory; and prepare the United States for any contingencies which may arise.[160] When Butler met with the Southern Rhodesian cabinet later in the month he drew its attention to the pressure Britain was under from 'Americans in the persons of Mr Adlai Stevenson and Mr Mennen Williams' over its Southern Rhodesian policies.[161]

The final death knell for the Federation came in March 1963 with the British government's decision that no country should be kept in the Federation against its will. This cleared the way for Northern Rhodesia to follow Nyasaland's lead and secede from the Federation, leaving the organisation obsolete. Welensky, in a moment of self-reflection believed he was responsible for the Federation's demise: 'I am to blame because I allowed myself to accept the views of men like Macmillan and Butler and by now I should have learnt that these men just cannot be trusted.'[162] Following this development, Macmillan's policy now rested in ensuring that Southern Rhodesia attended the Federal dissolution conference. He informed Robert Menzies, prime minister of Australia, that it would be a 'difficult proposition' to push independence for Southern Rhodesia through the Commons. At the same time he estimated that there were 'perhaps over 200 [Conservative backbenchers] who feel that we should now immediately recognise Southern Rhodesia's right to become independent'. Macmillan believed this problem could be overcome:

> by some sort of formula whereby Southern Rhodesia agreed to attend a conference to discuss the winding-up of the Federation on the understanding that such a Conference would not go on to discuss the future of the territories concerned or the links between them. That would give us a bit of time.[163]

In early March 1963 Butler formally invited the four central African governments to attend preparatory talks for a conference on the future of the Federation in London. Following these discussions, Butler announced that Northern Rhodesia would be allowed to secede from the Federation on 29 March and by doing so hammered the last nail into the coffin of the Federation of Rhodesia and Nyasaland. From this point onwards both Welensky and Field concerned themselves with ensuring Southern Rhodesia's independence once the Federation ended. Welensky doubted that Field 'will now have the courage to throw down the gauntlet' to the British over the issue of Southern Rhodesian independence. Furthermore, Welensky believed Field was 'not a frightfully well man and he doesn't like tough methods'. Welensky was adamant that Southern Rhodesia should receive its independence:

> I supported this line of thought under Whitehead four years ago at a time when a British Minister warned me I was putting too much power in Whitehead's hands by supporting this line. I thought it right then, I think it right now, and I've not hesitated to make it clear, both to the British Government and to the public here, how necessary I think it is for Southern Rhodesia to get its independence.[164]

Field's only effective bargaining tool would have been to make his government's attendance at the Federal dissolution conference dependent on the assurance that independence would be granted on the Federation's dissolution. Yet Field failed to realise this, and as Welensky summarised 'knocked the ground out from under his own feet' when he agreed in early June to attend the conference.[165] The evening before the conference was due to begin Butler met with Field and Ian Smith, his deputy and treasury minister. Both Field and Smith left the meeting believing that if they attended the conference the following morning Southern Rhodesia's independence would be 'dealt with immediately and would present no difficulties'.[166] Butler denied ever making such a promise and, irrespective of the truth of the matter, this encounter seemed another example of perfidious Albion in action to many Rhodesians.[167]

The Victoria Falls conference on the dissolution of the Federation took place during July and finished early in August. All outstanding issues were settled, and it was agreed that the Federation would be formally dissolved at midnight on 1 January 1964. According to Welensky, Butler handled the discussions with 'consummate skill'. Welensky perceived that his own decision to agree to a speedy dissolution – provided the federal civil service officials were protected – 'knocked the props out from under some of the African leaders'.[168] To all intents and purposes this was a hollow victory for the Rhodesian settlers as Southern Rhodesia did not manage to secure its independence from Britain. Over the following year, the accusations of duplicity which flew from Salisbury to London, and the numerous failed attempts to broker an agreement set the ground for the RF's new leader, Ian Smith, to make a unilateral declaration of independence on 11 November 1965.

Welensky made a final visit to Washington as federal prime minister in October 1963, where he addressed the Washington Press Club. The South African ambassador reported that Welensky made clear he still believed in 'the principles upon which the "British Commonwealth" was founded [...] but he had nothing but contempt for the present British government'. Welensky refused to be drawn into a discussion on events in the wider African region, nor would he comment on how racial tensions in the United States may have affected its African policy. He, however, clearly stated his belief that in the Rhodesias racial integration was the 'only valid solution'. When discussing Nyasaland's poor economic prospects, the South African ambassador noted that 'his [Welensky's] *schadenfreude* was patent'. This may not have been helped by the fact that attendance at Welensky's Press Club briefing was 'regrettably sparse'. The South African ambassador speculated on three reasons for this: Welensky had already addressed the Overseas Press Club in New York; the Federation's imminent demise had led to Welensky being considered *passé*; and 'Africa no longer excites the imagination in quite the same way' in Washington circles.[169]

CONCLUSION

The Federation of Rhodesia and Nyasaland, like the Crusader
Kingdom of Jerusalem, now looks like an aberration of history – a
curious deviation from the inevitable course of events, a backward
eddy in the river of time.

Lord Blake's foreword to the Welensky Papers[1]

The Central African Federation's existence spanned a decade which saw a
major reassessment of Britain's domestic, international and colonial
policies. The debates and issues which arose over its future played
an important role in shaping these changes. Lord Blake's beguiling
remark notwithstanding, the Federation was far from an aberration of
history. Its formation in 1953 fitted comfortably into the post-World
War II restructuring of European colonial possessions and raised few
serious objections outside those of the territories' African populations.
Similarly, its dissolution only a mere ten years later also faced little
criticism outside of its few remaining supporters. While the Federation's
birth and adolescence were relatively benign, its adulthood and death
provided the British government with one of its most intractable
problems during the period of decolonization.

This book has provided a detailed study of the factors which came to
the fore in deciding the Federation's fate. It has advanced a multi-causal
explanation to account for the Federation's ultimate failure, that sits
comfortably with John Hargreaves' observation that the 'European
powers were compelled, by complex and increasingly strong pressures
from both inside and outside Africa, to terminate their various colonial

regimes under conditions not of their choosing'.[2] Similarly, John Darwin has remarked that explanations of decolonization that 'depend upon one great cause, or upon particular developments in British or colonial society, are fundamentally unsatisfactory'.[3] There were several intertwined pressures which were crucial in determining the Federation's fate: namely, increased political mobilisation of both Africans and Europeans within the Federation, the economic and political influence of the copper industry, and British domestic and international concerns, particularly in regard to the United Nations. The significance of these factors differed, both temporally and territorially over the period.

To Sir Roy Welensky's Federal Party, the signs augured well at the beginning of 1957 for the Federation's future. The territory had enjoyed three years of solid economic growth, following the postwar copper boom, and there was little reason to question that dominion status would be awarded when the Federation underwent review in 1960. Yet attempts by the Federal government to reinforce their hold on power, through the Constitutional Amendment Bill, gave African nationalism a central issue on which to campaign. The Bill demonstrated to many Africans that the central theme of the Federation's approach to race relations, partnership, was little more than a smokescreen designed to firmly entrench settler rule, and in doing so convinced many Africans that they had lost British protection. As Clyde Sanger noted in 1960, 'this may not have been a correct assessment of the situation by Africans, but they certainly believed it to be correct, and acted on it'.[4] In addition the removal of the perceived liberal Southern Rhodesian Prime Minister, Garfield Todd also appeared to give credence to this claim.

The utility of the term partnership was in its imprecision. The deliberate ambiguity had allowed partnership to appeal to Africans, settlers and the British government simultaneously. It is perhaps unsurprising, however, that as the 1950s progressed, all parties found that partnership fell far short of their expectations. No amount of linguistic flexibility could escape the fact that the majority of settlers in the Federation were unwilling to view Africans, even potentially, as their equals. Over this period the number of Africans who were unwilling to accept anything less than majority rule grew. This growing confidence was in part due to the success of many of their fellow colonial subjects on the continent in wresting full independence from their former colonial masters. Consequently the whole concept of racial partnership became obsolete soon after its implementation in central Africa.

A key theme drawn out in this book is the increased effectiveness and mobilisation of African nationalist groups. In an attempt to decapitate organised African protest before the pending federal review, emergencies were declared in Southern Rhodesia and Nyasaland, during March 1959. Similarly the decision was taken in Northern Rhodesia to ban the Zambian African National Congress. Instead of the settlers' anticipated outcome, the emergencies acted as an accelerant which fuelled African nationalism. This was particularly the case in Nyasaland. The British government initially supported Sir Robert Armitage's decision to introduce emergency rule, however, the death of 51 Africans led to calls for an independent enquiry into events. African witness statements to the Devlin Commission revealed a commonly held fear that partnership was only a temporary forerunner to the introduction of apartheid by the Federal government. Dr Hastings Banda's evidence to the commission built on this with his impression that the sight of Southern Rhodesian troops operating in the territory signalled to Nyasalanders that the Southern Rhodesian settlers wished to take their land. In addition, Banda asserted that African nationalist tactics in Nyasaland were based on the Indian model of peaceful non-cooperation. Banda's sincerity on this issue could be questioned; however, his remark indicated the significance of the further internationalisation of anti-colonial protest during this period.

The Devlin Commission's report concluded that there was no evidence to support the justification for the state of emergency, nor that there had been a planned murder plot against the territory's European population. Most damningly it declared that the territory had been, albeit temporarily, a police state. This seriously damaged the Federation's image both in Britain and the wider world. Events in Kenya earlier that decade had demonstrated there was little, if any, will in the British government or general public to uphold a perceived privileged lifestyle of a small minority of their kith and kin in Africa. Events in Nyasaland were readily linked to the death of Mau Mau detainees at Hola camp and the worsening situation in South Africa. This ensured that the Federal review in 1960 could not simply hand over British responsibilities to the Federal government.[5] As Welensky later recognised, by the late 1950s colonialism had become a 'dirty word' in

Britain and the anachronistic idea of advancing Africans gradually towards majority-rule under the steady hand of benevolent white leadership was practically indefensible.[6] In response to their British kith and kin's apparent abandonment, and the rising effectiveness of African political organisation, many settlers' political ideology moved towards the right. This shift in political thought left Welensky progressively more isolated, and eventually led to the Rhodesian Front's success in the 1962 Southern Rhodesian territorial election.

After Godfrey Huggins retired as Federal prime minister the Federation became increasingly identified with the personality of Welensky. This was, in part, due to a dearth of effective international politicians within the Federation's settler community which was barely larger than the population of Brighton. Welensky's imposing frame and willingness to share his opinions candidly, both in private and public also contributed to this impression. As pressure built on the Federation, Welensky was forced to pursue a course which was too reactionary for most Africans, yet far too progressive for the majority of Europeans. This book provides a fresh interpretation of Sir Roy Welensky's role in central Africa. He is too easily caricatured as a reactionary white leader whose only concern was to ensure the continuation of white domination in Africa. It is suggested here that if Welensky himself recognised that the Federation did have to move further towards implementing partnership, his white electorate refused to accept this course.

This refusal by the Federation's white electorate to accept significant change in regard to race relations is crucial towards developing a full understanding of settler *mentalities* in this period. The UFP found itself increasingly out-of-step with European public opinion in the Federation, as their 'middle way' policies looked increasingly outdated. By 1962 they were unable to attract significant African support to replace its European base, which was drifting towards the Rhodesian Front. Therefore, Philip Murphy's argument that the UFP were 'unwilling' to implement limited advances required by the British and African nationalists should be qualified – rather than being unwilling, the UFP were unable.[7]

Sir Edgar Whitehead attempted, albeit unsuccessfully, to appease both Africans and Europeans in Southern Rhodesia. Whitehead proposed reform of the Land Apportionment Act to pacify African protest and simultaneously attempted to reassure Europeans with tougher legislation to control African protest, as evidenced by the Law and Order (Maintenance) Bill. Any concessions to Africans, however, infuriated Europeans, while any attempt to reassure Europeans further alienated Africans. In this volatile climate it was perhaps unsurprising that any attempt at compromise was rejected by both sides. By 1962 the Federal economy had slowed considerably, white immigration was falling, and white unemployment was becoming a problem for the first time since the 1930s. It is within this milieu that the Rhodesian Front (RF) formed from the amalgamation of several smaller Southern Rhodesian settler nationalist parties in March 1962, subsequently campaigning on a policy of independence for Southern Rhodesia.[8] The influence of elections, commissions, constitutional negotiations and referenda were therefore key in dictating the UFP's actions. During this period they had to contest two federal and three territorial elections, host both the Devlin and Monckton Commissions, and also take part in constitutional reviews in all three territories. The Monckton Commission's lukewarm assessment of the Federation's future pulled the rug out from under the Federal government in its ongoing negotiations with Britain.

The question remains as to whether there was a clear link between the Federation's economic performance and its political success. Although it is too crude an explanation to locate the Federation's failure with its economic fortunes, this book has argued that the sharp fall in copper prices on the world market significantly shaped the events that followed. It brutally exposed the Federation's over-reliance on a single commodity, and made it difficult, if not impossible, economically for the settlers to attempt to address African concerns. A further result of African political unrest was that it lowered the confidence of many settlers and external investors in the Federation's economic prospects. This led to capital flight from the Federation and reluctance from overseas capital to invest in the area.

A related issue concerns the role of big business at the end of empire. Nicholas White has previously argued that Malaya saw the loosening of ties between big business and government during the period of decolonization.[9] Unlike White's conclusion, in the Federation, however, the role of multinational business was more ambiguous. A key difference which separates multinational business in the Federation from White's work on Malaya and Sarah Stockwell's study of the Gold Coast was the strength of indigenous white nationalism.[10] Therefore, business did not just have the option of supporting the colonial government or aspirant nationalist movements. The initial confidence with which the Federal government conducted negotiations with the Anglo American Corporation and the Rhodesian Selection Trust (RST) over Kariba in 1955, demonstrated the confidence with which the settlers viewed their position before the fall in the price of copper. RST's liberal attitude towards African advancement was driven by the company's wish to secure cheaper competition for the copper industry's overpaid European workers, rather than for any altruistic reasons. Furthermore, it is clear that contrary to the existing historiography Anglo American and RST's company policies diverged after 1959. Anglo continued to provide support, albeit secretly to the UFP, while RST attempted to forge contacts with aspirant African nationalist leaders.

The role and influence of Harold Hochschild, the chairman of RST's parent company, the American Metal Climax Company (AMAX), was an important factor. This book has contended that Larry Butler's work on RST's chairman, Sir Ronald Prain, significantly overestimates the degree of autonomy he enjoyed when shaping his company's actions on the Copperbelt.[11] Instead, it suggests that Hochschild's influence was far greater on the policies than Butler credits. Hochschild's involvement with liberal organisations in the United States, as well as the close connections to the United States' State Department enjoyed by his political advisor, Taylor Ostrander, enabled Hochschild to independently assess and direct RST policy.

In contrast, Anglo American's chairman, Harry Oppenheimer, and several of the company's directors enjoyed close personal relationships with Welensky. This enabled the Federal Prime Minister to call upon these contacts to assist his party, both in Africa and Britain. The British South Africa Company, perhaps unsurprisingly due to the tenuous legality of its mineral claims, enjoyed a similar relationship with the Federal government. A further reason for Anglo's continued support was the ambiguous nature of the company's relationship with the apartheid regime in South Africa. The company was viewed with suspicion by many in the National Party and any pro-African approach adopted by Anglo could have damaged its ability to conduct its primary business in

South Africa. Oppenheimer appears to have believed in the ideal of partnership and hoped that its successful implementation in the Federation would provide a model that South Africa could one day follow. It is clear that the geographical location of the two mining companies shaped the policies they pursued. RST's American ownership ensured it was free of Anglo's regional ties, and it was this that allowed the former to follow a more pragmatic course.

The introduction to this book also raised the question of how Britain's domestic and international priorities affected the Federation. British public opinion conformed closely to Andrew Thompson's broad conclusion on the negligible influence of empire between 1959 and 1964, in that the British public were generally apathetic to the central African settlers' plight.[12] Welensky, however, failed to grasp this, and continued to place his faith in the support of the British public. The Macmillan government's support for the Federation in 1957 gradually rescinded, as its own electoral prospects took precedence. This supports John Darwin's observation that the British government saw its 'imperial' interests as distinct from the local interests of its settlers in central Africa.[13] Following the Conservative Party's re-election in 1959, Macmillan's own indifference to Britain's remaining colonial possessions and his wish for a closer association with Europe, combined with international opposition to colonialism, enabled his government to pursue a more flexible approach in central Africa.

In the two northern territories, Macmillan's flexible approach resulted in a rapid advance to independence under majority rule, in spite of Welensky's vocal protestations. Southern Rhodesia presented a more complex problem. The colony possessed a highly organised white settler community which had enjoyed de facto independence since 1923. The British government's approach to the Southern Rhodesian question was one of procrastination. It had been feasible to consider granting independence to the Southern Rhodesian settlers in the early 1950s, yet by the early 1960s it was virtually impossible. Similarly, Britain was in no position to force the settlers to accept majority rule. Therefore, the only realistic success for the British government was to ensure discussions between the African nationalists and settlers did not breakdown. This way Macmillan could avoid making a decision which would have little, if any, chance of achieving an orderly and peaceful resolution to the issue.

Macmillan's decision to appoint Iain Macleod as colonial secretary, to replace Alan Lennox-Boyd after the 1959 election, is often credited with accelerating the decolonization process. Yet in the central African context Macleod was primarily used as a lightning rod to channel criticism from the right of the Conservative party. Welensky attempted to influence opinion in Britain through the employment of the London public relations firm Voice and Vision and his contacts in the Conservative party. In the House of Commons, he could rely on the support of several backbenchers, the most prominent being Patrick Wall and Robin Turton, while Lord Salisbury offered the most vociferous criticism of the government's colonial policy in the House of Lords. As Philip Murphy has noted, for the pro-Federal supporters in Parliament 'a simple loyalty towards Welensky became a substitute for the coherent alternative vision in British policy in Africa which they had always lacked'.[14]

This support reached its zenith in February 1961 with Robin Turton's Early Day Motion, which expressed reservations over the government's constitutional proposals for Northern Rhodesia. This was the closest the central African settlers came to engineering a victory in the Commons. Although the government managed to prevent a rebellion, it clearly demonstrated that there was disquiet within the Conservative party over Macmillan's handling of the white settler communities in east and central Africa. Lord Salisbury's oft quoted attack in the Lords on Macleod, in which he labelled the colonial secretary 'too clever by half' emphasised this unease. Soon after, the settlers obtained a pyrrhic victory when Macleod was replaced by Reginald Maudling. The new colonial secretary, however, pursued a far more radical approach than Macleod towards the Northern Rhodesian constitution. Welensky later judged that the most effective British Minister involved during the final years of the Federation was R. A. Butler. Unlike Macleod or Maudling, Butler enjoyed wide appeal across all sides of the Conservative party and therefore found it easier to return backbench support for government policies after his appointment as minister of state for Central Africa.

In a general study of decolonization, Larry Butler noted that 'Britain's disengagement from empire cannot be comprehended unless proper consideration is given to wider developments in international politics, and particularly to the Cold War context in which it unfolded'.[15]

The argument advanced here supports Butler's statement and it has repeatedly stressed the importance of international factors on the Federation's fate. In doing so it reinforces elements of Ronald Hyam's claim that 'the international dimension was the most important of all'.[16] The final years of the Federation were not simply shaped in a bipolar process between metropole and periphery, however, events in Britain and the Federation were themselves crucial in formulating international opinion.

Regionally, the biggest influence on the Federation was its southern neighbour, South Africa. Suspicion, if not hostility, initially characterised the view of the two countries' settler populations. By the early 1960s, however, their relationship improved as they both found their policies under attack in the world community. This developing relationship allowed the Federal government to source military equipment, personnel and information from its southern neighbour and they offered information on African nationalist activities in return. It was equally important for the Federal government, however, to distance their policy of partnership from the South African practice of apartheid. This they struggled to do, as their attempts to stifle African protest though the introduction of more draconian legislation only exacerbated the criticism they received.

As R. A. Butler's observation to the Southern Rhodesian cabinet in 1962 revealed, the British government found representing the territory in the United Nations 'a difficult, tedious and unwanted task'.[17] This illustrates that the United Nations played a far more important role in determining the fate of the Federation than the Commonwealth. In part this was due to the changing nature of the Commonwealth in the postwar period. The very nature of Commonwealth membership had changed dramatically since World War II as newly independent colonies swelled its ranks. Consequently, it was increasingly difficult for the organisation to speak with one voice. Welensky understood that Macmillan's decision to apply for membership of the European Economic Community underscored the declining importance of the Federation for Britain.[18] Similarly, both Canada and Australia sought to cement their own bilateral relationships with the United States in this period. Following South Africa's decision to leave the Commonwealth in 1961, Welensky believed that only New Zealand, of the old Commonwealth members, retained any faith in the organisation.

As John Darwin has previously highlighted, the United Nations provided a forum in which the two Cold War blocs could compete for the allegiance of the Third World Nations.[19] Events in the Federation, particularly in Southern Rhodesia, were used in this wider debate. Resolution 1514 (IX), passed in 1960, and the formation of the Committee of Seventeen during 1961 clearly underlined the UN's commitment to advancing the world's remaining colonial territories towards independence. These developments allowed African nationalists in the Federation to effectively exploit the arena to raise world awareness of their plight. The United Nations not only provided a forum for debate, it also exerted influence through its actions in the breakaway Congolese state of Katanga. The sight of a United Nations army militarily engaged against a pro-western, anti-communist African president, Moise Tshombe, just across the border from Northern Rhodesia, infuriated Welensky. At the same time, the steady stream of European refugees entering the Federation with horrific stories of their treatment at the hands of Congolese and UN soldiers further exacerbated unease within the settler community. Meanwhile, many Africans in the Federation were emboldened by the sight of UN troops across the border, and this may have encouraged further use of the General Assembly as a forum for debate. Criticism reached fever pitch after the death of the UN Secretary General, Dag Hammarskjöld in an aeroplane crash in Northern Rhodesia during 1961. This led to the accusation that he had been killed by the Federal government, and brought additional criticism aimed at the central African settlers.

The role of the United States has also been discussed, both in relation to its role in the United Nations, and in its role as Britain's closest ally. The State Department attempted to foster greater liberalism without possessing the means to directly influence the situation. This study has further contended that both the Eisenhower and Kennedy administrations pursued policies designed to influence Britain and the Federal government to follow a more progressive line in Africa. The region was important to the United States in the context of the Cold War and with regard to American investment, particularly RST, in the region. Kennedy's Assistant Secretary of State for African Affairs, G. Mennen Williams clearly placed his hopes for Southern Rhodesia on Sir Edgar Whitehead securing victory in the 1962 territorial election. He significantly misjudged the mood of the majority of Europeans in the Federation, however, who were prepared to oppose any party which offered any meaningful concessions for Africans.

Settler claims for greater independence from Britain could not be settled due to the political realities of international relations at the end of the 1950s.[20] Britain could not be seen to concede independence to a white minority government in Africa, yet there were few, if any, benefits from allowing the Federation to drift along indefinitely. In the case of Northern Rhodesia and Nyasaland, by the early 1960s both British and African nationalist interests converged, and it became relatively easy to advance the two countries towards independence under majority rule. Few settler tears would have been shed in Salisbury at the prospect of Nyasaland leaving the Federation, had it not been for the worrying precedent it could set for Northern Rhodesia. This fear was proven true suggesting that Robert Holland is right to assert that Macmillan correctly calculated that 'while Southern Rhodesian whites might risk all to protect their homes, they were not likely to do so for the sake of their Northern Rhodesian cousins', and therefore the territory could follow Nyasaland towards majority rule.[21] Southern Rhodesia provided a more complex problem for Britain. Here, Whitehall's policy was generally more reactive than proactive and there was precious little, if any, chance of reconciling the competing claims of African and settler nationalism.

This conclusion corresponds with Ronald Hyam's point that the 'liquidation [of empire] was not a one-way process, neither solely driven by metropolitan policy and planning, nor by anti-colonial nationalist demand. The two elements needed to come into effective conjunction of interest'.[22] The settlers in the northern territories were too weak to stop, or even stall for very long, this process which was similar to other British territories in east and central Africa. On the other hand, Southern Rhodesia's settlers, although not strong enough to force through their own independence, could easily frustrate British and African moves towards greater African political rights. Therefore, during the period of Federation there was no clear locus of power in Southern Rhodesia; this would change following the settlers' successful UDI in November 1965.

The end of the Central African Federation is best explained by several intertwined pressures, of which increasing economic weakness in the face of the falling price of copper and international pressures proved decisive. This is not to say that British policy was dictated by the dour, anti-colonial rhetoric which poured forth in the committee rooms of the United Nations. Rather, it was the effect of this condemnation in the Federation itself which proved crucial. It helped foster both African protest and a sense of siege within the European community. This led to increased clashes between the two racial groups. Consequently, the relationship between local events and international criticism was cyclical and ultimately self-reaffirming. Britain had little, if any, interest in upholding a political system which eventually had precious few African or European supporters.

NOTES

Introduction

1. [W]elensky [P]apers 647/5, Welensky to Millin, 12 March 1963. File references are to Rhodes House Library, Oxford.
2. The term was first coined by D. A. Low and J. Lonsdale in 'Introduction: towards the new order, 1945–1963', in D. A. Low and Alison Smith (eds), *History of East Africa, Volume III* (Oxford: Clarendon Press, 1976), pp. 1–63.
3. See R. M. Creighton, *The Anatomy of Partnership: Southern Rhodesia and the Central African Federation* (Faber and Faber: London, 1960); C. Dunn, *Central African Witness* (London: Victor Gollancz Ltd., 1959); P. Keatley, *The Politics of Partnership: The Federation of Rhodesia and Nyasaland* (London: Penguin, 1963); P. Mason, *Year of Decision, Rhodesia and Nyasaland in 1960* (London: Oxford University Press, 1960); and W. M. Macmillan, *The Road to Self-Rule: A Study in Colonial Evolution* (London; Faber & Faber, 1959).
4. For the British perspective see H. Macmillan, *Pointing the Way* (London: Macmillan, 1972) and *At The End of the Day* (London: Macmillan, 1973); R. A. Butler, *The Art of the Possible* (London: Hamish Hamilton, 1971) and C. Alport, *The Sudden Assignment* (London: Hodder & Stoughton, 1965). The Federal stance is sketched out in R. Welensky, *4000 Days* (London: Collins, 1964) and J. Greenfield, *Testimony of a Rhodesian Federal* (Bulawayo: Books of Rhodesia, 1978). Similarly, an African nationalist interpretation of events can be found in K. Kaunda, *Zambia Shall Be Free* (London: Heinemann, 1962).
5. See J. Barber, *Rhodesia: The Road to Rebellion* (London: Oxford University Press, 1967); M. Perham, 'The Rhodesian crisis: the background', *International Affairs* 42/1 (Jan., 1966), pp. 1–13; R. C. Good, *UDI: The International Politics of the Rhodesian Rebellion* (London: Faber & Faber, 1973); and L. Bowman, *Politics in Rhodesia* (Cambridge, MA: Harvard University Press, 1973).
6. See J. G. Pike, *Malawi, A Political and Economic History* (London: F. A. Praegar, 1968); T. O. Ranger, 'African politics in twentieth-century Southern

Rhodesia', in T. O. Ranger (ed.), *Aspects of Central African History* (London: Heinemann, 1968); and A. Roberts, *A History of Zambia* (New York: Holmes and Meier Publishers Inc, 1976).

7. See J. Darwin, *Britain and Decolonisation, The Retreat from Empire in the Post-War World* (Basingstoke: Palgrave Macmillan, 1988); J. Hargreaves, *Decolonization in Africa* (London: Routledge, 1996) and R. F. Holland, *European Decolonization, 1918–1981* (London: Macmillan, 1985).

8. See for example L. J. Butler, *Britain and Empire: Adjusting to a Post-Imperial World* (London: I.B.Tauris, 2002); R. Hyam, *Britain's Declining Empire: The Road to Decolonisation 1918–1968* (Cambridge: Cambridge University Press, 2006); and S. Stockwell, 'Ends of empire', *The British Empire: Themes and Perspectives* (Oxford: Blackwell, 2008), pp. 269–94.

9. J. R. T. Wood, *The Welensky Papers* (Durban: Graham Publishing, 1983).

10. P. Murphy, *British Documents on the End of Empire, Vol. 9: Central Africa, Part I, Closer Association, 1945–1958* (London: Stationary Office, 2005) and *British Documents on the End of Empire, Vol. 9: Central Africa, Part II, Crisis and Dissolution, 1959–1965* (London: Stationary Office, 2005).

11. J. R. T. Wood, *So Far and No Further! Rhodesia's Bid for Independence During the Retreat from Empire 1959–1965* (Johannesburg: 30 Degrees South, 2005).

12. See for example J. Brownell: *Collapse of Rhodesia: Population Demographics and the Politics of Race* (London: I.B.Tauris, 2010); L. Butler 'Business and decolonisation: Sir Ronald Prain, the mining industry and the Central African Federation', *The Journal of Imperial and Commonwealth History* 35/3 (2007), pp. 459–84; A. Cohen, 'Business and decolonisation in Central Africa reconsidered, *The Journal of Imperial and Commonwealth History* 36/4 (2008), pp. 641–58; A. Cohen, '"Voice and Vision" – The Federation of Rhodesia and Nyasaland's public relations campaign in Britain: 1960–1963', *Historia* 54/2 (2009), pp. 113–32; A. Cohen, '"A difficult tedious and unwanted task": representing the Central African Federation in the United Nations, 1960–1963', *Itinerario* 34/2 (2010), pp. 105–28; K. Law, *Gendering the Settler State: White Women, Race, Liberalism and Empire in Rhodesia, 1950–1980* (London: Routledge, 2016); J. E. Lewis '"White man in a wood pile": race and the limits of Macmillan's great "wind of change" in Africa', in L. J. Butler and S. Stockwell (eds), *The Wind of Change: Harold Macmillan and British Decolonization* (London: Palgrave Macmillan, 2013), pp. 70–95; G. Macola, *Liberal Nationalism in Central Africa: A Biography of Harry Mwaanga Nkumbula* (London: Palgrave Macmillan, 2010); P. Murphy, 'Acceptable levels? the use and threat of violence in Central Africa, 1953–64', in M. B. Jerónimo and A. C. Pinto (eds), *The Ends of European Colonial Empires: Cases and Comparisons* (London: Palgrave Macmillan, 2015); I. Phimister, 'Corporate profit and race in central African copper mining, 1946–1958', *Business History Review* 85/4 (2011), pp. 749–74 and C. Watts, *Rhodesia's Unilateral Declaration of Independence: An International History* (London: Palgrave Macmillan, 2012).

13. J. Tischler, *Light and Power for a Multiracial Nation: The Kariba Dam Scheme in the Central African Federation* (London: Palgrave Macmillan, 2012).

14. J. Parker, *Brother's Keeper: The United States, Race and Empire in the British Caribbean, 1927–1962* (Oxford: Oxford University Press, 2008).

15. M. Collins, 'Decolonisation and the "Federal moment"', *Diplomacy and Statecraft* 24/1 (2013), pp. 21–40.

16. Creighton: *Anatomy*, p. 38; J. Darwin, 'British decolonization since 1945: a pattern or a puzzle?', *The Journal of Imperial and Commonwealth History* 12/2 (1984), p. 200; J. Gallagher, *The Decline, Revival and Fall of the British Empire* (Cambridge: Cambridge University Press, 1982), p. 149; R. Hyam, 'The geopolitical origins of the Central African Federation: Britain, Rhodesia and South Africa, 1948–1953, *The Historical Journal* 30/1(1987), p. 172 and C. Leys and C. Pratt, *A New Deal in Central Africa* (London: Heinemann, 1960), p. 50.

17. Hyam: 'Geopolitical origins', p. 169.

18. Bowman, *Rhodesia,* p. 18; and Murphy, *Closer Association*, p. xliv.

19. P. Murphy, '"Government by blackmail": the origins of the Central African Federation reconsidered', in M. Lynn (ed.), *The British Empire in the 1950s* (Basingstoke: Palgrave Macmillan, 2006), p. 73.

20. Darwin: *Britain and Decolonisation*, p. 195; T. M. Franck, *Race and Nationalism: The Struggle for Power in Rhodesia-Nyasaland,* (London: Allen & Unwin, 1960), p. 35; Good, *UDI*, p. 35.

21. B. V. Mtshali, *Rhodesia: Background to Conflict* (London: Hawthorn, 1968), p. 95.

22. Bowman: *Rhodesia*, p. 19; Roberts: *Zambia*, p. 207; and R. Rotberg, *The Rise of Nationalism in Central Africa: The Making of Malawi and Zambia 1873–1964* (Cambridge, MA: Harvard University Press, 1966), p. 220.

23. Bowman: *Rhodesia*, p. 18; and Keatley, *Politics of Partnership*, p. 424.

24. R. F. Holland, 'The imperial factor in British strategies from Attlee to Macmillan, 1945–63', *The Journal of Imperial and Commonwealth History* 12/2 (1984), p. 175.

25. Barber: *Rhodesia*, p. 27.

26. L. Butler, 'Britain, the United States, and the demise of the Central African Federation, 1959–1963', *Journal of Imperial and Commonwealth History* 28/3 (2000), pp. 131–51.

27. A. J. Hanna, *European Rule in Africa* (London: Routledge, 1961), p. 30.

28. Darwin, *Decolonisation*, p. 194.

29. P. Gifford, 'Misconceived dominion: the creation and disintegration of the Federation of British Central Africa', in P. Gifford and W. R. Louis (eds), *Transfer of Power in Africa: Decolonisation, 1940–1960* (New Haven, CT: Yale University Press, 1982), p. 396.

30. Ibid., p. 395.

31. Rotberg, *Nationalism*, p. 220.

32. E. Clegg, *Race and Politics, Partnership in the Federation of Rhodesia and Nyasaland* (London: Praeger, 1960), p. 176 and M. Perham: 'The Rhodesian crisis': the background', *International Affairs*, 42/1 (1966), p. 6.

33. Pike, *Malawi*, p. 112.
34. Ranger, 'African politics', p. 237.
35. Roberts, *Zambia*, pp. 208–11.
36. Ibid., p. 211.
37. Clegg, *Race*, pp. 188–9.
38. H. Franklin, *Unholy Wedlock: The Failure of the Central African Federation* (London: Allen & Unwin, 1963), p. 83; G. Jones, *Britain and Nyasaland* (London: Allen & Unwin, 1964), p. 187; J. McCracken, 'African politics in twentieth-century Malawi', in T. O. Ranger (ed.), *Aspects of Central African History* (London: Heinemann, 1968), p. 204; and Pike, *Malawi*, pp. 121–2.
39. See for example G. Macola's re-interpretation of the role played by the ANC in Northern Rhodesia during the final years of Federation, in *Liberal Nationalism*.
40. Gifford, 'Misconceived dominion', p. 395.
41. Leys and Pratt, *New Deal*, p. 51.
42. Creighton, *Anatomy*, pp. 39–40.
43. A. King, 'Identity and decolonisation: the policy of partnership in Southern Rhodesia, 1945–1962' (unpublished Oxford D. Phil thesis, 2001).
44. Ibid., p. 24.
45. S. Marks, 'Southern Africa', in J. Brown and W. M. Roger Louis (eds), *The Oxford History of the British Empire*, Vol. IV (Oxford: Oxford University Press, 1999), p. 569.
46. Bowman, *Rhodesia*, p. 18.
47. Leys and Pratt, *New Deal*, p. 48.
48. Holland, 'Imperial factor', p. 176.
49. Darwin, *Decolonisation*, p. 138.
50. Darwin, 'Pattern or a puzzle?', p. 200; and Mason, *Decision*, p. 237.
51. A. J. Willis, *An Introduction to the History of Central Africa: Zambia, Malawi and Zimbabwe* (Oxford: Oxford University Press, 1985), p. 322.
52. P. Murphy, *Party Politics and Decolonization: The Conservative Government and British Colonial Policy in Tropical Africa, 1951–1964* (Oxford: Oxford University Press, 1999), pp. 59–60.
53. A. Hazelwood, 'The economics of federation and dissolution in central Africa', in A. Hazelwood (ed.), *African Integration and Disintegration: Case Studies in Economic and Political Union* (London: Oxford University Press, 1967), pp. 188–95; D. S. Pearson and W. L. Taylor, *Break Up: Some Economic Consequences for the Rhodesias and Nyasaland* (Salisbury: Phoenix Group), 1963, p. 4.
54. Gifford, 'Misconceived dominion', pp. 401–402.
55. D. Birmingham and T. O. Ranger, 'Settlers and liberators in the south', in D. Birmingham and T. O. Ranger (eds), *History of Central Africa, Vol. 2* (London: Heinemann, 1983), pp. 363–4.
56. Leys and Pratt, *New Deal*, p. 81.
57. Franklin, *Unholy Wedlock*, p. 121.

58. R. Hyam and P. Henshaw, *The Lion and the Springbok: Britain and South Africa Since the Boer War* (Cambridge: Cambridge University Press, 2003), p. 223.

59. See for example the West Indies Federation which existed from 1958–1962. A concise examination is given in S. R. Ashton and D. Killingray, *British Documents on the End of Empire, Series B, Volume 6, The West Indies* (London: Stationery Office, 1999), pp. xxxvii–lxxxi.

60. J. Darwin, 'Was there a fourth British Empire?', in M. Lynn (ed.), *The British Empire in the 1950s* (Basingstoke: Palgrave Macmillan, 2006), p. 29 and Holland, 'The imperial factor', pp. 174–5.

61. Gifford, 'Misconceived dominion', p. 395.

62. Barber, *Rhodesia*, p. 13 and Leys and Pratt, *New Deal*, pp. 49–50.

63. Murphy, *Closer Association*, pp. xxxv–xxxvi.

64. E. L. Berger, *Labour, Race and Colonial Rule, The Copperbelt from 1924 to Independence* (Oxford: Oxford University Press, 1974), p. 9.

65. Barber, *Rhodesia*, p. 12; B. Raftopolous, 'Nationalism and labour in Salisbury 1953–1965', in *Journal of South African Studies* 21/1, (1995), p. 92.

66. Willis, *Central Africa*, p. 327.

67. Ibid.

68. R. Blake, *A History of Rhodesia* (London: Methuen, 1977), p. 285.

69. Franklin, *Unholy Wedlock*, p. 109.

70. Roberts, *Zambia*, p. 213.

71. Jones, *Britain and Nyasaland*, p. 161.

72. Tischler, *Light and Power*, p. 29.

73. Gifford, 'Misconceived dominion', pp. 401–2; and Holland, 'Imperial factor', p. 176.

74. Creighton, *Anatomy*, p. 65.

75. Bowman, *Rhodesia*, p. 26; Creighton, *Anatomy*, p. 65 and Leys and Pratt, *New Deal*, p. 117.

76. Gifford, 'Misconceived dominion', pp. 403–5.

77. Roberts, 'Zambia', p. 184.

78. Birmingham and Ranger, 'Settlers and liberators', p. 368; J. Darwin, 'The Central African Emergency, 1959', in *The Journal of Imperial and Commonwealth History* 21/3 (1993), p. 218; Mtshali, *Rhodesia*, p. 106 and Trevor Royle, *Winds of Change, The End of the Adventure in Africa* (London: John Murray, 1996), p. 230.

79. Barber, *Rhodesia*, p. 18.

80. Jones, *Britain*, p. 247.

81. Marks, 'Southern Africa', p. 570; Butler, 'Britain, the United States', p. 132.

82. Willis, *Central Africa*, p. 341.

83. Barber, *Rhodesia*, pp. 35–9.

84. Mtshali, *Rhodesia*, p. 108.

85. Ibid., and A. Verrier, *The Road to Zimbabwe, 1890–1980* (London: Jonathan Cape, 1986), p. 77.

86. Bowman, *Rhodesia*, p. 39.
87. Hazelwood, 'Economics of Federation', p. 227.
88. Ibid., p. 249.
89. Darwin, *Decolonisation*, pp. 273–4.
90. P. E. Hemming, 'Macmillan and the end of the British Empire in Africa', in R. Aldous and S. Lee (eds), *Harold Macmillan and Britain's World Role* (London: Palgrave Macmillan, 1996), p. 101.
91. D. Goldsworthy, *Colonial Issues in British Politics, 1945–1961* (Oxford: Oxford University Press, 1971), p. 361.
92. Franklin, *Unholy Wedlock*, p. 147 and Goldsworthy, *Colonial Issues*, p. 362.
93. R. Holland, *The Pursuit of Greatness: Britain and the World Role, 1900–1970* (London: Routledge, 1991), p. 298.
94. R. Blake, *The Decline of Power 1915–1964* (London: Faber, 1986), p. 392.
95. Ibid., p. 397.
96. S. J. Ball, 'Banquo's ghost: Lord Salisbury, Harold Macmillan, and the high politics of decolonization, 1957–1963', *Twentieth Century British History* 16/1 (2005); Goldsworthy, *Colonial Issues* and Murphy, *Party Politics*.
97. Ball, 'Banquo's ghost', p. 95.
98. D. Leonard, *A Century of Premiers: Salisbury to Blair* (London: Palgrave Scholar, 2005), p. 222.
99. R. Aldous and S. Lee, '"Staying in the game": Harold Macmillan and Britain's world role', in R. Aldous and S. Lee (eds), *Harold Macmillan and Britain's World Role* (Basingstoke: Palgrave Macmillan, 1996), p. 152.
100. Ibid., p. 153.
101. Verrier, *Zimbabwe*, p. 75.
102. FO 371/137972, no. 26, Record of US/UK talks on the future of Africa, 23 November 1959, cited in J. Kent, 'The United States and the decolonization of Black Africa, 1945–1963', in D. Ryan and V. Pungong (eds), *The United States and Decolonization* (London: Palgrave Macmillan, 2000), p. 178.
103. Darwin, *Decolonisation*, p. 248; R. Ovendale, 'Macmillan and the wind of change in Africa, 1957–1960', *The Historical Journal* 38/2 (1995), p. 477.
104. Ovendale, 'Macmillan', p. 477.
105. A. James, 'Britain, the cold war and the Congo crisis', *The Journal of Imperial and Commonwealth History* 28/3 (2000), p. 155.
106. Darwin, *Decolonisation*, p. 255.
107. Blake, *Decline*, pp. 400–1; Good, *UDI*, p. 39 and Perham: 'Rhodesian crisis', p. 8.
108. See R. Lipsey, *Hammarskjöld: A Life* (Ann Arbor, MI: University of Michigan Press, 2013) and S. Williams, *Who killed Hammarskjöld?* (London: Hurst, 2011).
109. *Guardian*, 11 September 1992, cited in D. Gibbs, 'Dag Hammarskjöld, the United Nations, and the Congo crisis of 1959–61: a reinterpretation', *The Journal of Modern African Studies* 31/1(1993), pp. 163–4.

110. L. J. Butler, *Copper Empire* (Basingstoke: Palgrave Macmillan), 2007.

111. M. Kahler, 'Political regime and economic actors: The response of firms to the end of colonial rule', *World Politics* 33/3 (1981), pp. 392–4 and Murphy, *Party Politics*, p. 86.

112. Ovendale, 'Macmillan', p. 466.

113. Holland, *Decolonization,* p. 230; W. P. Kirkman, *Unscrambling an Empire* (London: Chatto & Windus, 1966), p. 95.

114. P. Murphy, '"An intricate and distasteful subject": British planning for the use of force against the European settlers of central Africa, 1952–1965', *English Historical Review* 121/492 (June 2006), p. 776.

115. Bowman, *Rhodesia*, p. 43.

116. Ibid., pp. 33–4.

117. D. Austin, 'The British point of no return?', in P. Gifford and W. M. R. Louis (eds), *The Transfer of Power in Africa, Decolonization, 1940–1960* (New Haven, CT: Yale University Press, 1982), p. 238; Darwin, *Decolonisation*, p. 276; M. Kahler, *Decolonization in Britain and France: The Domestic Consequences of International Relations* (Princeton, NJ: Princeton University Press, 1984), p. 149; and Willis, *Central Africa*, pp. 350–1.

118. D. Horowitz, 'Attitudes of British Conservatives towards decolonization in Africa', *African Affairs* 69/274 (1970), p. 13.

119. Blake, *Rhodesia*, p. 285.

120. Creighton, *Anatomy* p. 121.

121. P. J. Griffiths, *Empire into Commonwealth* (London: Benn, 1969), p. 309.

122. Gifford, 'Misconceived dominion', p. 415 and C. M. B. Utete, *The Road to Zimbabwe: The Political Economy of Settler Colonialism, National Liberation and Foreign Intervention* (Washington, DC: Rowman and Littlefield, 1979), p. 51.

123. Roberts, *Zambia*, p. 208.

Chapter 1   Conception and the Early Years of Federation

1. Cited in R. Welensky, *4000 Days: The Life and Death of the Federation of Rhodesia and Nyasaland* (London: Collins, 1964), p. 35.

2. R. Blake, *A History of Rhodesia* (New York: Eyre Methuen, 1978), pp. 38–9.

3. Lobengula Khumalo (*c.*1835–93/4?) was king of the Ndebele from 1868 until his kingdom's defeat by the British South Africa Company in 1893. See I. Phimister, 'Lobengula Khumalo (*c.*1835–93/4?)', *Oxford Dictionary of National Biography* (Oxford: Oxford University Press 2004), {http://www.oxforddnb.com/view/article/52662, accessed 30 January 2014].

4. Cecil John Rhodes (1853–1902) was an imperialist, colonial politician and a mining entrepreneur. See S. Marks, S. Trapido, 'Rhodes, Cecil John (1853–1902)', *Oxford Dictionary of National Biography* (Oxford: Oxford University Press, 2004), online edn, September 2013 [http://www.oxforddnb.com/view/article/35731, accessed 17 January 2014].

5. Sir Hercules Robinson (1824–97) was governor of the Cape Colony and high commissioner for South Africa from 22 January 1881 to 21 April 1897. Robinson later held a substantial shareholding in the British South Africa Company and was described by Sir William Harcourt, the British chancellor of the exchequer (18 August 1892–21 June 1895) as 'the nominee of Rhodes to carry out his political ideas and financial interests'. See R. Rotberg, *The Founder: Cecil Rhodes and the Pursuit of Power* (Oxford: Oxford University Press, 1988) p. 527.

6. M. Chanock, *Unconsummated Union: Britain, Rhodesia and South Africa, 1900–1945* (Manchester: Manchester University Press, 1977), pp. 12–13.

7. Blake, *Rhodesia*, p. 39.

8. J. R. T. Wood, *The Welensky Papers: A History of the Federation of Rhodesia and Nyasaland* (Durban: Graham Publishing, 1983), p. 37.

9. Charles Dunell Rudd (1844–1916) was a friend of Cecil Rhodes and a founding director of the De Beers Mining Company. The Rudd Concession was not owned by the British South Africa Company, rather it was held privately by Rhodes, Rudd and others through the Central Search Association which they established in 1889. In 1890 this became the United Concessions Company which the British South Africa Company purchased by offering a million of its own shares, worth millions of pounds on the buoyant stock market at the time, as payment. Rudd enjoyed a holding of 66,800 shares in the United Concessions Company and consequently profited greatly from the sale. See R. T. Stern, 'Rudd, Charles Dunell (1844–1916)', *Oxford Dictionary of National Biography* (Oxford: Oxford University Press, 2004), online edn, May 2006 {http://www.oxforddnb.com/view/article/65577, accessed 15 April 2014}.

10. Blake, *Rhodesia*, pp. 43–7.

11. The British South Africa Company, *The Story of Rhodesia: Told in a Series of Historical Pictures* (Johannesburg: British South Africa Company, 1936), p. 9.

12. H. M. Hole, *The Making of Rhodesia* (London: Macmillan, 1926), p. 75.

13. I. Phimister, *An Economic and Social History of Zimbabwe 1890–1948* (London: Longman, 1988), p. 6.

14. R. Palmer, *Land & Racial Domination in Rhodesia* (London: Heinmann, 1977), p. 26.

15. Phimister, *Zimbabwe*, p. 6.

16. For a detailed account of the acquisition of the Charter see J. S. Galbraith, *Crown and Charter: The Early Years of the British South Africa Company* (Berkeley and Los Angeles, CA: University of California Press), 1974.

17. See H. W. Macmillan, 'The origins and development of the African Lakes Company, 1878–1908' (PhD Dissertation, University of Edinburgh, 1970).

18. C. Saunders and I. R. Smith, 'Southern Africa 1795–1910', in A. Porter (ed.), *Oxford History of the British Empire: The Nineteenth Century* (Oxford: Oxford University Press, 2001), p. 610.

19. Alfred Milner (1854–1925) was governor of the Cape Colony and high commissioner for Southern Africa from 5 May 1897 to 6 March 1901. He was also appointed as the Civil Administrator of the Orange River and Transvaal Colonies from 4 January 1901 to 23 June 1902 where he was crucially involved in the postwar integration of the Boer republics into the British Empire. See C. Newbury, 'Milner, Alfred Viscount Milner (1854–1925)', *Oxford Dictionary of National Biography* (Oxford: Oxford University Press, 2004), online edn, October 2008 [http://www.oxforddnb.com/view/article/ 35037, accessed 15 April 2014].

20. Milner to Percy Fitzpatrick, 28 Nov. 1899, in C. Headlam (ed.), *The Milner Papers* (South Africa), 1899–1905, 2 vols (London, 1933), II, pp. 35–6 cited in Shula Marks, 'Southern Africa', in Judith M. Brown and W. M. Roger Louis (eds), *The Oxford History of the British Empire: The Twentieth Century* (Oxford: Oxford University Press, 2001), p. 548.

21. Vindex, *Cecil Rhodes: His Political Life and Speeches 1881–1900* (London: Chapman and Hall, 1901), p. 719.

22. Phimister, *Zimbabwe*, pp. 7–8.

23. Ibid., p. 8.

24. Palmer, *Domination*, p. 24.

25. Blake, *Rhodesia*, p. 105.

26. Leander Starr Jameson (1853–1917) was Cecil Rhodes' medical practitioner, closest friend, confidant and 'alter ego'. See Rotberg, *Rhodes*, p. 126.

27. Phimister, *Zimbabwe*, pp. 9–10.

28. Ibid., p. 10.

29. Blake, *Rhodesia*, p. 114.

30. Phimister, *Zimbabwe*, pp. 13–16.

31. T. O. Ranger, *Revolt in Southern Rhodesia* (London: Heinmann, 1971), p. 74.

32. Paul Kruger (1825–1904) was president of the South African Republic from 9 May 1883 to 10 September 1900. See T. R. H. Davenport, 'Kruger, Stephanus Johannes Paulus (1825–1904)', *Oxford History of National Biography* (Oxford: Oxford University Press, 2004), online edn, May 2006 [http://www. oxforddnb.com/view/article/41290, accessed 15 April 2014].

33. Blake, *Rhodesia*, p. 124.

34. C. van Onselen, *Chibaro: African Mine Labour in Southern Rhodesia 1900–1933* (London: Pluto Press, 1976), p. 15.

35. Marks and Trapido, 'Rhodes'.

36. Phimister, *Zimbabwe*, pp. 17–20.

37. Earl Grey, 'The Matabeleland Rebellion', in *The British South Africa Company, The '96 Rebellions* (Bulawayo: Books of Rhodesia, 1975), p. 5.

38. Blake, *Rhodesia*, p. 147.

39. Joseph Chamberlain (1836–1914) was secretary of state for the colonies from 29 June 1895 to 16 September 1903 and was 'generally considered by the beginning of the twentieth century to be the first minister of the British empire'. See P. T. Marsh, 'Chamberlain, Joseph (1836–1914)', *Oxford*

Dictionary of National Biography (Oxford: Oxford University Press, 2004), online edn, September 2013 {http://www.oxforddnb.com/view/article/32350, accessed 15 April 2014}.

40. Marks and Trapido, 'Rhodes'.

41. C. Newbury, 'Milner, Alfred, Viscount Milner (1854–1925)', *Oxford Dictionary of National Biography* (Oxford: Oxford University Press, 2004), {http://www.oxforddnb.com/view/article/35037, accessed 22 January 2014].

42. Sir William Milton (1854–1930) was administrator of Mashonaland from 5 December 1898 to 20 December 1901 and administrator of Southern Rhodesia from 1 November 1914. In addition, he was an accomplished sportsman capped by England at rugby and South Africa at cricket. See J. Winch, 'Sir William Milton: A leading figure in public school games, colonial politics and imperial expansion, 1877–1914' (unpublished PhD thesis, University of Stellenbosch, 2013).

43. Albert, Earl Grey (1851–1917) succeeded Jameson as administrator of Southern Rhodesia on 2 April 1896 after the debacle of the Jameson Raid, a position he held until 5 December 1898 when he became administrator of Mashonaland and senior administrator of Southern Rhodesia. He was replaced by Milton on 20 December 1901. See C. Miller, 'Grey, Albert Henry George, fourth Earl Grey (1851–1917)', *Oxford Dictionary of National Biography* (Oxford: Oxford University Press, 2004), online edn, January 2008 {http://www.oxforddnb.com/view/article/33568, accessed 15 April 2014}.

44. Blake, *Rhodesia*, p. 148.

45. Ibid., p. 150.

46. Palmer, *Domination*, p. 58.

47. See for example the Government Notice 154 of 7 September 1897; the Land Ordinance of 1899; the 1900 Land Occupation Conditions Ordinance and Government Notice No. 274 of 29 October 1903.

48. Palmer, *Domination*, pp. 60–1.

49. Blake, *Rhodesia*, p. 166.

50. Sir Francis Percy Drummond Chaplin (1866–1933) served as administrator of Southern Rhodesia from 1 November 1914 to 1 September 1923. See his obituary in *The Times*, 17 November 1933.

51. Blake, *Rhodesia*, p. 174.

52. Jan Christiaan Smuts (1870–1950) was the prime minister of the Union of South Africa on two occasions, during 1919–24 and 1939–48. See S. Marks, 'Southern Africa', in J. M. Brown and W. M. R. Louis (eds), *The Oxford History of the British Empire: The Twentieth Century* (Oxford: Oxford University Press, 2001), p. 548 and S. Marks, 'Smuts, Jan Christiaan (1870–1950)', *Oxford Dictionary of National Biography* (Oxford: Oxford University Press, 2004), online edn, January 2011 {http://www.oxforddnb.com/view/article/36171, accessed 15 April 2014}.

53. Blake, *Rhodesia*, p. 175.

54. Sir Dougal Orme Malcolm (1877–1955) became a member of the Chartered Company's board in 1913 and subsequently its president in 1937. See J. G. Darwin, Malcolm, Sir Dougal Orme (1877–1955)', *Oxford History of National Biography* (Oxford: Oxford University Press, 2004), online edn, May 2009 [http://www.oxforddnb.com/view/article/34842, accessed 15 April 2014].

55. Chanock, *Unconsummated Union*, pp. 165–8.

56. Charles Coghlin (1863–1927) accepted the presidency of the Responsible Government Association in Southern Rhodesia during 1919 which went on to successfully oppose the territory's amalgamation with the Union of South Africa. He served as the territory's first premier from 1 October 1923 until his death on 28 August 1928. See D. Lowry, 'Coghlan, Sir Charles Patrick John (1863–1927)', *Oxford History of National Biography* (Oxford: Oxford University Press, 2004), online edn, January 2008 [http://oxforddnb.com/view/article/32477, accessed 15 April 2014].

57. Walter Hume Long (1854–1924) was secretary of state for the colonies from 10 December 1916 to 10 January 1919. See A. Jackson, 'Long, Walter Hume, first Viscount Long (1854–1924)', *Oxford Dictionary of National Biography* (Oxford: Oxford University Press, 2004), online edn, January 2011 [http://www.oxforddnb.com/view/article/34591, accessed 15 April 2014].

58. Blake, *Rhodesia*, p. 176.

59. For his work on the Commission George Cave (1856–1928) would later receive the award of a Knight Grand Cross (GCMG) honour. See T. S. Legg and M. Legg, 'Cave, George, Viscount Cave (1856–1928)', *Oxford Dictionary of National Biography* (Oxford: Oxford University Press, 2004), online edn, January 2011 [http://www.oxforddnb.com/view/article/32329, accessed 15 April 2014].

60. Blake, *Rhodesia*, p. 178.

61. Sydney Charles Buxton (1853–1934) was governor-general of South Africa from 8 September 1914 to 17 November 1920. See D. Waley, 'Buxton, Sydney Charles, Earl Buxton (1853–1934)', *Oxford Dictionary of National Biography* (Oxford: Oxford University Press, 2004), online edn, May 2006 [http://www.oxforddnb.com/view/article/32224, accessed 15 April 2014].

62. Blake, *Rhodesia*, p. 179.

63. Winston Churchill (1874–1965) was secretary of state for the colonies from 13 February 1921 to 19 October 1922. He later enjoyed two periods as prime minister, the first from 10 May 1940 to 26 July 1945. The second period ran from 26 October 1951 to 6 April 1955. See P. Addison, 'Churchill, Sir Winston Leonard Spencer (1874–1965)', *Oxford Dictionary of National Biography* (Oxford: Oxford University Press, 2004), online edn, January 2011 [http://www.oxforddnb.com/view/article/32413, accessed 15 April 2014].

64. Chanock, *Unconsummated Union*, pp. 158–64.

65. J. B. M. Hertzog (1866–1942) would later beat Smuts in the 1924 South African elections to become prime minister of a coalition government. See C. Saunders, 'Hertzog, James Barry Munnik (1866–1942)', *Oxford Dictionary*

of National Biography (Oxford: Oxford University Press, 2004), online edn, January 2011 [http://www.oxforddnb.com/view/article/33842, accessed 15 April 2014].

66. Wood, *Welensky Papers*, p. 46.

67. Blake, *Rhodesia*, p. 185.

68. Marks, 'Southern Africa', p. 548.

69. Chanock, *Unconsummated Union*, pp. 168–72.

70. Wood, *Welensky Papers*, p. 46.

71. P. Murphy (ed.), *British Documents on the End of Empire, Series B Volume 9: Central Africa Part 1: Closer Association, 1945–1958* (London: The Stationery Office, 2005), pp. xxx–xxxvi and T. M. Franck, *Race and Nationalism: The Struggle for Power in Rhodesia Nyasland* (New York: Fordham University Press, 1960), pp. 17–19.

72. Blake, *Rhodesia*, pp. 191–3.

73. 'Report of the Inter-Imperial Committee of the Imperial Conference, 1926', *The American Journal of International Law* 21/2 (1926), p. 21.

74. Blake, *Rhodesia*, p. 224.

75. Howard Unwin Moffat (1869–1951) was premier of Southern Rhodesia between 2 September 1927 and 5 July 1933. See Wood, *Welensky Papers*, p. 52.

76. H. I. Wetherell, 'Settler expansionism in central Africa: The imperial response of 1931 and subsequent implications', *African Affairs* 78/311 (1979), p. 212.

77. Ibid., pp. 212–13.

78. Sir Edmund Davis (1861–1939) was on the board of directors of the Bechuanaland Exploration Company, which became 'Managers in South Africa' for the Northern Territories (BSA) Exploring Company, registered (19 February 1895), and reorganised (June 1899) as the Northern Copper (BSA) Company; the Rhodesian Copper Company (31 January 1902); the Rhodesian Broken Hill Development Company (30 November 1904); the Rhodesia Copper & General Exploration & Finance Company (5 March 1909). The Bechuanaland Exploration Company was also the 'Agents in South Africa' for the Kafue Copper Development Company (31 May 1905) and the Bwana M'Kubwa Copper Mining Company (16 March 1910). By 1904, Davis' dubious business practices in Africa and China led *The Economist* to denounce him by name. See J. A. Bancroft, *Mining in Northern Rhodesia* (Bedford: British South Africa Company 1961), p. 56, and I. Phimister, 'Davis, Sir Edmund Gabriel (1861–1939)', *Oxford Dictionary of National Biography*, H. C. G. Matthew and Brian Harrison (eds) (Oxford: Oxford University Press, 2004), online edn, May 2006 [http://www.oxfordnb.com/view/article/40711, accessed 18 June 2007].

79. Sir Robert Williams (1860–1938) was asked by Cecil Rhodes to locate and develop the mineral prospects of Southern Rhodesia in 1890. Williams agreed, and subsequently registered the Zambesia Exploring Company in 1891 to finance this venture. He was favourably impressed with the results although he failed to find a suitable area for gold production, and in 1895 the British South

Africa Company gave him a permit to examine 300 square miles of land north of the Zambezi River. Again, no gold was found but Williams was sufficiently encouraged by the results to register Tanganyika Concessions Limited (Tanks) on the 20 January 1899. See Bancroft, *Mining*, p. 49 and S. Katzenellenbogen, 'Williams, Sir Robert, baronet (1860–1938)', *Oxford Dictionary of National Biography*, H. C. G. Matthew and Brian Harrison (eds) (Oxford: Oxford University Press, 2004), online edn, May 2006 [http://www.oxforddnb.com/view/article/50249, accessed June 18, 2007].

80. The finance for this 132-mile extension of the railway north from Broken Hill, was arranged by Robert Williams and reached the Belgian Congo border near Sakania in December 1909. This section of track was purchased by the Rhodesia and Mashonaland Railway for £975,000 in 1928. See Bancroft, *Mining,* pp. 51–2.

81. L. J. Butler, *Copper Empire: Mining and the Colonial State in Northern Rhodesia, c.1930–1964* (Basingstoke: Palgrave Macmillan, 2007), p. 14.

82. J. G. Phillips, 'Roan Antelope: big business in central Africa' (Unpublished Cambridge DPhil thesis, 2000), p. 57.

83. P. D. Curtin, *Disease and Empire* (Cambridge: Cambridge University Press, 1998); R. Kubicek, 'British expansion, Empire, and technological change', in A. Porter (ed.), *The Oxford History of the British Empire III: The Nineteenth Century* (Oxford: Oxford University Press, 1999), p. 263; and J. McKelvey, Jr., *Man Against Tsetse: Struggle For Africa* (Ithaca, NY: Cornell University Press, 1973), pp. 101–207.

84. Sir Alfred Chester Beatty (1875–1968), was born in New York and educated at Princeton and Columbia universities. In 1903 he became consulting engineer and assistant manager for the Guggenheim Exploration Company based in the United States. It is rumoured that despite their success, he never visited any of his investments in Central or West Africa. See R. L. Prain, 'Beatty, Sir (Alfred) Chester (1875–1968)' rev. A. McConnell, in *Oxford Dictionary of National Biography,* H. C. G. Matthew and Brian Harrison (eds) (Oxford: Oxford University Press, 2004), online edn, May 2006 [http://www.oxforddnb.com/view/article/30660, accessed 22 June 2007).

85. Anglo American Corporation archives, 44 Main Street, Johannesburg, South Africa, 'An Introduction to RST' (n.d), p. 6.

86. The Perkins Process was patented in 1926 and employs both non-selective floatation and oxidative leaching in the resulting concentrates to recover an increased amount of copper from porphyry copper ores.

87. Bancroft, *Mining,* p. 34.

88. 'Introduction to RST', pp. 6–8.

89. S. S. Bernfeld in collaboration with H. K. Hochschild, 'A short history of American Metal Climax Inc. 1887–1962', *American Metal Climax Inc. World Atlas* (Chicago: Rand McNally and Company, 1962), pp. 1–16.

90. A. D. Roberts, 'Notes towards a financial history of copper mining in Northern Rhodesia', *Canadian Journal of African Studies* 16/2 (1982), p. 348

and K. Bradley, *Copper Venture: The Discovery and Development of Roan Antelope and Mufulira* (London: Mufulira Copper Mines, 1952), p. 92.

91. Sir Ernest Oppenheimer (1880–1957), was born in Friedberg, Germany. In 1896 he began a clerkship with the London diamond merchants A. Dunkelsbuhler & Co. He became a British subject in 1901 and took up a position as Dunkelsbuhler's representative in Kimberley, soon after. Having served on Kimberley's Town Council and as Mayor between 1912 and 1915, he used his knowledge of Southern African mining to register the Anglo American Corporation on the 25 September 1917. See C. Newbury, 'Oppenheimer, Sir Ernest (1880–1957)', *Oxford Dictionary of National Biography* (Oxford: Oxford University Press, 2004), online edn, May 2006 [http://www.oxforddnb.com/view/article/35321, accessed 22 June 2007].

92. For a detailed, if rather dry, examination of the early development of the Anglo American Corporation see T. Gregory, *Ernest Oppenheimer and the Economic Development of Southern Africa* (Oxford: Oxford University Press, 1962).

93. Rhodesian Anglo American Corporation Limited was registered with an initial capital of £2,500,000 in shares of 10 shillings each. It had Ernest Oppenheimer as chairman and its board of directors included Sir Edmund Davis, Sir Henry Birchenough, Sir Drummond Chaplin, Carl R. Davies, W. McDermott, Leslie A. Pollack, Fred Searls, Jr., and J. S. Wetzlar. See Bancroft, *Mining*, p. 77.

94. Roberts, 'Financial history', p. 348 and Bancroft, *Mining*, p. 76.

95. Bancroft: *Mining*, p. 87.

96. Sir Edward Hilton Young (1879–1960) had previously chaired a commission on Indian finance that drew up the constitution of the Indian Reserve Bank. See W. Kennet, rev. A. May, 'Young (Edward) Hilton, first Baron Kennet (1879–1960)', *Oxford Dictionary of National Biography* (Oxford: Oxford University Press, 2004), online edn, January 2013 [http://www.oxforddnb.com/view/article/37071, accessed 15 April 2014].

97. Cmd. 3234 (1929), *Report of the Commission Closer Union of the Dependencies in Eastern and Central Africa.*

98. C. Andersen and A. Cohen, *The Government and Administration of Africa, 1880–1939*, Vol. 1. (London: Pickering and Chatto, 2013), p. xxix.

99. Murphy, *Central Africa*, p. xxxv.

100. Ibid., p. xxxv.

101. Blake, *Rhodesia*, pp. 222–3.

102. The Land Apportionment Act (1930) set aside 51 per cent of the best agricultural land and the major urban areas for European occupation. 22 per cent of the land was designated as African Reserves while 7.8 per cent of the land was available for African purchase. In 1931 it was estimated that the European population of the territory was 49,910; while the number of Africans was 937,000. See B. N. Floyd, 'Land apportionment in Southern Rhodesia, *Geographic Review* 52/4 (October 1962), pp. 566–82 and

A. Mlambo, 'Building a white man's country: aspects of white immigration into Rhodesia up to World War II', *Zambezia* 25/2 (1998), pp. 123–46.

103. Chanock, *Unconsummated Union*, pp. 214–17.

104. Blake, *Rhodesia*, pp. 224–5.

105. Franck, *Race*, pp. 34–8.

106. Murphy, *Central Africa Part 1*, p. xxxv.

107. Blake, *Rhodesia*, p. 226.

108. Murphy, *Central Africa Part 1*, p. xxxv.

109. (William) Malcolm Hailey (1872–1969) had served as the governor of the Punjab (1924–8) and the governor of the United Provinces (1928–34) in India before accepting the directorship of the Carnegie sponsored *African Survey* (1938), he consequently succeeded Frederick Lugard as the standard-bearer for the British Africanist establishment. See J. W. Cell, 'Hailey (William) Malcolm, Baron Hailey (1872–1969)', *Oxford History of National Biography* (Oxford: Oxford University Press, 2004), online edn, January 2010 [http://www.oxforddnb.com/view/article/33636, accessed 5 June 2014].

110. Murphy, *Central Africa Part 1: Closer Association*, p. xxxvi.

111. Evelyn Baring, first Baron Howick of Glendale (1903–73) was governor of Southern Rhodesia from 10 December 1942 to 26 October 1924. See https://www.dur.ac.uk/library/asc/collection_information/cldload/?collno (accessed 4 June 2014).

112. Oliver Frederick George Stanley (1896–1950) was secretary of state for the colonies from 22 November 1942 to 26 July 1945. See A. Whitfield, 'Stanley, Oliver Frederick George (1896–1950)', *Oxford Dictionary of National Biography* (Oxford: Oxford University Press, 2004), online edn, January 2011 [http://www.oxforddnb.com/view/article/36249, accessed 5 June 2014].

113. Wood, *Welensky Papers*, pp. 90–123.

114. Murphy, *Central Africa Part 1*, p. xxxvii.

115. Sir Andrew Cohen (1909–68) was assistant secretary in the Colonial Office from 1943 to 1947. See M. Lynn (ed.), *British Documents on the End of Empire, Series B Volume 7: Nigeria: Managing Political Reform, 1943–1963* (London: The Stationery Office, 2001), p. 770.

116. DO 35/1161, 'Central African Council', Minute by A. B. Cohen, 28 February 1945. See Murphy, *Central Africa Part 1*, p. 1.

117. DO 35/1161, Tate to Addison enclosing minutes of first Central African Council meeting, 13 August 1945. See Murphy, *Central Africa Part 1*, p. 5.

118. Murphy, *Central Africa Part 1*, p. xl.

119. CO 537/3607, Letter from Kennedy to Machtig, 2 March 1948. See Murphy, *Central Africa Part 1*, p. 72.

120. CO 795/156/5, Minute by Cohen, 16 July 1948. See Murphy, *Central Africa Part 1*, p. 83.

121. Wood, *Welensky Papers*, pp. 120–1.

122. Arthur Creech Jones (1891–1964) was a Labour Party member of parliament and secretary of state for the colonies from 4 October 1946 to 28 February 1950.

See P. M. Pugh, 'Jones, Arthur Creech (1891–1964)', *Oxford Dictionary of National Biography* (Oxford: Oxford University Press, 2004), online edn, January 2011 [http://www.oxforddnb.com/view/article/34224, accessed 4 May 2014].

123. Welensky, *4000 Days*, p. 23.

124. CO 537/3608, Colonial Office record of a meeting with representatives from Northern Rhodesia, 30 July 1948. See Murphy, *Central Africa Part 1*, p. 83.

125. Wood, *Welensky Papers*, p. 124.

126. Marks, 'Southern Africa', p. 569.

127. L. Bowman, *Politics in Rhodesia: White Power in an African State* (Harvard, Mass: Harvard University Press, 1973), p. 18.

128. C. Leys and C. Pratt, *A New Deal in Central Africa* (London: Heinemann, 1960), p. 48.

129. R. Holland, 'The imperial factor in British strategies from Atlee to Macmillan, 1945–1963', *Journal of Imperial and Commonwealth History* 22/2 (1984), p. 176.

130. See A. Jackson and K. Law, 'Influence in British Colonial Africa', in C. Tuck (ed.), *British Propaganda and Wars of Empire: Influencing Friend and Foe, 1900–2010* (London: Ashgate, 2014), pp. 97–122.

131. J. Darwin, *Britain and Decolonisation* (Basingstoke: Macmillan, 1988), p. 138.

132. J. Darwin, 'British decolonisation since 1945: a pattern or a puzzle?', *Journal of Imperial and Commonwealth History* 22/2 (1984), p. 200 and P. Mason, *Year of Decision: Rhodesia and Nyasaland 1960* (London: Oxford University Press, 1960), p. 237.

133. A. J. Willis, *An Introduction to the History of Central Africa: Zambia, Malawi and Zimbabwe* (Oxford: Oxford University Press, 1985), p. 322.

134. P. Murphy, *Party Politics and Decolonization: The Conservative Government and British Colonial Policy in Tropical Africa, 1951–1964* (Oxford: Oxford University Press, 1999), pp. 59–60.

135. A. Hazelwood, 'The economies of federation and dissolution in central Africa', in A. Hazelwood (ed.), *African Integration and Disintegration: Case Studies in Economic and Political Union* (London: Oxford University Press, 1967), pp. 188–95; D. S. Pearson and W. L. Taylor, *Break Up: Some Economic Consequences for the Rhodesias and Nyasaland* (Salisbury: Phoenix, 1963), p. 4.

136. Murphy, *Central Africa Part 1*, p. xlii.

137. Welensky, *4000 Days*, p. 30.

138. Murphy, *Central Africa Part 1*, p. xliii.

139. CO 537/5885, Minute by Lambert on the future of the Central African Council, 27 July 1950. See Murphy, *Central Africa Part 1*, p. 136.

140. R. M. Creighton, *The Anatomy of Partnership* (London: Faber & Faber, 1960), p. 38; Darwin, 'Pattern or a puzzle?', p. 200; J. Gallagher, *The Decline, Revival and Fall of the British Empire* (Cambridge: Cambridge University Press, 1982), p. 149; R. Hyam, 'The geopolitical origins of the Central African Federation: Britain, Rhodesia and South Africa, 1948–1953', *The Historical Journal* 30/1 (1987), p. 172; and Leys and Pratt, *New Deal*, p. 50.

141. Patrick Christen Gordon Walker (1907–80) was secretary of state for Commonwealth relations from 28 February 1950 to 26 October 1951. See R. Pearce, 'Walker, Patrick Chrestien Gordon, Baron Gordon-Walker (1907–1980)', *Oxford Dictionary of National Biography* (Oxford: Oxford University Press, 2004) online edn, January 2008 [http://www.oxforddnb.com/view/article/31161, accessed 8 May 2014].

142. R. Ovendale, 'The South African policy of the British labour government, 1947–51', *International Affairs* LIX (1983), pp. 51–8.

143. Murphy, *Central Africa Part 1*, p. xlv.

144. Hyam, 'Geopolitical origins', p. 153.

145. DO 35/3594, [Closer association in central Africa]: Note by G. H. Baxter on a conference of officials, 4 April 1951. See Murphy, *Central Africa Part 1*, p. 154.

146. Cited in Hyam, 'Geopolitical origins', p. 156.

147. James Griffiths (1890–1975) secretary of state for the colonies from 28 February 1950 to 26 October 1961. See http://www.archivesnetworkwales.info/cgi-bin/anw/search2?coll_id=206 [accessed 8 May 2014].

148. Hyam, 'Geopolitical origins', p. 153.

149. Murphy, *Central Africa Part 1*, p. xlvi.

150. Ibid.

151. P. Gifford, 'Misconceived dominion: Federation in British Central Africa', in P. Gifford and W. M. R. Louis (eds), *The Transfer of Power in Africa: Decolonization, 1940–1960* (Westford, CT: Yale University Press, 1982), p. 396.

152. Ibid., p. 395.

153. R. I. Rotberg, *The Rise of Nationalism in Central Africa* (Cambridge, MA: Harvard University Press, 1966), p. 220.

154. E. Clegg, *Race and Politics, Partnership in the Federation of Rhodesia and Nyasaland* (London: Praeger, 1960), p. 176 and M. Perham, 'The Rhodesian crisis: the background', *International Affairs* 42/1 (1966), p. 6.

155. J. G. Pike, *Malawi: A Political and Economic History* (London: Pall Mall, 1968), p. 112.

156. T. O. Ranger, 'African politics in twentieth-century Southern Rhodesia', in T. O. Ranger (ed.), *Aspects of Central African History* (London: Heinemann, 1980), p. 237.

157. A. Roberts, *A History of Zambia* (New York: Africana Publishing Company, 1976), pp. 208–11.

158. Cmnd 8233 (1951) *Report of the Conference on Closer Association in Central Africa*.

159. Clement Richard Attlee (1883–1967) was prime minister of the United Kingdom from 26 July 1945 to 26 October 1951. See R. C. Whiting, 'Attlee, Clement Richard, First Earl Attlee (1883–1967)', *Oxford Dictionary of National Biography* (Oxford: Oxford University Press, 2004), online edn, January 2011 [http://www.oxforddnb.com/view/article/30498, accessed 9 May 2014].

160. In the general election on 23 February 1950 Attlee came to power with a majority of just five seats. See H. Nicholas, *The British General Election of 1950* (London: Macmillan, 1951).

161. Oliver Lyttelton (1893–1972) was secretary of state for the colonies from 28 October 1951 to 28 July 1954. See P. Murphy, 'Lyttelton, Oliver, first Viscount Chandos (1893–1972)', *Oxford Dictionary of National Biography* (Oxford: Oxford University Press, 2004), online edn, January 2011 [http://www.oxforddnb.com/view/article/31385, accessed 9 May 2014].

162. Cmnd 8411 (1951) *Closer Association in Central Africa: Statement by HM Government*.

163. Sir Edgar Whitehead (1905–71) was minister of finance in the Southern Rhodesian government from 1946 to 1953. He was later the Southern Rhodesian prime minister from 17 February 1958 to 17 December 1962. See D. Lowry, 'Whitehead, Sir Edgar Cuthbert Freemantle (1905–71)', *Oxford Dictionary of National Biography* (Oxford: Oxford University Press, 2004), online edn, October 2005 [http://www.oxforddnb.com/view/article/31828, accessed 12 May 2014].

164. Sir Gilbert Rennie (1895–1981) was governor of Northern Rhodesia from 16 December 1947 to 1 April 1954. See Murphy, *Central Africa Part 1*, p. xxii.

165. Sir Geoffrey Colby (1901–58) was governor of Nyasaland from 30 March 1947 to 10 April 1956. See C. Baker, *Development Governor: A Biography of Sir Geoffrey Colby* (London: I.B.Tauris, 1994).

166. Hyam: 'Geopolitical origins', p. 163.

167. See for example the House of Commons debate on the proposed Central African Federation on 4 March 1952. *Hansard*, 4 March 1952. Cols. 208–339.

168. J. J. B. Somerville, 'The Central African Federation', *International Affairs* 39/3 (1963), p. 389.

169. Murphy, *Central Africa Part 1*, p. l.

170. Hyam, 'Geopolitical origins', p. 164.

171. Somerville, 'Federation', p. 389.

172. A detailed discussion of the constitutional development of Southern Rhodesia can be found in C. Palley, *The Constitutional History and Law of Southern Rhodesia, 1888–1965* (Oxford: Oxford University Press, 1966).

173. Robert Gascoyne-Cecil (1893–1972) was secretary of state for Commonwealth relations from 12 March 1952 to 24 November 1954. See D. Goldsworthy, 'Cecil, Robert Arthur James Gascoyne-, fifth marquess of Salisbury (1893–1972)', *Oxford Dictionary of National Biography* (Oxford: Oxford University Press, 2004), online edn, January 2008 [http://www.oxforddnb.com/view/article/30911, accessed 22 May 2014].

174. Maurice Harold Macmillan (1894–1986) was the prime minister from 10 January 1957 to 18 October 1963. See H. C. G. Matthew, 'Macmillan (Maurice) Harold, first earl of Stockton (1894–1986)', *Oxford Dictionary of National Biography* (Oxford: Oxford University Press, 2004), online edn, January 2011 [http://www.oxforddnb.com/view/article/40185, accessed 22 May 2014]; and Makarios III (1913–77) was a leader of the Cypriot National Organisation of Cypriot Fighters (EKOA) which pursued a policy of *enosis* (unity with Greece). He was placed in exile by the British government

from 9 March 1956 to March 1957. He returned to Greece and eventually became the first president of independent Cyprus on 3 December 1959.

175. Murphy, *Party Politics*, p. 92.

176. The Africa Bureau was established in London during 1952 to 'provide accurate information particularly on the aims and hopes of African nationalism, to oppose unfair discrimination, and to encourage development in Africa' by the Rev. Michael Scott. See P. Calvocoressi, 'The Africa Bureau, London', *The Journal of Modern African Studies* 2/2 (1964), pp. 292–4.

177. Harry Mwaanga Nkumbula (*c.*1917–83) was elected president of the Northern Rhodesian African Congress in 1951 and remained an active participant in African nationalist politics through the federal period. See G. Macola, *Liberal Nationalism in Central Africa: A Biography of Harry Mwaanga Nkumbula* (Basingstoke: Palgrave Macmillan, 2009), for details.

178. MSS.292.960.1.1, Central Africa Federation: Record of delegate conference held on behalf of the African National Congresses of Nyasaland and Northern Rhodesia by the Africa Bureau, 5 May 1952. All references to the Modern Records Centre, University of Warwick.

179. Cmnd. 8573, *Draft Federal Scheme* (1952).

180. Eventually signatories included John Dugdale; Dingle Foot; Victor Gollancz; Lord Listowel; Lady Pakenham and Lord Stansgate.

181. MSS.157.3.CEA.1.1.27, Hale to Gollancz, 3 July 1952. All file references to the Modern Records Centre, University of Warwick. UK.

182. MSS.157.3.CEA.1.1.27, Memorial on Central African Federation (n.d).

183. MSS.157.3.CEA.1.1.27, Hale to Gollancz, 9 March 1953.

184. Henry Lennox D'Aubigne Hopkinson (1902–96), first Baron Colyton was minister of state for colonial affairs from 1952 to 1955. See 'Obituary: Lord Colyton', the *Independent*, 8 January 1996.

185. MSS.292.960.1.1, Extracts from African National Congress Northern Rhodesia Presidential Address, 19–25 August 1952.

186. Hyam, 'Geopolitical origins', p. 165.

187. Wood, *Welensky Papers*, p. 308.

188. Murphy, *Central Africa Part 1*, p. 1.

189. T 220/253, 'Central African Federation conference: proposed white papers': Treasury Note by S. G. Charles. See Murphy, *Central Africa Part 1*, p. 232.

190. Welensky, *4000 Days*, p. 60.

191. Ibid., pp. 62–4.

192. Cmnd 8754, *Federal Scheme prepared by a Conference held in London in January 1953* (1953).

193. *Hansard*, 24 March 1953, col. 669.

194. Hyam, 'Geopolitical origins', pp. 167–8.

195. Sir (Reginald Stephen) Garfield Todd (1908–2002) was prime minister of Southern Rhodesia from 7 September 1953 to 17 February 1958. See D. Lowry, 'Todd, Sir (Reginald Stephen) Garfield (1908–2002)', *Oxford Dictionary of National Biography* (Oxford: Oxford University Press, January 2006), online edn,

January 2010 [http://www.oxforddnb.com/view/article/77353, accessed 27 May 2014]; while Julian Greenfield (1907–93) held several federal cabinet positions in both Huggins' and Welensky's administrations including the position of minister of law from 2 November 1956 until the Federation's dissolution on 31 December 1963. See J. Greenfield, *Testimony of a Rhodesian Federal* (Bulawayo: Books of Zimbabwe, 1978).

196. Wood, *Welensky Papers*, pp. 395–7.

197. Murphy, *Central Africa Part 1*, p. lx.

198. D. N. Waite, 'Copper', in C. Payer (ed.), *Commodity Trade of the Third World* (London: Macmillan, 1975), p. 42.

199. [R]onald [L]yndsay [P]rain Box 1, Amco/Hochschild, 1940–9, Letter from Prain to Harold Hochschild, 5 March 1947. All file references to the American Heritage Center, University of Wyoming, USA.

200. I. Phimister, *Wangi Kolia: Coal, Capitalism and Labour in Colonial Zimbabwe 1894–1954* (Harare: Baobab Books, 1994), pp. 99–100.

201. Butler, *Copper Empire*, p. 125.

202. Sir Ronald Lyndsay Prain (1907–91) was chairman of the Rhodesian Selection Trust from 1950 until his retirement in 1972. See Ian Phimister, 'Prain, Sir Ronald Lindsay (1907–1991)', *Oxford Dictionary of National Biography* (Oxford: Oxford University Press, May 2008), online edn, September 2010 [http://www.oxforddnb.com/view/article/49932, accessed 11 November 2014].

203. RLP Box 3, Correspondence with Sir William Murphy and Sir Harold Cartmel-Robinson, Cartmel-Robinson to Prain, 11 September 1953.

204. RLP Box 2, File, African Advancement, Prain to Welensky, 3 February 1955.

205. J. Tischler, *Light and Power for a Multiracial Nation: The Kariba Dam Scheme in the Central African Federation* (Basingstoke: Palgrave Macmillan, 2013), pp. 29–33.

206. [W]elensky [P]apers 342/6, Brief record of a meeting held in the Prime Minister's office on Friday, 16 December 1955. All file references to Rhodes House Library, University of Oxford, UK.

207. Ibid.

208. R. Prain, *Reflections of an Era: Fifty Years of Mining in Changing Africa: The Autobiography of Sir Ronald Prain* (Letchworth: Metal Bulletin Books, 1981), p. 132.

209. WP 339/6, Taylor to Welensky, 16 January 1958.

210. Ibid.

211. Wood, *Welensky Papers*, p. 463.

212. Murphy, *Central Africa Part 1*, p. lxii.

213. The discussions surrounding the financing of the Kariba project have been covered in detail in Tischler, *Kariba*, pp. 38–51.

214. [F]rank. [T]aylor [O]strander Papers, Box 39h, Chronological File, January–June 1955. Ostrander to Vogelstein, 24 March 1955. All references are to the American Heritage Center, University of Wyoming, USA.

215. Roberts, *Zambia,* pp. 208–11.

216. Clegg, *Race*, pp. 188–9.

217. Elena L. Berger, *Labour, Race and Colonial Rule, The Copperbelt from 1924 to Independence* (Oxford: Oxford University Press, 1974), p. 9.

218. In 1946 18 per cent of Africans worked in manufacturing; this had increased to 29 per cent by 1961. See *Report of the Advisory Committee: The Development of the Economic Resources of Southern Rhodesia with Particular Reference to the Role of African Agriculture* (Salisbury: Southern Rhodesian Ministry of Native Affairs, 1962), p. 382.

219. Bowman, *Politics*, p. 48.

220. See Ibid., p. 50 and D. C. Mulford, *Zambia: The Politics of Independence* (Oxford: Oxford University Press, 1967), p. 20.

221. J. Barber: *Rhodesia: The Road to Rebellion* (Oxford: Oxford University Press, 1967), p. 12; and B. Raftopolous, 'Nationalism and labour in Salisbury 1953–1965', *Journal of South African Studies* 21/1 (1995), p. 92.

222. For an African nationalist account of this process see Nathan M. Shamuyarira, *Crisis in Rhodesia* (London: Transatlantic Arts, 1965), pp. 15–57.

223. Joshua Nkomo (1917–99) was President of SRANC from 1952 and later President of the National Democratic Party from 1960. See T. O. Ranger, 'Nkomo, Joshua, Nyongolo (1917–1999) *Oxford Dictionary of National Biography* (Oxford: Oxford University Press, 2004), online edn, May 2006 [http://dx.doi.org/10.1093/ref:odnb/72535, accessed 31 May 2014].

224. Bowman, *Politics*, pp. 50–1.

225. The Native Land Husbandry Act was introduced in an attempt to deal with increased land pressure. African population growth had led to increased pressure on land in the African reserves and driven many Africans to squat on land reserved for European use. The LHA established standards for controlling land fragmentation and de-stocking African cattle. This proved unpopular as many Africans measured wealth and status through cattle ownership. African opposition was further encouraged by the LHA as it removed the right of African chiefs to allocate native reserved land amongst their people. See D. Birmingham and T. Ranger, 'Settlers and liberators in the south', in D. Birmingham and P. M. Martin (eds), *History of Central Africa*, Volume Two (London: Heinemann, 1983), p. 366.

226. George Bodzo Nyandoro (1926–94) was a founding member of the Southern Rhodesian African National Congress. See his obituary in the *New York Times*, 4 July 1994.

227. Bowman, *Politics*, p. 49.

228. M. West, *The Rise of an African Middle Class: Colonial Zimbabwe 1898–1965* (Bloomington: Indiana University Press, 2002), p. 2.

229. A. Mlambo, 'From the Second World War to UDI, 1940–1965', in B. Raftopolous and A. Mlambo (eds), *Becoming Zimbabwe: A History from the Pre-Colonial Period to 2008* (Harare: Weaver Press, 2009), p. 94.

230. Chad Chipunza; Herbert Chitepo; Enoch Dumbutshena Joshua Nkomo; Stanlake Samkange; Jasper Savanhu; Nathan Shamuyarira and Lawrence

Vambe were all involved with multiracial organisations during this period. See H. Holderness, *Lost Chance: Southern Rhodesia 1945–58* (Harare: Zimbabwe Publishing House, 1985), p. 107 and E. Mlambo, *Rhodesia: The Struggle for a Birthright* (London: C. Hurst, 1972), pp. 123–4.

231. Mlambo, 'Second World War to UDI', p. 95.

232. Mason, *Year of Decision,* p. 97 and K. Kaunda, *Zambia Shall be Free* (London: Heinemann, 1977), p. 76.

233. Rotberg, *Nationalism,* pp. 265–7.

234. Mason, *Year of Decision,* p. 176.

235. H. Franklin, *Unholy Wedlock: The Failure of the Central African Federation* (London: Allen & Unwin, 1963), p. 83; G. Jones, *Britain and Nyasaland* (London: Allen & Unwin, 1964), p. 187; J. McCracken, *A History of Malawi, 1859–1966* (Woodbridge: James Currey, 2012), pp. 336–65; and Pike, *Malawi*, pp. 121–2.

236. B. J. Phiri, 'The Capricorn Africa Society revisited: The impact of liberalism in Zambia's colonial history, 1949–1963', *The International Journal of African Historical Studies* 24/1 (1991), p. 66.

237. RLP Box 2, file, African Advancement. Prain's 'Notes on African advancement', 1 April 1954.

238. Ibid.

239. FTO Box 12, 'An appreciation of HKH as a businessman', paper read at discussion group on Overseas Business, Economic Development and the Cold War, Harvard Business School Association, 5 September 1958.

240. I. Phimister, 'Corporate profit and race in central African copper mining, 1946–1958', *Business History Review* 85/4 (2011), pp. 749–74.

241. Gifford, 'Misconceived dominion', pp. 401–2 and Holland, 'Imperial factor', p. 176.

242. Welensky, *4000 Days*, p. 67.

Chapter 2   The Pipe Dream of Partnership, 1957–9

1. South African Foreign Affairs Archives [BSB] S. 20 vols (5). Transcript of Welensky's address to the Executives' Association, Salisbury, 5 November 1959. All file references relate to the South African Foreign Affairs Archives, O. R. Tambo Building, Soutpansberg Road, Pretoria, South Africa.

2. Sir Pierson Dixon (1904–65) was Britain's permanent representative to the United Nations from March 1954 to 1960. See N. Piers Ludlow, 'Dixon, Sir Pierson John (1904–1965)', *Oxford Dictionary of National Biography* (Oxford: Oxford University Press, 2004), online edn, January 2008 [http://www.oxforddnb.com/view/article/32839, accessed 23 October 2014].

3. W. M. R. Louis, '"Public enemy number one": The British Empire in the dock at the United Nations, 1957–1971', in M. Lynn (ed.), *The British Empire in the 1950s: Retreat or Revival?* (Houndmills: Palgrave Macmillan, 2006), p. 192.

4. The influence of the Commonwealth reasserted itself over Rhodesia in the post-federal period see C. Watts, '"Moments of tension and drama": The Rhodesian problem at the Commonwealth Prime Ministers' Meetings, 1964–1965', *Journal of Colonialism and Colonial History* 8/1 (2007), pp. 98–146.

5. CO/926/1196, recalled by Martin, minute, 11 January 1960, cited in R. Hyam and W. M. R. Louis, *British Documents on the End of Empire, Series A Volume 4: The Conservative Government and the End of Empire, Part I, High Policy, Political and Constitutional Change*, p. lxxviii.

6. M. Beloff, 'Britain, Europe and the Atlantic Community', *International Organisation* 17/3 (1963), p. 575.

7. S. Ward, '"Worlds apart" three "British" prime ministers at empire's end', in P. Buckner and R. D. Francis (eds), *Rediscovery of the British World* (Calgary: Calgary University Press, 2005), p. 408.

8. [W]elensky [P]apers 671/4, Welensky to Spicer, 28 April 1960. All file references to Rhodes House Library, Oxford.

9. DO 35/6948, no. 14, 'The United Nations: a stocktaking': memorandum by I. T. M. Pink, 7 February 1957, cited in R. Hyam and W. M. R. Louis: *British Documents on the End of Empire, Series A, Volume Four, The Conservative Government and the End of Empire, 1957–1964 Part II, Economics, International Relations and the Commonwealth* (London: The Stationery Office, 2000), p. 306.

10. Louis: 'Public enemy number one', pp. 192–3.

11. Baron Llewellin (1893–1957) was the first governor-general of the Federation of Rhodesia and Nyasaland from September 1953 to 24 January 1957 when he died in office. See J. Lewis, 'Llewellin, John Jestyn, Baron Llewellin (1893–1957)', rev. *Oxford Dictionary of National Biography* (Oxford: Oxford University Press, 2004), online edn, January 2008 [http://www.oxforddnb.com/view/article/34563, accessed 23 October 2014].

12. J. R. T. Wood, *The Welensky Papers, A History of the Federation of Rhodesia and Nyasaland* (Durban: Graham Publishing, 1983), p. 502.

13. (Robert) Anthony Eden (1897–1977) was the Conservative Party prime minister from 6 April 1955 to 9 January 1957. See D. R. Thorpe, 'Eden (Robert) Anthony, first earl of Avon (1897–1977)', *Oxford Dictionary of National Biography* (Oxford: Oxford University Press, 2004), online edn, May 2011 [http://www.oxforddnb.com/view/article/31060 (accessed 31 October 2014).

14. J. Darwin, *Britain and Decolonisation: The Retreat from Empire in the Post-War World* (Basingstoke: Palgrave Macmillan, 1988), p. 226.

15. Hyam and Louis, *Conservative Government, Part I*, p. lxxvii.

16. I. Wallerstein, *Africa, The Politics of Independence* (New York: Vintage Books, 1961), p. 144.

17. L. Butler, *Britain and Empire: Adjusting to a Post-Imperial World* (London: I.B.Tauris, 2002), p. 153.

18. PREM 11/3239, PM(57)9 'Colonialism': minute by Lord Perth (CO) to Mr Macmillan. *Annex*: draft brief on British colonial policy and the attitude of

the USA, 23 February 1957 cited in Hyam and Louis: *Conservative Government, Part II,* pp. 224–6.

19. Bermuda during March and Washington, DC in October.

20. For a detailed examination of the Anglo-American relationship during Macmillan's governments see N. J. Ashton, 'Anglo-American revival and Empire during the Macmillan years, 1957–1963', in M. Lynn (ed.), *The British Empire in the 1950s: Retreat or Revival?* (Basingstoke: Palgrave Macmillan, 2006), pp. 164–87.

21. Butler, *Britain and Empire,* p. 153.

22. [R]ecord [G]roup 59, General Records of the Department of State, Bureau of African Affairs, Office of West African Affairs, Country Files 1951–63, Regional Correspondence to Williams European Talk (Box 8), Chronology – Bureau of African Affairs, 1 March 1963. All file references to the United States' National Archives and Records Administration, College Park, Maryland, United States of America.

23. FO 371/131189, no 24, 'The attitude of the United States to tropical Africa': dispatch (no 116; FO print) from Hood to Lloyd, 10 July 1958, cited in Hyam and Louis: *The Conservative Government, Part II,* pp. 241–3.

24. See *Northern Rhodesia Chamber of Mines Year Book, 1961* (Salisbury: Northern Rhodesia Chamber of Mines, 1962), p. 20.

25. Ibid., p. 21.

26. [R]onald [L]yndsay [P]rain Box 2, File, Correspondence with Sir Roy Welensky. Welensky to Prain, 20 January 1958. All file references relate to the American Heritage Center, University of Wyoming, Laramie, United States of America.

27. Elizabeth Henderson (*c.*1911–69) married Welensky on 28 April 1928. See Donal Lowry 'Welensky, Sir Roland (1907–1991)', *Oxford Dictionary of National Biography* (Oxford: Oxford University Press, 2004), [http://www.oxforddnb.com/view/article/50688/2004-09, accessed 24 October 2014]

28. WP 657/5, Welensky to Prain, 31 January 1957.

29. Walter Turner Monckton (1891–1965) was a former Conservative member of parliament who acted as chairman of the advisory committee on the constitution of the Federation of Rhodesia and Nyasaland during 1959–60. See M. Pugh, 'Monckton, Walter Turner, first Viscount Monckton of Brenchley (1891–1965)', *Oxford Dictionary of National Biography* (Oxford: Oxford University Press, 2004), online edn, January 2011 [http://www.oxforddnb.com/view/article/35061, accessed 27 October 2014].

30. RG 59 General Records of the Department of State, Bureau of African Affairs, Office of Eastern and Southern African Affairs, COUNTRY FILES, 1951–65, Kenya biographic data to Rhodesia desegregation (Box 1), Lloyd V. Steere, American Consul General, Salisbury to Fred L. Hadsel, Director, Office of Southern African Affairs, 22 March 1957.

31. RG 59 General Records of the Department of State, Records of G. Mennen Williams, 1961–6, Entry 719.3 Signature and Clearance File, 1961–6,

January–December 1961 (Box 9), Mennen Williams to Martin, 4 May 1961.

32. See A. DeRoche, 'Establishing the centrality of race: relations between the US and the Rhodesian Federation, 1953–1963', *Zambezia* 25/2 (1998), p. 211.

33. WP 647/3, Welensky to Millin, 13 June 1961.

34. (Courtney) Keith Acutt (1909–86) joined Anglo American in 1928 and was deputy chairman from 1957 to 1982. See http://oxfordindex.oup.com/view/10.1093/ww/9780199540884.013.U161338 {accessed 11 November 2014].

35. WP 349/3, Macintyre to Welensky, 19 February 1957.

36. Ibid.

37. See C. Palley, *The Constitutional History and Law of Southern Rhodesia 1888–1965* (Oxford: Oxford University Press, 1966), pp. 345–412.

38. P. Mason, *Year of Decision: Rhodesia and Nyasaland 1960* (London: Oxford University Press, 1960), p. 91.

39. [S]mith [P]apers Box 1/006, Southern Rhodesian Government Cabinet Memoranda 1957 part 1, Committee on Federal Franchise Qualifications, 7 February 1957. All file references refer to Cory Library, Grahamstown, Republic of South Africa.

40. The term 'partnership' was left deliberately vague so it could appeal to Africans, settlers and the British in equal measure. For a good summary of the various interpretations see C. Dunn, *Central African Witness* (London: Victor Gollancz, 1959), pp. 115–26.

41. Sir Robert Tredgold (1899–1977) was chief justice of the Federation of Rhodesia and Nyasland. See C. Palley, 'Tredgold, Sir Robert Clarkson (1899–1977)', rev. *Oxford Dictionary of National Biography* (Oxford: Oxford University Press, 2004), online edn, May 2006 [http://www.oxforddnb.com/view/article/31772, accessed 27 October 2014].

42. See H. Holderness, *Lost Chance: Southern Rhodesia, 1945–58* (Harare: Zimbabwe Publishing House, 1985).

43. SP Box 1/006, Southern Rhodesian Government Cabinet Memoranda Part I, Committee on Federal Franchise Qualifications, 14 March 1957.

44. SP Box 1/006, [S]outhern [R]hodesian [C]abinet Minutes 1957, Secret annexure to S.R.C. (57) thirteenth meeting, 28 March 1957.

45. SP Box 1/006, Southern Rhodesian Government Cabinet Memoranda 1957 Part I, Southern Rhodesia. Notes of a meeting held in the Federal Legislative Assembly, by Heads of Government with advisers, 30 March 1957.

46. Wood, *Welensky Papers*, p. 531.

47. Makarios III (1913–77) was a Greek Orthodox archbishop who became the first president of independent Cyprus. See C. M. Woodhouse, 'Makarios III (1913–1977)', rev. *Oxford Dictionary of National Biography* (Oxford: Oxford University Press; 2004), online edn, January 2011 {http://www.odnb.com/view/article/31401, accessed 31 October 2014].

48. See S. Ball, *The Guardsmen, Three Friends and the World They Made* (London: Harper Collins, 2005), pp. 333–6, and 'Banquo's ghost: Lord Salisbury,

Harold Macmillan and the high politics of decolonization, 1957–1963', *Twentieth Century British History* 16/1 (2005), pp 74–102 for details of Macmillan and Salisbury's relationship during this period.

49. WP 274/5, Welensky to Wynne, 7 January 1963.

50. Julius [Julian] Greenfield (1907–93) was the Federation's minister of law from 2 November 1956 to 31 December 1963. See J. Greenfield, *Testimony of a Rhodesian Federal* (Bulawayo: Books of Bulawayo, 1978).

51. Alexander Frederick [Alec] Douglas Home (1903–95) was secretary of state for Commonwealth relations from 7 April 1955 to 27 July 1960 and later prime minister from 19 October 1963 to 16 October 1964. See D. Hurd, 'Home Alexander Frederick Douglas – fourteenth Earl of Home and Baron Home of the Hirsel (1903–95)', *Oxford Dictionary of National Biography* (Oxford: Oxford University Press, 2004), online edn, January 2014 [http://www.oxforddnb.com/view/article/60455, accessed 31 October 2014].

52. Alan Lennox-Boyd (1904–83) was secretary of state for the colonies from 28 July 1954 to 14 October 1959. See P. Murphy, 'Boyd, Alan Tindal Lennox – first Viscount Boyd of Merton (1904–83)', *Oxford Dictionary of National Biography* (Oxford: Oxford University Press, 2004), online edn, January 2008 [http://www.odnb.com/view/article/31352, accessed 31 October 2014].

53. Home's account of events can be found in Lord Home, *The Way the Wind Blows* (London: Harper Collins, 1976), while Lennox-Boyd's career is covered in P. Murphy, *Alan Lennox-Boyd: A Biography* (London: I.B.Tauris, 1999).

54. Greenfield, *Testimony,* p. 154.

55. DO 35/7552, no 430, telegram from Lennox-Boyd to Benson and Armitage, 18 April 1957 cited in P. Murphy, *British Documents on the End of Empire, Vol. 9: Central Africa, Part I, Closer Association, 1945–58* (London: Stationery Office, 2005), p. 368.

56. A. King (ed.), *British Political Opinion 1937–2000: The Gallup Polls* (London: Politico's Publishing Ltd., 2001), p. 5.

57. R. Welensky, *4000 Days: The Life and Death of the Federation of Rhodesia and Nyasaland* (London: Collins, 1964), p. 76.

58. Ibid., p. 534.

59. WP 341/10, RST press release, 30 May 1957.

60. WP 341/10, Memorandum to Welensky from the Federal Economic Section, 1 June 1957.

61. Ibid.

62. *The Economist*, 1 June 1957.

63. Ibid.

64. R. Prain, *Reflections of an Era* (London: Metal Bulletin Books Ltd., 1981), p. 114.

65. *Union News*, 23 July 1957.

66. I. Phimister, 'Corporate profit and race in central African copper mining, 1946–1958', *Business History Review* 85/4 (2011), pp. 749–74.

67. E. Berger, *Labour, Race and Colonial Rule: The Copperbelt from 1924 to Independence* (Oxford: Oxford University Press, 1974), p. 190.

68. F. Bray, *Report of Facilities for Technical Education in the Federation* (Salisbury, 1958), p. 11, cited in Berger, *Labour*, p. 190.

69. Prain, *Reflections of an Era*, p. 114.

70. Leonard James [Jim] Callaghan (1912–2005) was in every Labour shadow cabinet while the party was in opposition between 1951 and 1964. He would later be prime minister of Britain from 5 April 1976 to 4 May 1979. See R. Hattersley, 'Callaghan Leonard James [Jim], Baron Callaghan of Cardiff (1912–2005)', *Oxford Dictionary of National Biography* (Oxford: Oxford University Press, January 2009), online edn, May 2013 [http://www.oxforddnb.com/view/article/94837, accessed 31 October 2014].

71. *{H}ouse of {C}ommons Deb*, 4 June 1957, Vol. 571, col. 1104–5.

72. Wood, *Welensky Papers*, p. 540.

73. Sir Archer Ernest Baldwin (1883–1966) was member of parliament for Leominster from 1945 to 1959. See *The Times*, Obituary, 29 March 1966.

74. *HC Deb*, 4 June 1957, Vol. 571, col. 1115.

75. James Johnson (1908–95) was Labour member of parliament for Rugby from 1950 to 1959 and had previously been an official of the National Union of General and Municipal Workers in Kenya, which may well have explained his qualified support for Welensky. See http://www.hull.ac.uk/oldlib/archives/mppapers/johnson.html [accessed 31 October 2014].

76. *HC Deb*, 4 June 1957, Vol. 571, col. 1186–9.

77. Africans in Northern Rhodesia and Nyasaland held the status of British Protected Persons.

78. Wood, *Welensky Papers*, p. 543.

79. Welensky, *4000 Days*, p. 77.

80. Wood, *Welensky Papers*, p. 544.

81. Welensky, *4000 Days*, p. 78.

82. The Constitutional Amendment Act provided for the enlargement of the Federal Assembly from 35 seats to 59 seats. Under the new arrangement the number of seats for representatives of Africans would increase; however, it was likely that the complex voting arrangements would ensure that, outside Nyasaland, an electorate that was predominantly European would nominate African representatives.

83. Murphy, *Central Africa: Part I*, p. lxvi.

84. RG 59 General Records of the Department of State, Bureau of African Affairs, Office of Eastern and Southern African Affairs, COUNTRY FILES, 1951–65, Kenya biographic data to Rhodesia desegregation (Box 1), LaMont to Palmer, 9 September 1957.

85. Ibid.

86. There is a rich literature dedicated to this subject, however for a good account see J. Williams, *Eyes on the Prize: America's Civil Rights Years, 1954–65* (London: Penguin, 2013).

87. WP 584/4, Acutt to Welensky, 18 October 1957.

88. WP 584/4, Welensky to Acutt, 23 October 1957.
89. WP 624/1, Hochschild to Welensky, 9 December 1957.
90. WP 624/1, Welensky to Hochschild, 19 December 1957.
91. Mason, *Year of Decision*, pp. 86–7.
92. Wood, *Welensky Papers*, p. 566.
93. Murphy, *Party Politics,* p. 71.
94. [D]eposit [P]atrick [W]all/48/168, Constitutional Amendment Bill & Papers, Bow Group report 'Crisis over Central Africa', 23 November 1957. All file references refer to the papers of Sir Patrick Wall, University of Hull Archives.
95. *HC Deb*, 25 November 1957, Vol. 578, col. 819.
96. John Dugdale (1905–63) was the Labour Party minister of state for the Colonies from 1950 to 1951. See *The Times*, 13 March 1963.
97. *HC Deb*, 25 November 1957, Vol. 578, col. 836.
98. Cuthbert 'Cub' Alport (1912–98) was under secretary of state for Commonwealth relations between 1957 and 1959; minister of state for the Commonwealth Relations Office between 1959 and 1961 and then British high commissioner to the Federation of Rhodesia and Nyasaland between 1961 and 1963. See J. Tomes, 'Alport, Cuthbert James McCall, Baron Alport (1912–1998)', *Oxford Dictionary of National Biography* (Oxford: Oxford University Press, 2004), online edn, January 2008 {http://www.oxforddnb.com/view/article/71022, accessed 27 October 2014].
99. *HC Deb*, 25 November 1957, Vol. 578, col. 830.
100. Frederic Bennett (1918–2002), represented the Torquay constituency from 1955 until it was abolished in 1974. See his obituary in the *Telegraph*, 18 September 2002.
101. *HC Deb*, 25 November 1957, Vol. 578, col. 909.
102. The Board was originally established in 1923 as the Joint East Africa Board to promote agricultural, industrial and commercial development in Britain's east and central African colonies. It supported the creation of the Central African Federation and after 1965 devoted its activities towards promoting settlement between the British and Rhodesian governments. For further details see http://www.hull.ac.uk/arc/collection/pressuregrouparchives/jab. html [accessed 5 September 2008].
103. DPW/48/168, The Joint East and Central African Board, Chairman's Letter No. 44, 2 December 1957.
104. DPW/48/170, Labour Party 'Statement on Central Africa', 28 March 1958.
105. Kenneth David Kaunda (1924–) was a member of the African National Congress before becoming dissatisfied with Harry Nkumbula's leadership and founding the Zambian African National Congress (ZANC) in 1958. In 1959 ZANC was banned and Kaunda imprisoned. Upon his release in January 1960 Kaunda assumed leadership of the United National Independence Party (UNIP) which had been formed in his absence by Mainza Chona. Kaunda became the first president of Zambia on 24 October 1964, a position he retained until 2 November 1991. For further details of Kaunda's influence

during the Federation see D. C. Mulford, *Zambia: The Politics of Independence, 1957–1964* (Oxford: Oxford University Press, 1967).

106. ANC 3/20, Symonds, to Kaunda, 21 February 1958. All file references refer to the Northern Rhodesian African National Conference located in the UNIP Archives, Sheki Sheki Road, Lusaka, Zambia.

107. John Hatch (1917–92) was secretary of the Commonwealth Department in the Labour Party from 1954 to 1961. See 'Obituary: Lord Hatch of Lusby', the *Independent*, 13 October 1992.

108. K. Kaunda, *Zambia Shall Be Free* (London: Heinemann, 1962), pp. 80–4.

109. The Conservative Overseas Bureau was founded in 1949 by Conservative Central Office to assist the parliamentary party in making its policies and principles known in overseas countries. See P. Murphy, *Party Politics and Decolonization: The Conservative Party and British Colonial Policy in Tropical Africa, 1951–64* (Oxford: Oxford University Press, 1995), p. 150.

110. Mainza (Mathias) Chona (1930–2001) was a prominent opponent of the Federation who went on to serve the Zambian government in various capacities, including terms as vice president (1970–3) and prime minister (1973–5). See H. Macmillan, 'Chona (Mathias) Mainza (1930–2001)', *Oxford Dictionary of National Biography* (Oxford: Oxford University Press, January 2005), {http://www.oxforddnb.com/view/article/76554, accessed 10 November 2014}.

111. UNIP 6/7/3, Milne to Chona, 6 October 1959.

112. H. Franklin, *Unholy Wedlock, The Failure of the Central and Nyasaland Federation* (London: Allen and Unwin, 1964), p. 187; J. McCracken, 'African politics in twentieth-century Malawi', in T. O. Ranger (ed.) *Aspects of Central African History* (London: Heinemann, 1968), p. 204; J. Pike, *Malawi; a Political and Economic History* (London: Praeger, 1968), pp. 121–2 and R. Rotberg, *The Rise of Nationalism in Central Africa: The Making of Malawi and Zambia, 1873–1964* (Cambridge, MA: Harvard University Press, 1966), p. 256.

113. A. Roberts, *A History of Zambia* (London: Holmes & Meier, 1976), p. 212.

114. The Federal Electoral Act provided for the creation of 'ordinary' and 'special' electoral rolls. They were to be differentiated through property and educational restrictions that were designed to ensure the 'ordinary' roll remained dominated by Europeans for the immediate future.

115. B. J. Phiri, 'The Capricorn Africa Society revisited: the impact of liberalism in Zambia's colonial history, 1949–1963', *The International Journal of African Historical Studies* 24/1 (1991), p. 66.

116. E. Mlambo, *Rhodesia: The Struggle for a Birthright* (London: C. Hurst, 1972), p. 129 and Holderness, *Last Chance*, pp. 165–230.

117. SP Box 1/006, Southern Rhodesia Cabinet Memoranda 1957, Letter from the Office of the Member for Education and Social Services, Lusaka, to the Secretary to the Prime Minister and the Cabinet Office, 27 May 1957.

118. SP Box 1/007, Southern Rhodesian Government Memorandum 1958, Part 1, Southern Rhodesia Cabinet (58) 78, memorandum on multiracial hotels, 11 April 1958.

119. B. N. Floyd, 'Land apportionment in Southern Rhodesia', *Geographical Review* 52/4 (1962), p. 580.

120. SP Box 1/007 Cabinet Memoranda part 2 1958, Annexure to Southern Rhodesia Cabinet (58) 103, 25 March 1958.

121. Ibid.

122. Berger, *Labour,* pp. 195–6.

123. Mason, *Year of Decision,* p. 156.

124. Murphy, *Central Africa: Part I,* p. lxvii and M. O. West 'Ndabaningi Sithole, Garfield Todd and the Dadaya school strike of 1947,' *Journal of Southern African Studies* 18/2 (1992), pp. 297–316.

125. George 'Herbert' Baxter (1894–1962) was assistant under-secretary of state for Commonwealth relations (1947–55) and the director of the Rhodesia and Nyasaland Committee (1957–62). See Murphy (ed.), *Central Africa Part 1,* p. 573.

126. The Rhodesia and Nyasaland Committee was a pro-federal pressure group founded in London during 1957. See WP 272/2, Cole to Welensky, 29 May 1957.

127. Major Sir Patrick Henry Bligh Wall (1916–98) was the Conservative MP for Haltemprice (and subsequently Beverley after the constituency was reorganised) from 1954 to 1987. Wall was also a senior member of the right-wing Conservative party Monday Club before he resigned in 1970, on the grounds that its members were incapable of serious thought. See 'Obituary: Major Sir Patrick Wall, The *Independent,* 20 May 1998.

128. Welensky later attributed this visit to moving Conservative Party policies to a position closer to those of the Labour Party. See Wood, *Welensky Papers*, p. 563.

129. DPW/48/170, Baxter to Wall, 24 January 1958.

130. Barbara Anne Castle (1910–2002) was the Labour Party MP for Blackburn from 1945 to 1979 and a firm critic of the Federation. See A. Howard, 'Castle, Barbara Anne, Baroness Castle of Blackburn (1910–2002)', *Oxford Dictionary of National Biography* (Oxford: Oxford University Press, January 2006), online edn, May 2012 [http://www.oxforddnb.com/view/article/76877, accessed 10 November 2014].

131. *HC Deb*, 18 February 1958, Vol. 582, col. 1137.

132. WP 672/1, Welensky to Stanley, 25 March 1958.

133. See N. M. Shamuyarira, *Crisis in Rhodesia* (London: Transatlantic Arts, 1965), p. 47.

134. Greenfield, *Testimony*, p. 157.

135. J. R. T. Wood, *So Far and No Further! Rhodesia's Bid for Independence during the Retreat from Empire 1959–65* (Johannesburg: 30 Degrees South, 2005), p. 14.

136. WP 655/2, Welensky to Pegrum, 23 January 1958.

137. Wood, *Welensky Papers*, p. 586.

138. SP Box 1/006 Southern Rhodesia Government Cabinet Minutes 1958, Southern Rhodesian Cabinet (58) nineteenth meeting, 19 April 1958.

139. The Dominion Party was formed in 1957 and was led by Winston Field. The party pursued a right-wing agenda and did not envisage substantial African advancement for the foreseeable future. Wood, *Welensky Papers*, p. 392. The difference between the UFP and the DP was, however, questioned by L. Bowman who contended that 'both favored continued white rule, domination status, economic expansion, and the social and industrial legislation that protected white privileges'. *Politics in Rhodesia: White Power in an African State* (Cambridge, MA: Harvard University Press, 1973), p. 31.

140. The first choice voting totals were as follows: Dominion Party, 18,314; United Federal Party, 17,064; United Rhodesia Party, 4,862. See Mason, *Year of Decision*, p. 199.

141. Welensky, *4000 Days*, p. 90.

142. Wood, *So Far and No Further!*, p. 14.

143. C. Alport, *The Sudden Assignment: Being a Record of Service in Central Africa During the Last Controversial Years of the Federation of Rhodesia and Nyasaland, 1961–1963* (London: Hodder & Stoughton, 1965), p. 36.

144. WP 662/4, Welensky to Robins, 25 June 1958.

145. WP 662/4, Welensky to Robins, 8 July 1958.

146. Mss.Afr.s.2125, Dick Hobson 'The Last Gasp' (1991), p. 12. File reference to Rhodes House Library, Oxford.

147. Clyde Sanger to Haddon. 11 December 1987, cited in A. King 'The *Central African Examiner*, 1957–65', *Zambezia* 23/2 (1996), p. 144.

148. WP 600/3, de Quehen to Parker, 14 March 1958.

149. WP 600/3, Cole to Welensky, 17 July 1958 and Welensky to Cole, 22 July 1958.

150. WP 600/3, de Quehen to Parker, 14 March 1958.

151. Ibid.

152. RLP Box 1 File 5, 'Notes on Mr. H. K. Hochschild' (n.d).

153. Roberts conducted a series of negotiations with Benson over the constitutional proposals to no avail. Agreement was finally reached at a meeting chaired by Lennox-Boyd during March 1958. The result of this meeting was released as *Proposals for Constitutional Change in Northern Rhodesia* (Lusaka, 28 March 1958) without Roberts' knowledge. Roberts was forced to protest to London that this had left him in an 'untenable position' with Welensky, as the federal prime minister believed the proposals ran counter to his plan to secure self-government for the territory under European control. See Wood, *Welensky Papers*, pp. 590–3.

154. Murphy, *Central Africa: Part I,* p. lxix.

155. Wood, *Welensky Papers*, p. 602.

156. CAB 129/95, C(58)232, Cabinet memorandum from Lord Home, 12 November 1958 cited in Hyam and Louis, *Conservative Government Part II,* pp. 540–1.

157. Hastings Kamazu Banda (*c*.1898–1997) led the African nationalist struggle for independence in Nyasaland. He was subsequently prime minister of

Malawi from 6 July 1964 to 6 July 1966 and then president of Malawi from 6 July 1966 to 24 May 1994. See J. McCracken, 'Banda, Hastings Kamuzu (*c*.1898–1997)', *Oxford Dictionary of National Biography* (Oxford: Oxford University Press, 2004), online edn, January 2008 [http://www.oxforddnb.com/view/article/68477, accessed 27 October 2014].

158. For an account of Banda's political activities before returning to Nyasaland see C. Sanger, *Central African Emergency* (London: Heinemann, 1960), pp. 182–202.

159. Darwin, *Decolonisation*, p. 270.

160. Sir Arthur Benson (1907–87) was governor of Northern Rhodesia from 1 May 1954 to 23 April 1959. See *The Times*, 19 October 1987.

161. Murphy, *Central Africa, Part I*, p. lxvii.

162. Cmnd. 530, *Northern Rhodesia: Proposals for Constitutional Change* (1958).

163. Murphy, *Central Africa: Part I*, p. lxviii.

164. For details of these meetings see Wood, *Welensky Papers*, pp. 618–19.

165. Cmnd 530, *Proposals for Constitutional Change in Northern Rhodesia* (1958).

166. *HC Deb*, 27 November 1958, Vol. 596, col. 576.

167. *HC Deb*, 27 November 1958, Vol. 596, col. 585.

168. *HC Deb*, 27 November 1958, Vol. 596, col. 600.

169. *HC Deb*, 27 November 1958, Vol. 596, col. 625.

170. WP 398/2, Wall to Welensky, 19 November 1958 and DPW/48/171.

171. Welensky, *4000 Days*, p. 89.

172. Mulford, *Politics of Independence*, p. 6.

173. Kaunda, *Zambia Shall Be Free*, p. 87.

174. Murphy, *Central Africa: Part I*, pp. lxviii – lxix.

175. Welensky, *4000 Days*, p. 105.

176. Wood, *Welensky Papers*, p. 625.

177. Mason, *Year of Decision*, p. 129.

178. Mulford, *Politics of Independence*, p. 74. Recent scholarship has challenged the nationalist portrayal of Nkumbula and his role in the independence struggle. See G. Macola, *Liberal Nationalism in Central Africa: A Biography of Harry Mwaanga Nkumbula* (London: Palgrave Macmillan, 2010).

179. Kaunda, *Zambia Shall Be Free*, p. 93.

180. Wood, *Welensky Papers*, p. 640.

181. Detailed studies of the Nyasaland emergency can be found in C. Baker, *State of Emergency: Crisis in Central Africa, Nyasaland 1959–60* (London: I.B.Tauris, 1997) and J. Darwin, 'The Central African Emergency, 1959', in R. F. Holland (ed.), *Emergencies and Disorder in the European Empires after 1945* (London: Routledge, 1994), pp. 217–34.

182. Robert Percival Armitage (1906–90) was governor of Nyasaland from 10 April 1956 to 10 April 1961. See C. Baker, *Retreat from Empire: Sir Robert Armitage in Africa and Cyprus* (London: I.B.Tauris, 1998).

183. Murphy, *Central Africa: Part I*, p. lxx.

184. Sir Peter William Youens (1916–2000) was deputy chief secretary of Nyasaland from 1953 to 1963 and subsequently secretary to the prime

minister and cabinet of Malawi from 1963 to 1966. After leaving Malawi he became a board member of the British multinational company Lonrho. See the *Telegraph,* 25 May 2000.

185. DP Box 5, Youens to Armitage, 5 January 1959, cited in Baker, *State of Emergency,* p. 11.

186. DP Box 1, NYC 1, Memorandum from Commissioner of Police, Nyasaland to The Hon. Chief Secretary, Nyasaland, 18 February 1959.

187. Darwin, 'Emergency', p. 223.

188. Ibid.

189. Joshua Nkomo (1917–99) became president of SRANC in 1957 and also of the National Democratic Party formed in 1960 and subsequently the Zimbabwe African Peoples Union formed in 1961. See T. O. Ranger, 'Nkomo, Joshua Mqabuko Nyongolo (1917–99)', *Oxford Dictionary of National Biography* (Oxford: Oxford University Press, 2004), online edn, May 2009 [http://www.oxforddnb.com/view/article/72535, accessed 10 November 2014].

190. (Arthur) Guy Clutton-Brock (1906–95) was a political activist from Middlesex who maintained friendships with many of the leading African nationalists in Southern Rhodesia. See T. O. Ranger, 'Brock (Arthur) Guy Clutton (1906–95)', *Oxford Dictionary of National Biography* (Oxford: Oxford University Press, 2004), online edn, January 2014 [http://www.oxforddnb. com/view/article/59788, accessed 10 November 2014].

191. Wood, *Welensky Papers,* p. 578.

192. This recourse to public confession and ceremony in the rehabilitation of subversive Africans had earlier been adopted in Kenya to deal with Mau Mau detainees. See D. Anderson, *Histories of the Hanged: Britain's Dirty War in Kenya and the End of Empire* (London: Orion, 2005), pp. 283–4.

193. SP Box 1/008, Southern Rhodesian Government Cabinet Minutes 1959, S.R.C (59) minutes of Seventeenth Meeting, 24 March 1959.

194. Wood, *So Far and No Further!,* p. 17.

195. Mulford, *The Politics of Independence,* p. 95.

196. John David Drummond, seventeenth Earl of Perth (1907–2002) was minister of state for the colonies from 1957 to 1962. See 'Obituary: The Earl of Perth', *Daily Telegraph,* 29 November 2002.

197. Murphy, *Central Africa: Part I,* p. lxxiii.

198. MSS. Macmillan dep. D. 33-5. Macmillan diary entry, 6 March 1959. All file references refer to the Bodleian Library, Oxford.

199. John Thomson Stonehouse (1925–88) was the Labour MP for Wednesbury from 28 February 1957 to 28 February 1974. He subsequently gained infamy by attempting to fake his own death in 1974. See J. Stonehouse, *Prohibited Immigrant* (London: Bodley Head, 1960).

200. Ibid., pp. 198–203.

201. Wood, *Welensky Papers,* pp. 646–7.

202. R. Hyam, *Britain's Declining Empire: The Road to Decolonisation 1918–1968* (Cambridge: Cambridge University Press, 2006), p. 263.

203. The *Guardian*, 16 December 1959.

204. BSB S.20 Vol. (5), Taswell to Secretary for External Affairs, Pretoria, 30 July 1959.

205. Ibid.

206. Ibid.

207. Darwin, 'Central African Emergency', p. 218.

208. WP 606/8, Savory to Welensky, 30 April 1959.

209. Harry Frederick Oppenheimer (1908–2000) was chairman of the Anglo American Corporation from 1957 until 1982.

210. WP 606/8, Welensky to Savory, 5 May 1959.

211. WP 657/5, Prain to Welensky, 16 January 1959; and RLP Box 2, File, Correspondence with Sir Roy Welensky. Welensky to Prain, 30 January 1959.

212. Ibid.

213. Ibid.

214. Ibid.

215. Ibid.

216. Ibid.

217. Ibid.

218. Ibid.

219. King, 'The *Central African Examiner*', pp. 133–7.

220. WP 657/5, Prain to Welensky, 16 October 1957.

221. WP 279/4, Macintyre to Welensky, 5 August 1959.

222. WP 279/4, Welensky to Acutt, 7 September 1959.

223. WP 279/4, Acutt to Welensky, 9 September 1959.

224. (Harold) Julian Amery (1919–96) was the Conservative Party MP for Preston North from 23 February 1950 to 31 March 1966 and a leading figure in the Conservative Party Monday Club. See P. Cosgrave, 'Amery (Harold) Julian, Baron Amery of Lustleigh (1919–1996)', *Oxford Dictionary of National Biography* (Oxford: Oxford University Press, 2004), online edn, January 2008 [http://www.oxforddnb.com/view/article/63313, accessed 10 November 2014]

225. CO 1015/1553, Minute from Amery to Lennox-Boyd, 11 March 1959 cited in Murphy, *Central Africa Part II,* pp. 34–5.

226. A. Thompson, *The Empire Strikes Back? The Impact of Imperialism on Britain from the Mid-Nineteenth Century* (Harlow: Routledge, 2005), p. 212.

227. WP 600/4, Thompson to Cole, 5 March 1959.

228. Welensky, *4000 Days*, p. 127.

229. Joseph Charles Satterthwaite (1900–90) was assistant secretary of state for African Affairs from 2 September 1958 until 31 January 1961. See https://history.state.gov/departmenthistory/people/satterthwaite-joseph-charles (accessed 11 November 2014).

230. RG 59 General Records of the Department of State, Bureau of African Affairs, Office of Eastern and Southern African Affairs, COUNTRY FILES, 1951–65, Kenya biographic data to Rhodesia desegregation (Box 1), Talking paper by Picard, African Affairs Dept to Satterthwaite 1 June 1959.

231. Ibid., Briefing Paper for Satterthwaite's conversation with Ambassador Whitney, 4 August 1959.

232. Ibid.

233. John Fitzgerald Kennedy (1917–63) was an American Democratic president who was in office from 20 January 1961 until his assassination on 22 November 1963.

234. RG 59 General Records of the Department of State, Bureau of African Affairs, Office of Eastern and Southern African Affairs, COUNTRY FILES, 1951–65, Kenya biographic data to Rhodesia desegregation (Box 1), Briefing Paper for Satterthwaite's conversation with Ambassador Whitney, 4 August 1959.

235. CAB 134/1935, no 15(28) 'The future of Anglo-American relations': FO note for Future Policy Study Working Group, 6 October 1959, cited in Hyam and Louis, *The Conservative Government: Part I*, p. 74.

236. BSB S. 20 Vol. (5), Transcript of Welensky's address to the Executives' Association, Salisbury, 5 November 1959.

237. RG 59 General Records of the Department of State, Bureau of African Affairs, Office of Eastern and Southern African Affairs, COUNTRY FILES, 1951–65, Kenya biographic data to Rhodesia desegregation (Box 1), Palmer to Satterthwaite, 11 December 1959.

238. RG 59 General Records of the Department of State, Bureau of African Affairs, Office of Eastern and Southern African Affairs, COUNTRY FILES, 1951–65, Kenya biographic data to Rhodesia desegregation (Box 1), Satterthwaite to Palmer, 30 December 1959.

239. RG 59 General Records of the Department of State, Bureau of African Affairs, Office of Eastern and Southern African Affairs, COUNTRY FILES, 1951–65, Kenya biographic data to Rhodesia desegregation (Box 1), Report by C. Vaughan Ferguson, Jr and Frederick Picard entitled, 'Approach to UK Government concerning the Federation of Rhodesia and Nyasaland', 3 August 1960.

240. Welensky, *4000 Days*, p. 137.

241. Patrick Arthur Devlin, Baron Devlin (1905–92) was a British lawyer, judge and jurist. See T. Honoré, 'Devlin, Patrick Arthur, Baron Devlin (1905–1992)', *Oxford Dictionary of National Biography* (Oxford: Oxford University Press, 2004), online edn, September 2012 [http://www.oxforddnb.com/view/article/50969, accessed 10 November 2014].

242. CO 1015/1533, no. 30, draft telegram from Home to Perth, 18 March 1959 cited in Murphy, *Central Africa Part II*, pp. 35–6.

243. Wood, *Welensky Papers*, p. 656.

244. Colonial policy towards Africa 'remained the Conservative party's most difficult problem in relation to the vital middle voters.' See R. Ovendale, 'Macmillan and the wind of change in Africa, 1957–1960', *The Historical Journal* 38/2 (1995), p. 472.

245. CO 1015/1533, minute from Amery to Lennox-Boyd, 20 March 1959 cited in Murphy, *Central Africa Part II*, pp. 36–7.

246. MSS. Macmillan dep. D, 35-5, Macmillan diary entry, 3 April 1959.

247. Wood, *Welensky Papers*, pp. 672–3.

248. Murphy, *Party Politics*, p. 203.

249. Welensky, *4000 Days*, p. 137.

250. DP Box 1, NYC 1, Metcalf to CRO, 4 April 1959.

251. Murphy, *Central Africa: Part I,* p. lxxiii.

252. Sir Percy Wyn-Harris (1903–79) had been governor of the Gambia from 7 December 1959 to 19 June 1958. See A. H. M. Kirk-Greene, 'Harris, Sir Percy Wyn (1903–79)', *Oxford Dictionary of National Biography* (Oxford: Oxford University Press, 2004) [http://www.oxforddnb.com/view/article/31861 accessed 10 November 2014].

253. Sir Edgar Trevor Williams (1912–95) was a historian who was warden of Rhodes House from 1952 until his retirement in 1980. See C. S. Nicholls, 'Williams, Sir Edgar Trevor [Bill] (1912–95)', *Oxford Dictionary of National Biography* (Oxford: Oxford University Press, 2004), online edn, May 2011 [http://www.oxforddnb.com/view/article/57959, accessed 10 November 2014].

254. Baker, *State of Emergency,* pp. 79–83.

255. DP Box 1, NYC 2, Chancy to the Secretary of the Devlin Commission, 30 April 1959.

256. DP Box 1, NYC 2, Kaunda to the Secretary of the Devlin Commission, 30 April 1959.

257. Ibid.

258. DP Box 1, NYC 1, Lennox-Boyd to Armitage, 27 March 1959.

259. DP Box 1, NYC 2, Magaguma, Mbulaula, Mlewa, Tembe, Mvimbo, Kamulaga and Herbert Zintambila [from Nakata Bay] to the Secretary of the Devlin Commission, 4 May 1959.

260. DP Box 1, NYC 2, Bandawe, to the Secretary of the Devlin Commission, 5 May 1959.

261. DP Box 1, NYC 2, Chisupe to the Secretary of the Devlin Commission, 8 May 1959.

262. DP Box 14, Transcripts File Vol. 8. Notes of a meeting between Devlin, Primrose, Harris, Williams and Nicholson, 11 May 1959.

263. DP Box 14, Note of a meeting between the Bishop of Nyasaland and Harris, Primrose and Williams, 20 May 1959.

264. Darwin, *Britain and Decolonisation*, pp. 271–3.

265. Sir Dingle Mackintosh Foot (1905–78) was a British lawyer and Liberal and Labour politician who defended Hastings Banda when he was gaoled. See R. Ingham, 'Foot, Sir Dingle Mackintosh (1905–1978)', *Oxford Dictionary of National Biography* (Oxford: Oxford University Press, 2004), online edn, January 2014 [http://www.oxforddnb.com/view/article/31115, accessed 11 November 2014].

266. The transcript of this interview amounts to 79 pages of foolscap and readers should see Baker, *State of Emergency*, pp. 127–9 for a brief summary of the points addressed.

267. DP, Box 14. Transcript of the interview of Banda, accompanied by Foot, Kellock and Mills Odoi, by Devlin, Primrose, Wyn-Harris and Williams, 16 May 1959.

268. Ibid.

269. DP, Box 14. Transcript of the interview of Armitage, accompanied by Ingham and the Solicitor General, by Devlin, Primrose, Wyn-Harris and Williams, 21 May 1959.

270. Murphy, *Central Africa: Part I,* p. lxxiii.

271. Ibid., p. lxxiv and Robert Shepherd, *Iain Macleod: A Biography* (London: Hutchinson, 1994), pp. 159–61.

272. WP 672/1, Welensky to Stanley, 27 July 1959.

273. Greenfield, *Testimony,* p. 173.

274. BSB S. 20 Vol. (5), Taswell to Secretary for External Affairs, 31 July 1959.

275. BSB S.20 Vol. (5), Secretary of State for External Affairs to Taswell, 25 March 1959.

276. Ibid., Taswell to Parry, 17 April 1959.

277. See for example BSB S.20 Vol. (5), Report entitled 'Review of secure intelligence within the Federation of Rhodesia and Nyasaland for the per January to March 1959', 22 April 1959.

278. Hendrik Frensch Verwoerd (1901–66) was the National Party prime minister of South Africa from 2 September 1958 until his assassination on 6 September 1966. See H. Giliomee, *The Last Afrikaner Leaders: A Supreme Test of Power* (Cape Town: Tafelberg), 2012.

279. Sir De Villiers Graaff (1913–99) was leader of the United Party from 1956 until it was dissolved in 1977. See 'Obituary: Sir De Villiers Graaf', the *Guardian*, 11 October 1999.

280. By the end of the 1950s South African society was becoming less concerned with sectional Afrikaner issues and more concerned about securing a 'white' South Africa. See R. Ross, *A Concise History of South Africa* (Cambridge: Cambridge University Press, 1999), pp. 114–43.

281. BSB S.20 Vol. (5) (n/k) to Fitt, 7 March 1959.

282. BSB S.20 Vol. (5), van Schalkwyk, to the Secretary for External Affairs, 17 July 1959.

283. Welensky, *4000 Days,* p. 147.

284. Hugh Todd Naylor Gaitskell (1906–63) was leader of the Labour Party from 14 December 1955 until his death on 18 January 1963. See B. Brivati, 'Gaitskell, Hugh Todd Naylor (1906–63)', *Oxford Dictionary of National Biography* (Oxford: Oxford University Press, 2004), online edn, January 2011 [http://www.oxforddnb.com/view/article/33309, accessed 11 November 2014].

285. *HC Deb,* 22 July 1959, Vol. 609, col. 1283–5.

286. *HC Deb,* 22 July 1959, Vol. 609, col. 1305.

287. *HC Deb,* 22 July 1959, Vol. 609, col. 1312.

288. *HC Deb,* 22 July 1959, Vol. 609, col. 1331–2.

289. *HC Deb,* 22 July 1959, Vol. 609, col. 1353.

290. SP 4/001(M), Whitehead to Home, 12 October 1959.
291. DPW/48/122, Conservative Research Department memorandum by Gerald Sayers, 17 November 1959.
292. BSB S. 20, Vol. (5), South African High Commissioner Salisbury to Secretary for External Affairs, Salisbury, 10 July 1959.
293. Ibid.
294. Ibid.
295. BSB S.20 Vol. (6), Taswell to Secretary of External Affairs, Pretoria (n.d) [July 1960].
296. Ibid.

Chapter 3 'The Wind of Change', 1960–1

1. WP 677/8, Welensky to van der Byl, 24 July 1961.
2. Macmillan visited Africa for a total of six weeks and visited all of the Federal territories. For Macmillan's own account of this trip see H. Macmillan, *Pointing the Way* (London: Macmillan, 1972), pp. 119–63.
3. For a study of Macmillan's speech and its effects on the wider British world see the essays contained in L. J. Butler and S. Stockwell (eds), *The Wind of Change: Harold Macmillan and British Decolonization* (Basingstoke: Palgrave Macmillan, 2013).
4. R. Ovendale, 'Macmillan and the wind of change in Africa, 1957–1960', *The Historical Journal* 38/2 (1995), p. 476.
5. J. R. T. Wood, *The Welensky Papers, A History of the Federation of Rhodesia and Nyasaland* (Durban: Graham Publishing, 1983), pp. 731–2.
6. WP 618/4, Welensky to Gore-Browne, 20 January 1960.
7. J. R. T. Wood, *So Far and No Further! Rhodesia's Bid for Independence during the Retreat from Empire 1959–65* (Johannesburg: 30 Degrees South, 2005), p. 25.
8. BSB S.16, Taswell to the Secretary of External Affairs, 1 February 1960.
9. WP 618/4, Welensky to Gore-Browne, 19 February 1960.
10. Soon after Lord Alport left his post as British High Commissioner in Rhodesia and Nyasaland he noted how he was 'conscious while in Salisbury that the realities of the situation in Central Africa were not always in clear focus as far as certain sections of public opinion here in Britain was concerned'. See Lord Alport, 'Britain in central Africa in the sixties', *African Affairs* 62/249 (October, 1963), p. 300.
11. PREM 11/3065, Telegram from Home to Macmillan, 17 January 1960 cited in P. Murphy, *British Documents on the End of Empire, Vol. 9: Central Africa, Part II, Crisis and Dissolution, 1959–65* (London: Stationary Office, 2005), p. 103.
12. See A. Cohen, 'Voice and Vision – The Federation of Rhodesia and Nyasaland's public relations campaign in Britain: 1960–1963', *Historia* 54/2 (2009), pp. 113–32.

13. P. Murphy, *Party Politics and Decolonization: The Conservative Government and British Colonial Policy in Tropical Africa, 1951–64* (Oxford: Oxford University Press, 1999), pp. 58–9.

14. The Voice and Vision campaign is covered in P. Keatley, *The Politics of Partnership: The Federation of Rhodesia and Nyasaland* (London: Penguin, 1963), pp. 446–50; D. Goldsworthy, *Colonial Issues in British Politics, 1945–61* (Oxford: Oxford University Press, 1971), p. 365 and Murphy, *Party Politics*, pp. 73–87.

15. The Colman, Prentis and Varley campaign is covered in D. Butler and R. Rose, *The British General Election of 1959* (London: Macmillan, 1960) and M. Rosenbaum, *From Soapbox to Soundbite: Party Political Campaigning in Britain since 1945* (Basingstoke: Macmillan, 1997).

16. David Cole was the head of a Salisbury public relations company and had worked for the Federal government since 1955.

17. WP 274/2, memorandum regarding public relations, 8 March 1960.

18. Ibid.

19. Goldsworthy, *Colonial Issues*, p. 367.

20. Keatley, *Partnership,* p. 447.

21. WP 274/2, public relations proposals, 25 January 1960.

22. Ibid., Brownrigg to Welensky, 18 February 1960.

23. MSS.Brit.Emp.s.527/2, Interview with Lord Home, December 1984. Transcript from Granada End of Empire series. File references relate to Rhodes House Library, Oxford.

24. Ibid.

25. Wood, *Welensky Papers*, pp. 751–2.

26. MSS. Macmillan dep. D. 38. Macmillan diary entry, 24 February 1960.

27. L. J. Butler, *Britain and Empire: Adjusting to a Post-Imperial World* (London: I.B.Tauris, 2002), p. 161.

28. WP 665/2, Welensky to Salisbury, 12 April 1960.

29. *The Times*, 2 April 1960, p. 7.

30. WP 628/6, Welensky to Joelson, 3 March 1960.

31. DPW/48/171, Wall to Stockil, 6 January 1958.

32. *HC Deb*, 28 March 1961, Vol. 637. col. 1162.

33. WP 274/2, Wynne to the acting secretary of home affairs, 6 October 1960.

34. WP 389/3, McWhinnie to Matthews, 13 September 1960.

35. Ibid.

36. *HC Deb*, 25 October 1960, Vol. 627, col., 2157.

37. *Reynolds News* cited in Ibid., col., 2157.

38. Ibid.

39. *HC Deb*, 25 October 1960, Vol. 627, col., 2157.

40. *HC Deb*, 3 November 1960, Vol. 629, col., 406.

41. Ibid.

42. *HC Deb*, 22 February 1961, Vol. 635. col. 552.

43. WP 274/3, Wynne to Parker, 18 May 1961.

44. Wood, *Welensky Papers*, p. 759.

45. WP 628/6, Welensky to Joelson, 3 March 1960.

46. SP Box 4/001 (M), folder 4-4a, Whitehead to Home, 16 March 1960.

47. BSB S.20 Vol. (6), Report on Lord Home's visit to the Federation, Taswell to the secretary for external affairs Pretoria, 29 February 1960.

48. Ibid.

49. Ibid.

50. BSB S.20 Vol. (6), Taswell to the secretary of state for external affairs, Cape Town (n.d) [but March 1960].

51. SP Box 4/001 (M), folder 4-4a, Whitehead to Home, 16 March 1960.

52. Ibid.

53. WP 628/6, Welensky to Joelson, 21 March 1960. Electoral issues considered important by the white electorate in Southern Rhodesia at the end of the 1950s are covered in C. Leys, *European Politics in Southern Rhodesia* (Oxford: Oxford University Press, 1959), pp. 241–82.

54. PREM 11/3076, no 16/60, [Situation in Nyasaland; ministerial visits]: letter from Lord Home to Sir W. Monckton, 22 March 1960, cited in R. Hyam and W. M. R. Louis: *British Documents on the End of Empire, Series A, Volume Four, The Conservative Government and the End of Empire, 1957–1964 Part II, Economics, International Relations and the Commonwealth* (London: The Stationery Office, 2000), p. 553.

55. Edwin Duncan Sandys (1908–87) was secretary of state for Commonwealth relations from 27 July 1960 to 13 July 1962 and secretary of state for the colonies from 13 July 1962 until 16 October 1964. See N. P. Ludlow, 'Sandys (Edwin) Duncan, Baron Duncan-Sandys (1908–1987)', first published 2004; online edn, January 2008 [http://dx.doi.org/10.1093/ref:odnb/39858] accessed 30 July 2015.

56. SP 1/012, Southern Rhodesia Government Cabinet Memorandum, 1960. Note of a discussion between Southern Rhodesian Ministers and Mr Duncan Sandys, secretary of state for Commonwealth relations, 20 September 1960.

57. J. Day, 'Southern Rhodesian African nationalists and the 1961 constitution', *The Journal of Modern African Studies* 7/2 (July 1969), pp. 221–2.

58. D. C. Mulford, *Zambia: The Politics of Independence* (Oxford: Oxford University Press, 1967), p. 123.

59. UNIP 6/7/5, Mwkemba, to Hoskyns, 17 November 1959.

60. Lawrence Katilingu led the powerful African Mine Workers Union on the Copperbelt, however his refusal to throw the full support of the unions behind the ANC's anti-Federation campaign prior to 1953 earned him many enemies amongst African nationalists in Northern Rhodesia. He ran for election to the legislative council in the March 1959 elections, and despite winning the popular vote by a large margin failed to take his seat due to preferenced European voting. This led to Katilingu taking a more active role in politics although he was closer to Harry Nkumbula's ANC than Kaunda's UNIP. During Nkumbula's detention in the early 1960s Katilingu took over

temporary leadership of the ANC. However, his foray into politics was cut short by his death in a car crash in November 1961. See Mulford, *Politics of Independence*, p. 240.

61. UNIP 6/7/5, Mweemba to Hoskyns, 26 November 1959.
62. UNIP 6/7/3, Chona to Milne, 1 December 1959.
63. Ibid.
64. WP 514/1, writing on placards held by members of UNIP in Fort Jameson on 16 March 1960.
65. UNIP 14/2/5, *Voice of UNIP,* April 1962.
66. Wood, *Welensky Papers*, p. 759 and B. A. Kosmin, *Majuta: A History of the Jewish Community in Zimbabwe* (Gwelo: Mambo Press, 1980), p. 120.
67. DO 35/7620, Macleod to Home, 27 June 1960.
68. WP 665/2, Welensky to Salisbury, 18 August 1960.
69. See for example *The Times*, 16 September 1960, p. 7 and 7 October 1960, p. 17.
70. WP 679/3, Wall to Welensky, 27 February 1961.
71. J. Hargreaves, *Decolonization in Africa* (London: Routledge, 1996), p. 213.
72. R. F. Holland, *European Decolonization, 1918–1981* (London: Macmillan, 1985), p. 225.
73. The final decision was that there would be 13 local members: four representing the Federal government and three members each representing the territorial governments; plus 13 further representatives from Britain and the Commonwealth, which gave the Commission a total membership of 26. Murphy *Part I: Closer Association,* p. lxxvii.
74. Butler, *Britain and Empire*, p. 161.
75. Lord Birkenhead, *Walter Monckton: The Life of Viscount Monckton of Brenchley* (London: Weidenfeld & Nicolson, 1969), p. 342.
76. J. Greenfield, *Testimony of a Rhodesian Federal* (Bulawayo: Books of Rhodesia, 1978), p. 167.
77. Hargreaves, *Decolonization in Africa*, p. 214.
78. WP 672/1, Welensky to Stanley, 15 December 1959.
79. Butler, *Britain and Empire,* p. 161.
80. WP 662/5, Welensky to Robins, 4 April 1960.
81. Murphy, *Closer Association*, p. lxxvi.
82. Hargreaves, *Decolonization in Africa,* p. 215
83. BSB S.20 Vol. (6), Review of security intelligence within the Federation of Rhodesia and Nyasaland for the period 16 April–30 June 1960 [n.d].
84. Ibid.
85. R. Welensky, *4000 Days* (London: Collins, 1964), p. 268 and Birkenhead, *Monckton,* p. 356.
86. Cmnd 1148, *Report of the Advisory Commission on the Review of the Constitution of Rhodesia and Nyasaland* (1960) para 82.
87. Keatley, *Partnership*, p. 457.
88. WP 679/3, Wall to Welensky, 17 October 1960.

89. Welensky, *4000 Days*, p. 272.
90. See H.D. Sills, 'The break-up of the Central African Federation: notes on the validity of assurances', *African Affairs* 73/290 (January 1974), pp. 50–62 for more details.
91. MSS. Macmillan dep. C. 358, fol. 54. Macmillan to Bligh, 22 September 1960.
92. Hargreaves, *Decolonization in Africa,* p. 215.
93. WP 679/3, Welensky to Wall, 14 October 1960.
94. Ibid., fol. 71, Welensky to Macmillan, 4 October 1960.
95. WP 679/3, Wall to Welensky, 4 November 1960.
96. J. Darwin, *Britain and Decolonisation, The Retreat from Empire in the Post-War World* (Basingstoke: Palgrave Macmillan, 1988), p. 273.
97. WP 274/2, Wynne to Parker, 10 November 1960.
98. Ibid.
99. DPW/48/181, Patrick Wall to the secretaries of state, 14 November 1960.
100. Wood, *Welensky Papers*, p. 846.
101. MSS. Macmillan dep. C. 358, fol. 87. Report on Welensky's speech to the Conservative Commonwealth Committee, 1 December 1960.
102. PREM 11/4608, Salisbury to Macmillan, 18 February 1961.
103. Ibid.
104. Welensky to Salisbury, 27 January 1961, cited in S. Ball, *The Guardsmen, Three Friends and the World They Made* (London: Harper Collins, 2005), p. 354.
105. Ball, *Guardsmen*, p. 352.
106. SP Box 4/001, folder 3/4a(M) Home to Whitehead, 19 July 1960.
107. For further details see F. Nehwati, 'The social and communal background to "Zhii": the African riots in Bulawayo, Southern Rhodesia in 1960', *African Affairs* 69/276 (July 1970), pp. 250–266 and T. O. Ranger, *Bulawayo Burning: The Social History of a Southern African City, 1893–1960* (Harare: Weaver Press, 2010).
108. Wood, *So Far and No Further!*, pp. 45–6.
109. Day, 'African nationalists', pp. 223–4.
110. BSB S.20 Vol. (6), Taswell to secretary for external affairs, Pretoria, 3 August 1960.
111. Ibid.
112. Wood, *So Far and No Further!,* p. 42.
113. Ibid., pp. 54–5.
114. WP 277/14, Welensky to Robins, 13 October 1960.
115. Wood, *So Far and No Further!,* p. 56.
116. See Ibid., p. 58 for a full list of measures.
117. UNIP 6/7/9, Sipalo to Nkomo, 1 November 1960.
118. BSB S.20 Vol. (6), Taswell to the secretary for external affairs, 12 November 1960.
119. BSB S.20 Vol. (6), Taswell to the secretary for external affairs, 3 November 1960. For Tredgold's account of this period see R. C. Tredgold, *The Rhodesia that Was my Life* (London: Allen & Unwin, 1968), pp. 202–66.

120. SP Box 4/001 (M), folder 3-4a, Sandys to Whitehead, 3 November 1960.
121. Ibid., Whitehead to Sandys, 5 November 1960.
122. Ibid., Welensky to Sandys, 7 November 1960.
123. Day, 'African nationalists', p. 227.
124. The proposals were for a 65-seat legislature, which would comprise 50 representatives elected by the majority white upper roll and 15 representatives elected by the largely African lower roll. Voters on each roll would have a 25 per cent influence over the choice made by the other roll. Racial discrimination would be guarded against through a declaration of rights. This would be enforced by a constitutional council which would be composed of members of all races. Britain agreed that it would only pass legislation for Southern Rhodesia at the request of the territory's government. Murphy, *Central Africa: Part I,* p. lxxx.
125. SP Box 4/001 (M), folder 2/4a, Dominion Party Statement to the Southern Rhodesia Constitutional Conference, 7 February 1961.
126. Ibid.
127. Ibid., Statement broadcast by Whitehead in Southern Rhodesia, 8 February 1961.
128. Day: 'African nationalists', p. 230.
129. SP Box 1/013, Southern Rhodesian Government Cabinet Minutes 1961, S.R.C. (61) Eleventh Meeting, 10 February 1961.
130. Ibid.
131. SP Box 1/013, Southern Rhodesian Government Cabinet Minutes 1961, S.R.C. (61), Fourteenth Meeting, 27 February 1961.
132. SP Box 4/001 (M), folder 2/4a, Sandys to Whitehead, 17 February 1961.
133. Day: 'African nationalists', p. 221.
134. Ibid., p. 244.
135. SP Box 4/001 (M), folder 2/4a, Whitehead to Sandys [n.d – its position in the file suggests at 17/18 April 1961].
136. WP 677/8, Welensky to van der Byl, 24 July 1961.
137. Murphy, *Closer Association,* p. lxxxi.
138. Wood, *So Far and No Further!,* p.90.
139. Goldsworthy, *Colonial Issues,* p. 367.
140. Holland, *European Decolonization*, p. 230.
141. PREM 11/3485, Macmillan to Macleod, 27 January 1961.
142. Ibid.
143. Ibid.
144. WP 679/3, Wall to Welensky, 10 February 1961.
145. Ibid.
146. DPW/48/181, Wall to Macmillan, 10 February 1961.
147. PREM 11/3076, Macleod to Macmillan, 31 March 1960, cited in Murphy, *Central Africa: Part II*, p. 130.
148. Murphy, *Central Africa: Part* II, pp. lxxxi–lxxxii.
149. Wood, *Welensky Papers*, p. 862.

150. The 15-15-15 proposal would give an upper roll 15 seats, a lower roll 15 seats and 15 more members based on the voting preferences of the other two rolls combined. In practice this would give a greater influence to the predominantly European upper roll, therefore Welensky believed it would be possible to still ensure a European majority under these proposals. See Murphy, *Central Africa: Part I,* p. lxxxiii.

151. Welensky, *4000 Days*, p. 293.

152. WP 665/3, Welensky to Salisbury, 27 February 1961.

153. See Philip Murphy, 'Operation KINGFISHER', in '"An intricate and distasteful subject": British planning for the use of force against the European settlers of central Africa, 1952–65', *English Historical Review* CXXI/492 (2006), pp. 746–77.

154. Wood, *The Welensky Papers*, p. 64.

155. WP 652/10, Welensky to Oppenheimer, 1 July 1961.

156. *HC Deb*, 22 February 1961, Vol. 635, col. 517.

157. Ibid., col. 518.

158. WP 665/3, Salisbury to Welensky, 25 February 1961.

159. Goldsworthy, *Colonial Issues*, pp. 368–9.

160. M. Kahler, *Decolonization in Britain and France: The Domestic Consequences of International Relations* (Princeton, NJ: Princeton University Press, 1984), p. 146.

161. A. King (ed.), *British Political Opinion 1937–2000: The Gallup Polls* (London: Politico's Publishing Ltd., 2001), p. 262.

162. Goldsworthy, *Colonial Issues*, p. 369.

163. WP 679/3, Wall to Welensky, 23 February 1961.

164. Murphy, *Central Africa: Part I,* p. lxxxiv.

165. WP 647/3, Welensky to Millin, 24 July 1961.

166. UNIP 14/1/3, *Dawn,* 1 July 1961, p. 6.

167. Welensky, *4000 Days*, p. 313.

168. Reginald Maudling (1917–79) was secretary of state for the colonies from 9 October 1961 until 13 July 1962. See R. Shepherd, 'Maudling, Reginald (1917–1979)', *Oxford Dictionary of National Biography* (Oxford: Oxford University Press, 2004), online edn, January 2008 {http://www.oxforddnb.com/view/article/31428, accessed 26 June 2015}.

169. C. Alport, *The Sudden Assignment: Being a Record of Service in Central Africa during the Last Controversial Years of the Federation of Rhodesia and Nyasaland, 1961–1963* (London: Hodder & Stoughton, 1965) p. 29.

170. Wood, *Welensky Papers*, p. 970.

171. WP 584/4, Welensky to Acutt, 20 September 1961.

172. WP 672/1, Welensky to Stanley, 21 September 1961.

173. WP 647/3, Welensky to Millin, 30 August 1961.

174. RLP Box 2, File, miscellaneous correspondence, including correspondence with Harry Oppenheimer. Oppenheimer to Prain, 6 March 1958.

175. RLP Box 1, File 5, Prain to H. Hochschild, 2 October 1959.

176. A. Hocking, *Oppenheimer and Son* (London: McGraw-Hill Inc., 1973), p. 303.
177. Ibid., p. 244.
178. RLP Box 1, File 5, Prain to Hochschild, 23 February 1963.
179. Hocking, *Oppenheimer*, p. 313.
180. *Optima*, September 1959, p. 132.
181. WP 584/4, Welensky to Acutt, 20 February 1960.
182. Ibid., Welensky to Acutt, 14 May 1962.
183. WP 502/4, Brickhill to Welensky, 16 May 1960.
184. Ibid., Welensky to Acutt, 20 May 1960.
185. WP 584/4, Welensky to Acutt, 20 September 1961.
186. Ibid., Welensky to Acutt, 14 May 1962.
187. Ibid., Welensky to Acutt, 21 May 1962.
188. D. Pallister, S. Stewart and I. Lepper, *South Africa Inc.: The Oppenheimer Empire* (New Haven, CT: Simon & Schuster, 1988), p. 17.
189. WP 662/4, Welensky to Robins, 12 August 1959.
190. WP 662/5, Robins to Welensky, 10 May 1960.
191. Anglo American chairman Harry Oppenheimer sat on the board of the British South Africa Company; the president of the Chartered Company, Ellis Robins, in turn sat on the board of Anglo American. Other members of the Chartered Company board included Lord Malvern, the previous federal prime minister; and the right-wing Conservative Party member, Lord Salisbury, the bête noire of Macmillan's colonial reformers. White's comment that business in Malaya was 'highly incestuous' is echoed in the case of central Africa. See N. White, *Business Government and the End of Empire: Malaya, 1942–57* (Oxford: Oxford University Press, 1997), p. 29.
192. The certificates awarded to the Chartered Company covered wide areas of Northern Rhodesia where the Company's treaty-gathering agents had never penetrated. P. Slinn 'The legacy of the British South Africa Company: the historical background', in M. Bostock and C. Harvey (eds), *Economic Independence and Zambian Copper* (London: Praeger, 1972), p. 25.
193. As Miles Kahler remarks: 'As a rentier, claiming royalties from mineral development and lacking the protective role of an agent of economic development, the BSA had clashed with the European settlers of Northern Rhodesia (prior to federation). Its strategy of opposition to rapid African advance, combined with efforts to strengthen its political position through diversifying its holdings and creating links, both to larger and more secure copper multinationals in the territory and to the political elite in Britain, ultimately failed to halt or even slow the transfer of power.' Kahler, *Decolonization in Britain and France*, p. 280.
194. BSB S.20 Vol. (5), Taswell to secretary for external affairs, Pretoria, 30 July 1959.
195. R. Prain, *Reflections of an Era: Fifty Years of Mining in Changing Africa: The Autobiography of Sir Ronald Prain* (Letchworth: Metal Bulletin Books, 1981), p. 144.

196. Ibid., p. 145.
197. Ibid.
198. RLP Box 2, File, Correspondence with Lord Monckton and Monckton Commission. Monckton to Prain, 20 February 1960.
199. RLP Box 1, File 5, Prain to Hochschild, 23 July 1959.
200. Welensky, *4000 Days*, p. 186.
201. Evans specifies 'either generally or on any of the particular functions mentioned: Education, Health, Agriculture with marketing, and Prisons'.
202. RLP Box 2, File, Correspondence with Lord Monckton and Monckton Commission. Evans to Prain, 4 November 1960.
203. Ibid., Prain to Evans, 15 November 1960.
204. Ibid.
205. Ibid.
206. Ibid.
207. WP 663/1, Robinson to Welensky, 13 June 1960.
208. Ibid., Welensky to Robinson, 13 June 1960.
209. Ibid.
210. Prain's factors were 'the possibility of irresponsible acts by Africans or Europeans, the tension which must accompany the next few weeks in the Congo, possible developments in Nyasaland, and the possibility of ill-considered statements by Government or company spokesmen or of African leaders'.
211. RLP Box 2, File, Correspondence with Harold Macmillan, Alan Lennox-Boyd and Iain Macleod. Prain to Macleod, 15 June 1960.
212. Ibid.
213. White, *Malaya, 1942–57*, p. 137.
214. RLP Box 1, File 5, H. Hochschild to Prain, 28 November 1959.
215. W. Rodney, *How Europe Underdeveloped Africa* (Cape Town: Pambazuka Press, 2012), p. 176.
216. RLP Box 1 File 5, H. Hochschild to Prain, 28 November 1959.
217. L. Butler, 'Business and decolonisation: Sir Ronald Prain, the mining industry and the Central African Federation', *The Journal of Imperial and Commonwealth History* 35/3 (2007), p. 470.
218. *African Mail*, 26 April 1960.
219. *Daily Herald*, 28 April 1960.
220. WP 600/5, Cole to Parker, 7 May 1960.
221. WP 251/7, L'Ange to Barrow, 10 May 1960.
222. RLP Box 1 File 5, Loft to H. Hochschild, 4 December 1959.
223. Wood, *Welensky Papers*, p. 765.
224. RLP Box 1 File 5, H. Hochschild to Loft, 24 November 1959.
225. Ibid., Loft to H. Hochschild, 5 November 1959.
226. RLP 1, unnumbered file, misc. 1949–62. Loft to Ostrander, 12 August 1961.
227. Butler, 'Business and decolonisation', p. 472.

228. Prain's statement pronounced that 'the first, and with no doubt the most important [factor], is the satisfactory evolution of the political future of the territories', and went on to conclude '[o]f one thing I am certain, that the copper mines of central Africa are an indispensable part of the structure of modern civilisation [...] The energies of your directors will continue to be addressed to ensuring, as far as it lies in their power, that these companies will play their full part in the development of central Africa and in the world copper industry.' *The Economist*, 28 November 1959.

229. RLP Box 1 File 5, H. Hochschild, 'Summary of talk with Dr Banda', 16 April 1960.

230. RLP 2, Correspondence, Governors of Rhodesia and Nyasaland, 1954–64. Armitage to Prain, 24 June 1960.

231. RLP Box 1 File 5, H. Hochschild 'Summary of talk with Dr Banda', 16 April 1960.

232. Ibid.

233. Ibid.

234. Ibid.

235. Ibid.

236. Ibid.

237. WP 647/4, Welensky to Millin, 13 May 1962.

238. WP 689/9, Ostrander to Jeffries, 1 December 1959.

239. Ibid., Jeffries to Welensky, 4 December 1959.

240. WP 690/4, 'Top secret' report, July 1960.

241. Ibid.

242. G. M. Houser, 'Meeting Africa's challenge: the story of the American Committee on Africa', *A Journal of Opinion* 6 2/3 Africanist Studies 1955–75 (Summer–Autumn, 1976), p. 19.

243. RLP 1, unnumbered file, miscellaneous correspondence, 1949–62. II. Hochschild to Prain, 17 January 1961.

244. WP 550/14, Parker to Wynne, 5 May 1961.

245. Ibid.

246. Ibid.

247. RG 59, General Records of the Department of State, Bureau of African Affairs, Office of Eastern and Southern African Affairs, COUNTRY FILES, 1951–65, Kenya biographic data to Rhodesia Desegregation, Box 1, Record of Conversation between Chester G. Dunham and F. Taylor Ostrander, 21 September 1961.

248. D. Lowry, 'Welensky, Sir Roland (1907–1991)', *Oxford Dictionary of National Biography* (Oxford: Oxford University Press, Sept. 2004), online edn, May 2006 [http://www.oxforddnb.com/view/article/50688, accessed 22 December 2007].

249. See for example RG 59, Office of Eastern and Southern African Affairs, COUNTRY FILES, 1951–65, Kenya biographic data to Rhodesia desegregation, Box 1. Report entitled 'The Southern Rhodesian question

at the UN', by E. H. Kloman, Jr. and F. Taylor Ostrander of American Metal Climax Inc., 2 Mar 1962; and Ibid. Report entitled 'The Northern Rhodesian question at the UN,' by E. H. Kloman, Jr. of American Metal Climax Inc., 28 May 1962.

250. Wood, *Welensky Papers*, p. 941.

251. WP 493/2, Welensky to Acutt, 28 August 1961.

252. WP 662/6, Welensky to Robins, 22 September 1961.

253. WP 493/2, Welensky to Acutt, 28 August 1961.

254. Ibid.

255. WP 584/4, Acutt to Welensky, 1 September 1961.

256. Ibid.

257. Ibid.

258. WP 662/6, Welensky to Robins, 10 September 1961.

259. WP 662/6, Robins to Welensky, 19 September 1961.

260. Ibid.

261. Ibid.

262. WP 502/4, Brownrigg to Welensky, 25 September 1961.

263. Ibid.

264. WP 502/4, Welensky to Brownrigg, 2 October 1961.

265. WP 484/7, Welensky to Etheridge, 19 December 1961.

266. Philip Murphy, *Alan Lennox-Boyd: A Biography* (London: I.B.Tauris, 1999), p. 90.

267. WP 494/2, Fox to Etheridge, 9 March 1962.

268. Ibid.

269. WP 494/2, Notes of a meeting held at 10 Upper Grosvenor Street, London regarding 'build-a-nation' campaign, 11 April 1962.

270. Ibid.

271. Ibid., Etheredge to Sharp, 11 May 1962.

272. Ibid.

273. H. Macmillan, *Susman Brothers & Wulfsohn, 1901–2005* (London: I.B.Tauris, 2005), pp. 221–45.

274. For a good summary of the Kennedy White House see D. Halberstam, *The Best and the Brightest* (New York, NY: Random House, 1972).

275. Butler, *Britain and Empire*, p. 153.

276. Williams was nicknamed 'Soapy' as his grandfather founded the Mennen Company, a large manufacturer of toiletries.

277. C. Watts, 'G. Mennen Williams and Rhodesian independence: a case study in bureaucratic politics', *Michigan Academician* XXXVI (2004), p. 232.

278. Wood, *Welensky Papers*, p. 944.

279. On this trip Williams visited Sudan, Ethiopia, Somalia, Kenya, Uganda, Tanganyika, Zanzibar, ex-Belgian Congo, ex-French Congo, Cameroon, Nigeria, Togo, Liberia, Ivory Coast, Ghana and Upper Volta.

280. RG 59 General Records of the Department of State, Records of G. Mennen Williams, 1961–6, Trips file, 1961–6, January–October 1961, 'Report on

trip to Africa' from G. Mennen Williams to the secretary of state (first draft, n.d.)

281. Ibid.

282. RG 59 General Records of the Department of State, Bureau of African Affairs, Office of Eastern and Southern African Affairs, COUNTRY FILES, 1951–65, Rhodesia, educational and culture to South Africa, Social, education (Box 2), memorandum on bilateral discussions with UK on the Federation of Rhodesia and Nyasaland, 31 January 1961.

283. Ibid.

284. Ibid., Picard to Williams, Penfield and Deming, 4 April 1961.

285. RG 59 General Records of the Department of State, Records of G. Mennen Williams, 1961–6, Entry 719.3 Signature and Clearance File, 1961–6, January–December 1961 (Box 9), Williams to Rusk, 1 May 1961.

286. RG 59 General Records of the Department of State, Records of G. Mennen Williams, 1961–6, Trips file, 1961–6, January – October 1961, Telegram (458) from Department of State, Washington to American Consulate, Salisbury, 26 May 1961.

287. Ibid.

288. RG 59 General Records of the Department of State, Records of G. Mennen Williams, 1961–6, Entry 719.3 Signature and Clearance File, 1961–6, January–December 1961 (Box 9), Letter from Williams to the Acting Secretary, 16 May 1961.

289. Ibid., Mennen Williams to Johnson, 4 May 1961.

290. Ibid., Mennen Williams to Rusk, 5 May 1961.

291. WP 493/2, Welensky to Acutt, 28 August 1961.

292. RG 59 General Records of the Department of State, Records of G. Mennen Williams, 1961–6, Trips file, 1961–6, January–October 1961, Telegram from American Consulate, Salisbury to State Department, Washington, DC, 31 August 1961.

293. Ibid.

294. RG 59 General Records of the Department of State, Bureau of African Affairs, Office of Eastern and Southern African Affairs, COUNTRY FILES, 1951–65, Kenya biographic data to Rhodesia desegregation (Box 1), Report on the Federation situation by F. Taylor Ostrander (nd).

295. Ibid.

296. Ibid.

297. Ibid.

298. RG 59 General Records of the Department of State, Bureau of African Affairs, Office of Eastern and Southern African Affairs, COUNTRY FILES, 1951–65, Rhodesia, educational and culture to South Africa, Social, education (Box 2), Memorandum of conversation between John Hemmings, Colonial Attaché British Embassy, Kenneth Luke, British Embassy, William L. Wright, AFE, Chester G. Dunham, AFE, 11 August 1961.

299. Ibid., p. 19.

300. R. A. Moore, Jr., *The United Nations Reconsidered* (Columbia, SC, 1963), p. 9.
301. J. H. Mittleman, 'Collective decolonisation and the UN Committee of 24', *The Journal of Modern African Studies* 14/1 (1976), p. 41.
302. Countries voting for abstention were Australia, Belgium, Dominican Republic, France, Portugal, Spain, South Africa, United Kingdom and the United States.
303. R. Emerson, 'Colonialism, political development and the UN', *International Organization* 19/3 (Summer, 1965), p. 495 and Mittleman, 'Collective decolonisation', p. 45.
304. Mittleman, 'Collective decolonisation', pp. 41–5.
305. Emerson, 'Colonialism', p. 497.
306. Ibid., p. 496.
307. FO 371/166819, no.8, Letter from Mr Maudling to Lord Home, 5 January 1962, cited in Hyam and Louis, *Conservative Government*: Part II, pp. 322–3.
308. Ibid.
309. Darwin, *Britain and Decolonisation*, p. 252.
310. Alport, *The Sudden Assignment*, pp. 95–7
311. H. Macmillan, *At The End of the Day* (London: Macmillan, 1973), p. 280.
312. Ibid., p. 211.
313. Welensky, *4000 Days*, p. 211.
314. The *Daily Telegraph*, 14 September 1961.
315. Ibid., 16 September 1961.
316. *The Times*, 14 September 1961.
317. The *Daily Mail*, 14 September 1961.
318. *Daily Express*, 15 September 1961.
319. See S. Williams, *Who Killed Hammarskjöld? The UN, the Cold War, and White Supremacy in Africa* (New York: Columbia University Press, 2011).
320. WP 584/5, Welensky to Adams, 18 September 1961.
321. WP 584/4, Welensky to Acutt, 20 September 1961.
322. Katema Yifru; J. Rudolph Grimes; Ibrahim Abboud; Mongi Slim; Kwame Nkrumah; Louis Lansana Beavogui; Leopold Sedar Senghor; Alhaji Sir Abubaker Tafawa Balewa, 'Africa speaks to the United Nations: a symposium of aspirations and concerns voiced by representative leaders at the UN', *International Organization* 16/2 (Spring, 1962), p. 319.
323. WP 234/8, Report by Benoy regarding his visit to Cape Town and Pretoria, 6 February 1961.
324. M. Hughes, 'The Central African Federation, Katanga and the Congo crisis', *Military and International History* 2 (2003), pp. 19–21.
325. Darwin, *Britain and Decolonisation*, p. 278.
326. A. Thompson, *The Empire Strikes Back? The Impact of Imperialism on Britain from the Mid-Nineteenth Century* (Harlow: Routledge, 2005), p. 216.
327. B. Porter: The Absent Minded Imperialists: What the British Really Thought About Empire (Oxford: Oxford University Press, 2004), p. 2.

Chapter 4 A Failed Experiment, 1962–3

1. Sarah Gertrude Millin (1889–1968) was a South African author who published both fiction and non-fiction including biographies of *Cecil Rhodes* (London: Chatto & Windus, 1933) and *General Jan Smuts* (London: Faber & Faber, 1936). See M. Rubin, *Sarah Gertrude Millin: A South African Life* (London: Ad Donker, 1977).
2. WP 647/4, Welensky to Millin, 16 March 1962.
3. R. Welensky, *4000 Days: The Life and Death of the Federation of Rhodesia and Nyasaland* (London, Collins, 1964), p. 317.
4. Ibid.
5. J. R. T. Wood, *The Welensky Papers* (Durban: Graham Publishing, 1983), p. 967.
6. Ibid., p. lxxxv.
7. CAB 128/36/1, CC 10(62)7, Cabinet Conclusions, 1 February 1962 cited in R. Hyam and W. M. R. Louis, *British Documents on the End of Empire, Series A, Volume Four, The Conservative Government and the End of Empire, 1957–1964 Part II, Economics, International Relations and the Commonwealth* (London: The Stationary Office, 2000), pp. 563–4.
8. P. Murphy, *British Documents on the End of Empire, Vol. 9: Central Africa, Part I, Closer Association, 1945–1958* (London Stationary Office, 2005), p. lxxxv.
9. R. Maudling, *Memoirs* (London: Sidgwick & Jackson, 1978), p. 99.
10. Welensky, *4000 Days*, p. 315.
11. RLP Box 2, misc. correspondence Harold Macmillan, Alan Lenox-Boyd and Iain Macleod. Prain to MacMillan, 18 January 1962.
12. Ibid.
13. Ibid.
14. Wood, *Welensky Papers*, p. 979.
15. C. Alport, *The Sudden Assignment: Being a Record of Service in Central Africa during the Last Controversial Years of the Federation of Rhodesia and Nyasaland, 1961–1963* (London: Hodder & Stoughton, 1965), p. 90.
16. Wood, *Welensky Papers*, pp. 1011–12.
17. WP 647/4, Welensky to Millin, 5 March 1962.
18. Ibid.
19. PREM 11/3943, Note by T. J. Bligh of a meeting at Admiralty House between Macmillan and Welensky, 1 March 1962 cited in P. Murphy, *British Documents on the End of Empire, Vol. 9: Central Africa, Part II, Crisis and Dissolution, 1959–1965* (London: Stationary Office, 2005), pp. 309–312.
20. DPW/48/198, Wall to Cleveland, 12 March 1962.
21. It was agreed that the Asian seat should remain, which in effect kept Asian voters on the upper roll and strengthened European influence. Maudling did manage to push through a lowering of the percentage of votes candidates in National seats were required to obtain from both rolls and the removal of the numerical alternative. Murphy, *Central Africa: Part I*, p. lxxxv.

22. Alport notes how Welensky was at this point 'under pressure from those quarters which normally attributed to him the infallibility of the Pope'. Alport, *Sudden Assignment*, p. 172.

23. WP 647/4, Welensky to Millin, 16 March 1962.

24. L. Bowman, *Politics in Rhodesia: White Power in An African State* (Cambridge, Mass.: Harvard University Press, 1973), p. 34.

25. Alport, *Sudden Assignment*, p. 178.

26. UNIP 14/2/4, *Voice of UNIP*, May 1962.

27. C. Baker, *Glyn Jones: A Proconsul in Africa* (London: I.B.Tauris, 2000), p. 124.

28. Murphy, *Central Africa: Part I*, p. xciii.

29. Ibid., p. xcii.

30. Richard Austen Butler, Baron Butler of Saffron Walden (1902–1982) was more generally known as R. A. Butler and familiarly known as 'Rab' was a Conservative politician who, amongst other positions in a long career, held the posts of deputy prime minister and first secretary of state from 13 July 1962 to 18 October 1963 and minister in charge of the Central Africa Office from March 1962 until October 1963. See Lord Butler, *The Art of the Possible: The Memoirs of Lord Butler* (London: Hamish Hamilton, 1971).

31. Welensky is said to have revealed to Lord Alport that he would never had called a federal election if he had known Butler would be taking over responsibility for the Federation. Alport, *Sudden Assignment*, p. 174.

32. Welensky, *4000 Days*, p. 331.

33. Butler, *Art of the Possible*, p. 209.

34. Murphy, *Central Africa: Part I*, p. xciii.

35. MSS. Macmillan dep. C. 358, fol. 273. Macmillan to Alport, 13 March 1962.

36. Ibid., fol. 275. Alport to Macmillan, 14 March 1962.

37. DPW/48/125, Patrick Wall to Grenfell, 16 March 1962.

38. Commander Thomas Fox-Pitt (1897–1980) had previously served in the Colonial Administrative Service in Northern Rhodesia between 1927 and 1951. See *https://www.soas.ac.uk/library/archives/collections/a-z/f/* [accessed 23 June 2015]

39. UNIP 9/1/37, Fox-Pitt to Mutti, 22 March 1962.

40. Ibid.

41. Simon Zukas was a European supporter of African nationalism in Northern Rhodesia, and was deported to Britain in 1952 as a result of his campaign against federation. See S. Zukas, *Into Exile and Back* (Lusaka: Bookworld Publishers, 2002).

42. Zukas Papers, HM 75/PP/1, Zukas to Mutti, 25 March 1962.

43. Ibid., Zukas to Kaunda, 3 June 1962.

44. SP Box 3/001, Memorandum from Southern Rhodesian Cabinet to Butler, 14 May 1962.

45. Ibid.

46. WP 677/8, Welensky to van der Byl, 25 May 1962.

47. WP 647/4, Welensky to Millin, 25 May 1962.

48. UNIP 16/1/6, Banda to UNIP Representative Dar-es-Salaam, 1 June 1962.

49. UNIP 16/1/13, Chona to Hone, 7 June 1962.

50. Wood, *Welensky Papers*, p. 1055.

51. Butler, *The Art*, p. 217.

52. Ibid., p. 216.

53. WP 679/4, Wall to Welensky, 23 July 1962.

54. J. Darwin, *Britain and Decolonization, The Retreat from Empire in the Post-War World* (Basingstoke: Palgrave Macmillan, 1988), p. 276.

55. Goldsworthy credits Turton's Early Day Motion as 'by far the most significant turning-point in the story of the inter-play between Conservative policies and Decolonization'. See D. Goldsworthy, 'Conservatives and decolonization: A note on the interpretation by Dan Horowitz', *African Affairs* 69/276 (Jul., 1970), p. 281.

56. WP 686/7, Welensky to Wynne, 12 March 1963.

57. Sir Albert Robinson (1915–2009) was the Federation's high commissioner in London from 1961 until the Federation was dissolved see http://www.telegraph.co.uk/news/obituaries/4980924/Sir-Albert-Robinson.html {accessed 23 June 2015}.

58. WP 665/4, Welensky to Salisbury, 18 March 1962.

59. WP 679/4, Welensky to Wall, 1 April 1962.

60. WP 274/4, Parker to Wynne, 12 July 1962.

61. Roy Mason (1924–2015) was Labour MP for Barnsley. See the *Yorkshire Post*, 20 April 2015.

62. *HC Deb.* 19 Jul 1962, Vol. 663, col. 89.

63. UNIP 6/7/13, Zaza to Castle, 14 April 1962.

64. Ibid., Mutti to Castle, 16 April 1962.

65. Ibid., Mutti to Castle, 17 April 1962.

66. *HC Deb.* 8 May 1962, Vol. 659, col. 276.

67. WP 647/4, Welensky to Millin, 20 October 1962.

68. Richard Aldous and Sabine Lee contend that Macmillan 'overestimated Britain's bargaining power' with regard to entry to the Common Market and 'by 1963 it had become clear that Britain's reorientation towards Europe had foundered not so much on doing little by way of concessions as doing it too late'. See R. Aldous and S. Lee, 'Staying in the game: Harold Macmillan and Britain's world role', in R. Aldous and S. Lee (eds), *Harold Macmillan and Britain's World Role* (Basingstoke: Palgrave Macmillan, 1996), p. 154.

69. WP 647/4, Welensky to Millin, 30 October 1962.

70. G. Mennen Williams (1911–1988) was assistant secretary of state for African Affairs from 1961 to 1966. See *http://articles.chicagotribune.com/1988-02-03/news/8803270440_1_mennen-supreme-court-democratic-party* {accessed 25 June 2015}.

71. RG 59 General Records of the Department of State, Records of G. Mennen Williams, 1961–1966, Entry 719.3 signature and clearance file, 1961–6,

January – December, 1962 (Box 10), Mennen Williams to Paul Geren, 19 September 1962.

72. Ibid., Report from Mennen Williams to Matthews and Martin, 12 October 1962.

73. Ibid.

74. Ibid.

75. See A. Cohen, '"A difficult, tedious and unwanted task": representing the Central African Federation at the United Nations, 1960–1963', *Itinerario* 34/2 (2010), pp. 105–28.

76. J. R.T. Wood, *So Far and No Further! Rhodesia's Bid for Independence During the Retreat from Empire 1959–1965* (Johannesburg: 30 Degrees South, 2005), p. 117.

77. BSB S.12/5 Vol. (1), South African high commissioner, Salisbury to secretary of external affairs, Pretoria, 25 June 1962.

78. Ibid., South African high commissioner, Salisbury to secretary of external affairs, Pretoria, 26 June 1962.

79. T. Hovet, *Africa in the United Nations System* (Evanstan, III: Northwestern University Press, 1963), p. 4.

80. WP 677/8, Welensky to van der Byl, 10 January 1962.

81. BSB S.20/6 Vol. (1), Memorandum from the Permanent South African Mission to the United Nations to the secretary of foreign affairs, Pretoria, 7 March 1962.

82. Ibid.

83. Ibid.

84. WP 647/4, Welensky to Millin, 3 May 1962.

85. RG 59, Office of Eastern and Southern African Affairs, COUNTRY FILES, 1951–1965, Kenya biographic data to Rhodesia desegregation, Box 1. Report entitled 'The Southern Rhodesian question at the UN', by E.H. Kloman, Jr. and F. Taylor Ostrander of American Metal Climax Inc., 2 March 1962.

86. WP 647/4, Welensky to Millin, 13 May 1962.

87. Welensky, *4000 Days*, pp. 340–2.

88. David Dean Rusk (1909–1994) was the United States Secretary of State from 1961 until 1969, served under both President Kennedy and President Johnson. See http://www.independent.co.uk/news/people/obituaries–dean-rusk-1390416.html [accessed 25 June 2015]

89. RG 59, Presidential and Secretary of State Correspondence with Foreign Heads of State, 1953–1964, Rusk's Correspondence with UK Officials, Vol. 4, Box 19. Douglas-Home to Rusk, 18 October 1962.

90. RG 59, Records of G. Mennen Williams, 1961–66, Entry 719.3 Signature and Clearance File, 1961–66, January to December 1962, Box 10. Mennen Williams to Secretary of State, 10 March 1962.

91. Ibid.

92. BSB S.20/6 Vol. (1). Permanent South African Mission to the United Nations to the secretary of foreign affairs, Pretoria, 29 March 1962.

93. Ibid.

94. Voting in favour were: Cambodia, Ethiopia, India, Mali, Poland, Syria, Tanganyika, Tunisia, the USSR, Uruguay, Venezuela and Yugoslavia. Opposing were: Australia, Italy, the United Kingdom and the United States. Madagascar was absent.

95. RG 59, Office of Eastern and Southern African Affairs, COUNTRY FILES, 1951–1965, Kenya biographic data to Rhodesia desegregation, Box 1. Report entitled 'The Northern Rhodesian question at the UN', by E.H. Kloman, Jr. of American Metal Climax Inc., 28 May 1962.

96. WP 647/4, Welensky to Millin, 27 June 1962.

97. Welensky, *4000 Days*, pp. 340–2.

98. Wood, *So Far and No Further!*, pp. 109–10.

99. Welensky, *4000 Days*, pp. 340–2.

100. Wood, *So Far and No Further!*, p. 118.

101. Accusations of big business conspiring together were not just confined to southern Africa. 'I am convinced that all the various Mining Companies in this country form one whole block in a particular London Office', the Convention Peoples Party member for Kumasi East, Fori Dwumah, declared in the Gold Coast during March 1952. See S. Stockwell, *The Business of Decolonization* (Oxford: Oxford University Press, 2000), p. 93.

102. RLP Box 1, File 5, Prain to Hochschild, 19 February 1963.

103. Ibid.

104. Ibid., Hochschild to Oppenheimer, 5 March 1963.

105. WP 274/1, Grenfell to Parker, 13 July 1959.

106. WP 662/5, Robins to Welensky, 26 February 1960.

107. Ibid.

108. Ibid., Welensky to Robins, 1 March 1960.

109. Ibid.

110. P. Murphy, *Party Politics and Decolonization: The Conservative Government and British Colonial Policy in Tropical Africa, 1951–1964* (Oxford: Oxford University Press, 1999), p. 112.

111. P. Keatley, *The Politics of Partnership: The Federation of Rhodesia and Nyasaland* (London: Penguin, 1963), pp. 462–4.

112. Murphy, *Party Politics,* p. 112.

113. K. S. Petersen, 'The business of the United Nations Security Council: history (1946–1963) and prospects', *The Journal of Politics* 27/ 4 (Nov., 1965), p. 824.

114. Hovet, *Africa*, p. 216.

115. Petersen, 'United Nations Security Council', p. 830.

116. CAB 128/36/2, CC 64 (62) 2, Cabinet conclusions, 29 October 1962, cited in Hyam and Louis, *The Conservative Government: Part II,* pp. 224–226.

117. CAB 128/37, CC21 (63), Cabinet conclusions, 1 April 1963, cited in Ibid., pp. 597–598.

118. RG 59 General Records of the Department of State, Bureau of African Affairs, Office of Eastern and Southern African Affairs, COUNTRY FILES,

1951–1965, Rhodesia, educational and culture to South Africa, Social, education (Box 2), Research Memorandum from Hilman to Rusk, 29 October 1962.

119. Ibid.

120. Ibid.

121. RG 59 General Records of the Department of State, Records of G. Mennen Williams, 1961–1966, Entry 719.3 Signature and Clearance File, 1961–1966, January – December 1962 (Box 10), Mennen Williams to the Secretary of State, 21 November 1962.

122. WP 647/4, Welensky to Millin, 22 November 1962.

123. WP 670/15, Welensky to Solomon, 31 December 1962.

124. WP 647/4, Welensky to Millin, 18 December 1962.

125. WP 652/10, Welensky to Oppenheimer, 2 January 1963.

126. WP 652/10, Oppenheimer to Welensky, 25 December 1962.

127. Ibid.

128. Ibid.

129. Ibid.

130. Ibid.

131. Ibid., Welensky to Oppenheimer, 2 January 1963

132. WP 677/8, Welensky to van der Byl, 4 April 1963.

133. SP 3/001, Annexure to SRC (F) (63) 20th Meeting, 8 April 1963.

134. WP 665/5, Welensky to Salisbury, 9 May 1963.

135. WP 149/6, Memorandum from the Federal Office of Race Affairs, 5 January 1959.

136. BTS 22/2/27 Vol. (1), Taswell to secretary for foreign affairs, Pretoria, 13 May 1963.

137. For details on Federal-South African economic ties, particularly in relation to secondary industry in this period, see A. Mlambo and I. Phimister, 'Partly protected: origins and growth of colonial Zimbabwe's textile industry, 1890–1965', *Historia* 52/2 (November 2006), pp. 145–75.

138. BTS 22/2/27 Vol. (1), Taswell to secretary for foreign affairs, Pretoria, 13 May 1963.

139. WP 647/5, Welensky to Millin, 25 May 1963.

140. DO 183/305, no 19, 'Southern Rhodesia: first months of Mr Field's government': dispatch no 2. from Alport to Butler, 6 May 1963 cited in Murphy, *Central Africa, Part II*, pp. 372–3.

141. Rev Ndabaningi Sithole (1920–2000) became the first president of the Zimbabwe Africa National Union and later played a prominent role in the African nationalist struggle for majority rule in Rhodesia. See http://www.telegraph.co.uk/news/obituaries/1378211/The-Reverend- Ndabaningi-Sithole.html [accessed 25 June 2015]

142. BSB S.20/6 Vol. (2), Report from A. L. Hattingh, acting permanent representative at the South African Mission to the United Nations to the secretary of external affairs, Pretoria, 5 March 1963.

143. Darwin, *Decolonization*, p. 277.
144. PREM 11/4419, draft minute from Macmillan to Butler, 21 March 1963, cited in Hyam and Louis, *The Conservative Government: Part II*, p. 591.
145. BSB S.12/5 (1), The South African ambassador Washington, to the secretary of state for foreign affairs, Pretoria, 25 April 1963.
146. WP 647/5, Welensky to Millin, 7 January 1963.
147. WP 647/5, Welensky to Millin, 7 January 1963 and Welensky to Millin, 16 January 1963.
148. SP Box 2/001, Cabinet Memorandum, S.R.C. (F) (63) 35: Note of a Second Meeting between the First Secretary of State, the Rt. Hon. R. A. Butler, C.H., M.P., and the Prime Minister of Southern Rhodesia, the Hon. W. J. Field, C. M.G., O.B.E., M.P., held in the Prime Minister's Office, 25 Central Avenue, Salisbury, at 2.30 pm on Tuesday, 22 January, 1963, dated 25 January 1963.
149. Ibid.
150. Ibid.
151. WP 647/5, Welensky to Millin, 24 January 1963.
152. SP Box 3/001 (SSF) Vol. 1 – 1962–1963, Annexure to S.R.C. (F) (63) 8th Meeting, 30 January 1963.
153. SP Box 2/001 (A), Cabinet Memorandum, S.R.C. (F) (63) 47: Note of a fourth meeting between the Prime Minister of Southern Rhodesia and the First Secretary of State, held on Wednesday, 30 January, 1963, at 'Northward', Chancellor Avenue, Salisbury at 3.30 p. m. 4 February 1963.
154. Wood, *So Far and No Further!*, p. 128.
155. SP Box 3/001 (SSF) Vol. 1 1962–1963, Annexure to Southern Rhodesia cabinet (f) (63) twelfth meeting, 26 February 1963.
156. RG 59, General Records of the Department of State, Records of G. Mennen Williams, 1961–1966, Chronological file of G. Mennen Williams, 1961–6 January–December 1963 (Box 3), Williams to Geren, 1 March 1963.
157. DO 183/462, no 26 [Federation and the USA], letter from R. W. H. du Boulay (Washington) to N. D. Watson, 6 March 1963. cited in Murphy, *Central Africa, Part II,* pp. 359–61.
158. WP 590/3, Bennett to Welensky, 7 March 1963.
159. RG 59, General Records of the Department of State, Records of G. Mennen Williams, 1961–1966, Chronological file of G. Mennen Williams, 1961– 1966 January–December 1963 (Box 3), Williams to Secretary of State, 25 February 1963.
160. RG 59 General Records of the Department of State, Records of G. Mennen Williams, 1961-66, Entry 719.3 Signature and clearance file, 1961–6, January – December 1963 (Box 11), United States Strategy in British Central Africa, 1 May 1963
161. SP 2/001 (A), First meeting between Field, DuPont and Butler, 27 May 1963.
162. WP 686/7, Wynne to Welensky, 16 April 1963.
163. MSS. Macmillan dep. C. 358, fol. 333. Macmillan to Menzies, 28 April 1963.
164. WP 647/5, Welensky to Millin, 16 April 1963.

165. WP 665/5, Welensky to Salisbury, 24 June 1963.
166. See K. Young, *Rhodesia and Independence* (London: Eyre & Spottiswoode, 1969), p. 89 and I. Smith, *The Great Betrayal* (London: Blake, 1997), pp. 53–4.
167. R. A. Butler, *The Art of the Possible* (London: Hamish Hamilton, 1971), p. 226.
168. WP 584/5, Welensky to Adams, 11 July 1963.
169. BSB S.12/5 Vol. (1) South African Ambassador, Washington to Secretary for Foreign Affairs, 10 October 1963.

Conclusion

1. J. R. T. Wood, *The Welensky Papers* (Durban: Graham Publishing, 1983), p. 15.
2. J. Hargreaves, *Decolonization in Africa* (London: Routledge, 1996), p. 248.
3. J. Darwin, *Britain and Decolonisation, The Retreat from Empire in the Post-War World* (Basingstoke: Palgrave Macmillan, 1988), p. 330.
4. C. Sanger, *Central African Emergency* (London: Heinemann, 1960), p. 179.
5. The link between the Nyasaland Emergency and the subsequent Monckton Commission has been emphasised by Hargreaves, *Decolonization in Africa*, p. 213.
6. R. Welensky, *4000 Days* (London: Collins, 1964), p. 137.
7. P. Murphy, *Party Politics and Decolonization: The Conservative Government and British Colonial Policy in Tropical Africa, 1951–1964* (Oxford: Oxford University Press, 1999), p. 232.
8. L. Bowman, *Politics in Rhodesia: White Power in an African State* (Cambridge, MA; Harvard University Press, 1973), pp. 33–4.
9. N. White, *Business Government and the End of Empire: Malaya, 1942–1957* (Oxford: Oxford University Press, 1997).
10. S. Stockwell, *The Business of Decolonization* (Oxford: Oxford University Press, 2000).
11. L. J. Butler, *Copper Empire* (Basingstoke: Palgrave Macmillan, 2007) and 'Business and decolonisation: Sir Ronald Prain, the mining industry and the Central African Federation', *The Journal of Imperial and Commonwealth History* 35/3 (2007), pp. 459–84.
12. A. Thompson, *The Empire Strikes Back? The Impact of Imperialism on Britain from the Mid-Nineteenth Century* (Harlow: Routledge, 2005), p. 216.
13. Darwin, *Britain and Decolonisation*, p. 278.
14. Murphy, *Party Politics*, p. 237.
15. L. J. Butler, *Britain and Empire: Adjusting to a Post-Imperial World* (London: I.B.Tauris, 2002), p. 190.
16. R. Hyam, *Britain's Declining Empire: The Road to Decolonisation 1918–1968* (Cambridge: Cambridge University Press, 2006), p. xiv.
17. SP Box 2/001 (A), Cabinet Memorandum S.R.C (F) (63) 36: Note of a meeting between R. A. Butler and the Southern Rhodesian cabinet, 25 January 1963.

18. See especially W. M. R. Louis and R. Robinson, 'The imperialism of decolonization', *The Journal of Imperial and Commonwealth History* 22/3 (September 1994), p. 487.

19. J. Darwin, *The End of Empire: The Historical Debate* (Oxford: Basil Blackwell, 1991), p. 73.

20. The influence of international relations has been emphasised in two studies: Butler, *Britain and Empire*, pp. 190–1 and Hyam, *Britain's Declining Empire*, pp. 301–26.

21. R. F. Holland, *European Decolonization, 1918–1981* (London: Macmillan, 1985), pp. 230–1.

22. R. Hyam, *Britain's Declining Empire*, p. 403.

BIBLIOGRAPHY

Archival Sources

American Heritage Center, *University of Wyoming, 2111 Willett Drive, Laramie, Wyoming, United States of America*

RONALD PRAIN PAPERS

BOX	FILE
Box 1	Miscellaneous file, 1949–62.
Box 1/2	AMAX – 1959–60.
Box 1/5	Correspondence with Amco, H. K. Hochschild 1955–69.
Box 2	Correspondence with Sir Roy Welensky.
Box 2	Correspondence with the Governor of Northern Rhodesia 1954–64.
Box 2	African Advancement.
Box 2	Miscellaneous correspondence, including correspondence with Harry Oppenheimer.
Box 2	Correspondence with Lord Monckton and the Monckton Commission.
Box 2	Correspondence with Harold Macmillan, Alan Lennox-Boyd and Iain Macleod.

FRANK TAYLOR OSTRANDER PAPERS

BOX	FILE
Box 12	An Appreciation of HKH as a Businessman.
Box 39h	Chronological File, January–June 1955.

Anglo American Archives, 44 Main Street, Johannesburg, Republic of South Africa

Annual Reports, The Rhodesian Broken Hill Development Company Limited, 1957–8.
Annual Reports, Nchanga Consolidated Copper Mines Limited, 1957–60.

'An Introduction to RST', [n.d].

Optima, 1957–63.

'The Attitudes of White Mining Employees towards Life and Work at Broken Hill, Northern Rhodesia', (December, 1961).

Theodore Gregory Papers.

Brynmor Jones Library, The University of Hull, Cottingham Road, Hull, United Kingdom

PATRICK WALL PAPERS

BOX/FILE

48/122	Africa. Correspondence, list of Contacts in Africa and of MPs interested in African affairs, November 1959–December 1966.
48/125	Report of Visit to Central and Southern Africa by Patrick Wall, June 1961–July 1962.
48/168	Central African Federation. Correspondence and background papers covering the Federal Constitutional Amendment Bill and the Federal Electoral Bill, August–December 1957.
48/170	Central African Federation. Background papers and relative correspondence, about the Federation of Rhodesia and Nyasaland Election Bill, December 1957–December 1958.
48/171	Central African Federation. Correspondence, January 1958–February 1959.
48/181	Central African Federation. Correspondence, including with Harold Macmillan, Prime Minister, Iain Macleod, Colonial Secretary, MPs, Lords, July 1960–April 1961.
48/198	Nyasaland. Notes, statistics of violent incidents and correspondence, March–October 1963.

Bodleian Library, Broad Street, Oxford, United Kingdom

HAROLD MACMILLAN PAPERS

BOX/FILE

Mss. C.358   Conservative Commonwealth Committee, 1960.
Mss. D.33–5   Personal Diary, 1959.
Mss. D.38   Personal Diary, 1960.
Mss. D.C.358   Central Africa Correspondence, 1960.

GENERAL

Mss. Afi.s.2125 Dick Hobson, 'The Last Gasp' (1991).

GRANADA END OF EMPIRE DEPOSIT

BOX/FILE

MSS.Brit.Emp.s.572/2   Interview Transcripts.

PATRICK DEVLIN PAPERS

BOX/FILE

BOX 1, NYC 1   Nyasaland Commission Correspondence, 1959.
BOX 1, NYC 2   Nyasaland Commission Correspondence, 1959.
BOX 14, Vol. 8   Transcripts File, 1959.

SIR ROY WELENSKY PAPERS

BOX/FILE

WP 149/6   Correspondence regarding Partnership, 1959.
WP 233/4   Defence and Security, 1961.
WP 234/8   Defence and Security, 1961.
WP 251/7   Correspondence regarding African Advancement, 1960.
WP 272/2   Correspondence with D. Cole, copper companies and others regarding
              public relations, 1957.
WP 274/1   Correspondence with D. Cole, copper companies and others regarding
              public relations, 1959.
WP 274/2   Correspondence with D. Cole, copper companies and others
              regarding public relations, 1960.
WP 274/3   Correspondence with D. Cole, copper companies and others regarding
              public relations, 1961.
WP 274/4   Correspondence with D. Cole, copper companies and others
              regarding public relations, 1962.
WP 274/5   Correspondence with D. Cole, copper companies and others regarding
              public relations, 1963.
WP 277/14   Correspondence concerning African newspapers, 1955–63.
WP 279/4   Correspondence regarding the *Central African Examiner*, 1959–60.
WP 339/6   Correspondence concerning the financing of the Kariba Dam, 1958.
WP 341/10   Correspondence regarding Copper Pricing, 1957.
WP 342/6   Copper Companies and Loans, 1955–61.
WP 349/3   Correspondence concerning Federal Loan, 1957.
WP 398/2   Correspondence regarding London/Lisbon visits, 1958.
WP 471/4   Correspondence with Spicer, 1960–3.
WP 484/7   Correspondence regarding organisation and finance, 1961–2.
WP 493/2   Correspondence regarding African Membership of the UFP, 1961.
WP 494/2   Correspondence regarding 'Build-a-Nation', 1962.
WP 502/4   Correspondence regarding UFP, 1960–1.
WP 514/1   Security, 1960.
WP 550/14   Correspondence with Wynne, 1961.
WP 584/4   Correspondence with Acutt, 1957–62.
WP 584/5   Correspondence with Adams, 1961–3.
WP 590/3   Correspondence with Bennett, 1963.

WP 600/3   Correspondence with Cole, 1958.
WP 600/4   Correspondence with Cole, 1959.
WP 600/5   Correspondence with Cole, 1960.
WP 606/8   Correspondence with Savory, 1959.
WP 618/4   Correspondence with Gore-Browne, 1960.
WP 624/1   Correspondence with Harold K. Hochschild and Walter Hochs-
            child, 1957.
WP 628/6   Correspondence with Joelson, 1960.
WP 635/9   Correspondence with Lambton, 1960–1.
WP 647/3   Correspondence with Millin, 1961.
WP 647/4   Correspondence with Millin, 1962.
WP 647/5   Correspondence with Millin, 1963.
WP 652/10   Correspondence with H. Oppenheimer, 1960–3.
WP 655/2   Correspondence with Pegrum, 1958–60.
WP 657/5   Correspondence with Prain, 1957–62.
WP 662/4   Correspondence with Robins, 1958–9.
WP 662/5   Correspondence with Robins, 1960.
WP 662/6   Correspondence with Robins, 1961.
WP 663/1   Correspondence with Robinson, 1960.
WP 665/2   Correspondence with Salisbury, 1960.
WP 665/3   Correspondence with Salisbury, 1961.
WP 665/4   Correspondence with Salisbury, 1962.
WP 665/5   Correspondence with Salisbury, 1962–3.
WP 670/15   Correspondence with Solomon, 1962.
WP 672/1   Correspondence with Stanley, 1957–63.
WP 677/8   Correspondence with van der Byl, 1961–3.
WP 679/3   Correspondence with Wall, 1960–1.
WP 679/4   Correspondence with Wall, 1962.
WP 686/7   Correspondence with Wynne, 1963.
WP 689/9   Correspondence concerning Enoch Dumbutshena, 1959.
WP 690/4   'The Hochschild Papers', 1960.

Cory Library, Eden Grove Building, Rhodes University, Grahamstown, South Africa

IAN SMITH PAPERS

BOX/FILE

1/006   Southern Rhodesia Government Cabinet Minutes, 1957.
1/007   Southern Rhodesia Government Cabinet Memoranda, 1958.
1/008   Southern Rhodesia Government Cabinet Minutes, 1959.
1/010   Southern Rhodesia Government Cabinet Minutes, 1960.
1/012   Southern Rhodesia Government Cabinet Memoranda, 1960.
1/013   Southern Rhodesia Government Cabinet Minutes, 1961.
2/001   Southern Rhodesia Government Cabinet Memoranda, 1963.
3/001   Secretary's Standard File.
4/001 (M)   Anglo-Rhodesian Relations, 1959–65.

National Archives, Kew, Richmond, Surrey, United Kingdom

DO: RECORDS CREATED OR INHERITED BY THE DOMINIONS OFFICE AND THE COMMONWEALTH RELATIONS AND FOREIGN AND COMMONWEALTH OFFICES

BOX/FILE

35/7620	Sir Ronald Prain's ideas on advancement of Africans in the Federation, 1959–60.

PREM: RECORDS OF THE PRIME MINISTER'S OFFICE

BOX/FILE

11/3414	Kenya independence: correspondence from Chairman and Leader of the United Party, 1960–1.
11/3485	Constitutional Development in Africa, Federation of Rhodesia and Nyasaland: part 12, 1961.
11/3490	Constitutional Development in Africa, Federation of Rhodesia and Nyasaland: part 17, 1961.
11/3495	Rhodesia and Nyasaland, Conservative Commonwealth Committee, 1961.
11/4608	Developments in Africa: setting up of Lord Salisbury's 'Watching Committee'; Correspondence and Records of Meetings with Lord Salisbury and Others, 1961–4.

National Archives, 8601 Adelphi Rd, College Park, Maryland, United States of America

RECORD GROUP 59 GENERAL RECORDS OF THE DEPARTMENT OF STATE

Office of Eastern and Southern African Affairs COUNTRY FILES, 1951–65, Kenya Biographic Data to Rhodesia Desegregation (Box 1).

Office of Eastern and Southern African Affairs, COUNTRY FILES, 1951–65, Rhodesia, Educational and Culture to South Africa, Social, Education (Box 2).

Office of West African Affairs, Country Files 1951–63, Regional Correspondence to Williams European Talk (Box 8).

Presidential and Secretary of State Correspondence with Foreign Heads of State, 1953–64, Macmillan to Eisenhower Correspondence 1960–1, Vol. 5 (Box 3).

Presidential and Secretary of State Correspondence with Foreign Heads of State, 1953–64, Macmillan to Eisenhower Correspondence 1960–1, Vol. 3 (Box 4).

Presidential and Secretary of State Correspondence with Foreign Heads of State, 1953–64, Rusk's Correspondence with UK Officials, Vol. 4 (Box 19).

Central Decimal File, 320/12–1462, 1962 (Box 507).

Central Decimal File, 321/1–560, 1962 (Box 507).

Records of G. Mennen Williams, 1961–6, Chronological File of G. Mennen Williams, 1961–6, January–December 1963 (Box 3).

Records of G. Mennen Williams, 1961–6, Entry 719.3, Signature and Clearance File, 1961–6, January–December 1961 (Box 9).

Records of G. Mennen Williams, 1961–6, Entry 719.3, Signature and Clearance File, 1961–6, January–December 1961 (Box 10).

Records of G. Mennen Williams, 1961–6, Entry 719.3 Signature and Clearance file, 1961–6, January–December 1963 (Box 11).

Records of G. Mennen Williams, 1961–6, Miscellaneous Files, 1961–6 (Box 29).

Records of G. Mennen Williams, 1961–6, Trips file, 1961–6, January–October 1961.

National Archives and Records Service of South Africa, 24 Hamilton Street, Arcadia, Pretoria, South Africa

FOREIGN AFFAIRS ARCHIVES

BOX/FILE

BSB S.12/5 Vol. (1)	High Commission Correspondence, 1959–62.
BSB S.16	Visits to the Federation of Rhodesia and Nyasaland.
BSB S.20 Vol. (5)	Federation of Rhodesia and Nyasaland, 1959.
BSB S.20 Vol. (6)	Federation of Rhodesia and Nyasaland, 1960.
BSB S.20/6 Vol. (1)	United Nations, 1962.
BSB S.20/6 Vol. (2)	United Nations, 1963.
BSB S.41 Vol. (1)	External Affairs, 1960–1.
BSB S.41.2 Vol. (1)	Defence, 1961.
BTS 22/2/27 Vol (1)	Secretary of Foreign Affairs, 1963.

National Archives of Zambia, Lusaka, Zambia

SIMON ZUKAS PAPERS

BOX/FILE

HM 75/PP1   Correspondence 1962.

United National Independence Party Archives, Sheki Sheki Road, Lusaka, Zambia

UNITED NATIONAL INDEPENDENCE PARTY PAPERS

BOX/FILE

UNIP 6/7/3	External Relations.
UNIP 6/7/5	External Relations.
UNIP 6/7/9	External Relations.
UNIP 6/7/11	External Relations.

UNIP 6/7/13   External Relations.
UNIP 9/1/37   Foreign Representatives.
UNIP 14/1/3   Newsletters.
UNIP 14/2/4   UNIP publications.
UNIP 14/2/5   UNIP publications.
UNIP 16/1/6   Correspondence, 1962 (incl. Administrative
               Secretary, National Secretary, Director of Youth Movement).
UNIP 16/1/13 Correspondence, 1960–3 (mainly Correspondence with the
               Governor of Northern Rhodesia).

NORTHERN RHODESIAN AFRICAN NATIONAL CONGRESS PAPERS

BOX/FILE

3/20   External Correspondence, 1958.

University of Warwick Modern Records Centre

MSS.292.960.1.1   Central African Federation.
MSS.157.3.CEA.1.1.27 Central African Federation.

Printed Primary Sources

UNITED KINGDOM GOVERNMENT PUBLICATIONS:
Cmnd 298, *Federation of Rhodesia and Nyasaland Constitutional Amendment Bill* (1957).
Cmnd 362, *Federation of Rhodesia and Nyasaland Electoral Bill* (1958).
Cmnd 530, *Proposals for Constitutional Change in Northern Rhodesia* (1958).
Cmnd 707, *State of Emergency* (1959).
Cmnd 814, *Report of the Nyasaland Commission of Enquiry* (1959).
Cmnd 1148, *Report of the Advisory Commission on the Review of the Constitution of Rhodesia and Nyasaland* (1960).

SOUTHERN RHODESIAN GOVERNMENT PAPERS:
Report of the Advisory Committee: The Development of the Economic Resources of Southern Rhodesia with Particular Reference to the Role of African Agriculture (Salisbury, 1962).

UNITED KINGDOM PARLIAMENTARY DEBATES:
Hansard House of Commons Debates [571], May–June 1957.
Hansard House of Commons Debates [578], November 1957.
Hansard House of Commons Debates [582], February 1958.
Hansard House of Commons Debates [596], November–December 1958.
Hansard House of Commons Debates [609], July 1959.
Hansard House of Commons Debates [627], July 1960.
Hansard House of Commons Debates [629], November 1960.
Hansard House of Commons Debates [635], February–March, 1961.
Hansard House of Commons Debates [637], March 1961.

Hansard House of Commons Debates [659], May 1962.
Hansard House of Commons Debates [663], July 1962.
Hansard House of Lords Debates [229], February–March 1961.

NEWSPAPERS:
African Mail.
Daily Express.
Daily Herald.
Daily Mail.
Daily Mirror.
Daily Telegraph.
Evening Standard.
Sunday Express.
The Economist.
The *Independent.*
The *New York Times.*
The Times.
Union News.

Secondary Sources: Books

Alport, C., *The Sudden Assignment: Being a Record of Service in Central Africa during the Last Controversial Years of the Federation of Rhodesia and Nyasaland, 1961–1963* (London: Hodder & Stoughton, 1965).

American Metal Climax Inc. World Atlas (Chicago: Rand McNally and Company, 1962).

Andersen, C., and Cohen, A., *The Government and Administration of Africa, 1880–1939, Vol. 1* (London: Pickering and Chatto, 2013).

Anderson, D., *Histories of the Hanged: Britain's Dirty War in Kenya and the End of Empire* (London: Orion, 2005).

Ashton, S.R. and Killingray, D., *British Documents on the End of Empire, Series B, Volume 6, The West Indies* (London: Stationery Office, 1999).

Baker, C., *State of Emergency: Crisis in Central Africa, Nyasaland 1959–1960* (London: I.B.Tauris, 1997).

———, *Development Governor: A Biography of Sir Geoffrey Colby* (London: I.B.Tauris, 1994).

———, *Retreat from Empire: Sir Robert Armitage in Africa and Cyprus* (London: I.B.Tauris, 1998).

———, *Glyn Jones: A Proconsul in Africa* (London: I.B.Tauris, 2000).

Ball, S., *The Guardsmen, Three Friends and the World They Made* (London: Harper Collins, 2005).

Bancroft, J.A., *Mining in Northern Rhodesia* (Bedford: British South Africa Company 1961).

Barber, J., *Rhodesia: The Road to Rebellion* (London: Oxford University Press, 1967).

Berger, E.L., *Labour, Race and Colonial Rule, The Copperbelt from 1924 to Independence* (Oxford: Oxford University Press, 1974).

Birkenhead, Lord, *Walter Monckton: The Life of Viscount Monckton of Brenchley* (London: Weidenfeld & Nicolson, 1969).

Blake, R., *A History of Rhodesia* (London: Methuen, 1977).

———, *The Decline of Power 1915–1964* (London: Faber & Faber, 1986).

Bowman, L., *Politics in Rhodesia: White Power in An African State* (Cambridge, MA: Harvard University Press, 1973).

Bradley, K., *Copper Venture: The Discovery and Development of Roan Antelope and Mufulira* (London: Mufulira Copper Mines, 1952).

Bray, F., *Report of Facilities for Technical Education in the Federation* (Salisbury: Rhodesia and Nyasaland Ministry of Education, 1958).

British South Africa Company, *The Story of Rhodesia: Told in a Series of Historical Pictures* (Johannesburg: British South Africa Company, 1936).

———, *The '96 Rebellions* (Bulawayo: Books of Rhodesia, 1975).

Brownell, J., *Collapse of Rhodesia: Population Demographics and the Politics of Race* (London: I.B.Tauris, 2010).

Butler D., and Rose, R., *The British General Election of 1959* (London: Palgrave Macmillan 1960).

Butler, L.J., *Copper Empire* (Basingstoke: Palgrave Macmillan, 2007).

———, *Britain and Empire: Adjusting to a Post–Imperial World* (London: I.B.Tauris, 2002).

Butler, R.A., *The Art of the Possible* (London: Hamish Hamilton, 1971).

Chanock, M., *Unconsummated Union: Britain, Rhodesia and South Africa, 1900–1945* (Manchester: Manchester University Press, 1977).

Clegg, E., *Race and Politics, Partnership in the Federation of Rhodesia and Nyasaland* (London: Praeger, 1960).

Creighton, R.M., *The Anatomy of Partnership: Southern Rhodesia and the Central African Federation* (London: Faber & Faber, 1960).

Curtin, P.D., *Disease and Empire* (Cambridge: Cambridge University Press, 1998).

Darwin, J., *Britain and Decolonisation, The Retreat from Empire in the Post-War World* (Basingstoke: Palgrave Macmillan, 1988).

———, *The End of Empire: The Historical Debate* (Oxford: Basil Blackwell, 1991).

Dunn, C., *Central African Witness* (London: Victor Gollancz Ltd., 1959).

Franck, T.M., *Race and Nationalism: The Struggle for Power in Rhodesia-Nyasaland* (London: Allen & Unwin, 1960).

Franklin, H., *Unholy Wedlock: The Failure of the Central African Federation* (London: Allen & Unwin, 1963).

Galbraith, J.S., *Crown and Charter: The Early Years of the British South Africa Company* (Berkeley and Los Angeles, CA: University of California Press, 1974).

Gallagher, J., *The Decline, Revival and Fall of the British Empire* (Cambridge: Cambridge University Press, 1982).

Giliomee, H., *The Last Afrikaner Leaders: A Supreme Test of Power* (Cape Town: Tafelberg, 2012).

Goldsworthy, D., *Colonial Issues in British Politics, 1945–1961* (Oxford: Oxford University Press, 1971).

Good, R.C., *UDI: The International Politics of the Rhodesian Rebellion* (London: Faber & Faber, 1973).

Greenfield, J. *Testimony of a Rhodesian Federal* (Bulawayo: Books of Rhodesia, 1978).

Gregory, T., *Ernest Oppenheimer and the Economic Development of Southern Africa* (Oxford: Oxford University Press, 1962).

Griffiths, P.J., *Empire into Commonwealth* (London: Benn, 1969).

Halberstam, D., *The Best and the Brightest* (New York: Random House, 1972).

Hanna, A.J., *European Rule in Africa* (London: Routledge, 1961).

Hargreaves, J., *Decolonization in Africa* (London: Routledge, 1996).

Hocking, A., *Oppenheimer and Son* (London: McGraw-Hill Inc., 1973).

Holderness, H., *Lost Chance: Southern Rhodesia 1945–58* (Harare: Zimbabwe Publishing House, 1985).

Hole, H.M., *The Making of Rhodesia* (London: Macmillan, 1926).

Holland, R.F., *European Decolonization, 1918–1981* (London: Macmillan, 1985).

———, *The Pursuit of Greatness: Britain and the World Role, 1900–1970* (London: Routledge, 1991).

Home, Lord, *The Way the Wind Blows* (London: Harper Collins, 1976).

Hovet, T., *Africa in the United Nations System* (Evanstan, IL: Northwestern University Press, 1963).

Hyam, R., *Britain's Declining Empire: The Road to Decolonisation 1918–1968* (Cambridge: Cambridge University Press, 2006).

Hyam R., and Henshaw, P., *The Lion and the Springbok: Britain and South Africa Since the Boer War* (Cambridge: Cambridge University Press, 2003).

Hyam R., and Louis, W.M.R., *British Documents on the End of Empire, Series A, Volume 4: The Conservative Government and the End of Empire, Part I, High Policy, Political and Constitutional Change* (London: The Stationery Office, 2000).

———, *British Documents on the End of Empire, Series A, Volume Four, The Conservative Government and the End of Empire, 1957–1964 Part II, Economics, International Relations and the Commonwealth* (London: The Stationery Office, 2000).

Jones, G., *Britain and Nyasaland* (London: Allen & Unwin, 1964).

Kahler, M., *Decolonization in Britain and France: The Domestic Consequences of International Relations* (Princeton, NJ: Princeton University Press, 1984).

Kaunda, K., *Zambia Shall Be Free* (London: Heinemann, 1962).

Keatley, P., *The Politics of Partnership: The Federation of Rhodesia and Nyasaland* (London: Penguin, 1963).

Kosmin, B.A. *Majuta: A History of the Jewish Community in Zimbabwe* (Gwelo: Mambo Press, 1980).

Law, K., *Gendering the Settler State: White Women, Race, Liberalism and Empire in Rhodesia, 1950–1980* (London: Routledge, 2016).

Lynn, M. (ed.), *British Documents on the End of Empire, Series B Volume 7: Nigeria: Managing Political Reform, 1943–1963* (London: The Stationery Office, 2001).

King, A. (ed.), *British Political Opinion 1937–2000: The Gallup Polls* (London: Politico's Publishing Ltd, 2001).

Kirkman, W.P., *Unscrambling an Empire* (London: Chatto & Windus, 1966).

Koorts, L., *D. F. Malan and the Rise of Afrikaner Nationalism* (Cape Town: Tafelberg, 2014).

Leonard, D., *A Century of Premiers: Salisbury to Blair* (London: Palgrave Schol, 2005).

Leys, C., *European Politics in Southern Rhodesia* (Oxford: Oxford University Press, 1959).

Leys C., and Pratt, C., *A New Deal in Central Africa* (London: Heinemann, 1960).

Lipsey, R., *Hammarskjöld: A Life* (Ann Arbor, MI: University of Michigan Press, 2013).

Macmillan, H., *Pointing the Way* (London: Macmillan, 1972).

———, *At The End of the Day* (London: Macmillan, 1973).

Macmillan, W.M., *The Road to Self–Rule: A Study in Colonial Evolution* (London: Faber & Faber, 1959).

Macola, G., *Liberal Nationalism in Central Africa: A Biography of Harry Mwaanga Nkumbula* (London: Palgrave Macmillan, 2010).

Mason, P., *Year of Decision, Rhodesia and Nyasaland in 1960* (London: Oxford University Press, 1960).

Maudling, R., *Memoirs* (London: Sidgwick & Jackson, 1978).

McCracken, J., *A History of Malawi, 1859–1966* (Woodbridge: James Currey, 2012).

McKelvery, J., *Man Against Tsetse: Struggle for Africa* (Ithaca, NY: Cornell University Press, 1973).

Millin, S.G., *Cecil Rhodes* (London: Chatto & Windus, 1933).

———, *General Jan Smuts* (London: Faber & Faber, 1936).

Mlambo, E., *Rhodesia: The Struggle for a Birthright* (London: C. Hurst, 1972).

Moore, R.A. Jr., *The United Nations Reconsidered* (Columbia, SC: University of South Carolina Press, 1963).

Mtshali, B.V., *Rhodesia: Background to Conflict* (London: Hawthorn, 1968).

Mulford, D.C., *Zambia: The Politics of Independence* (Oxford: Oxford University Press, 1967).

Murphy, P., *Party Politics and Decolonization: The Conservative Government and British Colonial Policy in Tropical Africa, 1951–1964* (Oxford: Oxford University Press, 1995).

———, *Alan Lennox–Boyd: A Biography* (London: I.B. Tauris, 1999).

———, *British Documents on the End of Empire, Vol. 9: Central Africa, Part I, Closer Association, 1945–1958* (London: The Stationery Office, 2005).

———, *British Documents on the End of Empire, Vol. 9: Central Africa, Part II, Crisis and Dissolution, 1959–1965* (London: The Stationery Office, 2005).

Nicholas, H., *The British General Election of 1950* (London: Macmillan, 1951).

van Onselen, C., *Chibaro: African Mine Labour in Southern Rhodesia 1900–1933* (London: Pluto Press, 1976).

Palley, C., *The Constitutional History and Law of Southern Rhodesia, 1888–1965* (Oxford: Oxford University Press, 1966).

Pallister, D., Stewart S., and Lepper, I., *South Africa Inc.: The Oppenheimer Empire* (New Haven, CT: Simon & Schuster, 1988).

Palmer, R., *Land & Racial Domination in Rhodesia* (London: Heinemann, 1977).

Parker, J., *Brother's Keeper: The United States, Race and Empire in the British Caribbean, 1927–1962* (Oxford: Oxford University Press, 2008).

Pearson, D.S., and Taylor, W.L., *Break Up: Some Economic Consequences for the Rhodesias and Nyasaland* (Salisbury: Phoenix Group, 1963).

Phimister, I., *An Economic and Social History of Zimbabwe 1890–1948* (London: Longman, 1988).

———, *Wangi Kolia: Coal, Capitalism and Labour in Colonial Zimbabwe 1894–1954* (Harare: Baobab Books, 1994).

Pike, J.G., *Malawi, A Political and Economic History* (London: F.A. Praeger, 1968).

Porter, B., *The Absent Minded Imperialists: What the British Really Thought About Empire* (Oxford: Oxford University Press, 2004).

Prain, R., *Reflections of an Era: Fifty Years of Mining in Changing Africa: The Autobiography of Sir Ronald Prain* (Letchworth: Metal Bulletin Books, 1981).

Ranger, T.O., *Revolt in Southern Rhodesia* (London: Heinemann, 1971).

———, *Bulawayo Burning: The Social History of a Southern African City, 1893–1960* (Harare: Weaver Press, 2010).

Roberts, A., *A History of Zambia* (New York: Holmes and Meier Publishers Inc., 1976).

Rodney, W., *How Europe Underdeveloped Africa* (Cape Town: Pambazuka Press, 2012).

Rosenbaum, M., *From Soapbox to Soundbite: Party Political Campaigning in Britain since 1945* (Basingstoke: Macmillan, 1997).

Ross, R., *A Concise History of South Africa* (Cambridge: Cambridge University Press, 1999).

Rotberg, R., *The Rise of Nationalism in Central Africa: The Making of Malawi and Zambia 1873–1964* (Cambridge, MA: Harvard University Press, 1966).

———, *The Founder: Cecil Rhodes and the Pursuit of Power* (Oxford: Oxford University Press, 1988).

Royle, T., *Winds of Change, The End of the Adventure in Africa* (London: John Murray, 1996).

Rubin, M., *Sarah Gertrude Millin: A South African Life* (London: Ad Donker, 1977).

Sanger, C., *Central African Emergency* (London: Heinemann, 1960).

Shamuyarira, N.M., *Crisis in Rhodesia* (London: Transatlantic Arts, 1965).

Smith, I., *The Great Betrayal* (London: Blake, 1997).

Stockwell, S., *The Business of Decolonization* (Oxford: Oxford University Press, 2000).

Stonehouse, J., *Prohibited Immigrant* (London: Bodley Head, 1960).

Thompson, A., *The Empire Strikes Back? The Impact of Imperialism on Britain from the Mid–Nineteenth Century* (Harlow: Routledge, 2005).

Tischler, J., *Light and Power for a Multiracial Nation: The Kariba Dam Scheme in the Central African Federation* (London: Palgrave Macmillan, 2012).

Tredgold, R.C., *The Rhodesia that was my Life* (London: Allen & Unwin, 1968).

Unknown, *Northern Rhodesia Chamber of Mines Year Book 1961* (Salisbury: Northern Rhodesia Chamber of Mines, 1962).

Utete, C.M.B., *The Road to Zimbabwe: The Political Economy of Settler Colonialism, National Liberation and Foreign Intervention* (Washington, DC: Rowman and Littlefield, 1979).

Verrier, A., *The Road to Zimbabwe, 1890–1980* (London: Jonathan Cape, 1986).

Vindex, *Cecil Rhodes: His Political Life and Speeches 1881–1900* (London: Chapman and Hall, 1901).

Wallerstein, I., *Africa, The Politics of Independence* (New York: Vintage Books, 1961).

Watts, C., *Rhodesia's Unilateral Declaration of Independence: An International History* (London: Palgrave Macmillan, 2012).

Welensky, R., *4000 Days, The Life and Death of the Federation of Rhodesia and Nyasaland* (London: Collins, 1964).

West, M., *The Rise of an African Middle Class: Colonial Zimbabwe 1898–1965* (Bloomington, IN: Indiana University Press, 2002).

White, N., *Business Government and the End of Empire: Malaya, 1942–1957* (Oxford: Oxford University Press, 1997).

Williams, J., *Eyes on the Prize: America's Civil Rights Years, 1954–1965* (London: Penguin, 2013).

Williams, S., *Who killed Hammarskjöld?* (London: Hurst, 2011).

Willis, A.J., *An Introduction to the History of Central Africa: Zambia, Malawi and Zimbabwe* (Oxford: Oxford University Press, 1985).

Wood, J.R.T., *The Welensky Papers* (Durban: Graham Publishing, 1983).

————, *So Far and No Further! Rhodesia's Bid for Independence during the Retreat from Empire 1959–1965* (Johannesburg: 30 Degrees South, 2005).

Young, K., *Rhodesia and Independence* (London: Eyre & Spottiswoode, 1969).

Secondary Sources: Articles

Aldous R., and Lee, S., '"Staying in the game": Harold Macmillan and Britain's world role', in R. Aldous and S. Lee (eds), *Harold Macmillan and Britain's World Role* (Basingstoke: Palgrave Macmillan, 1996), pp. 147–59.

Ashton, N.J., 'Anglo–American revival and empire during the Macmillan years, 1957–1963', in M. Lynn (ed.), *The British Empire in the 1950s: Retreat or Revival?* (Basingstoke: Palgrave Macmillan, 2006), pp. 164–87.

Austin, D., 'The British point of no return?', in P. Gifford and W.M.R. Louis (eds), *The Transfer of Power in Africa, Decolonization, 1940–1960* (New Haven, CT: Yale University Press, 1982), pp. 225–47.

Ball, S.J., 'Banquo's ghost: Lord Salisbury, Harold Macmillan, and the high politics of decolonization, 1957–1963', in *Twentieth Century British History* 16/1 2005, pp. 74–102.

Beloff, M., 'Britain, Europe and the Atlantic Community', *International Organisation* 17/3, 1963, pp. 574–91.

Birmingham D., and Ranger, T.O., 'Settlers and liberators in the South', in D. Birmingham and T.O. Ranger (eds), *History of Central Africa*, Vol. 2 (London: Heinemann, 1983), pp. 336–82.

Butler, L., 'Britain, the United States, and the demise of the Central African Federation, 1959–1963', *Journal of Imperial and Commonwealth History* 28/3 (2000), pp. 131–51.

————, 'Business and decolonisation: Sir Ronald Prain, the mining industry and the Central African Federation', *The Journal of Imperial and Commonwealth History* 35/3 (2007), pp. 459–84.

Calvocoressi, P., 'The Africa Bureau, London', *The Journal of Modern African Studies* 2/2 (1964), pp. 292–4.

Cohen, A., 'Business and decolonisation in central Africa reconsidered', *The Journal of Imperial and Commonwealth History* 36/4 (2008), pp. 641–58.

————, '"Voice and Vision" – The Federation of Rhodesia and Nyasaland's public relations campaign in Britain: 1960–1963', *Historia* 54/2 (2009), pp. 113–32.

————, '"A difficult tedious and unwanted task:" representing the Central African Federation in the United Nations, 1960–1963', *Itinerario* 34/2 (2010), pp. 105–28.

Collins, M., 'Decolonisation and the "federal moment"', *Diplomacy and Statecraft* 24/1 (2013), pp. 21–40.

Darwin, J., 'British decolonization since 1945: a pattern or a puzzle?', *The Journal of Imperial and Commonwealth History* 12/2 (1984), pp. 187–209.

————, 'The Central African emergency, 1959', *The Journal of Imperial and Commonwealth History* 21/3 (1993), pp. 217–34.

————, 'The Central African emergency, 1959', in R.F. Holland (ed.), *Emergencies and Disorder in the European Empires after 1945* (London: Routledge, 1994), pp. 217–34.

————, 'Was there a fourth British Empire?', in M. Lynn (ed.), *The British Empire in the 1950s* (Basingstoke: Palgrave Macmillan, 2006), pp. 16–31.

Day, J., 'Southern Rhodesian African nationalists and the 1961 Constitution', *The Journal of Modern African Studies* 7/2 (1969), pp. 221–47.

DeRoche, A., 'Establishing the centrality of race: relations between the US and the Rhodesian Federation, 1953–1963', *Zambezia* 25/2 (1998), pp. 131–51.

Emerson, R., 'Colonialism, political development and the UN', *International Organization* 19/3 (1965), pp. 484–503.

Floyd, B.N., 'Land apportionment in Southern Rhodesia, *Geographic Review* 52/4 (1962), pp. 566–82.

Gibbs, D., 'Dag Hammarskjöld, the United Nations, and the Congo crisis of 1959–61: a reinterpretation', *The Journal of Modern African Studies* 31 (1993), pp. 163–74.

Gifford, P., 'Misconceived dominion: the creation and disintegration of the Federation of British Central Africa', in P. Gifford and W.M.R. Louis (eds), *Transfer of Power in Africa: Decolonization, 1940–1960* (New Haven, CT: Yale University Press, 1982), pp. 387–416.

Goldsworthy, D. 'Conservatives and decolonization: a note on the interpretation by Dan Horowitz', *African Affairs* 69/276 (1970), pp. 278–81.

Hazelwood, A., 'The economies of federation and dissolution in Central Africa', in A. Hazelwood (ed.), *African Integration and Disintegration: Case Studies in Economic and Political Union* (London: Oxford University Press, 1967), pp. 188–95.

Hemming, P.E., 'Macmillan and the end of the British Empire in Africa', in R. Aldous and S. Lee (eds) *Harold Macmillan and Britain's World Role* (London: Palgrave Macmillan, 1996), pp. 97–121.

Holland, R.F., 'The imperial factor in British strategies from Attlee to Macmillan, 1945–63', *The Journal of Imperial and Commonwealth History* 12/2 (1984), pp. 165–86.

Horowitz, D., 'Attitudes of British Conservatives towards decolonization in Africa', *African Affairs* 69/274 (1970), pp. 9–26.

Houser, G.M., 'Meeting Africa's challenge: The story of the American Committee on Africa', *A Journal of Opinion* 6/2-3 (1976), pp. 16–26.

Hughes, M., 'The Central African Federation, Katanga and the Congo crisis', *Military and International History* 2 (2003), pp. 7–33.

Hyam, R., 'The geopolitical origins of the Central African Federation: Britain, Rhodesia and South Africa, 1948–1953', *The Historical Journal* 30/1 (1987), pp. 145–72.

Jackson, A., and Law, K., 'Influence in British colonial Africa', in C. Tuck (ed.), *British Propaganda and Wars of Empire: Influencing Friend and Foe, 1900–2010* (London: Ashgate, 2014), pp. 97–122.

James, A., 'Britain the Cold War and the Congo crisis', *The Journal of Imperial and Commonwealth History* 28/3 (2000), pp. 152–68.

Kahler, M., 'Political regime and economic actors: The response of firms to the end of colonial rule', in *World Politics* 33/3 (1981), pp. 383–412.

Kent, J., 'The United States and the decolonization of Black Africa, 1945–1963', in D. Ryan and V. Pungong (eds), *The United States and Decolonization* (London: Palgrave Macmillan, 2000), pp. 168–87.

King, A., 'The *Central African Examiner*, 1957–1965', *Zambezia* 23/2 (1996), pp. 133–56.

Kubicek, R., 'British expansion, empire, and technological change', in A. Porter (ed.) *The Oxford History of the British Empire III: The Nineteenth Century* (Oxford: Oxford University Press, 1999), pp. 247–69.

Lewis, J.E., '"White man in a wood pile": race and the limits of Macmillan's great "wind of change" in Africa', in L.J. Butler and S. Stockwell (eds), *The Wind of Change: Harold Macmillan and British Decolonization* (London: Palgrave Macmillan, 2013), pp. 70–95.

Low, D.A., and Lonsdale, J., 'Introduction: towards the new order, 1945–1963', in D.A. Low and A. Smith (eds), *History of East Africa, Volume III* (Oxford: Clarendon Press, 1976), pp. 1–63.

Louis, W.M.R., '"Public enemy number one": The British empire in the dock at the United Nations, 1957–1971', in M. Lynn (ed.), *The British Empire in the 1950s: Retreat or Revival?* (Houndmills: Palgrave Macmillan, 2006), pp. 186–213.

Louis W.M.R., and Robinson, R., 'The imperialism of decolonization', *The Journal of Imperial and Commonwealth History* 22/3 (1994), pp. 462–511.

Marks, S., 'Southern Africa', in J. Brown and W.M.R. Louis (eds), *The Oxford History of the British Empire*, Vol. IV (Oxford: Oxford University Press, 1999), pp. 545–73.

McCracken, J., 'African politics in twentieth-century Malawi', in T.O. Ranger (ed.), *Aspects of Central African History* (London: Heinemann, 1968), pp. 97–111.

Mittleman, J.H., 'Collective decolonisation and the UN Committee of 24', *The Journal of Modern African Studies* 14/1 (1976), pp. 41–64.

Mlambo, A., 'Building a white man's country: aspects of white immigration into Rhodesia up to World War II', *Zambezia* 25/2 (1998), pp. 123–46.

———, 'From the Second World War to UDI, 1940–1965', in B. Raftopolous and A. Mlambo (eds), *Becoming Zimbabwe: A History from the Pre-Colonial Period to 2008* (Harare: Weaver Press, 2009), pp. 75–114.

Mlambo A., and Phimister, I., 'Partly protected: origins and growth of colonial Zimbabwe's textile industry, 1890–1965', *Historia* 52/2 (2006), pp. 145–75.

Murphy, P. '"Government by blackmail": The origins of the Central African Federation reconsidered', in M. Lynn (ed.), *The British Empire in the 1950s* (Basingstoke: Palgrave Macmillan, 2006), pp. 53–76.

———, '"An intricate and distasteful subject": British planning for the use of force against the European settlers of Central Africa, 1952–1965', *English Historical Review* 121/492 (2006), pp. 746–77.

———, 'Acceptable levels? The use and threat of violence in central Africa, 1953–1964', in M.B. Jerónimo and A.C. Pinto (eds), *The Ends of European Colonial Empires: Cases and Comparisons* (London: Palgrave Macmillan, 2015), pp. 178–96.

Nehwati, F., 'The social and communal background to "Zhii": The African riots in Bulawayo, Southern Rhodesia in 1960', *African Affairs* 69/276 (1970), pp. 250–66.

Ovendale, R., 'Macmillan and the wind of change in Africa, 1957–1960', *The Historical Journal* 38/2 (1995), pp. 455–77.

———, 'The South African policy of the British Labour government, 1947–51', *International Affairs* LIX (1983), pp. 51–8.

Perham, M., 'The Rhodesian crisis: The background', *International Affairs* 42/1 (1966), pp. 1–13.

Petersen, K.S., 'The business of the United Nations Security Council: history (1946–1963) and prospects', *The Journal of Politics* 27/4 (1965), pp. 818–38.

Phimister, I., 'Corporate profit and race in central African copper mining, 1946–1958', *Business History Review* 85/4 (2011), pp. 749–74.

Phiri, B.J., 'The Capricorn Africa Society revisited: The impact of liberalism in Zambia's colonial history, 1949–1963', *The International Journal of African Historical Studies* 24/1 (1991), pp. 65–83.

Raftopolous, B., 'Nationalism and labour in Salisbury 1953–1965', in *Journal of South African Studies* 21/1 (1995), pp. 79–93.

Ranger, T.O., 'African politics in twentieth-century Southern Rhodesia', in T.O. Ranger (ed.), *Aspects of Central African History* (London: Heinemann, 1968), pp. 210–45.

Roberts, A.D., 'Notes towards a financial history of copper mining in Northern Rhodesia', *Canadian Journal of African Studies* 16/2 (1982), 347–59.

Saunders C., and Smith, I.R., 'Southern Africa 1795–1910', in A. Porter (ed.), *Oxford History of the British Empire: The Nineteenth Century* (Oxford: Oxford University Press, 2001), pp. 597–623.

Sills, H.D., 'The break-up of the Central African Federation: notes on the validity of assurances', *African Affairs* 73/290 (1974), pp. 50–62.

Slinn, P., 'The legacy of the British South Africa Company: The historical background', in M. Bostock and C. Harvey (eds), *Economic Independence and Zambian Copper* (London: Praeger, 1972), pp. 23–52.

Somerville, J.J.B., 'The Central African Federation', *International Affairs* 39/3 (1963), pp. 386–482.

Stockwell, S., 'Ends of empire', *The British Empire: Themes and Perspectives* (Oxford: Blackwell, 2008), pp. 269–94.

Unknown, 'Report of the Inter-Imperial Committee of the Imperial Conference, 1926', *The American Journal of International Law* 21/2 (1927), pp. 21–38.

Waite, D.N., 'Copper', in C. Payer (ed.), *Commodity Trade of the Third World* (London: Macmillan, 1975), pp. 40–57.

Ward, S., '"Worlds apart" three "British" prime ministers at empire's end', in P. Buckner and R.D. Francis (eds), *Rediscovery of the British World* (Calgary: Calgary University Press, 2005), pp. 399–420.

Watts, C., 'G. Mennen Williams and Rhodesian independence: a case study in bureaucratic politics', *Michigan Academician* XXXVI (2004), pp. 225–46.

———, '"Moments of tension and drama": The Rhodesian problem at the Commonwealth prime ministers' meetings, 1964–1965', *Journal of Colonialism and Colonial History* 8/1 (2007), pp. 98–146.

West, M.O., 'Ndabaningi Sithole, Garfield Todd and the Dadaya school strike of 1947', *Journal of Southern African Studies* 18/2 (1992), pp. 297–316.

Wetherell, H.I., 'Settler expansionism in central Africa: The imperial response of 1931 and subsequent implications', *African Affairs* 78/311 (1979), pp. 210–27.

Unpublished sources

Horowitz, D., 'Attitudes of British Conservatives towards decolonization in Africa during the period of the Macmillan government 1957–1963' (Oxford, D.Phil. thesis, 1967).

King, A., 'Identity and decolonisation: the policy of partnership in Southern Rhodesia, 1945–1962' (Oxford, D. Phil thesis, 2001).
Phillips, J.G., 'Roan Antelope: big business in central Africa' (Cambridge, D.Phil thesis, 2000).

Internet Sources

OXFORD DICTIONARY OF NATIONAL BIOGRAPHY

Addison, P., 'Churchill, Sir Winston Leonard Spencer (1874–1965)', *Oxford Dictionary of National Biography* (Oxford: Oxford University Press, 2004), online edn, January 2011 [http://www.oxforddnb.com/view/article/32413, accessed 15 April 2014].
Brivati, B., 'Gaitskell, Hugh Todd Naylor (1906–1963)', *Oxford Dictionary of National Biography* (Oxford: Oxford University Press, 2004), online edn, January 2011 [http://www.oxforddnb.com/view/article/33309, accessed 11 November 2014].
Cell, J.W., 'Hailey, (William) Malcolm, Baron Hailey (1872–1969)', *Oxford Dictionary of National Biography* (Oxford: Oxford University Press, 2004), online edn, January 2010 [http://www.oxforddnb.com/view/article/33636, accessed 5 June 2014].
Cosgrave, P., 'Amery, (Harold) Julian, Baron Amery of Lustleigh (1919–1996)', *Oxford Dictionary of National Biography* (Oxford: Oxford University Press, 2004), online edn, January 2008 [http://www.oxforddnb.com/view/article/63313, accessed 10 November 2014].
Darwin, J.G., Malcolm, Sir Dougal Orme (1877–1955)', *Oxford Dictionary of National Biography* (Oxford: Oxford University Press, 2004), online edn, May 2009 [http://www.oxforddnb.com/view/article/34842, accessed 15 April 2014].
Davenport, T.R.H., 'Kruger, Stephanus Johannes Paulus (1825–1904)', *Oxford Dictionary of National Biography* (Oxford: Oxford University Press, 2004), online edn, May 2006 [http://www.oxforddnb.com/view/article/41290, accessed 15 April 2014].
Goldsworthy, D., 'Cecil, Robert Arthur James Gascoyne–, fifth marquess of Salisbury (1893–1972)', *Oxford Dictionary of National Biography* (Oxford: Oxford University Press, 2004), online edn, January 2008 [http://www.oxforddnb.com/view/article/30911, accessed 22 May 2014].
Grenfell, H. St. L., 'Robins, Thomas Ellis, Baron Robins (1884–1962)', rev. *Oxford Dictionary of National Biography*, (Oxford, 2004), online edn, May 2006 [http://www.oxforddnb.com/view/article/35789, accessed 25 June 2007].
Hattersley, R., 'Callaghan Leonard James [Jim], Baron Callaghan of Cardiff (1912–2005)', *Oxford Dictionary of National Biography* (Oxford: Oxford University Press, January 2009) online edn, May 2013 [http://www.oxforddnb.com/view/article/94837, accessed 31 October 2014].
Honoré, T., 'Devlin, Patrick Arthur, Baron Devlin (1905–1992)', *Oxford Dictionary of National Biography* (Oxford: Oxford University Press, 2004), online edn, September 2012 [http://www.oxforddnb.com/view/article/50969, accessed 10 November 2014]
Howard, A., 'Castle, Barbara Anne, Baroness Castle of Blackburn (1910–2002)', *Oxford Dictionary of National Biography* (Oxford: Oxford University Press,

Jan 2006), online edn, May 2012 [http://www.oxforddnb.com/view/article/
76877, accessed 10 November 2014].

Hurd, D., 'Home Alexander Frederick Douglas –, fourteenth Earl of Home and
Baron Home of the Hirsel (1903–1995)', *Oxford Dictionary of National Biography*
(Oxford: Oxford University Press, 2004) online edn, January 2014 [http://www.
oxforddnb.com/view/article/60455, accessed 31 October 2014].

Ingham, R., 'Foot, Sir Dingle Mackintosh (1905–1978)', *Oxford Dictionary of
National Biography* (Oxford: Oxford University Press, 2004), online edn, January
2014 [http://www.oxforddnb.com/view/article/31115, accessed 11 November
2014].

Jackson, A., 'Long, Walter Hume, first Viscount Long (1854–1924)', *Oxford Dictionary
of National Biography* (Oxford: Oxford University Press, 2004), online edn, January
2011 [http://www.oxforddnb.com/view/article/34591, accessed 15 April 2014].

Katzenellenbogen, S., 'Williams, Sir Robert, baronet (1860–1938)', *Oxford
Dictionary of National Biography*, ed. H.C.G. Matthew and Brian Harrison
(Oxford University Press, 2004), online edn, May 2006, [http://www.
oxforddnb.com/view/article/50249, accessed June 18, 2007].

Kennet, W., rev. A. May, 'Young, (Edward) Hilton, first Baron Kennet (1879–
1960)', *Oxford Dictionary of National Biography* (Oxford: Oxford University Press,
2004), online edn, January 2013 [http://www.oxforddnb.com/view/article/
37071, accessed 15 April 2014].

Kirk-Greene, A.H.M., 'Harris, Sir Percy Wyn (1903–1979)', *Oxford Dictionary of
National Biography* (Oxford: Oxford University Press, 2004), [http://www.
oxforddnb.com/view/article/31861, accessed 10 November 2014].

Legg, T.S, and Legg, M., 'Cave, George, Viscount Cave (1856–1928)', *Oxford
Dictionary of National Biography* (Oxford: Oxford University Press, 2004), online
edn, January 2011 [http://www.oxforddnb.com/view/article/32329, accessed
15 April 2014].

Lewis, J., 'Llewellin, John Jestyn, Baron Llewellin (1893–1957)', rev. *Oxford
Dictionary of National Biography* (Oxford: Oxford University Press, 2004), online
edn, January 2008 [http://www.oxforddnb.com/view/article/34563, accessed
23 October 2014].

Lowry, D., 'Coghlan, Sir Charles Patrick John (1863–1927)', *Oxford History of National
Biography* (Oxford: Oxford University Press, 2004), online edn, January 2008
[http://oxforddnb.com/view/article/32477, accessed 15 April 2014].

———, 'Whitehead, Sir Edgar Cuthbert Freemantle (1905–1971)', *Oxford
Dictionary of National Biography* (Oxford: Oxford University Press, 2004), online
edn, October 2005 [http://www.oxforddnb.com/view/article/31828, accessed
12 May 2014].

———, 'Todd, Sir (Reginald Stephen) Garfield (1908–2002)', *Oxford Dictionary of
National Biography* (Oxford: Oxford University Press, January 2006), online edn,
January 2010 [http://www.oxforddnb.com/view/article/77353, accessed 27 May
2014].

———, 'Welensky, Sir Roland (1907–1991)', *Oxford Dictionary of National
Biography* (Oxford: Oxford University Press, 2004), [http://www.oxforddnb.
com/view/article/50688/2004–09, accessed 24 October 2014].

Ludlow, N.P., 'Sandys, (Edwin) Duncan, Baron Duncan–Sandys (1908–1987)', first
published 2004; online edn, January 2008 [http://dx.doi.org/10.1093/ref:odnb/
39858 accessed 30 July 2015].

——, 'Dixon, Sir Pierson John (1904–1965)', *Oxford Dictionary of National Biography* (Oxford: Oxford University Press, 2004), online edn, January 2008 [http://www.oxforddnb.com/view/article/32839, accessed 23 October 2014].

Macmillan, H., 'Chona (Mathias) Mainza (1930–2001)', *Oxford Dictionary of National Biography* (Oxford: Oxford University Press, January 2005), [http://www.oxforddnb.com/view/article/76554, accessed 10 November 2014].

Marks, S., 'Smuts, Jan Christiaan (1870–1950)', *Oxford Dictionary of National Biography* (Oxford: Oxford University Press, 2004), online edn, January 2011 [http://www.oxforddnb.com/view/article/36171, accessed 15 April 2014].

Marks, S. and Trapido, S., 'Rhodes, Cecil John (1853–1902)', *Oxford Dictionary of National Biography* (Oxford: Oxford University Press, 2004), online edn, September 2013 [http://www.oxforddnb.com/view/article/35731, accessed 17 January 2014].

Marsh, P.T., 'Chamberlain, Joseph (1836–1914)', *Oxford Dictionary of National Biography* (Oxford: Oxford University Press, 2004), online edn, September 2013 [http://www.oxforddnb.com/view/article/32350, accessed 15 April 2014].

Matthew, H.C.G., 'Macmillan (Maurice) Harold, first earl of Stockton (1894–1986)', *Oxford Dictionary of National Biography* (Oxford: Oxford University Press, 2004) online edn, January 2011 [http://www.oxforddnb.com/view/article/40185, accessed 22 May 2014].

McCracken, J., 'Banda, Hastings Kamuzu (c.1898–1997)', *Oxford Dictionary of National Biography* (Oxford: Oxford University Press, 2004), online edn, January 2008 [http://www.oxforddnb.com/view/article/68477, accessed 27 October 2014].

Miller, C., 'Grey, Albert Henry George, fourth Earl Grey (1851–1917)', *Oxford Dictionary of National Biography* (Oxford: Oxford University Press, 2004), online edn, January 2008 [http://www.oxforddnb.com/view/article/33568, accessed 15 April 2014].

Murphy, P., 'Lyttelton, Oliver, first Viscount Chandos (1893–1972)', *Oxford Dictionary of National Biography* (Oxford: Oxford University Press, 2004), online edn, January 2011 [http://www.oxforddnb.com/view/article/31385, accessed 9 May 2014].

——, 'Boyd, Alan Tindal Lennox – first Viscount Boyd of Merton (1904–1983)', *Oxford Dictionary of National Biography* (Oxford: Oxford University Press, 2004), online edn, January 2008 [http://www.odnb.com/view/article/31352, accessed 31 October 2014].

Newbury, C., 'Milner, Alfred Viscount Milner (1854–1925)', *Oxford Dictionary of National Biography* (Oxford: Oxford University Press, 2004), online edn, October 2008 [http://www.oxforddnb.com/view/article/35037, accessed 15 April 2014].

——, 'Oppenheimer, Sir Ernest (1880–1957)', *Oxford Dictionary of National Biography*, Oxford, 2004), online edn, May 2006 [http://www.oxforddnb.com/view/article/35321, accessed 22 June 2007].

Nicholls, C.S., 'Williams, Sir Edgar Trevor [Bill] (1912–1995)', *Oxford Dictionary of National Biography* (Oxford: Oxford University Press, 2004), online edn, May 2011 [http://www.oxforddnb.com/view/article/57959, accessed 10 November 2014].

Palley, C., 'Tredgold, Sir Robert Clarkson (1899–1977)', rev. *Oxford Dictionary of National Biography* (Oxford: Oxford University Press, 2004), online edn,

May 2006 [http://www.oxforddnb.com/view/article/31772, accessed 27 October 2014].

Pearce, R., 'Walker, Patrick Chrestien Gordon, Baron Gordon-Walker (1907–1980)', *Oxford Dictionary of National Biography* (Oxford: Oxford University Press, 2004), online edn, January 2008 [http://www.oxforddnb.com/view/article/31161, accessed 8 May 2014].

Phimister, I., 'Lobengula Khumalo (*c.*1835–1893/4?)', *Oxford Dictionary of National Biography* (Oxford: Oxford University Press 2004), [http://www.oxforddnb.com/view/article/52662, accessed 30 January 2014].

———, 'Davis, Sir Edmund Gabriel (1861–1939)', *Oxford Dictionary of National Biography*, eds H.C.G. Matthew and Brian Harrison (Oxford: Oxford University Press, 2004), online edn May, 2006, [http://www.oxforddnb.com/view/article/40711, accessed 18 June 2007].

———, 'Prain, Sir Ronald Lindsay (1907–1991)', *Oxford Dictionary of National Biography* (Oxford: Oxford University Press, May 2008), online edn, September 2010 [http://www.oxforddnb.com/view/article/49932, accessed 11 November 2014].

Prain, R.L.P., 'Beatty, Sir (Alfred) Chester (1875–1968)' rev. A. McConnell, *Oxford Dictionary of National Biography,* ed. H.C.G. Matthew and Brian Harrison. (Oxford: Oxford University Press, 2004), [*http://www.oxforddnb.com/view/article/30660*, accessed 22 June 2007].

Pugh, P.M., 'Jones, Arthur Creech (1891–1964)', *Oxford Dictionary of National Biography* (Oxford: Oxford University Press, 2004), online edn, January 2011 [http://www.oxforddnb.com/view/article/34224, accessed 4 May 2014].

———, M., 'Monckton, Walter Turner, first Viscount Monckton of Brenchley (1891–1965)', *Oxford Dictionary of National Biography* (Oxford: Oxford University Press, 2004), online edn, January 2011 [http://www.oxforddnb.com/view/article/35061, accessed 27 October 2014].

Ranger, T.O., 'Nkomo, Joshua, Nyongolo (1917–1999), *Oxford Dictionary of National Biography* (Oxford: Oxford University Press, 2004), online edn, May 2006 [http://dx.doi.org/10.1093/ref:odnb/72535, accessed 31 May 2014].

———, 'Brock, (Arthur) Guy Clutton (1906–1995)', *Oxford Dictionary of National Biography* (Oxford: Oxford University Press, 2004), online edn, January 2014 [http://www.oxforddnb.com/view/article/59788, accessed 10 November 2014].

Saunders, C., 'Hertzog, James Barry Munnik (1866–1942)', *Oxford Dictionary of National Biography* (Oxford: Oxford University Press, 2004), online edn, January 2011 [http://www.oxforddnb.com/view/article/33842, accessed 15 April 2014].

Shepherd, R., 'Maudling, Reginald (1917–1979)', *Oxford Dictionary of National Biography* (Oxford: Oxford University Press, 2004), online edn, January 2008 [http://www.oxforddnb.com/view/article/31428, accessed 26 June 2015].

Stern, R.T., 'Rudd, Charles Dunell (1844–1916)', *Oxford Dictionary of National Biography* (Oxford: Oxford University Press, 2004), online edn, May 2006 [http://www.oxforddnb.com/view/article/65577, accessed 15 April 2014].

Thorpe, D.R., 'Eden (Robert) Anthony, first earl of Avon (1897–1977)', *Oxford Dictionary of National Biography* (Oxford: Oxford University Press, 2004), online edn, May 2011 [http://www.oxforddnb.com/view/article/31060 accessed 31 October 2014].

Tomes, J., 'Alport, Cuthbert James McCall, Baron Alport (1912–1998)', *Oxford Dictionary of National Biography* (Oxford: Oxford University Press, 2004), online edn, January 2008 [http://www.oxforddnb.com/view/article/71022, accessed 27 October 2014].

Waley, D., 'Buxton, Sydney Charles, Earl Buxton (1853–1934)', *Oxford Dictionary of National Biography* (Oxford: Oxford University Press, 2004), online edn, May 2006 [http://www.oxforddnb.com/view/article/32224, accessed 15 April 2014].

Whitfield, A., 'Stanley, Oliver Frederick George (1896–1950)', *Oxford Dictionary of National Biography* (Oxford: Oxford University Press, 2004), online edn, January 2011 [http://www.oxforddnb.com/view/article/36249, accessed 5 June 2014].

Whiting, R.C., 'Attlee, Clement Richard, First Earl Attlee (1883–1967)', *Oxford Dictionary of National Biography* (Oxford: Oxford University Press, 2004), online edn, January 2011 [http://www.oxforddnb.com/view/article/30498, accessed 9 May 2014].

Woodhouse, C.M., 'Makarios III (1913–1977)', rev. *Oxford Dictionary of National Biography* (Oxford: Oxford University Press, 2004), online edn, January 2011 [http://www.odnb.com/view/article/31401, accessed 31 October 2014].

Websites

https://www.dur.ac.uk/library/asc/collection_information/cldload/?collno [accessed 4 June 2014].

http://oxfordindex.oup.com/view/10.1093/ww/9780199540884.013.U161338 [accessed 11 November 2014].

http://www.archivesnetworkwales.info/cgi–bin/anw/search2?coll_id=206 [accessed 8 May 2014].

http://www.hull.ac.uk/oldlib/archives/mppapers/johnson.html [accessed 31 October 2014].

http://www.hull.ac.uk/arc/collection/pressuregrouparchives/jab.html [accessed 5 Sepember 2008].

http://quod.lib.umich.edu/b/bhlead/umich–bhl–85365?rgn=main;view=text [accessed 11 November 2014].

INDEX

AAI (African American Institute), 139, 141, 143, 144
ACOA (American Committee on Africa), 144
Acutt, Keith, 62, 69, 89, 134–5, 146, 148
Africa
  independence of African colonies, 1, 15, 18, 60, 194–5
  self-determination, 2, 170
  UN, 154, 172
  United States, 60, 170
African advancement, 5, 53–6, 87, 133, 140, 198
  Britain, 92–3, 150
  copper industry, 55, 66
  Macmillan, Harold, 158–9
  railway, 87, 140
  resistance to, 76, 78
  RST, 78, 141–2, 161, 198
  settler and, 133, 138, 149, 202–3
  United States, 92–3, 152
  Welensky, Sir Roy, 87
  Whitehead, Sir Edgar, 133, 179–80
African Affairs Board, 2, 43, 45, 49, 68, 69, 70, 71
  discriminatory legislature, 12, 72
African Mail, 139

African National Congress, 13, 71, 82, 84, 85, 113, 179
Nyasaland African National Congress, 13, 79, 83, 95, 96, 98, 99–100
  see also SRANC; ZANC
African nationalism, 6, 7, 138, 182, 195
  African nationalist protest, 8, 113
  decolonization, 18
  emergencies in Southern Rhodesia, Nyasaland, Northern Rhodesia, 13, 195
  Federation, challenges and failure, 18, 19, 54, 72, 112, 152, 194
  growth of, 13
  Prain, Sir Ronald, 139–40, 141, 147
  RST, 141–3, 144, 146, 147, 198
  Southern Rhodesia, 113, 124, 126, 162, 171, 180, 189
  UN, 173, 202
  United States, 144–5, 151, 170
  see also nationalism
African protest, 2, 12, 13, 115, 139, 195, 201, 204
  African nationalist protest, 8, 113
  reduction/relaxation of, 7, 9, 53, 56, 72

rural/urban Africans front, 7, 11, 53, 97
Southern Rhodesia, 121, 122, 196–7
urban discontent, 53
AFSC (American Friends Service Committee), 140, 144
Aitken-Cade, Stewart, 86, 103
Albert, Earl Grey, 26, 27
Aldous, Richard, 15
Alport, Lord (Cuthbert 'Cub'), 71, 77, 123, 124, 132, 162, 164, 184
AMAX (American Metal Climax Company), 69, 140, 143–5, 153, 177, 198 see also RST
AMC (American Metal Company), 34
Amery, Julian, 89, 93
Amery, Leo, 35
Anglo American Corporation, 16, 34–5, 36, 62, 85–6, 89, 134, 177, 178
  African/European wages disparity, 55
  coal, 50
  copper pricing, 65–6
  diamonds, 34
  Kariba Dam, 51–2, 198
  Rhodesian Anglo American Limited, 35
  South Africa's apartheid, 198–9
  UFP, 69, 77, 85, 133–6, 145, 147–8, 198
  Welensky, Sir Roy, 77, 134–5, 145, 147–8, 198
  see also mining; Oppenheimer, Ernest; Oppenheimer, Harry
Anglo-Boer Wars, 21, 27
anti-colonialism, 99, 150, 195, 199, 203, 204
  UN, 155–6
  UN Resolution 1514, 155
  United States, 59, 149–50
Armitage, Sir Robert, 13, 83–5, 89, 94, 96, 116, 195
  Devlin Commission, 97, 98
  see also Nyasaland Emergency

Attlee, Clement, 4, 44
Australia, 155, 175, 176, 190, 201

Baldwin, Archer, 67
Balfour Declaration, 32
Ball, Simon, 15
Banda, Hastings, Dr, 83, 99, 109, 140, 141–3, 160
  Devlin Commission, 97–8, 195
  Monckton Commission, 108, 116
  Nyasaland African National Congress, 13, 79
  Nyasaland's Prime Minister, 183, 185, 187
  Nyasaland's secession, 152, 160, 163–4, 167, 168
  release from detention, 108, 112, 116, 117
  return to Nyasaland, 2, 13, 79, 82, 117
  United States, 144, 151, 152, 170
Barber, James, 6
Baring, Evelyn, 38
Baxter, Herbert, 43, 44, 75
Beatty, Alfred Chester, 33–4
Belgium, 16 see also Congo
Beloff, Max, 58
Bennett, Frederic, 71
Bennett, Oliver, 188
Benson, Sir Arthur, 42, 79–80, 81, 84
Blake, Lord, 193
Blake, Robert, 11, 15, 18
Bledisloe, Lord, 10, 37, 38
Bow Group, 70, 93–4, 120
Britain
  1959–1964 'third implosion of empire', 158
  Anglo-American relations, 59–60, 69, 91, 92, 145, 150, 171, 173, 174, 202
  Britain/Europe/EEC relationship, 15, 58, 59, 154, 169–70, 199, 201

colonial policy, 59, 91, 99, 109, 131, 150, 154, 158, 172, 189, 193, 195–6, 203–4
colonial withdrawal, 1, 2, 16, 17, 200–1, 203–4
decolonization, 3, 189, 193, 194, 200
economy, 1, 9
postwar reconstruction, 9, 41
'second colonial occupation', 1, 9, 41
UN, 57–8, 156, 158, 171–6, 179, 194, 201
see also Britain/Federation relationship
Britain/Federation relationship, 44, 59, 61–2, 105–6, 107–10, 127–8, 129–30, 150, 152, 159, 164, 165, 193, 201
African advancement, 92–3, 150
Anglo-settler relationship, 17, 40, 77–9, 91, 109, 111, 158, 203
anti-British feeling, 112
British domestic politics, 15, 193, 199
British opposition, 46–7, 85, 119
British support, 43, 44, 200
economic issues, 62, 150, 153, 165, 193
Federation, dissolution of, 189, 203–4
Northern Rhodesia, 31, 48, 161
Nyasaland, 48, 195
recasting the Federation's public image in Britain, 107–10
rights, 7, 12, 17
Southern Rhodesia, 17, 121, 153, 171–2, 184, 189, 191, 199, 203
Welensky/Britain clash, 17, 79, 132–3, 156, 162, 164, 168–9, 172, 185
see also Britain; Federation
British Protected Persons, 67–8
Brownrigg, Philip, 147, 176–7
BSAC (British South Africa Company), see Chartered Company

'build-a-nation' campaign, 77, 145, 146, 147–8
Butler, Larry, 6, 139, 141, 143, 200–1
Butler, Richard Austen, 164–8, 169, 179, 183, 198, 201
Central Africa Office, 164, 168
Federation, dissolution of, 167, 186–8, 189–91
Welensky, Sir Roy, 166–8, 200

Callaghan, James, 66–7, 70, 75, 80, 102, 130–1
Canada, 173, 176, 201
Cartmel-Robinson, Harold, 51
CAST (Consolidated African Selection Trust Limited), 34
Castle, Barbara, 75, 102, 169
Cave Commission, 29, 30
Cave, Lord, 29
Central Africa Office, 164–5, 168
see also Butler, Richard Austen
Central Africa Party, 72–3, 76, 103
Central African Council, 38–9, 42
Central African Examiner, 77, 88–9
Chamberlain, Joseph, 26
Chaplin, Sir Drummond, 28–9
Chartered Company (BSAC/British South Africa Company), 22–31, 34, 36, 146, 147, 148, 177, 178
1898 Southern Rhodesia Order-in-Council, 24, 26–7, 28
forced labour, 25
gold, 22–3
Jameson Raid, 25, 26
Kariba Dam, 52
land expropriation, 23–4, 27, 29
Mashonaland, 23, 24–5, 26, 27
murder, theft, injustice, 25, 26
Rhodesia, 24
Royal Charter, 26
settlement with the Colonial Office, 31
settler discontent, 26, 27

Southern Rhodesia, future after
Company rule, 28–31
UFP, 135, 146, 148, 198
see also LegCo
Chitepo, Herbert, 54–5
Chona, Mainza, 72, 113, 167
Churchill, Winston, 4, 30, 44, 47, 160,
215n63
City Youth League, 53–4
Clutton-Brock, Guy, 84
coal, 9, 34, 36, 50–1
Wankie Colliery, 50–1, 54
Coghlan, Charles, 29, 32–3
Cohen, Sir Andrew, 38–9, 42, 43
Colby, Sir Geoffrey, 45
Cold War, 15, 16, 155, 200
UN, 6, 174, 202
Cole, David, 77–8, 107, 143–4
Collins, Michael, 4
Colman, Prentis and Varley, 107
Colonial Office, 8, 10, 41, 89
concessions to Africans, 78–9
settlement with the Chartered
Company, 31
colonial policy, 13, 16, 91, 155, 200
Britain, 59, 91, 99, 109, 131, 150,
154, 158, 172, 189, 193, 195–6,
203–4
colonialism, 59–60, 93–4, 109, 155,
195–6
international nature of, 3
Commonwealth, 58, 90, 201
Britain, 59
Britain/Europe relationship, 58, 59
Federation, 5, 65, 93, 115, 201
integration into, 5, 65, 93
membership, 58
Welensky, Sir Roy, 58, 191
Commonwealth Affairs Committee,
81, 128
Commonwealth Relations Office,
78–9, 123
communism, 1, 6, 16, 59, 60, 93, 154,
155, 202

Congo, 16, 23, 33, 88, 115, 138, 157,
176, 177–8
independence, 87, 156
UN, 156
Conservative Party, Britain, 15, 44,
72, 81, 89, 93–4, 102–3, 107,
119, 200
Conservative government, 4, 14–15,
44, 102, 108, 158, 167–8, 199
Conservative Overseas Bureau, 72
Constitutional Amendment Act, 70
pro-federal motion, 131
Constitutional Amendment Act, 2,
12–13, 72, 194, 231n82
Conservative Party, 70
criticism, 69, 70, 71
debate on, 70–1, 72, 75
Labour Party, 66–7, 70, 71
passage of the Bill, 70, 71, 72
racial discrimination, 68, 69–71
Welensky, Sir Roy, 62
copper, 9, 36, 104, 153–4, 194
African advancement, 55, 66
Apprentice Ordinance Act, 74
copper boom, 11, 53, 56, 72, 194
demand for, 33, 50, 69
European population's obstinacy, 66
Federation, challenges and failure,
61, 194, 197, 203
Kariba Dam, 51–2
Northern Rhodesia, 32
price fall, 2, 56, 61, 65, 74, 197,
198, 203
production cut, 65–6
strike, 66
see also Anglo American Corporation;
RST
Copper Ventures Limited, 33–4
Copperbelt, 9, 11, 134, 156, 176
colour bar, 38, 47, 74, 141
large-scale development of, 34
Northern Rhodesia, 33, 36, 40, 50
Creech Jones, Arthur, 41, 102
Creighton, Thomas R.M., 18

Daily Express, 157
Daily Herald, 139
Daily Mail, 157
Daily Telegraph, 157
Darwin, John, 97, 119, 158, 167,
    194, 199, 202
Davis, Edmund, 33, 34
Day, John, 126
De Quehen, Basil 'Bob', 77–8
decolonization, 15, 18, 158, 193–4
    British decolonization, 3, 189, 193,
        194, 200
    coming to terms with African
        nationalism, 18
    European decolonization, 3
    Federation, 19
    multinational business, 197–8
    self-decolonization, 8
    Southern Rhodesia, 18, 189
Devlin Commission, 93–100, 195, 197
    Armitage, Sir Robert, 97, 98
    Banda, Hastings, Dr, 97–8, 195
    Devlin Report, 13, 96, 99, 116,
        117, 195
    Devlin, Sir Patrick, 13, 93, 94, 98
    intimidation reported by witnesses, 96
    members, 94–5, 97
    see also Nyasaland Emergency
Dixon, Sir Pierson, 57–8
Dominion Party, 76, 86, 103, 112,
    122, 124–5, 135, 152,
    153, 163
Dominions Office, 32
Dugdale, John, 70, 101–2

Earl Buxton, 29, 30
Eden, Anthony, 2, 59
EEC (European Economic Community),
    15, 59, 169–70, 201
Eisenhower, Dwight David, 60,
    92–3, 202
Etheridge, Dennis, 147, 148
European, *see* settler/European
Evans, Athol, 136, 137

Federal Assembly/Parliament, 16–17,
    45, 49, 68, 70
    African MP, 12, 17, 88, 123, 138
    Constitutional Amendment Act, 12,
        231n82
    European MP, 12, 45, 62
    Monckton Report, 136, 137
    see also Constitutional Amendment
        Act; Federal electoral law;
        Federation
Federal Constitution, 45
Federal Constitution review, 12, 14, 17,
    49, 65, 79, 93–4, 118, 120, 195
    Labour Party, 101
    Macmillan, Harold, 101, 115, 127
    preparatory commission, 100, 101–2
    Wall, Patrick, 101, 128
    Welensky, Sir Roy, 49, 65, 100–1,
        120, 127
    see also Federation
Federal electoral law, 45
    dual-roll system, 64, 68, 80, 83
    Federal Electoral Bill, 62
    Federal franchise, 45, 62–4, 66–7
    oath-taking, 67–8
    racial discrimination, 68, 69–71
    Welensky, Sir Roy, 64, 67–70
Federal Party, 2, 50, 51, 66, 67, 68,
    75, 194
Federation (Federation of Rhodesia and
    Nyasaland), 1–2, 193
    1957, 12, 70, 194, 199
    1962 Federal election, 162–3
    Commonwealth, 5, 65, 93, 115, 201
    division of powers, 48, 49
    dominion status, 5, 12, 95, 104, 115,
        133, 194
    economic issues, 2, 9–10, 11, 12,
        14, 197
    economic performance/political
        success link, 9, 41, 197–9
    fiscal structure/issues, 45, 48, 50, 61
    historiographical approaches to,
        3–19

international context, 2, 10, 14–15, 58, 199, 200–1, 203
liberalism, 4, 42
Northern Rhodesia, 5, 8, 10, 16–17, 48, 53
Nyasaland, 1, 8, 10, 16, 37, 48
pro-Federation factions, 1, 5, 6, 7, 9, 10, 36, 41, 44, 200
Salisbury as Federal capital, 11, 12, 51, 56, 73
South Africa, 90, 99–100, 111, 113, 121, 182–4, 201
South Africa, apartheid, 2, 4–5, 42
South Africa, expansion of, 1, 5, 10, 42, 43
Southern Rhodesia, 5, 8, 10, 11, 48, 51
territorial rivalry, 11, 32
UN, 2, 16, 154–8, 171–5, 179, 201–2, 204
United States, 61–2, 68–9, 90–3, 143–4, 149–54, 170–1, 188, 202
see also the entries below for Federation; Britain/Federation relationship; Constitutional Amendment Act; Federal Assembly; Federal Constitution review
Federation, beginning and early years, 20–56, 193
1936 Victoria Falls conference, 37
1949 Victoria Falls conference, 41–2
1951 Victoria Falls conference, 44
1952 Lancaster House conference, 45
1953 Carlton House conference, 48–9
1953 referendum, 49
1953 Rhodesia and Nyasaland Federation Act, 49
antecedents, 20–38
British support, 43, 44
campaign for Federation, 41
early years, 7, 9, 10–12, 49–53
racial issues, 45–6

Southern Rhodesia/Northern Rhodesia amalgamation, 32–3, 35, 36–40
see also Chartered Company; Federation, motivations for
Federation, challenges and failure, 7, 10–11, 18–19, 117–18, 193
African discontent, 55, 56, 87, 95
African nationalism, 18, 19, 54, 72, 112, 152, 194
apartheid, 67, 195
constitutional differences and incompatibility of legal status, 37, 47
copper, 61, 194, 197, 203
criticism, 15, 48, 49, 64, 73, 89–90, 99, 107, 109, 139–40, 157, 193, 202, 204
debt, 52–3
economic issues, 9–10, 17, 18, 53, 61, 194, 197, 203
economic performance/political success link, 197
independence by African colonies, 18, 194–5
native policies, 10, 37, 38
political stability, 87, 91, 110–11, 197
racial discrimination, 3, 54–5, 73
racial partnership, 18, 53, 54–5, 68, 72–4, 75, 91–2, 95, 104, 194–5
settler discontent, 56, 123, 132, 133
settler population's obstinacy, 66, 70
Southern Rhodesian/Northern Rhodesian settlers clash, 50
UN, 194, 204
Federation, dissolution of, 2, 14, 17–18, 49, 55, 184–92, 193, 201, 203–4
1963 Victoria Falls conference/ Federal dissolution conference, 18, 190, 191
articles of dissolution, 18
Britain, 189, 203–4

Butler, Richard Austen, 167, 186–8, 189–91
Field, Winston, 185–7, 190–1
Kaunda, Kenneth, 187
Macmillan, Harold, 185, 189–90
Monckton Report, 14, 114, 116, 118, 119, 127, 136, 137
Northern Rhodesia's secession, 182, 186, 189, 190, 203
Nyasaland's secession, 97, 127, 133, 152, 160, 163–4, 175, 182, 183, 186, 203
secession, 93, 109, 114, 116, 119, 136, 137, 160, 189
secession, right to, 14, 117, 168, 175, 179, 183
settler, 87
Welensky, Sir Roy, 118, 164, 187, 189, 190–1
Whitehead, Sir Edgar, 112
see also Federation, challenges and failure; Federation, opposition to
Federation, economic issues, 2, 11, 12, 14, 69, 78, 87, 166
American investment in, 61–2, 68
Britain, 62, 150, 153, 165, 193
copper, 61, 104
economic advantages of the Federation, 5, 8–10, 14, 40–1, 48, 117
economic failure, 9–10, 17, 18, 53, 61–2, 65, 69
fiscal income, 45, 48, 50, 61, 65
see also copper
Federation, motivations for, 4–10
economic advantages, 5, 8–10, 14, 40–1, 48
liberalism, 42
nation-building, 10, 60
racial partnership, 4, 7–8, 9, 42, 48, 54, 63, 87
see also Federation, beginning and early years

Federation, opposition to, 16, 47
African opposition, 2, 6, 8, 12–13, 40, 44, 46, 53–5, 62, 67, 68, 117
Britain, 46–7, 85, 119
failed opposition, 6, 7, 72
Northern Rhodesia, 6, 44, 62, 68, 82, 157, 181, 185
Nyasaland, 47, 62, 68, 82, 181, 185
Southern Rhodesia, 5, 47, 62, 103, 181, 185
Field, Winston, 135–6, 163
Federation, dissolution of, 185–7, 190–1
Southern Rhodesian Prime Minister, 181–2, 183–4
FISB (Federal Intelligence and Security Bureau), 77, 100, 117
Fiscal Commission, 45, 48
Fox-Pitt, Thomas, 165
France, 15, 16, 59

Gaitskell, Hugh, 101
Germany, 15
Ghana, 2, 172, 176
gold, 20, 22–3, 34, 47, 79, 97, 198
Goldsworthy, David, 107–8
Gordon Walker, Patrick, 42–3, 44, 102
Greater Rhodesia, 28
Greenfield, Julian, 49, 64–5, 80, 99, 116, 127–8
Grenfell, Harry, 148, 177
Griffiths, James, 43
Guardian, 85–6

Hailey, Lord, 38
Hale, Leslie, 46–7, 102
Hammarskjöld, Dag, 16, 157–8, 202
Hargreaves, John, 193–4
Hazelwood, Arthur, 9–10, 14
Hilton-Young Commission, 35, 36
Hilton-Young, Sir Edward, 35
Hochschild, Harold, 55, 69, 78, 85, 134, 136, 138–45, 177, 198
Hole, Marshall, 22

Holland, Robert, 127, 203
Home, Alec Douglas, 64–5, 67, 79, 93,
    107, 108, 112, 129, 174
    visit to the Federation, 110, 111
Hopkinson, Henry, 47–8
Horner, Preston K., 33–4
Huggins, Godfrey, 37, 38, 39, 50
    Federal Prime Minister, 49, 57, 196
    Federation, 40, 41, 42, 44–5, 46
    Malvern of Rhodesia and Bexley,
        Lord, 2, 51–2, 57
Hyam, Ronald, 5, 10, 43, 85, 201, 203

IBRD (International Bank for
    Reconstruction and Development),
    52–3

Jameson, Leander Starr, 24, 26, 28
Jameson Raid, 25, 26
Johnson, James, 67, 80–1, 102
Jones, Griff, 11

Kafue River/Dam, 11, 51, 52
Kahler, Miles, 16
Kapwepwe, Simon, 153, 188
Kariba Dam, 4, 11, 51–3, 198
Katanga, 16, 112, 129, 176–8, 202
    mineral wealth, 33, 177
    UN, 156–7, 202
Kaunda, Kenneth, 71–2, 81, 82, 106,
    113, 114, 129, 132, 139, 141,
    142–3, 179, 185
    Federation, dissolution of, 187
    non-violence policy, 153
    Northern Rhodesian Constitution,
        128, 152
    Northern Rhodesian independence,
        71
    Oppenheimer/Kaunda meeting, 182
    'prohibited immigrant', 188
    UN, 173
    United States, 144–5, 151, 152, 170
Kennedy, John F., 91, 144, 149, 151,
    170, 202

Kent, John, 15–16
Kenya, 130, 141, 153, 195
    Kenyan settlers, 107
    see also the Mau Mau
Korean War, 6, 50

Labour Party, Britain, 44, 46–7, 49,
    65, 71–2, 79, 81, 102–3, 159
    Complaint of Privilege, 109–10
    Constitutional Amendment Act,
        66–7, 70, 71
    Federal Constitution review, 101
    Labour government, 4, 93
    Plural Society, 64
land
    African reserves, 27, 28, 31
    land alienation, 11, 53
    Land Apportionment Act, 36, 73,
        122, 163, 196–7
    land expropriation, 23–4, 27, 29
    Land Husbandry Act, 54
Lee, Sabine, 15
LegCo (Legislative Council), 27–30,
    33, 35, 36, 37, 39, 42, 50
    members, 27–8, 38
    settler representation, 27
    see also Chartered Company
Lennox-Boyd, Alan, 14, 64–5, 67,
    80, 89, 96, 108, 129, 131, 148,
    168, 200
Liberal Party, 39, 46, 152–3
liberalism, 12, 14, 70, 171, 177
    Central African Examiner, 88
    Federation, 4, 42
    Macmillan, Harold, 158–9
    Maudling, Reginald, 161
    Northern Rhodesia, 7
    Nyasaland, 7
    Prain, Sir Ronald, 139–40
    RST, 85–6, 139–40, 198
    settler/European, 5, 67
    Southern Rhodesia, 7–8, 76, 103,
        179, 180, 181
    Todd, Garfield, 75, 103

United States, 92, 139, 144,
  198, 202
Welensky, Sir Roy, 80–1
Whitehead, Sir Edgar, 122–3, 180
Limpopo/Limpopo River, 20, 21,
  28, 42
Llewellin, Lord, 59, 61
Lobengula, Ndebele king, 21, 24, 25
  Rudd Concession, 22
Loft, George, 140, 141, 145
Long, Walter, 29
Lyttelton, Oliver, 44, 49

Macintyre, Donald, 62, 69, 89
Macleod, Iain, 14–15, 108, 115,
  127–8, 133, 140–1, 200
  Northern Rhodesian Constitution,
  128–31
  visit to the Federation, 116–17
Macmillan, Harold, 58, 101, 115, 154,
  158, 161, 199–200
  1959 emergencies, 85
  African policy, 13, 14, 15, 16
  Britain/Europe relationship, 15, 58,
  154, 199, 201
  British Prime Minister, 2, 14, 59
  Central Africa Office, 164
  Eisenhower/Macmillan meeting,
  92–3
  Federal Constitution review, 101,
  115, 127
  liberalism, 158–9
  Monckton Report, 117, 118
  Northern Rhodesia, 129–30
  Southern Rhodesia, 127, 190, 203
  UN, 156
  visit to the Federation, 105–6, 107
  'wind of change', 105–6, 128,
  133–49, 158, 170
Malan, D.F., 4, 5
Malawi, 3 see Nyasaland
Malaya, 1, 2, 58, 138, 197–8
Malcom, Dougal, 28
Martin, Sir Richard, 26

the Mau Mau, 1, 67, 89
  death of Mau Mau detainees at Hola
  camp, 13, 85, 89, 99, 102, 195
Maudling, Reginald, 132, 156, 160–4,
  169, 200
MCP (Malawi Congress Party), 13–14,
  117, 133, 140, 142, 145–6, 167
Metcalf, Maurice, 94, 106
migration, 17, 114
  European immigration, 12, 46, 56,
  197
  'prohibited immigrant', 85, 141, 188
  urban migration, 11, 53
the military, 1, 17, 60, 129, 154,
  184, 201
Millin, Sarah, 143
Milner, Alfred, 23, 26, 29, 30
Milton, William, 27, 28
mining, 16
  mineral wealth, 5, 8, 33
  mining company, 16, 138–9
  Rudd Concession, 22
  see also Anglo American Corporation;
  copper; Copperbelt; gold; RST
Mlambo, Alois, 54
Moffat, Howard, 32–3
Moffat, John, 21, 69
  Moffat Treaty, 21
Monckton Commission, 10, 104, 106,
  109, 136, 137, 164, 197
  Banda, Hastings, Dr, 108, 116
  members of, 116, 118, 119,
  136, 137
  Minority Report, 118
  Monckton Commission in the
  Federation, 115–20
  Monckton, Sir Walter, 14, 61,
  116, 136
  preparing for, 110–15
  UNIP, 113–14
  see also Monckton Report
Monckton Report, 14, 104, 117,
  119, 121
  Federal Assembly, 136, 137

Federation, dissolution of, 185,
    189–90
Macmillan, Harold, 117, 118
Monckton's recommendations, 14,
    17, 118, 129, 136–7
Prain, Sir Ronald, 136–7
secession issue, 114, 116, 119, 127,
    136, 137
Welensky, Sir Roy, 117, 118, 119
see also Monckton Commission
multinational business, 2, 86, 138–9,
    197–9
see also Anglo American Corporation;
    RST
Murphy, Philip, 5, 16, 38, 43, 45, 48,
    68, 94, 107, 164, 196, 200
British Documents on the End of
    Empire, 4

nationalism, 3
Afrikaner nationalism, 8, 28, 104
indigenous white nationalism, 198
Northern Rhodesia, 82
Nyasaland, 47, 79, 117, 195
settler nationalism, 6, 7, 17, 182,
    197, 203
see also African nationalism
the Ndebele, 21, 22, 24, 25–6
NDP (National Democratic Party),
    13–14, 113, 121, 124, 125–6,
    127, 146, 152
New Zealand, 37, 201
Nkomo, Joshua, 54, 84, 121, 122, 124,
    125–6, 176
United States, 151
Nkumbula, Harry, 46, 47, 81, 82, 113,
    163, 179, 185
Northern Rhodesia, 1, 23, 152–3, 189
1962 Northern general election,
    179–82
African National Congress, 13
Britain, 31, 48, 161
Constitution, 39, 78–82, 120, 128–
    32, 152, 153, 161–3, 166, 200

copper, 32
Copperbelt, 33, 36, 40, 50
Emergency (1959), 83, 84–93
Federation, 5, 8, 10, 16–17, 48, 53
Federation, opposition to, 6, 44, 62,
    68, 82, 157, 181, 185
independence, 18, 199, 203
liberalism, 7
Macmillan, Harold, 129–30
Maudling and the Northern Rhodesia
    proposals, 160–4
nationalism, 82
'Operation KINGFISHER', 130
secession, 182, 186, 189, 190, 203
self-government, 6, 35, 44, 46
settler, 28, 36, 39, 128, 161, 175,
    203
Southern Rhodesia/Northern
    Rhodesia amalgamation, 32–3,
    35, 36–40
UN, 175
Welensky, Sir Roy, 80–2, 129–30,
    132, 153–4
see also Zambia
Nyasaland, 23, 46
1961 election, 133, 145
Britain, 48, 195
Constitution, 79, 83, 116–17, 121,
    167, 168
Federation, 1, 8, 10, 16, 37, 48
Federation, opposition to, 47, 62, 68,
    82, 181, 185
independence, 18, 168, 183, 195,
    199, 203
liberalism, 7
nationalism, 47, 79, 117, 195
Nyasaland African National
    Congress, 13, 79, 83, 95, 96,
    98, 99–100
secession, 97, 127, 133, 152, 160,
    163–4, 175, 182, 183, 186, 203
self-government, 90, 97
settler, 82, 96, 97, 203
UN, 175

Welensky, Sir Roy, 133, 164
Whitehead, Sir Edgar, 112
  see also Malawi; Nyasaland Emergency
Nyasaland Emergency (1959), 13, 16,
    83–4, 85, 89, 98, 99, 195
  African insurrection, 83–4
  consequences, 13, 85–93, 107, 195
  murder plot, 13, 83, 97, 98, 99, 195
  Nyasaland as a police state, 13, 96,
    99, 195
  R-Plan, 83, 96, 97, 98
  Welensky, Sir Roy, 90
  see also Devlin Commission

'one man, one vote', 65, 113, 173, 176
Oppenheimer, Ernest, 34, 36, 134
  see also Anglo American
    Corporation
Oppenheimer, Harry, 51, 86, 130,
    133–4, 135, 147, 177, 178, 182,
    198–9 see also Anglo American
    Corporation
Ostrander, Taylor, 140, 143–5, 153–4,
    177, 198

Palmer, Joseph, 92
Parker, Jason, 4
Parker, Stewart, 77–8, 144–5, 169, 177
Passfield, Lord, 35
Perth, Lord, 85, 93, 94
Phimister, Ian, 24, 55
Prain, Sir Ronald, 51, 55, 66, 78,
    86–7, 88, 133, 137–41, 143, 145,
    161, 198
  African nationalism, 139–40,
    141, 147
  liberalism, 139–40
  Monckton Report, 136–7
  UFP, 139
  see also RST

racial discrimination, 3, 7–8, 31, 46,
    84, 122, 144, 176, 247n.124
  Apprentice Ordinance Act, 74

censorship laws, 73
colour bar, 38, 47, 74, 141
Constitutional Amendment Act, 68,
    69–71
Federal electoral law, 68, 69–71
Federation, challenges and failure, 3,
    54–5, 73
Land Apportionment Act, 73
Liquor Act, 73–4
political action and, 55
RST, 55
Southern Rhodesia, 36, 46, 47,
    152, 176
racial equality, 55, 70, 74, 75, 92,
    101, 130, 149
racial issues, 10, 11, 40, 138–9, 172
  see also racial discrimination;
    racial equality; racial partnership;
    white racial issues
racial partnership, 87, 139, 150, 196
  African/European wages disparity,
    55, 56, 74
  ambiguity of the term, 194
  Capricorn Africa Society, 54, 72
  failed partnership, 18, 53, 54–5,
    68, 72–4, 75, 91–2, 95, 104,
    194–5
  Inter-Racial Association, 54
  as motivation for Federation, 4, 7–8,
    9, 42, 48, 54, 63, 87
  partnership in practice, 72–4
  purposes, 8, 63
  resistance to, 73
  settlers' inability to view Africans as
    their equals, 72, 194
  Welensky, Sir Roy, 73–4
railway, 11, 21, 32–3, 36, 53, 57, 61,
    65, 166, 177
  African advancement, 87, 140
  Chartered Company, 27, 28, 31
  Copperbelt, 33
  Rhodesia Railways, 50–1
RCBC (Rhodesian Congo Border
    Concessions Limited), 34, 35

Rennie, Sir Gilbert, 45
Reynolds News, 109
RF (Rhodesian Front), 17, 163, 183, 191, 196, 197
  1962 Southern Rhodesian general election, 17, 163, 180, 181, 182–3, 185, 196
  UDI, 3, 191, 203
RGA (Responsible Government Association), 29
responsible-government campaign, 29–30
Rhodesia Agriculture Union, 29
Rhodes, Cecil John, 21–8, 54, 63, 94, 160
  British South Africa Company, 22–3
  'equal rights for all civilized men', 54, 63
Rhokana Corporation Ltd, 35
rights/African rights, 151
  1957 Constitutional Amendment Act, 12
  American civil rights movement, 69
  Britain, 7, 12, 17
  'equal rights for all civilized men', 54, 63
  political rights, 20, 130
  voting rights, 63, 178
Roberts, John, 78, 127–8
Robins, Sir Ellis, 52, 77, 135, 146–7, 177–8
Robinson, Roland, 119
Robinson, Sir Albert, 135, 137, 168
Robinson, Sir Hercules, 21, 22
Rodney, Walter, 139
RST (Rhodesian Selection Trust), 16, 34, 50, 51, 65, 85–6, 133–4, 138
  African advancement, 78, 141–2, 161, 198
  African/European wages disparity, 55
  African nationalism, 141–3, 144, 146, 147, 198
  Beatty, Alfred Chester, 34

coffee development scheme, 142
  copper pricing, 65–6
  Federal government/RST link, 77, 141–2, 198
  Kariba Dam, 51–2, 198
  liberalism, 85–6, 139–40, 198
  racial discrimination, 55
  UFP, 69, 85, 86, 88, 133, 135, 139, 147
  United States, 198, 199, 202
  see also AMAX; mining; Prain, Sir Ronald
RUA (Rhodesia Unionist Association), 29
Rudd, Charles, 22
Rudd Concession, 22
Rusk, Dean, 152, 174

Salisbury, Lord, 46, 64, 115, 168
  Watching Committee, 120
Sandys, Duncan, 113, 119, 123–6, 129, 161, 163–4
Sanger, Clyde, 194
Satterthwaite, Joseph, 90, 91, 92
self-determination, 2, 151, 170
self-government, 15, 23, 26, 35, 39, 47, 67, 155, 159
  Northern Rhodesia, 6, 35, 44, 46
  Nyasaland, 90, 97
  Southern Rhodesia, 31, 32, 48, 49, 124, 172, 174–6
settler/European, 196, 200
  African advancement, 133, 138, 149, 202–203
  Anglo-settler relationship, 17, 40, 77–9, 91, 109, 111, 158, 203
  anti-British feeling, 111, 203
  development in European areas, 53
  discontent, 26, 27, 56, 123, 132, 133
  European immigration, 12, 46, 56, 197
  Federal Parliament, European MP, 12
  Federation's dissolution, 87

inability to view Africans as their equals, 72, 194
Kenyan settlers, 107
LegCo, 27
liberalism, 5, 67
Northern Rhodesia, 28, 36, 39, 128, 161, 175, 203
Nyasaland, 82, 96, 97, 203
obstinacy/intransigence, 66, 70
political power, 50, 62, 82, 91
pro-Federation settler faction, 1, 5, 6, 7, 9, 10, 36, 41, 44
right-wing political ideology, 76, 112, 123, 153, 163, 196
settler community, 30, 121, 196
settler government, 63, 76, 90, 115
settler mentality, 196
settler nationalism, 6, 7, 17, 182, 197, 203
settler supremacy/rule, 14, 17, 139, 172, 173, 177, 194, 203
Southern Rhodesia, 17, 32, 36, 44, 47, 82, 111, 112, 122, 123, 126, 133, 139, 171, 172, 173, 179, 186–7, 191, 197, 199, 203
trade union, 66, 87
UN, 202
see also racial discrimination; racial partnership; white racial issues
Shona, the, 24, 25, 26
Smith, Ian, 4, 191
Smuts, Jan, General, 28, 30, 36
South Africa, 1, 58, 103–4, 134, 201
Afrikaner nationalism, 8, 28, 104
apartheid, 4, 172, 198–9, 201
British refusal to condemn apartheid regime, 16, 42
expansion of, 1, 5, 10, 42, 43
Federation, 90, 99–100, 111, 113, 121, 182–4, 201
Federation and apartheid, 2, 4–5, 42
Federation/South Africa intelligence sharing, 99–100, 201

South Africa/Southern Rhodesia relations, 29, 30–1, 36–8, 42, 103, 111–13, 118, 179, 182–3
UN, 59, 171, 175
Welensky, Sir Roy, 183–4
Whitehead, Sir Edgar, 103–4, 113
Southern Rhodesia, 1, 23, 26
1898 Southern Rhodesia Order-in-Council, 24, 26–8
1922 referendum, 30–1
1961 referendum, 126–7, 132, 153, 181
1962 Southern Rhodesian general election, 17, 163, 179–83, 185, 196, 202
African nationalism, 113, 124, 126, 162, 171, 180, 189
African protest, 121, 122, 196–7
apartheid, 171
Britain, 17, 121, 153, 171–2, 184, 189, 191, 199, 203
Constitution, 17, 48, 102, 120, 121, 123, 124–7, 153, 170–1
decolonization, 18, 189
dominion status, 8
Emergency Powers Bill, 122, 123
emergency state in, 84, 195
Federation, 5, 8, 10, 11, 48, 51
Federation, opposition to, 5, 47, 62, 103, 181, 185
financial issues, 35–6, 40, 166, 186
future of, after Chartered Company rule, 28–31
independence, 124–5, 153, 173, 176, 179, 181–2, 185, 189, 190–1, 197, 199, 203
land alienation, 11, 53
Law and Order (Maintenance) Bill, 122, 197
liberalism, 7–8, 76, 103, 179, 180, 181
Macmillan, Harold, 127, 190, 203
pro-Federation faction, 6
racial practices, 36, 46, 47, 152, 176

responsible government, 29,
30–8, 48
self-government, 31, 32, 48, 49, 124,
172, 174–6
settler, 17, 32, 36, 44, 47, 82, 111,
112, 122, 123, 126, 133, 139, 171,
172, 173, 179, 186–7, 191, 197,
199, 203
South Africa/Southern Rhodesia
relations, 29, 30–1, 36–7,
38, 42, 103, 111–13, 118,
179, 182–3
Southern Rhodesia/Northern
Rhodesia amalgamation, 32–3,
35, 36–40
UN, 171–6, 179, 202
United States, 180, 188–9, 202
Vagrancy Bill, 123
Welensky, Sir Roy, 39–40, 124,
126–7, 190
a 'white man's country', 6, 36, 44
see also Zimbabwe
Soviet Union, 149, 155, 173, 174
SRANC (Southern Rhodesian African
National Congress) 13, 53–4, 71,
82, 84, 113
Stanley, Oliver, 38
Stockwell, Sarah, 198
Stonehouse, John, 85, 102, 169
Suez crisis, 2, 14, 57–9, 60

Taswell, Harold, 86, 99, 103–4, 106,
111–12, 121, 122–3, 135–6,
183–4
Thompson, Andrew, 89, 158, 199
Thompson, Jack, 89–90
Times, The, 109, 157
Tischler, Julia, 4, 11, 51
tobacco, 9, 36, 41, 48, 153
Todd, Garfield, 49, 54, 64, 76–7, 103
removal as Southern Rhodesian Prime
Minister, 75–9, 194
Tredgold, Sir Robert, 63, 119,
123–4

Tshombe, Moise, 156, 157, 158, 202
Turton, Robin: Early Day Motion, 131,
158, 167, 200

UCAA (United Central Africa
Association), 39
UFP (United Federal Party), 15, 74,
75, 78, 82, 103, 112, 146, 153,
163, 197
1958 Federal election campaign, 146
1962 elections, 162–3, 179, 196
Anglo American Corporation, 69, 77,
85, 133–6, 145, 147–8, 198
Chartered Company, 135, 146, 148,
198
Prain, Sir Ronald, 139
RST, 69, 85, 86, 88, 133, 135,
139, 147
UN (United Nations), 2, 16, 58–9, 151
Africa, 154, 172
African nationalism, 173, 202
Afro-Asian bloc, 16, 58, 155, 156,
158, 171, 173–6, 178
anti-colonialism, 155–6
Britain, 57–8, 156, 158, 171–6,
179, 194, 201
Cold War, 6, 174, 202
Committee of Seventeen/Special
Committee, 155, 172–5, 176,
202, 204
Congo, 156
Federation, 2, 16, 154–8, 171–5,
179, 201–2
Federation, challenges and failure,
194, 204
Ghana, 2, 172, 176
Katanga, 156–7, 202
Macmillan, Harold, 156
membership, 2, 154, 175
Northern Rhodesia, 175
Nyasaland, 175
settler, 202
South Africa, 59, 171, 175
Southern Rhodesia, 171–6, 179, 202

UN Charter, 155, 176
UN General Assembly, 59, 154–5, 172, 173, 175
UN Resolution 1514, 155, 202
UN Resolution 1654, 155
UN Security Council, 178
United States, 173, 174, 202
Welensky, Sir Roy, 156–7, 171, 173, 175, 202
unemployment, 17, 110, 166, 197
Union Minière du Haut Katanga, 33, 177, 178
Union of South Africa, *see* South Africa
UNIP (United National Independence Party), 13–14, 106, 113, 125, 132, 146, 152, 153, 165, 179
aim, 113
Monckton Commission, 113–14
The Voice of UNIP, 114
United Party, 39, 50, 100
United Rhodesia Party, 50, 75, 78
United States, 2, 15, 50, 90
Africa, 60, 170
African advancement, 92–3, 152
African nationalism, 144–5, 151, 170
AMAX, 145, 198
Anglo-American relations, 59–60, 69, 91, 92, 145, 150, 171, 173, 174, 202
anti-colonialism, 59, 149–50
Assistant Secretary for African Affairs, 60, 90, 149, 170, 202
Banda, Hastings, Dr, 144, 151, 152, 170
civil rights movement, 69
Federation, 61–2, 68–9, 90–3, 143–4, 149–54, 170–1, 188, 202
Kaunda, Kenneth, 144–5, 151, 152, 170
liberalism, 92, 139, 144, 198, 202
Nkomo, Joshua, 151
RST, 198, 199, 202

Southern Rhodesia, 180, 188–9, 202
UN 173, 174, 202
Welensky, Sir Roy, 151–2, 191–2

Verwoerd, Hendrik, South African Prime Minister, 100, 183, 184
Voice and Vision, 77, 107–10, 115, 117, 119, 169, 200
aim of the campaign, 108

Wall, Patrick, 75, 81, 103, 109, 117–20, 131, 162, 167, 168–9, 200
Central Africa Office, 165
Federal Constitution review, 101, 128
Ward, Stuart, 58
Welensky, Elizabeth (née Henderson), 61, 135
Welensky, Michael, 134–5
Welensky, Sir Roy, 1, 57, 105, 160, 196
1962 Federal election, 162–3
Acutt, Keith, 134–5
African advancement, 87
Anglo American Corporation, 77, 134–5, 145, 147–8, 198
anti-Semitic attack, 114–15
Commonwealth, 58, 191
Constitutional Amendment Act, 62
corruption, 145
criticism, 68, 114, 168, 170, 196
Federal Constitution review, 49, 65, 100–1, 120, 127
Federal electoral law, 64, 67–70
Federal Party, leadership of, 2
Federal Prime Minister, 56, 57, 59, 61, 62, 67, 80–2, 87–8, 104, 112, 191, 196
Federation, 40, 41, 42, 115
Federation, dissolution of, 118, 164, 187, 189, 190–1
liberalism, 80–1
Monckton Report, 117, 118, 119
Northern Rhodesia, 80–2, 129–30, 132, 153–4

Nyasaland, 133, 164
Nyasaland Emergency, 90
political rights, 20
racial equality, 75
racial partnership, 73–4
South Africa, 183–4
Southern Rhodesia, 39–40, 124,
   126–7, 190
UN, 156–7, 171, 173, 175, 202
United States, visit to, 151–2,
   191–2
Welensky/Britain clash, 17, 79,
   132–3, 156, 162, 164, 168–9,
   172, 185
White, Nicholas, 197–8
white racial issues
   white electorate, 31, 68, 71, 196
   white identity politics, 11
   white immigration, 17, 197
   white labour, high remuneration of,
      55
   white minority rule, 12, 15–16,
      74, 203
   white paternalism, 54
   white unemployment, 17, 197
   see also racial issues; settler/European
Whitehead, Sir Edgar, 44–5, 61, 92,
   112, 121, 171, 173, 174
   1962 Southern Rhodesian general
      election, 17, 179–81
   African advancement, 133, 179–80
   African rights, 17

Federation, dissolution of, 112
liberalism, 122–3, 180
Nyasaland, 112
South Africa, 103–104, 113
Southern Rhodesian emergency, 84
Southern Rhodesian Prime Minister,
   76–7, 102, 110, 122–5, 196–7,
   203
Williams, Mennen 'Soapy', 149–50,
   151–2, 170–1, 174, 188–9,
   202–203
Williams, Robert, 33
Wood, Richard, 40, 129, 130
   So Far and No Further!, 4
   The Welensky Papers, 4
World Bank, 144–5
World War II, 4, 20, 35–6, 38, 46,
   50, 51, 53, 60, 201
Wynne, Sydney, 169

Youens, Peter, 83

Zambia, 3, 18 see also Northern
   Rhodesia
ZANC (Zambia African National
   Congress), 82, 84, 113, 195
ZAPU (Zimbabwe African Peoples
   Union), 171, 174, 176
ZAR (Boer South African Republic),
   20–1, 25
Zimbabwe, see Southern Rhodesia
Zukas, Simon, 165